D1400050

*Principal Diseases of
Marine Fish and Shellfish*

SH
171
.S53
1970
c.2

noaalnc
3-19-2010

Principal Diseases of
Marine Fish and Shellfish

CARL J. SINDERMANN

DIRECTOR, TROPICAL ATLANTIC BIOLOGICAL LABORATORY
BUREAU OF COMMERCIAL FISHERIES
MIAMI, FLORIDA

AND

ADJUNCT PROFESSOR OF BIOLOGY
UNIVERSITY OF MIAMI AND
MEMBER OF THE AFFILIATE FACULTY IN BIOLOGY
FLORIDA ATLANTIC UNIVERSITY

WALFORD LIBRARY

1970

ACADEMIC PRESS   New York and London

#39288100153309

Copyright © 1970, by Academic Press, Inc.
ALL RIGHTS RESERVED
NO PART OF THIS BOOK MAY BE REPRODUCED IN ANY FORM,
BY PHOTOSTAT, MICROFILM, RETRIEVAL SYSTEM, OR ANY
OTHER MEANS, WITHOUT WRITTEN PERMISSION FROM
THE PUBLISHERS.

ACADEMIC PRESS, INC
111 Fifth Avenue, New York, New York 10003

United Kingdom Edition published by
ACADEMIC PRESS, INC. (LONDON) LTD.
Berkeley Square House, London W1X 6BA

LIBRARY OF CONGRESS CATALOG CARD NUMBER: 75-86365·

PRINTED IN THE UNITED STATES OF AMERICA

Preface

The present work offers opportunity to expand the consideration of diseases of marine fish and shellfish included in two previous reviews and to explore areas such as internal defense mechanisms of invertebrates, relation of human diseases to those of marine animals, and diseases in captive marine populations.

Regardless of the degree of success or failure of the product, the processes of conception and birth involved in this book have been rewarding in many ways. I have encountered, for the first time, the full sweep of literature in the general field of my own research. Particularly enjoyable is some of the older more leisurely work, with detail of observation and small personal glimpses usually missing in today's literature. Individuals, regardless of the decade in which they were active, often emerged with personal characteristics such as "exhaustively thorough," "capable of brilliant syntheses," "waspish," and "gentlemanly." Some authors may appear suddenly, produce quantities of papers, and quickly disappear; others, such as J. Johnstone, C. B. Wilson, R. P. Dollfus, R. F. Nigrelli, S. M. Shiino, may dominate the literature in their areas of interest for decades. Many personal stories are suggested by the accumulated literature—the permanent disappearance of certain Polish and other European names from the literature before and during World War II; the long association of certain names as co-authors; the weddings announced by sudden hyphenation of a female scientist's name; or the laboratory cat immortalized by Plehn and Mulsow because it ate one of the three diseased fish on which they based their first report of *Ichthyophonus*. More important of course are the solid impressive lists of major contri-

butions by a core of prolific dedicated research people who have been
challenged by disease problems in the sea. Their work, in many languages
and in countless journals, is available, and demands adequate attention
in any attempted summarization.

A number of important papers, symposia, and books have appeared
since this manuscript was completed which augment the information
contained herein. A symposium volume "Immunity to Parasitic Animals"
(G. J. Jackson and I. Singer, eds.) was published by Appleton-Century
Crofts. Of particular note in this volume is a chapter on "Mechanisms
and General Principles of Invertebrate Immunity" by M. R. Tripp. An
issue of the *Journal of the Fisheries Research Board of Canada* (Vol. **26**,
No. 4, 1969), dedicated to T. W. M. Cameron, was devoted entirely to
parasitological papers—many of them marine. An "Annotated Bibliography of Pathology in Invertebrates Other than Insects" by Phyllis T.
Johnson was published by Burgess. Other useful bibliographies that have
appeared include a "Partial Bibliography on the Bacterial Diseases of
Fish" by D. A. Conroy (FAO Fisheries Technical Paper No. 73, 1968), a
"Bibliography of the Literature on Neoplasms of Invertebrate Animals"
by G. E. Cantwell *et al.* (Gann Monograph 5: "Experimental Animals in
Cancer Research," Maruzen Co., Tokyo, 1968), and "Neoplasia in Fish—
a Bibliography" by L. E. Mawdesley-Thomas (*J. Fish Biol.* **1**, 187–207,
1969). A sampling of recently published research papers includes
Minchinia nelsoni disease syndrome in the American oyster *Crassostrea
virginica* by C. A. Farley (*J. Protozool.* **15**, 583–599, 1968); Outbreak of
cryptocaryoniasis in marine aquaria at Scripps Institution of Oceanography by D. W. Wilkie and H. Gordin (*Calif. Fish Game* **55**, 227–236,
1969); and the fine structure of *Nosema* sp. *Sprague*, 1965 Microsporida,
Nosematidae, with particular reference to stages in sporogony by V.
Sprague, S. H. Vernick, and B. J. Lloyd (*J. Invertebr. Pathol.* **12**, 105–117,
1968). The 1969 volume (**59**) of *Proceedings of the National Shellfisheries
Association* contains four papers (Sprague *et al.*, Sparks *et al.*, Myhre, and
Sawyer) on diseases of shellfish. And so the development and publication
of information about disease in marine populations continue to accelerate,
and we move closer to full understanding of the role that disease plays
in the sea.

This manuscript was completed during my tenure as Director, U. S.
Bureau of Commercial Fisheries Biological Laboratory, Oxford, Maryland.
Many of the staff members there contributed to my information on diseases of marine invertebrates. I wish to thank all those interested in diseases of aquatic animals (as listed by the Food and Agriculture Organization of the United Nations) who responded generously to my requests
for information pertinent to the subject matter of this book. The Branch of

Foreign Fisheries, Bureau of Commercial Fisheries, U. S. Fish and Wild-life Service, aided in translations of certain Japanese and Russian papers. Drafts of portions of the manuscript were kindly read by Drs. S. F. Snieszko, Z. Kabata, A. Rosenfield, G. E. Krantz, J. R. Uzmann, S. H. Hopkins, and E. S. Iversen. Their comments have been important, and have undoubtedly strengthened the final product. Drs. R. A. Hile and P. H. Eschmeyer, Biological Editors of the Bureau of Commercial Fisheries, examined the entire manuscript and made many valuable sug-gestions. There is, however, no implication of responsibility for statements or conclusions on the part of anyone but me.

I hope that errors or omissions will be brought to my attention so that any future revisions will more closely appromixate reality. I hope too that this book will serve to stimulate increased research in a fascinating and very significant aspect of marine biology—the role of disease in marine populations.

CARL J. SINDERMANN

Miami, Florida
December, 1969

Contents

Principal Diseases of
Marine Fish and Shellfish

GIFT OF
A.V. FARMANFARMAIAN
PROFESSOR OF PHYSIOLOGY

I

Introduction

Man's scientific probes of the marine environment have increased in frequency and intensity in recent decades. As a result, our knowledge about the factors that affect abundance of sea animals has increased significantly. Quantitative ecological studies of estuarine, continental shelf, and high seas populations have led to elaboration of population models for exploited species. Often, however, an incomplete understanding of ecological factors influencing abundance has led to major deficiencies in analyses of population dynamics.

One environmental factor in the sea, about which significant new information has been emerging, is disease. The important role of diseases and parasites in affecting the abundance of marine species—particularly those of commercial importance—can now be demonstrated. One of the many purposes of this book is to assemble the widely scattered evidence for the important, and at times dominant, part played by disease in marine ecology.

Much of the available knowledge about diseases of marine animals concerns commercial species, so it is logical that most of this book will be oriented toward commercial species of fish and shellfish. There are, in addition, scattered through the world literature, studies of the parasites of many marine animals that have no direct economic importance. Since some of these animals, such as the copepods and chaetognaths, have significance in the complex food webs of the sea, it is necessary to understand factors such as disease, which can cause imbalances or disruption in food relations by affecting population abundance at any trophic level.

1

Consideration of diseases of noncommercial species is not included in this book, however, because of the inadequacy of available information and the need to concentrate on marine animals of economic importance. It is obvious that more studies of noncommercial invertebrates—particularly of their infectious diseases—are needed.

It might be well to establish guidelines and provide definitions early in this introduction. Disease is here defined in its broadest possible sense —as any departure from normal structure or function of the animal. Included are the conditions resulting from infectious diseases and parasite invasion, as well as genetic or environmentally induced abnormalities. Emphasis has been placed on infectious diseases—those caused by microbial pathogens capable of direct transmission and multiplication within the host. Certain of the larger animal parasites can cause serious abnormalities in their hosts, but many other parasites are innocuous unless present in large numbers. There is an extensive literature, however, on such relatively nonpathogenic parasites of marine animals, particularly the fishes. The emphasis of many of these papers is on description and taxonomy of the parasites, with little attention to the pathology they produce. Some of the papers are discussed, but most have not been included.

The proper extent of the marine environment to be considered also becomes a matter of definition. Diseases of estuarine animals and those of anadromous or catadromous species have been included if such diseases or parasites are acquired in salt water. Similarly, disease and parasite problems in saline inland seas have been included, since many of the hosts and their parasites are of marine origin. Many of the diseases discussed are characteristic of inshore or estuarine waters, where abnormal conditions are more readily noted and examined than in the open sea. Carcasses of marine animals washed up on beaches or floating in shoals near shore are much more likely to elicit action, scientific or otherwise, than would similar events a hundred miles from shore. Also, scientific studies of marine animals in the past have often varied inversely with distance from shore. As a result, much of the world literature on marine diseases concerns inshore events.

The world literature encompassed by this book is diverse and voluminous but can be categorized as: (1) original research papers; (2) reviews of literature on particular diseases, groups of disease organisms, or host species; and (3) monographic works, symposium volumes, or textbooks which include some treatment of diseases and parasites of marine species. The first category—original research reports—is obviously the most significant and challenging source of material for a book of this kind, but is also the most difficult to examine adequately, since papers are in many languages and in many journals throughout the world. Publications in the second category—reviews of literature—are less abundant, although a number of studies dealing with selected aspects of disease in the sea or with particular parasite groups are available. Examples are Dollfus' superb study and review of the tetrarhynchid cestodes (1942), and his review of cod parasites (1953); Kudo's classic work on myxosporidan and microsporidan Protozoa (1920, 1924, 1933); and Sindermann's review of marine fish diseases (1966). Publications in the third category—textbooks and symposium volumes—contain material on diseases or parasites of marine species, particularly the fishes. Examples are "Proceedings of a Conference on Fish Diseases" (Pavlovskii, 1959), "Parasitology of Fishes" (Dogiel *et al.*, 1958); "Symposium on Fish Diseases" (Altara, 1963), and Schäperclaus' classic "Fischkrankeiten" (1954).

A body of literature is slowly accumulating about diseases and treatment of diseases in marine aquaria and in other situations in which marine populations are held captive (e.g., lobsters in pounds and oysters on planted beds). Studies oriented toward prophylaxis and treatment of diseases in marine aquaria have been prompted by losses of individual expensive specimens, by persistent problems such as bacterial fin rot which disfigures specimens, or by mass mortalities, usually of undetermined causes. Conditions in captive marine populations are often conducive to rapid spread of pathogenic microorganisms or parasites which can proliferate quickly. Usually the captive population is crowded into too little space, often with inadequate food and poor water circulation; also many individuals may be slightly injured during capture or transport. Such conditions enhance destructive effects not only of pathogens, but also of facultative organisms not normally pathogenic in the natural populations.

With the recent heightened interest in sea farming—the cultivation of commercial fishes and invertebrates—there will be concurrent great need to cope with disease problems that are certain to develop. In the limited cultivation of marine animals already practiced, serious disease and predator problems have already been encountered (Sindermann, in press), in addition to the many other difficulties inherent in a farming operation. Disease control must be a major effort in the development of marine aquaculture.

As far as possible, consideration of diseases and parasites of each group of economically important marine animals in this book will follow a sequence beginning with viruses and proceeding through bacteria, fungi, protozoa, and larger animal parasites, to tumors and other abnormalities. Stress has been placed deliberately on diseases of microbial etiology, since these are responsible for mass mortalities. Other parasites may cause mortalities, if present in sufficient numbers, but their effects are mostly indirect, rendering the host animal more vulnerable to predation. The reference sections for each chapter, because of space limitations, contain only those literature citations referred to in the text. A great body of published information about the more benign parasites of commercial fish and shellfish, or diseases and parasites of non-commercial species, has thus been excluded. The references listed therefore constitute only a small—but hopefully a representative—fraction of the literature available. A separate bibliography of parasites and diseases of marine fish and shellfish will be published by the Bureau of Commercial Fisheries (Sindermann, in press).

Although supporting data are sometimes inadequate and fragmentary, I believe that the following hypotheses about the role of disease in marine populations can be stated: (1) Disease may exert profound effects on population size, and may at times be one of the most important factors of environmental limitation to the biotic potential of certain marine species. (2) Epizootic disease in one species may have pronounced negative or positive effects on other species—predators, scavengers, or competitors. (3) Disease levels may be influenced by a number of factors, including change in susceptibility of the host population, or increase in infection pressure on the host population. (4) Certain diseases and parasites common in one geographical area may be rare or absent in other areas. Microhabitats within hosts with cosmopolitan distribution may be occupied by different representatives of a genus or family of parasites in different parts of the world. (5) Some of the great past fluctuations in sea fisheries may have been caused by disease. (6) Epizootics in marine animals may occur at times of high population density. (7) Disease may be significant at any age; there are some indications that the earliest life history stages—eggs, larvae, and juveniles—may at times be seriously affected. (8) Close scrutiny of a marine species usually discloses one or more diseases which might be considered "characteristic" of that species in a given geographic area, although other diseases may occur. (9) At least some disease problems in marine populations are amenable to solution.

Diseases of marine fishes are less well known than those of freshwater species because: (a) Mortalities and epizootics are so much less apparent and so much less frequently observed in the sea than are those in the more restricted freshwater habitat, that the true role of disease in the sea has not been fully appreciated. (b) Freshwater hatcheries and aquaria are much more numerous than comparable saltwater facilities. Research on problems associated with crowding, artificial feeding, and disease control has been much less intensive for saltwater than for freshwater species. Much of the impetus for research, and the advances in understanding of disease in freshwater fishes have originated in the hatchery or aquarium environment; this impetus has been largely lacking for marine species. (c) The marine environment is less amenable to manipulation than is the freshwater environment, and problems of disease control in the sea have seemed insurmountable to some people.

The widely scattered world literature on marine fish diseases encompasses a body of knowledge that is growing rapidly with increasing scrutiny of the oceans and their inhabitants as actual and potential food sources for an expanding human population. The species of fishes studied are primarily members of commercially important groups such as gadoids and clupeoids, and attention has been paid to those conditions which affect survival or marketability. Diseases of marine fishes are important economically because they reduce the number of fish available to man, or they reduce the quality of fish as food. Important to reduction in numbers are epizootics and resultant mass mortalities caused by infectious agents. Less conspicuous but also important are "background" effects of disease that result in continuous direct or indirect subtraction of individuals from a population. Important to reduction in quality are parasites that inhabit and sometimes degrade the flesh of marine fishes. Conspicuous in this group are the Microsporida, Myxosporida, larval worms, and tissue-invading copepods.

Infectious diseases produce dramatic effects, such as epizootics and mass mortalities. Bacteria, fungi, and protozoans have all been implicated in marine diseases of serious consequence. Severe short-term effects of outbreaks on population size and on commercial landings have been observed in Atlantic herring, *Clupea harengus* L., white perch, *Roccus americanus* (Gmelin), and other species.[*] Repeated outbreaks of certain infectious diseases, such as "red disease" of eels and *Ichthyophonus* disease of herring, have been recorded.

Among the invasive diseases, larval cestodes, trematodes, and nematodes can be found (often in large numbers) in the flesh and viscera of marine fishes, where they may interfere with metabolic activities and with growth, or they may otherwise reduce the value of the parasitized

[*] Throughout the book an attempt has been made to give common and scientific names of fish and shellfish when they are first mentioned, and only the common name thereafter. In some cases this is not possible, as for example when the same common name is applied to several different species in different geographical areas, or when a species may have a different common name in different areas. Scientific names of fishes from North American waters follow the recommendations of the American Fisheries Society (1960).

fish to man. Tissue-invading copepods may act in similar ways. Enzootic centers exist for certain parasites, for example larval nematodes and some copepods; occasionally parasites such as monogenetic trematodes increase in abundance locally to produce epizootics.

Abnormalities, including tumors and skeletal deformities, are known for many marine species. Most of the morphological variations other than tumors can probably be attributed to defects in embryonic development; in fact a wide range of abnormalities has been seen in larval fishes, especially those reared in environments in which oxygen, salinity, light, or other factors deviated from normal.

Studies of captive marine fishes have provided much information about diseases. Many pathogens multiply rapidly in the aquarium environment to produce epizootics; other organisms, which may be insignificant in the natural habitat, may assume pathogenic roles. *Vibrio* infections are common in marine aquaria, and may quickly destroy captive populations. The dinoflagellate *Oodinium* and the ciliate *Cryptocaryon* have been causes of epizootics in marine aquaria, but, as far as it is known, are not significant pathogens in natural populations.

Among the invertebrates, molluscan and crustacean species of economic value as food have been affected by diseases, some of which have produced epizootics with resultant mass mortalities. Much attention has been directed toward oyster diseases, possibly because oysters have been cultivated more intensively than most other inshore or estuarine species. Microbial diseases—including those of bacterial, fungal, and protozoal etiology—have affected oyster stocks in many parts of the world. Bacterial diseases have had serious effects on lobsters, and a number of Protozoa—particularly Microsporida—affect crab and shrimp populations. Recent summaries of information about diseases and parasites of shellfish can be found in Cheng (1967) and Sindermann and Rosenfield (1967).

It is often difficult to establish the precise cause of death of marine invertebrates—to determine whether a suspected pathogen is a primary or secondary invader. Environmental and physiological factors can be inextricably associated with apparent disease; their relative effects are often not easy to assess. Thus, the literature on mass mortalities contains measurements of many environmental variables, descriptions of physiological conditions of host animals, and reports of suspected disease agents, but too frequently the studies have been unable to point to a single cause of death. The search for a single cause may have been an oversimplified approach to a complex problem. In other situations, epizootics of specific pathogens, possibly influenced to some extent by environmental factors, can be directly related to the state of resistance of the host population, the virulence and infectivity of the pathogen, and infection pressure.

Mass mortalities, many of undetermined origin but some definitely the result of disease, have occurred in populations of commercial invertebrates. These mortalities are a natural method of regulating population size; they have received increasing scrutiny in recent years. The development of methods of cultivation and of limited manipulation of the inshore environment should make it possible to reduce or eliminate the serious threat of disease to populations of commercial shellfish.

Gratifying recent increases in research efforts concerned with diseases of marine animals indicate that we may soon be able to assess with some reliability the role of disease in the sea. The following pages represent an attempt to summarize some of the background upon which we must build.

REFERENCES

Altara, I. (1963). Symposium européen sur les maladies des poissons et l'inspection des produits de la pêche fluviale et maritime. *Bull. Office Intern. Epizooties* **59**, 1–152.

Cheng, T. C. (1967). Marine molluscs as hosts for symbioses with a review of known parasites of commercially important species. *Advan. Marine Biol.* **5**, 1–424.

Dogiel, V. A., Petrushevskii, G. K., and Polyanski, Y. I., eds. (1958). "Parasitology of Fishes." Leningrad Univ. Press, Leningrad (in Russian) (Transl. by Z. Kabata. Oliver & Boyd, Edinburgh and London, 1961).

Dollfus, R. P. (1942). Etudes critiques sur les tétrarhynques du Muséum de Paris. *Arch. Museum Hist. Nat.* (*Paris*) [6] **19**, 1–466.

Dollfus, R. P. (1965). Aperçu général sur l'histoire naturelle des parasites animaux de la morue atlanto-arctique, *Gadus callarias* L. *Encyclopedie Biol.* No. 43, 428 pp.

Kudo, R. R. (1920). Studies on Myxosporidia. A synopsis of genera and species of Myxosporidia. *Illinois Biol. Monographs* **5**, 1–265.

Kudo, R. R. (1924). A biologic and taxonomic study of the Microsporidia. *Illinois Biol. Monographs* **9**, 1–268.

Kudo, R. R. (1933). A taxonomic consideration of Myxosporidia. *Trans. Am. Microscop. Soc.* **52**, 195–216.

Pavlovskii, E. N., ed. (1959). "Proceedings of a Conference on Fish Diseases," 224 pp. (In Russian.) Ikhtiol. Kom., Akad. Nauk SSSR, Moscow-Leningrad.

Schäperclaus, W. (1954). "Fishkrankheiten," 708 pp. Akademie Verlag, Berlin.

Sindermann, C. J. (1966). Diseases of marine fishes. *Advan. Marine Biol.* **4**, 1–89.

Sindermann, C. J. (in press). Disease and parasite problems in marine aquiculture. *Proc. Oregon State Univ. Conf. Marine Aquicult., 1968* (in press).

Sindermann, C. J. (in press). A bibliography of diseases and parasites of marine fish and shellfish. *U. S. Fish Wildlife Serv. Spec. Sci. Rept., Fisheries.*

Sindermann, C. J., and Rosenfield, A. (1967). Principal diseases of commercially important marine bivalve Mollusca and Crustacea. *U. S. Fish Wildlife Serv., Fishery Bull.* **66**, 335–385.

II

Diseases of Marine Fishes

A. INTRODUCTION

Studies of marine fish diseases have been sporadic and inadequate until recently. Although knowledge of freshwater fish diseases—particularly those of hatchery fish—has progressed rapidly in the past few decades, little incentive has existed for a comparable development of understanding of the role of disease in marine species. The vastness of the oceans, the complexity of natural factors regulating the size of fish populations, and the lack of methods to control and manipulate such factors have tended to discourage adequate continuing studies of such specific aspects of the marine environment as disease. Growing awareness that the human population is increasing at an alarming rate, that over two thirds of the earth's surface is ocean, and that we understand little of the dynamics of production in the sea, has led to increasing scrutiny in recent years of the variables that might at any particular time become overriding in their influence on population size. Disease is one such variable.

Diseases of food fishes have logically received greatest attention in past research—as they will in this chapter. Parasites and disease, in addition to killing the host, can materially reduce the value of fish as food for humans; this fact serves as a further incentive to examine disease of commercial species. Nonutilized fish may receive attention because of some academic interest, but the preponderance of research has been and is concerned with food species with large biomass. The term "disease" is used here in its broadest possible sense, to include any departure from normal structure or function of the organism—encompassing those states that result from activities of infectious agents, parasite invasion, and genetic or environmentally induced abnormalities. Such a broad definition of disease in marine fishes requires the inclusion of a surprising amount of widely scattered literature—certainly more than might be expected in view of the apparent neglect of the field.

Access to the literature on marine fish diseases is at present indirect. Several general texts on fish parasites and diseases have appeared in the German language (Hofer, 1904; Plehn, 1924; Schäperclaus, 1954; Amlacher, 1961; Reichenbach-Klinke, 1966). Schäperclaus' excellent text contains information on disease in marine as well as freshwater fishes. Recently several shorter texts on diseases of lower vertebrates by Reichenbach-Klinke have been translated into English, expanded, and combined into a more comprehensive work (Reichenbach-Klinke and Elkan, 1965). Russian texts, symposium volumes, and reviews (Liaiman, 1949, 1957; Dogiel, 1945, 1955; Petrushevskii, 1957; Dogiel et al., 1958; Pavlovskii, 1959, 1962; Polyanski, 1955) contain summarizations of marine studies and have appeared in English translations. Other nations have also made significant summarizing contributions to the general literature on fish diseases. Bergman (1922) published an early monograph in Swedish; Fujita (1943) published a text on diseases of fish and shellfish in Japanese; H. S. Davis (1953) published an English language text on culture and diseases of freshwater game fishes; and Ghittino (1963) recently published a handbook of fish diseases in Italian. A symposium on fish diseases held at Turin, Italy, in 1962 has been published by the Office International des Epizooties (Altara, 1963). English-language reviews and symposia on selected aspects of fish-disease research, usually including references to marine diseases, have appeared (Kudo, 1920, 1924, 1933; Sproston, 1946; Nigrelli, 1952a; Oppenheimer and Kesteven, 1953; Snieszko, 1954; Manter, 1955; Hoffman and Sindermann, 1962; Oppenheimer, 1962; Sindermann, 1963, 1966; Post, 1965; Putz et al., 1965; Snieszko et al., 1965; Wolf, 1966). Textbooks which include considerations of marine fish diseases and parasites include Breed et al. (1957), bacteria; Johnson and Sparrow (1961), fungi; Kudo (1966), protozoa; Pellérdy (1965), Coccidia; Shulman (1966), Myxosporida; Yamaguti (1958–1963), helminths; Dawes (1946, 1947) and Skrjabin (1947–1962), trematodes; Wardle and McLeod (1952), cestodes; and Yorke and Maplestone (1926), nematodes.

The general plan of this chapter is to consider examples of the significant diseases of marine fishes, concentrating sensibly on those that have received somewhere near adequate scientific attention, and attempting to include those caused by a wide variety of pathogens and parasites.

In the necessary process of selection at least two things happen: (1) Many examples and much literature must be neglected or not treated in sufficient depth, and (2) a natural tendency arises to choose examples close at hand or drawn from the author's research. Thus, illustrative material has been taken to a large extent from studies in the North Atlantic, although comparable material could be obtained from other geographical areas. Omitted is much of the great but scattered fund of published information from parasite surveys, including a large part of the ecological parasitology of the USSR, which has been effectively summarized by Dogiel *et al.* (1958). Many taxonomically oriented descriptions of parasites of fishes have not been considered, even though effects of such parasites may be properly included in the broad definition of disease used in this book. The literature cited thus includes only a small part of the often extensive published information on any particular parasite group. The references, extensive as they may seem, represent a too small sampling of the world literature—particularly the older literature, which for groups such as the Myxosporida and Microsporida is voluminous and elaborate. References to some of the early literature have been compiled by McGregor (1963); access to other early work can be gained through bibliographies included in more recent papers. For such parasite groups as the monogenetic trematodes, the cestodes, the nematodes, or the parasitic copepods, the consideration in this chapter therefore represents only a tiny, but hopefully a representative, fraction of the whole.

B. MICROBIAL DISEASES

Included in the category of microbial diseases, and aggregated here largely for convenience, are those of viral, bacterial, fungal, and protozoal etiology. They include the infectious diseases of fishes caused by parasites capable of destruction of host tissue and multiplication within the fish. Resultant pathology and the course of disease may depend on such factors as infective dose, virulence, and resistance of the individual host animal, as well as host nutrition and other environmentally influenced variables (Snieszko, 1957, 1964). The disease condition may range from chronic to acute, with varying degrees of host response.

1. Viruses

Virus diseases of fishes have received increasing attention in the past few decades. The present state of knowledge has been admirably reviewed by Wolf (1966). Much of our information concerns propagated freshwater fishes; virus diseases of marine fishes, although not unknown, are not reported abundantly in the scientific literature. This lack of knowledge probably stems in part from the absence, until recently, of adequate techniques for study. With the successful establishment of fish cells in culture (Wolf and Dunbar, 1957; Clem *et al.*, 1961; Wolf and Quimby, 1962), a most important tool has become available, and understanding of the role of viruses in marine fish populations should increase greatly in the next decade. Viruses are best known in marine fishes as suspected or known etiological agents of several neoplastic, hyperplastic, and hypertrophic diseases. Lymphocystis disease and certain papillomas have long been believed to be of viral origin, on the basis of epizootiological and transmission studies, and the presence of inclusions in affected cells.

Lymphocystis is probably the best known virus disease of marine and freshwater fishes. It was first described from the European flounder, *Pleuronectes flesus* (L.), by Lowe (1874), and soon after from other species (McIntosh, 1885, 1886; Sandeman, 1893; Woodcock, 1904a,b); the disease has since been reported from the orange filefish, *Alutera schoepfii* (Walb.), by Weissenberg (1938) and Nigrelli and Smith (1939); from the mummichog, *Fundulus heteroclitus* L., by Weissenberg (1939a); from the striped mullet, *Mullus surmuletus* (L.), by Alexandrowicz (1951); and from other marine and freshwater species by Bergman (1922), G. M. Smith and Nigrelli (1937), Weissenberg *et al.* (1937), and Weissenberg (1945). Recently several cases of presumed lymphocystis in striped bass, *Roccus saxatilis* (Walb.), have been observed (Anonymous, 1951; Sindermann, 1966). The disease was originally thought to be caused by parasitic protozoa or by the deposition of eggs of another animal under the skin of fish (Sandeman, 1893; Woodcock, 1904a). Weissenberg (1914b, 1920) and Joseph (1917, 1918) were the first to recognize lymphocystis cells as hypertrophied fibroblasts. Transmission studies (Rašín, 1927, 1928; Weissenberg, 1939b, 1951b; Wolf, 1962) have demonstrated the infectious nature of the disease and have suggested some degree of host specificity. Definitive evidence that a virus is responsible for lymphocystis was obtained by electron microscopy (Walker, 1962; Walker and Wolf, 1962) and by transmission of the disease with ultracentrifugates and bacteria-free filtrates (Weissenberg, 1951a; Wolf, 1962). Manifestations of lymphocystis include whitish nodules on body and fins caused by hypertrophy of fibroblasts and osteoblasts (Fig. 1A). The connective tissue cells grow to enormous size (5 mm in some cases) and become surrounded by a thick hyaline capsule. In severe cases most of the body surface may be involved. Weissenberg

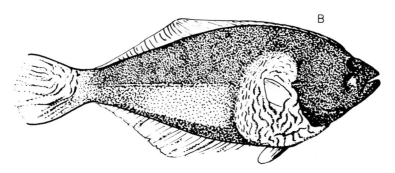

FIG. 1. (A) Lymphocystis disease of the dorsal fin of a flounder; (B) papilloma of a flounder.

(1921a) reported that in some areas up to one third of a population of fish could be affected. A great body of literature has accumulated on lymphocystis; much of the early work was well summarized by Nigrelli and Smith (1939). Two very important papers on lymphocystis appeared in 1965. Weissenberg published a history of research on the disease covering half a century, and Nigrelli and Ruggieri published an excellent and concise summary of knowledge about the disease with a list of known hosts and an annotated bibliography. Lymphocystis has been reported in 49 species of fishes, representing 20 families.

A recent and apparently sharply defined outbreak of lymphocystis in American plaice, *Hippoglossoides platessoides* (Fabr.), of the Grand Bank was reported by W. F. Templeman (1965b). Infected fish were first seen in 1960, and in 1964 the infection level in American plaice on the eastern slope of the Grand Bank was approximately 1%. Badly infected fish, called "scabby" or "seedy" by fishermen, were thrown overboard; estimates of such discards ran as high as 300 to 400 pounds per set in areas of heavy infections. Trawlers usually moved to other locations where fewer fish were diseased. Templeman suggested several possible explanations for the outbreak, including the possibility that the disease is enzootic in the population and may increase in intensity periodically. Awerinzew (1911) found annual prevalence levels of 11% in flounders, *Pleuronectes flesus,* from the Murmansk coast, and Nordenberg (1962) found infections as high as 12% in the same species from the Öresund, with some indication of higher prevalence in the warmer months of the year.

Neoplastic or hyperplastic diseases, some thought to be of virus origin, include dermal and epidermal papillomas of many flatfish species (Fig. 1B). Such diseased conditions have been reported from Atlantic halibut, *Hippoglossus hippoglossus* L., by Johnstone (1912a); plaice, *Pleuronectes platessa* (L.), by Johnstone (1925); sole, *Solea solea* (L.), by Thomas (1926); winter flounder, *Pseudopleuronectes americanus* (Walb.), by G. M. Smith (1935); flathead sole, *Hippoglossoides elassodon* Jord. and Gilb., by Wellings and Chuinard (1964) and Wellings *et al.* (1964, 1965); as well as from other pleuronectids. An epizootic level of epithelial tumors has been reported by Nigrelli *et al.* (1965) in juvenile sand soles, *Psettichthys melanosticus,* from the coast of British Columbia in which up to 40% of individuals were affected at certain sampling locations. The authors suggested that the disease may contribute to high natural mortality of the species. A similar epidermal papilloma was described from a Japanese witch flounder, *Glyptocephalus stelleri* (Schmidt), by Honma and Kon (1968) and from Japanese soles, *Limanda herzensteini* and *Hippoglossoides dubius,* by Kimura *et al.* (1967). Suspected viral particles have been described from the cytoplasm in some cases (Wellings *et al.,* 1967), but transmission has not been reported. Similar epidermal hyperplasia, of suspected viral etiology, is common in freshwater among European cyprinids. Characterized by irregular, white, raised patches on the skin, the disease is often referred to as "fish pox" (Roegner-Aust and Schleich, 1951; Roegner-Aust, 1953).

Skin tumors, described as sarcomas, were reported from northern pike, *Esox lucius* L., taken in brackish water of the Baltic (Ljungberg and Lange, 1968). The tumors had been noted since 1959, and, according to fishermen, occurred in up to 10% of pike in certain areas. The average diameter of tumors was 5–6 cm, and infiltration of underlying musculature was frequently observed. Viral etiology was indicated but not

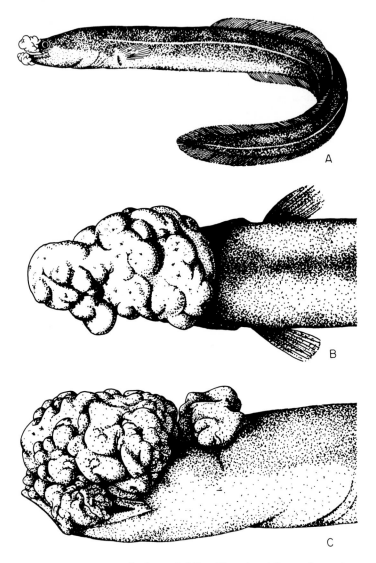

FIG. 2. Progressive stages of *Blumenkohlkrankheit* (cauliflower disease) in eels.

demonstrated, although viral particles were demonstrated in a concurrent study of other epidermal proliferations in pike from the same population (Winqvist *et al.*, 1968).

A remarkable tumorous growth of eels is aptly labeled *Blumenkohlkrankeit* or cauliflower disease (Fig. 2). This common chronic fibroepithelial tumor, often of dramatic proportions, occurs principally in the head region of European eels, *Anguilla anguilla* (L.). Reports of the disease in European rivers and coastal waters have increased in recent years (Schäperclaus, 1954; Lühmann and Mann, 1957; Engelbrecht, 1958; Koops and Mann, 1966).

According to Christiansen and Jensen (1950) the disease appeared in 1944 in Sweden and Bornholm, and was found in Polish Baltic waters in 1947. Prevalences were low (0.1–2%). Mann (1967) has recently summarized information about the spread of cauliflower disease in northern Europe—information which suggests that the disease is now epizootic in parts of the North Sea and the Baltic Sea. On the German coast of the North Sea prevalences have risen from a first report in 1953 (Schäperclaus, 1953b), to 1.8% in 1957, and 4.5% in 1964 and 1965—all in adult eels (over 30 cm long). During the period 1957–1965 the disease occurred in from 9 to 16% of small eels. On the German Baltic coast the disease was known as early as 1910 and was common in 1950 (Schäperclaus, 1953b; Mann, 1967). It now occurs on the entire Baltic coast, and is most abundant in low-salinity waters. It has been reported also from The Netherlands. Transmission has not yet been effected, but virus etiology is strongly suspected (Christiansen and Jensen, 1950). Eels with progressive tumors become emaciated and die. Schäperclaus (1953b) also found comparable growths in cod, *Gadus morhua* L., and papillomas have been reported from smelts, *Osmerus eperlanus* (L.), taken in the Baltic Sea, with characteristics very similar to cauliflower disease of eels (Breslauer, 1916).

A number of highly pathogenic viruses of freshwater fishes do not cause tumors (Wolf, 1964). The diseases produced include infectious stomatitis in fishes from South American rivers (Torres and Pacheco, 1934; Pacheco, 1935), viral hemorrhagic septicemia of salmonids in Europe (Jensen, 1963), and infectious pancreatic necrosis of brook trout, *Salvelinus fontinalis* (Mitchill) and rainbow trout, *Salmo gairdneri* Richardson (Wolf et al., 1960). Among the anadromous species, viral etiology has been indicated for a disease of Chinook salmon, *Oncorhynchus tshawytscha* (Walb.), from the Sacramento River, California (Ross et al., 1960; Parisot and Pelnar, 1962), and for a more widespread disease of sockeye salmon *Oncorhynchus nerka* (Walb.), in the Pacific Northwest (Watson et al., 1954; Guenther et al., 1959). Transovarian transmission was hypothesized for the Chinook disease, and the feeding of fingerlings with diets including salmon carcasses was implicated in the sockeye disease. The discreteness of the viruses involved, and the pathological changes in host tissue have been summarized by Parisot et al. (1965) and Yasutake et al. (1965).

Viruses that do not cause tumors have not yet been clearly demonstrated in marine fishes. Moewus (1963) reported studies of a ciliate parasite, *Miamiensis avidus* Thompson and Moewus, which was isolated from tumor-like nodules on seahorses, *Hippocampus erectus* Perry. The organism was studied as a possible vector of virus; poliovirus was used in absence of a suitable laboratory strain of marine virus. Results were inconclusive, but the author's suggestion of parasites as possible vectors of fish viruses does not seem unreasonable; in fact it was made previously by Thomas (1931) and Nigrelli (1938) in reference to epidermal hyper-plasias of cyprinids. Transmission of viral and rickettsial agents by parasites is known for certain diseases of mammals, e.g., swine influenza and salmon poisoning of dogs. The salmon poisoning example is of particular interest, because the pathogen, *Neorickettsia helminthoeca*, carried by the heterophyid trematode, *Nanophyetus salmincola*, can persist in salmon in the sea for several years (Farrell *et al.*, 1964; Mil-lemann *et al.*, 1964). An extensive literature on the disease has accumulated.

Moewus-Kobb (1965) also reported that the virus of infectious pan-creatic necrosis of freshwater fishes multiplied when introduced into cell cultures derived from a marine fish, the bluestriped grunt, *Haemulon sciurus* (Shaw). The same cell line of grunt was found to harbor a presumed "orphan virus" destructive to primary explants as well as fish cell lines (Clem *et al.*, 1965).

2. Bacteria

Critical problems in the study of bacterial pathogens of fish are the correct identification of the infectious agent and the determination of its role as primary or secondary invader. Not only is bacterial classification confused (Krasilnikov, 1949; Breed *et al.*, 1957; Prévot, 1961), but type cultures may be unavailable, and often biochemical and physiological characterization is incomplete. G. L. Bullock (1961, 1964) has made important contributions to the systematization of methods to identify bacterial pathogens in freshwater, and Colwell and Liston (1960), Shewan (1961, 1963), Shewan *et al.* (1954, 1958, 1960), G. H. G. Davis and Park (1962), and Scholes and Shewan (1964) have attempted similar systematization for marine bacteria. Bacterial pathogens most commonly reported from sea fishes are species of *Pseudomonas*, *Vibrio*, or *Mycobacterium*. Many of the bacteria normally present in seawater, or on the surface of fish, can invade and cause pathological effects if fish are injured or subjected to other severe environmental stresses.

Bacteria associated with fish and other marine animals can be categorized as: (1) primary pathogens; (2) secondary invaders, often with proteolytic abilities, that may be pathogenic for weak hosts; (3) heterotrophs, proteolytic, which invade dying animals and which, if cultured and injected experimentally in massive quantities, may kill some experimental hosts; or (4) normal marine flora, halophilic, that may occur on body surfaces or even within tissues of the host, but are not pathogenic.

Reports of bacterial epizootics in marine fishes are surprisingly infrequent, and relatively few bacterial pathogens have been recorded from natural populations of marine fish. Scarcity of information is probably due to lack of observation or to inadequate examination rather than lack of occurrence. Two examples support this view: Oppenheimer and Kesteven (1953) reported underwater observations of fish schools in which up to 10% of individuals exhibited lesions indicative of bacterial infections later demonstrated by smears and cultures; and Sindermann and Rosenfield (1954a) in their study of bacterial tail rot of Atlantic herring reported observation of typical disease signs in natural populations of immature fish from the Maine coast (Fig. 3).

Among the widespread bacterial epizootics, one caused by a species of *Pasteurella* resulted in extensive and selective mortalities of white perch, *Roccus americanus* (Gmelin), in Chesapeake Bay during the summer of 1963 (Snieszko *et al.,* 1964). Lesser mortalities of striped bass also occurred. The pathogen was isolated consistently in pure culture from moribund white perch, and was identified as a member of the genus *Pasteurella* on the basis of morphology and biochemical tests. Catch statistics and unpublished observations by the author in 1964 suggested that significant population decimation had resulted from the epizootic. This very recent and as yet only partially documented example undoubtedly has its counterparts caused by other bacterial pathogens in various parts of the world. Most of the outbreaks, because of location, or because they may not involve food fish, probably escape scientific scrutiny, and are viewed by local inhabitants with the same dismay and bewilderment that must have characterized the great human plagues and epidemics of past centuries.

Of all the known bacterial diseases of marine fishes, none has a longer or more fascinating history than the "red disease" of eels, caused by *Vibrio anguillarum* Bergman. The disease occurs during the warmer months in brackish and saltwater; reports have been most numerous from the Danish, German, Italian, and Swedish coasts, and the Baltic and North Seas. According to Hofer (1904), the disease was known and reported as early as 1718 from the Italian coast, and epizootics occurred repeatedly during the nineteenth century (reports date from 1825, 1850,

Fig. 3. Bacterial dermatitis and tail rot in juvenile Atlantic herring.

1864, 1884, 1885, 1889, and 1892). Disease signs include progressive reddening of fins and skin, visceral hemorrhages, reduced activity, and death —often preceded by loosening and fraying of the skin. *Vibrio anguillarum* appears to be a truly marine pathogen, limited to salinities above 9‰ and unable to survive in freshwater. Infection may occur through the gills or digestive tract of eels. Effects of the disease are most pronounced and mortalities are most common in late summer, in areas where sea temperatures exceed 16°C.

The term "red disease" was introduced by Feddersen (1896a,b) in reporting an outbreak of the disease in Scandinavian waters. Comparable outbreaks have occurred repeatedly to the present time (Feddersen, 1897a,b); Bergman, 1909; Brunn and Heiberg, 1932, 1935; Ljungberg, 1963), often causing significant mortalities and economic losses. The disease has also been reported from The Netherlands (Schäperclaus, 1927), Poland (Kocylowski, 1963), and Germany (Schäperclaus, 1934; Mattheis, 1960; Wolter, 1961). Characteristically, infections become evident among eels stored, even for short periods, in live boxes. Dead eels may be found in nets, traps, and impoundments during epizootics; the disease apparently spreads very rapidly among captive fish. An extensive survey conducted by Brunn and Heiburg (1932) documented the widespread occurrence of the disease in Scandinavian waters at the time and provided information about previous outbreaks dating back to 1880—outbreaks that sometimes brought the fishery to a standstill. Information from fishing industry sources in Denmark in the autumn of 1968 indicated exceptionally high prevalence of red disease and extensive mortalities in coastal waters, trap nets, and live boxes. The outbreak began earlier than usual and seemed much more virulent, as suggested by the amount of tissue damage and number of deaths. Many eels bore extensive ulcers that penetrated the musculature and rendered the eels unsalable. The disease signs suggest a possible mixed infection, or even a new disease entity, since the common form of red disease causes superficial red spots and reddening of the fins.

Brunn and Heiberg raised other questions in their report on the 1931 epizootic in Danish waters by suggesting that several pathogens may be involved in red disease from different geographical areas. They pointed out that only a few of the early studies (Canestrini, 1893; Inghilleri, 1903, Bergman, 1909) included bacterial examinations, and that at least three bacterial disease entities may be involved. Schäperclaus (1930) also demonstrated that red disease of eels in freshwater may be caused by *Pseudomonas* (*Aeromonas*) *punctata* Zimmerman. Other observations suggest that reddening of the skin of eels may be a generalized response to abnormal temperatures and reduced availability of oxygen, as well as to bacterial invasion. There seems to be little doubt, however, that a common infectious agent is involved in many of the outbreaks reported, since *Vibrio anguillarum* has been isolated repeatedly (Bergman, 1909; Schäperclaus, 1927; Nybelin, 1935). Two types, A and B, of the vibrio have been identified, and a toxin has been demonstrated. *Vibrio anguillarum* has also been found to be pathogenic to cod and plaice (Dannevig and Hansen, 1952; Bagge and Bagge, 1956; Ljungberg, 1963), to pike

(Schäperclaus, 1928; Ojala, 1963), and to brown trout, *Salmo trutta* L. (I. W. Smith, 1961).

Other vibrio diseases of marine and freshwater fishes have been reviewed by Rucker (1959). He suggested that vibrio infections may be much more prevalent than had been previously recognized, pointing out as examples that vibrio infections often kill Pacific herring, *Clupea pallasi* Val., held as live bait, and that a study by Bückmann (1952) disclosed natural vibrio infections in almost half of a sample of 117 European plaice. Recent studies of cultured marine fish of Japan, discussed in Chapter V, indicate a major role for vibrios in mortalities of captive populations.

Bacterial dermatitis, sometimes accompanied by ulcerations and fin rot, and usually associated in the literature with *Vibrio* or *Pseudomonas*, has been reported from wild populations of marine fishes. *Pseudomonas ichthyodermis* infections have been observed by Wells and ZoBell (1934), ZoBell and Wells (1934), and Hodgkiss and Shewan (1950). ZoBell and Wells reported evidence of the infection in California killifish, *Fundulus parvipinnis* Girard, in their natural habitat on the Pacific Coast, and stated that 90% of these fish died of the disease when brought into aquaria during the summer. Other species, such as gobies, *Gillichthys mirabilis* Cooper, blennies, *Hypsoblennius gilberti* (Jordan), and topsmelt, *Atherinops affinis* (Ayres), also exhibited lesions. Characteristics of the disease included an initial whitish spot on the body surface which expanded rapidly, disintegration of melanophores, raising and sloughing of scales, minute hemorrhages, and death. Smears from lesions revealed almost pure cultures of *Pseudomonas ichthyodermis*, but there was no evidence of systemic invasion, nor could the organism be demonstrated in the blood. Reinfections from cultures were made repeatedly; initial lesions occurred within 18 hours and death within 14 days. Mortality of fish infected from cultured pathogens was not as high as that of fish infected directly with material from lesions. The pathogen was described as a motile, gram-negative, nonspore-forming, halophilic bacillus, with a temperature optimum for infectivity, growth, and virulence near 20°C. A significant finding was that fish kept in water above 30°C did not become infected and that badly diseased fish recovered rapidly if acclimated successfully to water of 32°–35°C. Hodgkiss and Shewan (1950) described an intramuscular lesion in plaice and obtained presumptive evidence that *Pseudomonas ichthyodermis* was the etiological agent. More recently, Shewan (1963) has suggested that the pathogen should be placed in the genus *Vibrio*, and that its correct designation is *Vibrio ichthyodermis*.

Tuberculous lesions with acid-fast bacilli have been reported from a number of commercial marine fishes, including halibut (Sutherland, 1922; Johnstone, 1927; Hodgkiss and Shewan, 1950), cod (Alexander, 1913; Johnstone, 1913), and plaice (Hodgkiss and Shewan, 1950). Spontaneous lesions of this type in marine fishes have been thought until recently to be rare, so that single cases have warranted descriptions in the literature. Aronson (1926) characterized and named *Mycobacterium marinum* from several species of marine fishes, including Atlantic croaker, *Micropogon undulatus* (L.), and black sea bass, *Centropristes striatus* (L.), in the Philadelphia Aquarium; this bacillus remains as the only fully characterized *Mycobacterium* of marine fish origin, although others are known to exist and have been partially characterized (Alexander, 1913; Sutherland, 1922; Griffith, 1930; Reichenbach-Klinke, 1955a,b). Aronson (1938) pointed out that mycobacteria responsible for spontaneous tuberculosis in marine fishes differ from acid-fast bacilli known as human pathogens, but the classification of pathogenic mycobacteria is at present very confused (McMillen and Kishner, 1959; McMillen, 1960; Nigrelli and Vogel, 1963). A recent review by Vogel (1958) reported acid-fast bacillus disease, principally in the form of visceral lesions, in 120 species of marine and freshwater teleosts throughout the world. Parisot (1958) has also reviewed the literature on tuberculosis in fish. He suggested that this disease may be serious in adult Pacific salmonids, and that it may be partly responsible for recent decreases in the catch. Wood and Ordal (1958), Ross *et al.* (1959), and Ross (1960) found high prevalence of tuberculosis in salmon returning from the sea, but attributed much of it to early exposure to bacilli in hatchery diets which included carcasses of tuberculous fish. Walford (1958) listed tuberculosis as a disease of young Pacific salmon, and believed that the pathogen may have been acquired in the sea. Infected fish were characterized by reduced growth, incomplete gonad development, and kidney lesions containing acid-fast bacilli.

In addition to tuberculosis, Walford (1958) considered several other interesting bacterial diseases of young Pacific salmon from saltwater: (1) "Hemorrhagic septicemia" occurred repeatedly and caused extensive mortalities in young salmon held in saltwater. Outbreaks were found to be caused by a vibrio that was enzootic in Pacific herring and was thought to be responsible for outbreaks and mortalities in herring and Pacific sardines, *Sardinops sagax* (Jenyns), of the Pacific Northwest. Other organisms, such as *Pseudomonas* (*Aeromonas*) *punctata*, have been reported to cause hemorrhagic septicemia in freshwater pond fishes. (2) "Eye disease" of salmon, cod, and other bottom fishes was also caused by a vibrio. The disease was characterized by initial destruction of the eyes, followed by bacteremia and death. This malady may be similar or identical to *Augenkrankheit* of North Sea cod (Bergman, 1912). (3) "Boil disease" was found to be a progressive and usually fatal disease of young salmon, characterized by muscle abscesses. The pathogen was a diplobacillus resembling the causative agent of kidney disease of salmon in freshwater. (4) A myxobacterial disease similar to "columnaris disease" of freshwater salmonids was characterized by development of gray-white lesions anterior to the tail. The lesions progressed with sloughing of skin and fins. The myxobacterium, *Chondrococcus columnaris* (Davis), has been described as infecting skin, gills, and fins of *Fundulus heteroclitus* (Nigrelli and Hutner, 1945) and other marine species (H. S. Davis, 1922; Garnjobst, 1945).

This array of infectious diseases, either of saltwater origin or enhanced by saltwater phases of the life history of salmon, indicates the possibilities for disease studies in this and other anadromous fish (Rucker *et al.*, 1954).

Some appreciation of the undoubtedly important role of bacteria as pathogens of marine fishes can be gained from papers and discussions presented during a recent Symposium on Bacterial Fish Diseases (summarized in the *Bulletin of the Japanese Society of Scientific Fisheries* 34, No. 3, 271–277). Although oriented primarily toward bacterial diseases of cultivated fish (to be considered in Chapter V), the symposium included information on several bacterial diseases found in natural waters. Among these, "ulcer disease" was very common during the warmer months of the year on the west coast of Japan (Akazawa, 1968). Large numbers of fry died, and vibrios were isolated in almost all cases. Three species were identified: *Vibrio parahemolyticus, V. alginolyticus,* and *V. anguillarum.* Kusuda (1968) discussed the same or a similar vibrio disease which occurred in wrasses, dolphins, yellowtails, and mackerel from the Sea of Japan, in open waters as well as in coastal regions. The vibrio was isolated from seawater samples and from healthy fish as well.

3. Fungi

The role of fungi in the oceans was admirably summarized by Johnson and Sparrow (1961). Fungus diseases of marine organisms received excellent coverage by the authors, and it is startling to note that with the single exception of *Ichthyophonus hoferi* (Plehn and Mulsow), often referred to as *Ichthyosporidium hoferi,* which is discussed in detail in various sections of this book, fungus diseases of marine fishes are almost unknown.

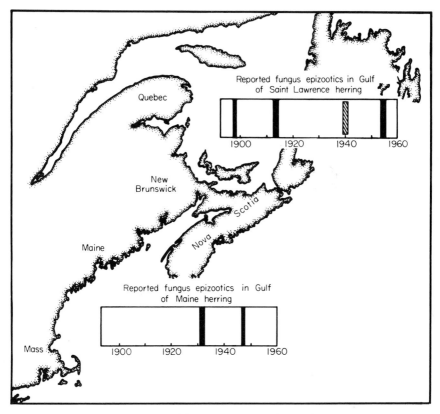

FIG. 4. Reported epizootics of fungus disease (*Ichthyophonus hoferi*) in herring of the western North Atlantic. The 1940 outbreak was included on the basis of verbal reports from fishermen and other residents of the area. (From Sindermann, 1963.)

Half a century of sporadic study in Europe and North America has provided evidence that one of the most serious fungus pathogens of fishes, marine or freshwater, is *Ichthyophonus hoferi*. Systemic infections, found in mackerel in England (Johnstone, 1913; Sproston, 1944), rainbow trout in Germany (Plehn and Mulsow, 1911), and herring and mackerel in Canada (Sindermann, 1958), can result in widespread mortalities in these and other species. Epizootics of the disease are characteristic of herring, *Clupea harengus,* of the western North Atlantic (Cox, 1916; F. W. Fish, 1934; Scattergood, 1948). Six such outbreaks have been reported since 1898 (Sindermann, 1963; see Fig. 4). Drastic reduction in herring abundance due to disease has been documented, and the postulation made that this disease may be the most important single limiting factor to population growth of herring in the western North Atlantic.

Whether a single species, or a complex of related forms (Schäperclaus, 1953a; Sprague, 1965), *Ichthyophonus* is known as a menace to aquarium fishes in Europe (Lederer, 1936), as an introduced pathogen in trout hatcheries of western United States (Rucker and Gustafson, 1953), as a long-recognized pathogen of wild salmonids in western Europe, and as a pathogen of many other marine and freshwater fishes. Reichenbach-Klinke (1954, 1955a) has assembled a list of more than 80 species that have been found to be infected by the fungus.

The disease is systemic, with foci of infection in the heart, viscera, and lateral somatic muscles (Figs. 5, 6, 7, 8). A simple sequence of life-history stages, described from herring (Sindermann and Scattergood, 1954), involves multiple germination of heavy-walled spores, hyphal invasion of host tissues (Fig. 9), formation of "hyphal bodies," and sequential germination of these entities. The disease has been reported in Atlantic herring in chronic and acute phases. Acute infections were characterized by massive tissue invasion, necrosis, and death within 30 days. Chronic infections exhibited cell infiltration, progressive connective tissue encapsulation of spores (Fig. 10), and accumulation of melanophores. The disease was rarely arrested completely, however, and deaths occurred in most fish within 6 months. During the most recent epizootics, infections averaged about 25% of all herring sampled, and many cases were acute (Fig. 11). Enzootic prevalence was usually well under 1% and infections during this phase have been chronic in all cases examined.

Transmission of the disease has been achieved by feeding massive spore doses, derived either from cultures or from diseased fish. Increase of experimental spore doses resulted in increasing numbers of chronic infections and, beyond a certain dosage, the appearance of acute infections (Sindermann, 1963, 1965). Experimental epizootics, produced in populations of immature herring held in large seawater aquaria, duplicated many of the events observed in nature. Herring varied individually in responses to identical spore doses; some acquired acute infections, some acquired chronic infections, and some remained uninfected.

A more complex life cycle for *Ichthyophonus* has been described from mackerel by Sproston (1944). This is the only study in which indications of sexual reproduction, in the form of hyphal fusions, were observed. Other authors have described the occasional appearance of conida-like bodies, and the occurrence of macro- and microhyphae. Reichenbach-Klinke (1956a) and others have raised the question of several possible species, but definitive culture studies have yet to be carried out. Reichenbach-Klinke (1956b,c, 1958) found *Ichthyophonus* to

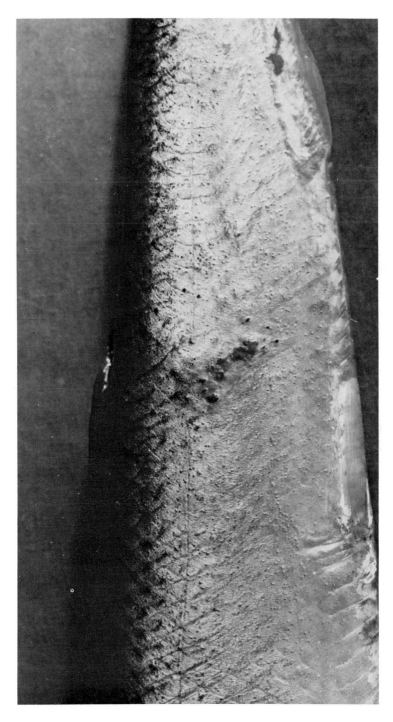

FIG. 5. External signs of *Ichthyophonus hoferi* infection in Atlantic herring: "sandpaper effect" and ulceration.

FIG. 6. Effects of *Ichthyophonus hoferi* infection on body muscles of Atlantic herring: uninfected (top); acute infection with extensive necrosis (center); and chronic infection with pigment deposition around fungus nodules (bottom).

Fig. 7. Internal signs of *Ichthyophonus hoferi* infection in Atlantic herring; white nodules on and in all visceral components.

be very common in Mediterranean fish. A similar organism has recently been seen in cultured marine fish in Japan.

Other than *Ichthyophonus,* reports of fungus pathogens of marine fishes are very scarce in the scientific literature. Reichenbach-Klinke (1956b) briefly described a species of *Cladosporium* found associated with hypertrophy of the epithelium of a cod, *Gadus morhua,* taken in the North Sea, but the disease was apparently rare. He also mentioned a *Cladosporium* from the body cavity of two South American species of the characid genus *Hyphessobrycon* that may be found in brackish water. Apstein (1910) described infection of lumpfish, *Cyclopterus lumpus* (L.), by *Cycloptericola marina.* Cysts containing the fungus were found in the stomach wall of over half the specimens examined.

It is not uncommon for diseases and parasites of freshwater origin, including fungi, to be carried downstream with the anadromous host to the estuary and the sea, where survival is often limited. Such appears to have been the situation in the observation of Aleem *et al.* (1953) of *Isoachlya parasitica* in *Atherina riqueti* in southern France. External signs of fungus infection have been seen in alewives, *Alosa pseudoharengus* (Wilson), and smelts, *Osmerus mordax* (Mitchill), as they enter the sea after spawning (Sindermann, 1966). *Saprolegnia* infections of Pacific salmon disappeared when the fish were placed in seawater

(Earp *et al.*, 1953), although Vishniac and Nigrelli (1957) have suggested that brackish-water fishes may be parasitized by Saprolegniaceae.

Saprolegnia parasitica, an important parasite of freshwater fishes, grew in seawater base media (Stuart and Fuller, 1968a), and grew and sporulated in slightly saline water if other environmental factors were suitable (Te Strake, 1959). Stuart and Fuller observed also that Atlantic salmon recently returned from the ocean, as evidenced by presence of "sea lice," have been taken from estuarine waters with signs of ulcerative dermal necrosis, thought to be caused by *Saprolegnia*. The possible role of *Saprolegnia* as a disease agent in estuaries, however, is still in doubt (Dick, 1968; Stuart and Fuller, 1968b).

Representatives of the genus *Dermocystidium* have been reported as parasites of fishes, particularly salmonids (Dunkerley, 1914; Léger, 1914; H. S. Davis, 1947). An epizootic in Chinook salmon was described by Allen *et al.* (1968). In all examples cited, however, the infections were confined to freshwater, or were acquired by anadromous hosts in freshwater.

FIG. 8. Hearts of normal (left) and fungus-infected Atlantic herring.

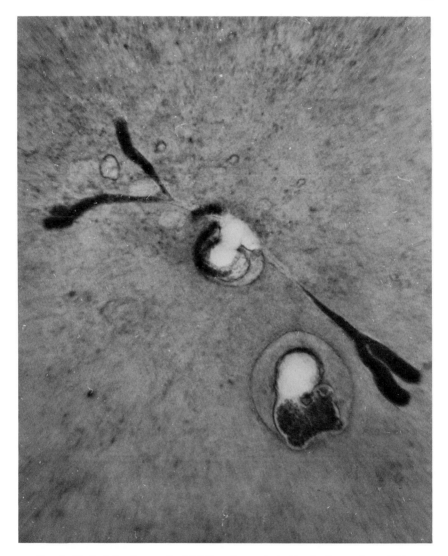

FIG. 9. Hyphal development of *Ichthyophonus hoferi* in the heart of a redfish.

4. Protozoa

Sporozoa and Cnidospora* are among the best-known and most serious pathogens of marine fishes, although studies have been made of repre-

---

* An attempt has been made to conform to the revised system of classification of the Protozoa (Honigberg *et al.*, 1965), with suggested modifications of Sprague (1966).

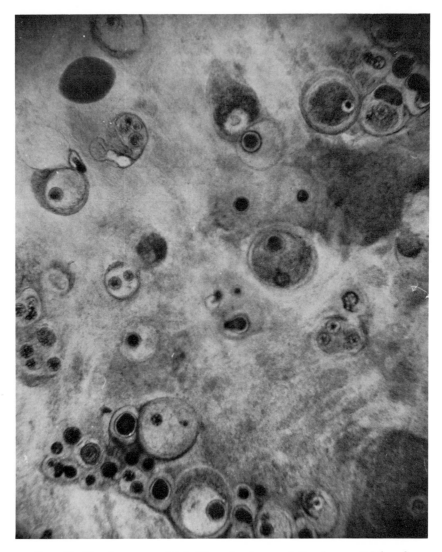

Fig. 10. Heavily encapsulated life-cycle stages of the fungus *Ichthyophonus hoferi* from the heart of a redfish.

sentatives of other protozoan groups, such as the dinoflagellates, hemo-flagellates, and ciliates (Laveran and Mesnil, 1902a,b; Neumann, 1909; Tripathi, 1948; Brown, 1951; Laird, 1951a,b; Reichenbach-Klinke, 1956d). Ciliates and dinoflagellates which assume pathogenic roles in marine aquaria are considered in Chapter V. Coccidia, Myxosporida, and Micro-sporida have various but often severe effects on their hosts, ranging from castration to nerve and muscle degeneration. Many of the representatives of these three groups that have been studied have characteristic and readily recognizable spore stages, which facilitate identification (Fig. 12). Most are specific for particular host tissues. For some, life cycles and transmission are adequately understood, but for many, much remains to be learned, particularly about their ecology.

a. Hemoflagellates

Trypanosomes are occasional inhabitants of the blood of marine fishes. Transmission from fish to fish is thought to be effected by blood-sucking invertebrates, particularly leeches. Pathogenicity is unknown, but infections are usually light. From the studies of Laveran and Mesnil (1902a), Henry (1913), Fantham (1930), Laird (1951b), and others, it is obvious that marine fishes have an extensive hematozoan fauna, and that the trypanosomes are represented in various groups of teleosts.

Eels, *Anguilla anguilla* (L.), from Europe were found infected by

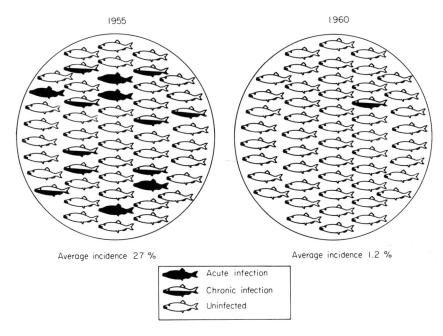

FIG. 11. Relative frequencies of infected individuals in samples of Atlantic herring from the Gulf of Saint Lawrence during (1955) and after (1960) the last epizootic of the fungus *Ichthyophonus hoferi*. (From Sindermann, 1963.)

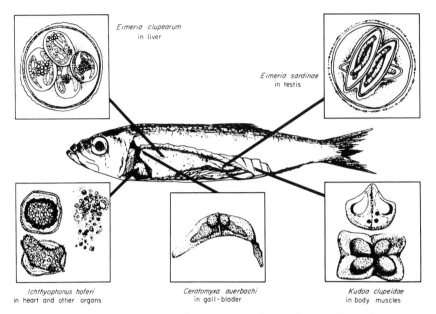

Fig. 12. Protistan parasites of immature Atlantic herring from the western North Atlantic.

Trypanosoma granulosum (Laveran and Mesnil, 1902a), whereas *Anguilla mauritanica, A. bengalensis,* and *A. reinhardtii* in Australia harbor *T. auguillicola* (Johnston and Cleland, 1910).

Javelin fish, *Coelorhynchus australis* (Richardson), and red cod, *Physiculus bachus* (Forster), from New Zealand waters were found by Laird (1951b) to be parasitized by *Trypanosoma coelorhynchi.* The half-banded sea perch, *Gilbertia semicincta,* also from New Zealand, was parasitized by *T. pulchra* (Mackerras and Mackerras, 1925), and the European haddock, *Melanogrammus aeglefinus,* was infected by *T. aeglefini* (Henry, 1913).

Two pleuronectids, the witch flounder, *Caulopsetta scapha,* and the sand flounder, *Rhombosolea plebeia,* from New Zealand were infected by *Trypanosoma caulopsettae* (Laird, 1951b). All infections were heavy, with from 10 to 40 parasites per thin smear. Trypanosomes have been reported from other flatfishes: *T. soleae* from European flounder, *Pleuronectes flesus* (Lebailly, 1904); and *T. platessae* from European plaice, *Pleuronectes platessa* (Lebailly, 1905).

Blennies harbor trypanosomes also. Cockabullies, *Tripterygium medium* Günther and *T. varium* (Forster), from New Zealand were infected by *Trypanosoma tripterygium* (Laird, 1951b), the European blenny *Blennius pholis* was infected by *T. delagei* (Brumpt and Lebailly,

1904), and the South African *Blennius cornutus* by *T. blenniclini* (Fantham, 1930).

Other New Zealand trypanosomes described by Laird include *T. congiopodi* from the pigfish, *Congiopodus leucopaecilus* (Richardson), and *T. parapercis* from the blue cod, *Parapercis colias* (Forster).

Saunders (1959) described *T. balistes* from Florida gray triggerfish, *Balistes capriscus Gmelin*. It is notable that these were the only trypanosomes encountered in examining blood smears from 1677 fish.

b. *Coccidia*

Severe and often fatal coccidian infections of mammals and birds have some counterparts in freshwater fishes (Bespalyi, 1959; Pellérdy, 1965), particularly in cultured fish, in which they may affect the digestive tract, but also the liver, kidney, and air bladder. All fish coccidians are members of the genus *Eimeria*. The group is widely distributed among marine fish also, but effects of parasitization are less well known.

A widely distributed disease of clupeoid fishes is that caused by *Eimeria sardinae* (Thélohan). The parasite localizes, often in massive numbers, in the testes, where it may reduce reproductive capacity or cause complete sterility of the host (Pinto, 1956; Letaconnoux, 1960; Pinto and Barraca, 1961; Pinto *et al.*, 1961; see Fig. 13). *Eimeria sardinae* has been reported from the European sardine, *Sardina pilchardus* Walb., off Portugal (Pinto, 1956), the sprat, *Sprattus sprattus* (L.), from the eastern North Atlantic (Thomson and Robertson, 1926), and the Atlantic herring, *Clupea harengus*, from the Baltic Sea (Dogiel, 1939; Dollfus, 1956), Barents Sea (Polyanski, 1955), White Sea (Shulman and Shulman-Albova, 1953), North Sea (Kabata, 1963a), and the western North Atlantic (Sindermann, 1961). It occurred in over 50% of sardine samples examined by Pinto (1956) and thus must be considered a significant limitation to the reproductive potential of that species.

Other coccidian parasites of the testes of marine clupeoids have been reported. Spores of *Eimeria brevoortiana* occur in the testes of Atlantic menhaden, *Brevoortia tyrannus* (Latrobe), according to Hardcastle (1944), and spores of *E. nishin* have been described from Pacific herring by Fujita (1934). *Eimeria brevoortiana* was found in 42% of 700 male fish examined, and was more common in adults than in juveniles. No spores were seen in females. *Eimeria nishin* occurred in even higher percentages, and heavy infections were common. *Eimeria etrumei* was described by Dogiel (1948) from round herring, *Etrumeus micropus*.

Eimeria may occur in other organs. *Eimeria clupearum* (Thélohan) is found in the liver of clupeoids, often in abundance, but is usually not considered seriously pathogenic. Livers of sticklebacks, *Gasterosteus*

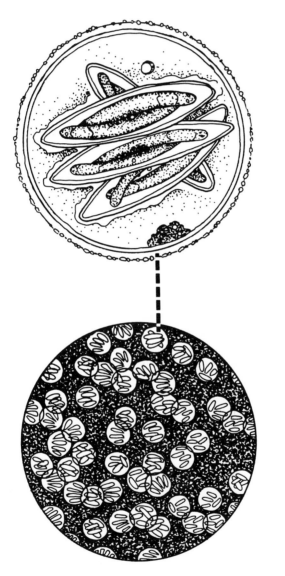

Fig. 13. Invasion of testes of sea herring by the coccidian *Eimeria sardinae*. Low-power view (left) and single mature oocyst (right). (Redrawn from Dogiel *et al.*, 1958, and Kabata, 1963a.)

aculeatus and *G. clupeatus,* are invaded by *E. gasterostei* (Thélohan, 1890). Grossly visible lesions in the liver of kingfish, *Caranx trachurus,* can be caused by *E: cruciata* (Thélohan, 1892; Yakimoff, 1929).

The intestine and pyloric caeca of a number of fish are invaded by coccidians. *Eimeria cristalloides* and *E. motellae* occur in rocklings of the genus *Motella* (Thélohan, 1893; Labbé, 1893, 1896); *E. evaginata* occurs in rockfish, *Sebastodes taczanowskii,* and sculpin, *Myxocephalus stelleri* (Dogiel, 1948). *Eimeria anguillae* was described by Léger and Hollande (1922) from the intestine of the European eel, *Anguilla anguilla.*

The air bladders of several gadoids, haddock, *Melanogrammus aeglefinus,* cod, *Gadus morrhua,* and pollock, *Gadus virens,* are occasionally heavily infected by *Eimeria gadi* (Fiebiger, 1913). *In situ* germination of sporocysts of the pathogen are thought to produce such heavy infections. *Eimeria auxidis* was described by Dogiel (1948) from the kidney of the Pacific saury, *Cololabis saira,* and from *Auxidis mafu.*

c. *Haemogregarina*

Members of another coccidian group, the Haemogregarinidae, have long been recognized as of widespread occurrence in blood cells of fishes, and are the most common blood parasites of marine fishes. Although the parasites were first reported in 1901 by Laveran and Mesnil, the complete life history and method of transmission of marine members of the group are still unknown, and their pathogenicity for the fish host is undetermined. A number of biologists have published extensively on the group (Laveran and Mesnil, 1901, 1902b; Neumann, 1909; Laird, 1952, 1953, 1958; Saunders, 1955, 1960, 1964, 1966). Most haemogregarines have been described from marine, anadromous, and catadromous fishes, rather than from freshwater species. Leeches are thought to be vectors. Laird (1952) pointed out that a number of species have been described as new on the basis of occurrence in a new host or in a new geographical area. Considering possible host-induced morphological variation, this practice has resulted in appreciable confusion and probably extensive synonymy. Haemogregarines have been described from menhaden in Florida by Saunders (1964), from sea-run arctic char, *Salvelinus alpinus* (L.), in nothern Canada by Laird (1961), from javelinfish, *Coelorhynchus australis* (Richardson), in New Zealand by Laird (1952); and from many other fishes from diverse habitats (Laveran, 1906; Lebailly, 1905; Kudo, 1966).

Several haemogregarines have been described from eels. *Haemogregarina lignieresi* was described by Laveran (1906) from Argentinian eels; *H. bettencourti* was described from European eels by França (1908); and *H. thyrosideae* was described from an Indian eel by De

Mello and Valles (1936).

Blennies from several widely separated localities have been found to be infected by haemogregarines. Laveran and Mesnil (1901), in the earliest report on these parasites, described *Haemogregarina bigemina* from European *Blennius pholis* L. and *B. gattorugine* Bloch. *Haemogregarina londoni* was described by Kohl-Yakimoff and Yakimoff (1915) from *Blennius trigloides* at Naples; *H. salariasi* was described by Laird (1951a) from the blenny *Salarias periophthalmus* Val. from Fiji; and *H. fragilis* was described from *Blennius cornutus* (L.) from South Africa by Fantham (1930). The Atlantic wolffish, *Anarhichas lupus* is parasitized by *H. anarhichadis* (Henry, 1912).

Mullets in various parts of the world are infected by haemogregarines. Carini (1932) described *Haemogregarina mugili* from *Mugil brasiliensis* Agassiz in Brazil. The same parasite was reported by Laird (1958) from *Mugil* sp. taken at Guadalcanal Island in the South Pacific. Another haemogregarine was reported but not identified in South African *Mugil capito* Cuvier (Fantham, 1919).

Haemogregarina bigemina, identified by Laveran and Mesnil (1901), is a cosmopolitan species, having been reported from Europe, Canada, United States, South Africa, the Red Sea, and the South Pacific. It is nonspecific, having been reported from many families (Laveran and Mesnil, 1901; Laird, 1953, 1958; Saunders, 1955, 1958, 1960). Among 1677 Florida fish (representing 26 species) examined by Saunders (1958b), for example, *H. bigemina* was present in 116. The haemogregarines have not been reported as responsible for mortalities.

d. *Myxosporida*

Diseases caused by Myxosporida are common in marine as well as freshwater fishes. The myxosporidans inhabiting organs such as the gallbladder are most frequently studied and described; consequently the proportion of described coelozoic species in marine fishes in higher than the histozoic species (Meglitsch, 1952). Those localizing in the somatic muscles, however, must be considered the most destructive and of greatest economic significance. Statements exist in the literature to the effect that Myxosporida as a group are not particularly injurious (H. S. Davis, 1917). This may be true of some of the coelozoic members, but it is certainly not true of histozoic forms, which are numerous and which destroy the flesh of many hosts. Muscle-inhabiting Myxosporida are of worldwide distribution and economic significance. Of particular importance are members of the genus *Kudoa,* which was created by Meglitsch (1947) to include species removed from the genus *Chloromyxum* that are histozoic, usually in the skeletal muscles of fish, and have quadrate or stellate spores broader than they are long. These species are associated with necrosis of the flesh of living fish, and with rapid postmortem deterioration and liquefaction.

Meglitsch removed eight species of *Chloromyxum* to his new genus *Kudoa*. Since then other *Chloromyxum* species have been described that clearly fit the criteria for *Kudoa*. For simplicity, I have retained *Chloromyxum* if the species was so designated in the literature, except for the species removed by Meglitsch.

The flesh of clupeoid fishes is often parasitized by Myxosporida that produce opaque white cysts and necrotic areas. A *Chloromyxum* occurs in the pilchard, *Sardinops ocellata*, from South Africa (Rowan, 1956). Juvenile Atlantic herring, *Clupea harengus*, menhaden, *Brevoortia tyrannus*, and blueback herring, *Alosa aestivalis* (Mitchill), from the Atlantic coast of North America are often parasitized by *Kudoa* (=*Chloromyxum*) *clupeidae* (Hahn, 1918; Meglitsch, 1947; Sindermann, 1961a). Several authors (Tyzzer, 1900; Linton, 1901; Sindermann, 1957) have noted that the parasite occurred only in smaller and younger members of the host species (Fig. 14). As many as 75% of 1-year-old Atlantic herring from certain parts of the United States (Maine) coast were parasitized, but adults were not infected (Fig. 15). Linton speculated that there were fewer infections among older fish because the vitality of the diseased fish was so impaired that they fell victim to predators in larger proportional numbers than did healthy fish. It seems equally likely that invasion occurs early in the life of the host, that spores mature and escape from cyst areas, and that evidence of disease is absent by the time the host reaches maturity.

Other pelagic fishes may be parasitized by muscle-invading Myxosporida. Spanish mackerel, *Scomberomorus maculatus*, from the Florida coast were found by Iversen and Van Meter (1967) to be infected by a previously undescribed myxosporidan that they named *Kudoa crumena*. Numerous cysts were found throughout the body musculature, but the prevalence of the parasite in Spanish mackerel from Florida waters was considered to be low. Pérard (1928) has described the degeneration of muscles of Atlantic mackerel, *Scomber scombrus* L., resulting from parasitization by *Kudoa* (=*Chloromyxum*) *histolyticum*.

Extensive necrosis of the body muscles characterizes invasion of halibut, *Hippoglossus stenolepis* Schmidt, by two Myxosporida: *Unicapsula muscularis* Davis, which causes a condition known as "wormy" halibut, and *Kudoa* (=*Chloromyxum*) sp., which causes "mushy" halibut (Thompson, 1916; H. S. Davis, 1924). Both reduce the value of the fish as food. Muscle necrosis in swordfish, *Xiphias gladius* L., from Japan has been reported by Matsumoto (1954) to be caused by the myxosporidan *Chloromyxum musculoliquefaciens;* a similar "jellied" con-

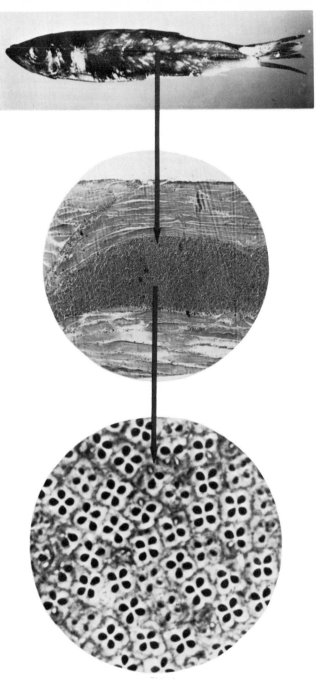

Fig. 14. Infection of immature Atlantic herring by the myxosporidan *Kudoa clupeidae*. Opaque white intramuscular cysts (top): low-power photomicrograph of cyst, showing masses of mature spores (center): and oil immersion photomicrograph of stained spores (bottom).

dition of swordfish from the North Atlantic has been observed by Mc-Gonigle and Leim (1937). Another cnidosporan, *Hexacapsula neothunni*, has been associated by Arai and Matsumoto (1953) with a jellied condition of the body muscles in yellowfin tuna, *Thunnus albacores*. The condition had apparently been known for a long time by fisherman and dealers, since it was a cause of considerable economic losses. Liquefied muscle was first noted adjacent to the vertebral column of infected fish. The process of liquefaction was very rapid, involving most of the body of some iced fish within 3 days. The phenomenon was observed only rarely in recently killed fish, but developed in many iced fish by the time they reached the market. *Hexacapsula neothunni* spores were found in jellied flesh of tuna from the Tokyo market, taken in the Bunda Sea. Bluefin tuna, *Thunnus thynnus* (L.), from Moroccan waters were found to be parasitized by a myxosporidan identified as *Kudoa clupeidae* by Dollfus (1955).

A condition known as "milkiness"—a softening and liquefaction of the flesh—in several species of fishes from the African coast has been associated with the presence of *Kudoa* (=*Chloromyxum*) *thyrsites* (Gil-

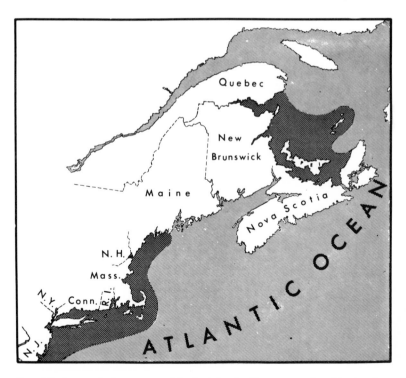

FIG. 15. Areas of the western North Atlantic (heavy crosshatching) where the myxosporidan *Kudoa clupeidae* occurs in immature herring.

christ). The parasite has been reported in barracuda, *Thyrsites* (*Sphy-raena*) *atun* (Euphr.), by Gilchrist (1924); in stockfish, *Merluccius capensis,* by Fletcher *et al.* (1951); and in the John Dory, *Zeus faber* L., by Davies and Beyers (1947). The same condition and parasite have been reported in *Thyrsites atun* from Australia by Johnston and Cleland (1910) and Willis (1949). Milky flesh deteriorates rapidly after the fish is caught, probably due in part to a proteolytic enzyme secreted by the parasite, as postulated by Willis. In South African waters, Davies and Beyers found that three fourths of the John Dory and stockfish were infected with *Kudoa thyrsites.* About 25% of all John Dory were too heavily in-fected to be suitable for filleting. The same parasite occurred in 5% of Australian barracuda (Roughley, 1951).

Milkiness of the flesh of lemon sole, *Paraphrys vetulus* Girard, and other species, was reported from the Canadian Pacific coast by Margolis (1953) and Forrester (1956) as due to a species of *Chloromyxum.* Milky condition of several other Pacific coast flatfishes was recently ex-amined by Patashnik and Groninger (1964). Pacific halibut, *Hippoglossus stenolepis,* Dover sole, *Microstomus pacificus,* petrale sole, *Eopsetta jordani,* and starry flounder, *Platichthys stellatus,* were found with the condition. A myxosporidan with four polar capsules was identified that resembled *Kudoa thyrsites* in many details.

Among the anadromous fishes, Iversen (1954) described a myxo-sporidan, *Myxosoma squamalis,* that caused external pustules on the body surfaces of coho salmon (*Oncorhynchus kisutch* Walbaum) and chum salmon (*Oncorhynchus keta* Walbaum). Prevalence was about 5% in coho salmon, and some fish contained several hundred cysts. Another myxosporidan, *Henneguya salminicola* Ward, invades the flesh of several species of Pacific salmon, producing opaque white cysts described as "tapioca disease" (H. B. Ward, 1919; F. F. Fish, 1939). Ward described *H. salminicola* from Alaskan coho salmon, and the parasite was sub-sequently reported from other Pacific coast species of *Oncorhynchus* by Fish. Fantham *et al.* (1939) described another species, *H. salmonis,* from Atlantic salmon, *Salmo salar,* taken in Quebec. Spores of *Henneguya salminicola* have also been seen in milky necrotic pockets in salmon from the eastern Pacific (Patashnik and Groninger, 1964), and the milky condition was thought to be an advanced stage of the tapioca-like cysts commonly found in salmon. Similar pathological conditions and high prevalences have been described in salmon from the western Pacific by Akhmerov (1954, 1955). Prevalences in Kamchatkan salmon were as high as 40% in chum salmon, 25% for sockeye salmon, and 26% for coho salmon. The coho salmon seemed most seriously affected with the necrotic phase of the disease. Dogiel *et al.* (1958) discussed the final ulcerative stage of *H. salminicola* infection, and reported that severe parasitization (40–50 cysts per fish) caused emaciation and death.

Other representatives of the myxosporidan genus *Henneguya* (characterized by spores with two polar capsules; spore body compressed parallel to sutural plane, often with heavy sutural ridge; usually with iodinophilous vacuole and caudal prolongations of each valve) are histozoic in many marine and freshwater fishes. Iversen and Yokel (1963) described *H. ocellata* from the red drum, *Sciaenops ocellata*, taken in Florida waters. The parasites produced cysts in pyloric ceca and intestine. The same parasite was seen earlier (Linton, 1905) in red drum from North Carolina. Heavy infection, with cysts "completely covering the pyloric caeca and beginning of the intestine" were reported. Another sciaenid, the weakfish, *Cynoscion regalis*, a close relative of the red drum, is also parasitized by a species of *Henneguya* (Jakowska *et al.*, 1954). Cysts occur between the rays of the dorsal and anal fins. Still other species of the genus are known from marine fishes. *Henneguya lagodon* was described from pinfish from Florida, *Lagodon rhomboides*, by Hall and Iversen (1967). Cysts occurred in tissues surrounding the eyes, often forming conspicuous external bulges. Laird (1950) described *H. vitiensis* from the heart of the Fijian marine fish, *Leiognathus fasciatus* (Lacépède). *Henneguya otolithi* was described from the bulbus arteriosus of two Indian marine fishes, *Otolithus ruber* (Bloch and Schneider) and *O. maculatus* (Cuvier and Valenciennes), by Ganapati (1936, 1938, 1941). Sea bream, *Box salpa* (Cuvier and Valenciennes), from Naples were infected by *H. neapolitana* (Parisi, 1912) and black rockfish, *Sebastodes melanops* (Girard), from California were infected by *Henneguya* sp. (Jameson, 1929).

Myxosporida that inhabit the gallbladder and urinary bladder—of which there are many species (Kudo, 1919)—are widespread in marine fishes. Several genera (particularly *Ceratomyxa*, *Chloromyxum*, *Myxidium* and *Leptotheca*) are common in gallbladders and urinary bladders of teleosts, and gallbladders of elasmobranchs (Fig. 16). Since examination of such structures for Myxosporida is much easier than examination of tissues, particularly in preserved specimens, it is not surprising that the misconception has arisen that most of the Myxosporida are relatively innocuous coelozoic parasites. In freshwater ponds certain gallbladder-inhabiting myxosporidans may cause epizootics, for example, *Chloromyxum truttae* in trout (Léger, 1906), but comparable effects are not known in the marine environment. Light infections do not cause significant pathology, but heavy infections in the gallbladder may cause enlargement, discoloration, and disruption of function of the organ. Fantham and Porter (1912), who examined the widespread occurrence

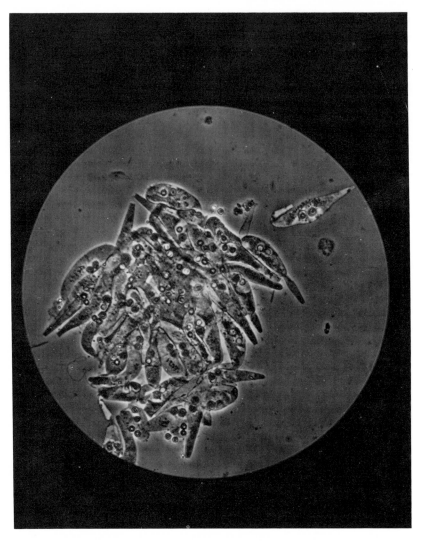

Fig. 16. Spores of the myxosporidan *Ceratomyxa sphaerulosa* from the gall-bladder of Atlantic herring.

of gallbladder parasites in elasmobranchs and teleosts from the English and French coasts, found that myxosporidan parasitization caused inflammation, excess secretion of mucus, increase in viscosity of bile, enlarged livers, and emaciation of the host.

Gill-invading Myxosporida are not usually of serious consequence to marine fishes. However, Shulman (1957) described an epizootic of

Myxobolus exiguus Thélohan in the gills of mullet, *Mugil cephalus* (L.), from the Black Sea, in which 500 to 600 kg of fish per kilometer were washed up on the western shore of the Crimean Peninsula during the spring of 1949. Mechanical disruption of gill function was characteristic of the disease. Often entire gill filaments were filled with cysts. Rupture of cysts caused tissue damage and often extensive hemorrhage. Death was thought to be due to asphyxia from loss of respiratory surfaces, or to severe loss of blood. No abnormalities were noted in the viscera. According to Dogiel *et al.* (1958) infection with *M. exiguus* has been reported from many parts of the Black and Azov Seas.

Several species of Myxosporida invade the cranial cartilages of fishes. One, *Myxobolus aeglefini* (Auerbach), occurs in plaice, *Pleuronectes platessa* (L.), hake, *Merluccius merluccius* (L.), and haddock, *Melanogrammus aeglefinus* L., of the North Sea (Johnstone, 1906; Auerbach, 1906, 1912; Kabata, 1957b). Erosion and (in some instances) hypertrophy of head cartilage result. Effects of *M. aeglefini* do not seem as severe as those caused by *Myxosoma cerebralis* (Hofer) in salmonid fishes, *Myxosoma*, a highly infectious disease agent acquired early in life in freshwater, causes "whirling disease" of juvenile salmon and trout, as well as gross skeletal abnormalities (Bogdanova, 1960; Hoffman *et al.*, 1962). The disease has long been known in central Europe, and has recently been found in Russia and United States. Dannevig and Hansen (1952) have reported symptoms indicating possible *M. cerebralis* infections in very young herring reared in aquaria.

The general occurrence of histozoic Myxosporida in pelagic hosts (especially in species such as the tunas, which have little association with inshore waters) naturally raises questions about the method of transmission from fish to fish. Histozoic spores deep in the musculature would seem to require death and decay of the host for release, or cannibalism by larger fish on smaller members of the species. It should be noted, however, that exit pores were found in *Kudoa clupeidae* infections of the somatic muscles of sea herring, and similar methods of spore release may exist for other histozoic species. Also, it is possible that the life cycle of myxosporidans includes an intermediate host. In pelagic fishes, the intermediate host could be a member of the zooplankton community.

e. *Microsporida*

Several serious diseases of marine fishes result from microsporidan invasion. The Microsporida, unlike the Myxosporida, are intracellular parasites, which cause enough hypertrophy of host cells to form grossly visible cysts or tumorlike areas. Serious crippling and disfiguring diseases

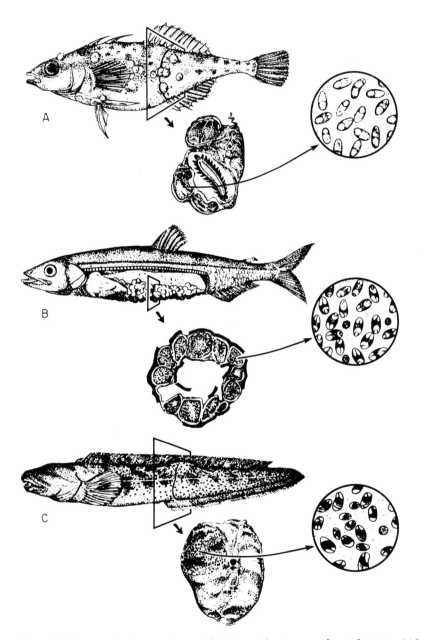

FIG. 17. Gross and microscopic manifestations of microsporidan infections. (A) *Glugea anomala* infection of stickleback; (B) *Glugea hertwigi* infection of smelt; and (C) *Plistophora macrozoarcidis* infection of ocean pout.

of marine and freshwater fish are caused by microsporidans; most seriously affected are muscles, skin, digestive tract, and nerves (Fig. 17). The genera *Glugea, Plistophora,* and *Nosema* all contain severe pathogens of marine fishes. Although Polyanski (1955, p. 28) stated ". . . . the Microsporidia group of parasitic protozoa have relatively small distribution in marine fish," recent (and not so recent) publications indicate not only that Microsporida are widely distributed in marine and estuarine fishes, but also that their effects on the host are among the most severe of any parasite group.

Smelts, *Osmerus eperlanus* from Europe (Weissenberg, 1911c) and *Osmerus mordax* from North America (Schrader, 1921; Fantham *et al.,* 1941), are often parasitized by *Glugea hertwigi* Weissenberg, which produces varying degrees of visceral involvement, to the extreme condition in which the body cavity is packed full of microsporidan cysts up to 9 mm in diameter. Heavy infections have been reported to prevent reproduction by mechanical occlusion of the vent (Haley, 1954; Sindermann, 1963), and lesser infections destroy parts of the digestive tract and gonad and impair metabolic functions of other organs. Haley found that 23% of the smelt he examined were infected; because of the serious pathological manifestations of the disease he suggested that it could be an important factor in the recently observed decline of the smelt fishery on the New Hampshire coast. Bogdanova (1957) reported that massive infections with *G. hertwigi* caused degenerative changes in sexual organs and death of the host. Dogiel *et al.* (1958) stated that infection of *O. eperlanus* caused functional disturbances in several organs, growth retardation, decline in fertility, and mass mortality. Incidence of *Glugea* reached 25–50% and decline in stocks of *Osmerus* was attributed to the parasite (Annenkova-Khlopina, 1920). W. Templeman (1948) found a *Glugea,* probably *G. hertwigi,* in capelin, *Mallotus villosus* (Müller), spawning on the Newfoundland coast. Almost one fourth of all fish examined carried cysts beneath the peritoneum or in the mesenteries.

The digestive tracts of several flatfishes are invaded by the microsporidan, *Glugea stephani.* As with *G. hertwigi* in smelts, the walls of the intestine and pyloric caeca are often covered with layers of cysts, sometimes abundant enough to occlude the lumen (Fig. 18). Hagenmüller (1899) described the parasite from small *Pleuronectes flesus* from the coast of France. Johnstone (1901) and Woodcock (1904a,b) reported a similar parasite in plaice, *Pleuronectes platessa,* from the Irish Sea and the English coast, and Linton (1901) saw a similar form in winter flounders, *Pseudopleuronectes americanus,* from Massachusetts waters. Half of all winter flounders examined at Woods Hole, Massachusetts, by Mavor (1915) were infected with *G. stephani,* and extensive parasitization of *Pleuronectes limanda* from Helgoland was reported by Reichenow

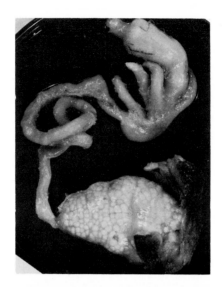

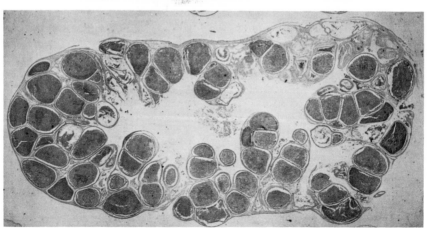

46

(1929). Fantham *et al.* (1941) found the microsporidan in *Limanda ferruginea* from the Nova Scotia coast. Recently Stunkard and Lux (1965) reexamined the parasite and its abundance in winter flounders at Woods Hole. They found that infections were acquired very early in life, and that fish heavily infected during the first year of life probably did not survive. The authors considered it probable that a second or intermediate host is required in the life cycle of the parasite.

Another species of the same genus, *G. anomala* (Moniez), was reported earlier (Weissenberg, 1913, 1914a, 1921b) from two European sticklebacks, *Gasterosteus aculeatus* L. and *Pungitius pungitius* (L.). Hypertrophy of connective tissue cells, resulting in thick-walled cysts up to 4 mm in diameter, occurs externally and internally. External white nodules develop in the subepidermal connective tissue, particularly in areas overlying the coelomic cavity. Cysts contain spores and developmental stages of the microsporidan. Early stages in cyst development can be found in hypertrophying mesenchymal cells around the host digestive tract. The parasite undergoes schizogony and the host cell nuclei proliferate so that a storage area for mature spores, the *Glugea* cyst, is eventually formed. Kudo (1924) and others described gross deformation of the host's body as a result of intensive *G. anomala* infection. The parasite has been reported as a contributing factor in mass mortality of sticklebacks from the White Sea (Dogiel *et al.,* 1958). The environmental situation was somewhat unusual though, since the sticklebacks were trapped in tide pools after an unusually high tide. Most of the population died as a result of severe infections with *G. anomala* and monogenetic trematodes.

The pollock, *Pollachius pollachius* (L.), is infected with *Glugea punctifera*, which occurs in the connective tissue of the eye musculature (Thélohan, 1895). This microsporidan has also been reported as a serious intramuscular parasite of walleye pollock, *Theragra chalcogramma*, from the Okhotsk and Japan Seas (Akhmerov, 1951). Cod from the Okhotsk Sea were also infected with this *Glugea*.

Another microsporidan, *Plistophora macrozoarcidis* Nigrelli, is an important parasite of the ocean pout, *Macrozoarces americanus* (Bloch and Schneider). Extensive tumor-like intramuscular cysts, often several centimeters in diameter, seriously reduce the marketability and use of this

---

FIG. 18. *Glugea stephani* infection in digestive tract of the winter flounder: digestive tract with heavy infection of rectal wall (top); heavily infected pyloric caeca and intestine, showing characteristic chalk-white pebbled appearance (center); and photomicrograph (×100) of the heavily infected intestine (bottom). (Photographs provided by Mr. Fred Lux, U. S. Bureau of Commercial Fisheries, Woods Hole, Massachusetts.)

fish in the United States. Appearance of fillets containing parasite cysts on the market during 1943–1944 was responsible in part for curtailment of a developing fishery for ocean pout, and in a few years led to complete disappearance of the species as a food fish in the United States (Fischthal, 1944; Sandholzer *et al.*, 1945). Recent interest in reviving the fishery seems contingent on development of a suitable method of eliminating parasitized fish from processing procedures.

Plistophora cysts in the ocean pout can often be recognized by conspicuous bulges on the body of the host. The lesions are usually exposed during filleting, and a puslike exudate of spores and tissue debris occurs when such areas are cut. Life-cycle stages have been described by Nigrelli (1946). Since no ulceration has been seen, the method of spore liberation has been postulated as death and decay of the host. The massive involvement of individual fish suggests sporulation *in situ*. Repeated autoinfection is possible in some species of Microsporida, according to Kudo (1966), and some suggestion of it was found in ocean pout. Many specimens were characterized by immense numbers of minute infections involving single muscle fibers (Olsen and Merriman, 1946).

Plistophora macrozoarcidis was originally described as a haplosporidan—an *Ichthyosporidium*—by Fischthal (1944), but Nigrelli (1946) demonstrated that it is a microsporidan. Recently another presumed *Ichthyosporidium* causing pathology in fish has also been placed in the Microsporida. Schwartz (1963) reported that the huge abdominal bulges frequently found in spot, *Leiostomus xanthurus*, from Chesapeake Bay (Fig. 19) are actually cysts containing large numbers of spores. Although he designated the forms as *Ichthyosporidium* sp., Sprague (1966) reexamined the material and demonstrated polar filaments, indicating that the parasite is a microsporidan rather than a haplosporidan.

Other species of *Plistophora* invade the flesh of fish also. Body muscles overlying the visceral cavity of the long rough dab, *Drepanopsetta hippoglossoides* Gill, are invaded by *P. hippoglossoideos* Bosanquet, which forms cysts up to 10 mm long. Kabata (1959) found the parasite to be widely distributed in the North Sea, but believed that no great damage to the host resulted from infection with this parasite. Cod of the Barents Sea were found to be infected with another species, *P. gadi* (Polyanski, 1955). The parasite produced large tumors (5–8 mm in diameter) in the body muscles. *Plistophora ehrenbaumi* was reported by Reichenow (1929), Claussen (1936), and A. Meyer (1951, 1952) from the wolffish, *Anarhichas lupus*, in which it causes intramuscular lesions.

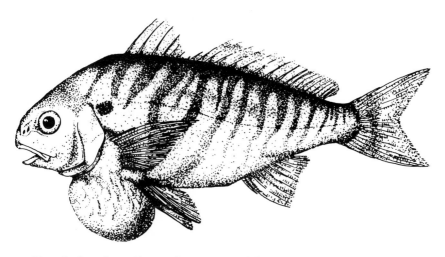

Fig. 19. Spot from Chesapeake Bay with abdominal bulge resulting from microsporidan infection. (Redrawn from Schwartz, 1963.)

Bond (1937) identified a *Plistophora* from the mummichog, *Fundulus heteroclitus*, from Chesapeake Bay.

The microsporidan *Nosema lophii* (Doflein) produces large tumorlike cysts in the central nervous system of the goosefish or angler-fish, *Lophius piscatorius* L. Parasitization results in extensive hypertrophy of processes of host ganglion cells as the cyst develops, producing dark grape-like enlargements on the nerves. Weissenberg (1909, 1911a,b,c) found abundant infections at Naples; the parasite has also been reported from England and France. Weissenberg observed multiple infections in single host nerve cells. In advanced stages, hypertrophy of the cell, with its contained areas of spores and schizonts, continues, and much connective tissue infiltrates the ganglia. The parasites remain restricted to the cell processes, and do not invade the cell body proper, even though it too is much hypertrophied.

Another species of *Nosema, N. branchiale,* was described by Nemeczek (1911) as an intracellular parasite of the gills of the haddock, *Melanogrammus aeglefinus* L. Small white cysts, grossly visible, were produced (Fig. 20). The parasite was found by Bazikalova (1932), Dogiel (1936), and Shulman (1950) in Baltic cod, *Gadus morhua callarias* L.; by Shulman and Shulman-Albova (1953) in White Sea cod, *Gadus morhua maris-albi* Derrugin; and by Fantham *et al.* (1941) in cod from the Gulf of Saint Lawrence, Canada. Kabata (1959) reported *N. branchiale* from cod caught off Iceland. Over 60 cysts were found on one gill arch, but

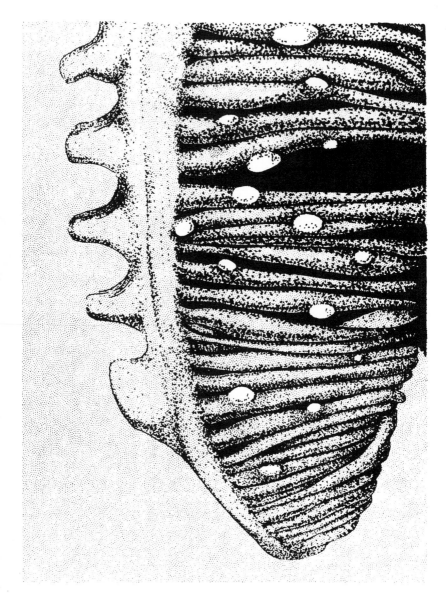

Fig. 20. Cysts of the microsporidan *Nosema branchiale* on gills of haddock. (Redrawn from Nemeczek, 1911.)

even the most heavily parasitized fish did not seem to be seriously damaged.

f. *Ciliata*

Ectoparasitic ciliates represent a little known field of marine fish parasitology, according to Lom (1962). Members of the peritrich genus *Trichodina* are commonly found on marine hosts from natural populations (Kahl, 1934, 1935), and the holotrich *Cryptocaryon irritans* is common in aquarium populations. Studies of trichodinids on marine fish extend back in time to Robin (1879). Tripathi (1948) and Lom (1963) have summarized information on the species of *Trichodina*. Lom (1962) examined 20 species of fish from the Black Sea, and found 10 infected with trichodinids; they were localized principally on the gills, and only rarely on the skin, unlike the freshwater species, which are found principally on the skin. Laird (1953), who examined 458 intertidal zone fishes of 10 species from New Zealand, found the prevalence of *Trichodina* (98%) much higher than that of any other protozoan group.

Padnos and Nigrelli (1942) examined 300 puffers, *Spheroides maculatus*, from the New Jersey coast and found 82% parasitized with two trichodinids. *T. spheroidesi* and *T. halli*. Intensity of parasitization varied from fish to fish; the ciliates were found principally on gills, but occasionally on the skin. Other marine fishes from the same sampling area harbored trichodinids (Nigrelli, 1940) but infestation was not as intense as on puffers. Presence of host red blood cells in vacuoles of the ciliates indicated that they cause tissue destruction. In very heavy infestations the gill epithelium was completely destroyed, leaving large denuded areas among the filaments. Padnos and Nigrelli (1942) stated that such a condition resulted in death of the fish.

Another example of pathogenicity of trichodinids was given by Reichenbach-Klinke (1956a). Describing *T. dohrni* from Mediterranean *Bathygobius capito* Cuv. et Val., he noted that in some infections the gills were covered by a grayish layer of hundreds of ciliates, and that the filaments were hypertrophied.

Representatives of other genera of peritrichous ciliates also occur on marine or brackish-water fishes. Precht (1935) described *Scyphidia gasterostei* from the stickleback, *Gasterosteus aculeatus*, taken in Kiel Harbor. Laird (1953) described *Scyphidia acanthoclinia* from kelpfish, *Acanthoclinus quadridactylus*, and *Caliperia longipes* from the clingfish, *Oliverichtus melobesia*, of New Zealand.

Cryptocaryon irritans, a ciliate pathogenic to fish in marine aquaria, is considered in Chapter V.

C. DISEASES CAUSED BY HELMINTHS AND
PARASITIC CRUSTACEA

The invasive diseases, as considered in this chapter, include those caused by the larger parasites, those that are nonmultiplicative in the fish host. Of primary concern in marine fishes are the various parasitic worms and the tissue-invading copepods. Omitted from this discussion are leeches, most ectoparasitic copepods, and lampreys, which, although of occasional concern, probably do not often exert serious effects on marine fish populations. Since the worms and copepods are large, conspicuous, and often abundant, they have been observed and studied extensively.

1. Helminths

The helminths—trematodes, cestodes, nematodes, and acanthocephalans—are common parasites of marine fishes. Usually it is as larvae that the worms are of greatest significance. Adults occur in the digestive tract, but larvae are usually in the flesh or in the viscera. The effects of worm larvae on the host include growth retardation, tissue disruption, metabolic disturbances, and even death in heavy infestations. Added economic effects include discarding of otherwise edible fish products, delay in processing operations, and possible loss in oil yields.

a. *Trematoda*

Adult digenetic trematodes are common in the digestive tracts of marine fishes. Yamaguti (1958) recognized 367 genera and 1390 species from fish, but it is as larvae (as migrating cercariae and as metacercariae) that trematodes seem to be of greatest significance to the fish host. Marine teleosts serve as intermediate hosts for many trematodes, particularly those whose definitive hosts are shore-inhabiting or fish-eating birds and mammals. Metacercariae of such worms encyst beneath the skin or in the body of inshore fishes. An excellent example is the trematode *Cryptocotyle lingua* (Creplin), whose life cycle in the western North Atlantic involves the periwinkle, *Littorina littorea* (L.), the Atlantic herring, and the gull, *Larus argentatus* Pontoppidan (Fig. 21). Originally a parasite of comparable species in northwestern Europe (Christensen and Roth, 1949), the parasite was introduced into North American waters near the middle of the nineteenth century, probably with its snail host (Stunkard, 1930). Cercariae of *Cryptocotyle* invade and encyst in the fins and integument of herring, cunner, *Tautogolabrus adspersus,* and a number of other inshore western Atlantic species, causing the formation of conspicuous cysts or "black spots" (Fig. 22). It has been demonstrated experimentally (Sindermann and Rosenfield, 1954b) that massive cercarial invasion will blind and kill immature herring, and it has been postulated that invasions of comparable magnitude are possible in the inshore habitat of the fish (Fig. 23).

Another larval fluke, *Stephanostomum baccatum* (Nicoll), occurs in a number of marine fishes, particularly flatfishes, from the Canadian Atlantic coast to the Baltic Sea. The life cycle, as elucidated by Wolfgang (1954a,b, 1955a,b), involves gastropods of the family Buccinidae, the winter flounder and other pleuronectids, and the sea raven, *Hemitripterus americanus* (Gmelin) (Fig. 24). Metacercariae occur in unpigmented cysts, concentrated on the blind side of the flatfish and in the fins, often in great numbers in larger fish. The parasite was originally reported from a halibut from the English coast by Nicoll (1907) and was later found in American plaice, *Hippoglossoides platessoides* (Fabr.), by Nicoll (1910). Dawes (1947) recorded six species of European flatfish as hosts.

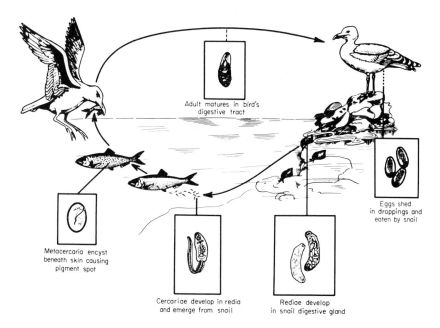

FIG. 21. Life cycle of the trematode *Cryptocotyle lingua.* (Based on Stunkard, 1930.)

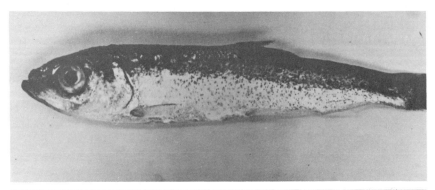

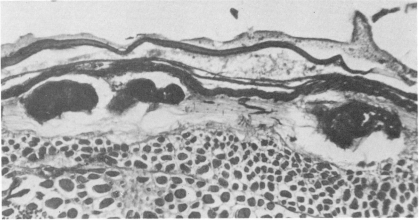

FIG. 22. Heavy invasion of immature Atlantic herring by the larval trematode, *Cryptocotyle lingua* (above), and photomicrograph of metacercariae in the skin (below).

A number of larval trematodes encyst in the hearts of fish. Burton (1956) described *Ascocotyle leighi*, whose metacercariae inhabit the bulbus arteriosus of the brackish-water *Mollienesia latipinna* from Florida. Sogandares-Bernal and Bridgman (1960) found the same parasite in Louisiana. Sogandares-Bernal and Lumsden (1964), after observing mortalities of heavily infected hosts, suggested that reduced circulatory capacity could reduce survival under conditions of environmental stress. Dead fish each harbored over 80 metacercariae; fibrosis of cardiac tissue was extensive, and the lumen of the bulbus was partially occluded. Other members of the genus *Ascocotyle* occur as metacercariae in brackish-water Mugilidae, Poeciliidae, and Cyprinodontidae, usually in close association with the circulatory system of the host (Timon-David, 1961; Lumsden, 1963; Sogandares-Bernal and Lumsden, 1963).

Hopkins (1968) described a dip-netted sample of sheepshead minnow, *Cyprinodon variegatus* at Grand Isle, Louisiana, that was 100% infected with heavy-walled *Ascocotyle* cysts in the bulbus, which was much enlarged. A later seine collection in the same area was only about 10% infected. This suggests that heart infections slow the hosts, rendering them more susceptible to predation.

Many other larval trematodes occur in marine fishes. Bykhovskaya-Pavlovskaya and Petrushevskii (1959), for example, have listed 46 species of metacercariae from the USSR, of which almost half occurred in marine or estuarine species. Fish-eating birds and mammals have been identified as definitive hosts of most of these parasites. Mass mortalities due to larval trematode invasion have been reported from the Aral and Caspian Seas (Dogiel and Bykhovskii, 1939; Dubinin, 1949). Red mullet, *Mullus barbatus* (L.) and striped mullet, *M. surmuletus* (L.), in the Mediterranean Sea are often parasitized by larval trematodes (Orlandini, 1957).

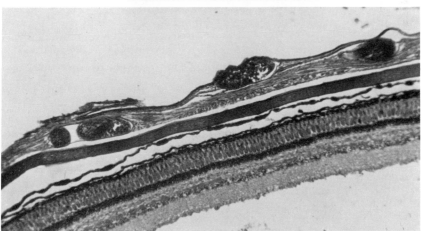

Fig. 23. Exophthalmia induced in juvenile Atlantic herring by invasion of the larval trematode *Cryptocotyle lingua* (above), and photomicrograph of eye tissues showing metacercarae (below).

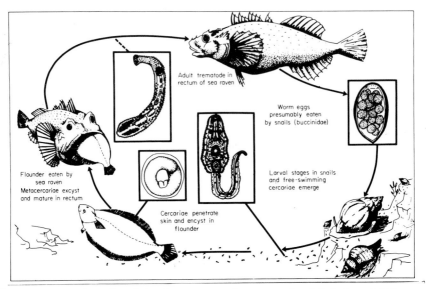

Fig. 24. Life cycle of *Stephanostomum baccatum*. (Modified from Wolfgang, 1955a.)

Adult digenetic trematodes are common parasites of the digestive tract, but are usually not a cause of serious disease. The literature containing descriptions of trematodes from fishes is voluminous, but much of it must remain outside the confines of this book. Cosmopolitan fish species harbor a number of adult trematodes throughout their range. Manter (1955), who reviewed the zoogeography of many, including the 20 species from Atlantic eels, found that most of the trematodes in eels were of marine origin, and that those characteristic of the eel in Europe were different from those reported in America. Apparently the parasites were acquired after the larval eels had separated in the Atlantic. Many of the trematode species in marine fishes of a given geographical region are peculiar to that region, although similarities exist in faunas from major ocean areas such as the European Atlantic and the Mediterranean.

Manter (1934, 1940, 1947) identified a number of adult digenetic trematodes from the dolphin, *Coryphaena hippurus* L., including the giant leech-like *Hirudinella marina* Garcin. H. L. Ward (1954) found this trematode, which may reach 3 cm in length, in sailfish, *Istiophorus americanus* Cuv. and Val., and in bonito, *Euthynnus* sp., from Florida. Earlier, Nigrelli and Stunkard (1947) concluded from a review of the genus *Hirudinella* that forms from wahoo, *Acanthocybium solandri*, belonged to the species *H. ventricosa* Pallas, and those from all other hosts belonged to *H. marina*.

Monogenetic trematodes, ectoparasitic for the most part, have been studied extensively in marine fishes by Price (1934, 1963), Yamaguti (1934, 1953, 1958, 1963), Sproston (1946), Hargis (1954, 1957), Manter (1955), Bykhovskii (1957), Euzet (1957), Hargis and Dillon (1965), and Euzet and Oliver (1967).

Among the monogenetic trematodes parasitic on gills and body surfaces of marine fishes, a number become serious parasites in aquaria, where conditions for reinfestation are optimum. Only rarely, and under unusual conditions, have members of this group been demonstrated to be pathogenic to fish in natural habitats. Heavy infestation of sticklebacks in the White Sea by two parasite species, *Gyrodactylus arcuatus* Bykhovskii and *G. bychowskyi* Sproston, was believed to be partially responsible (along with Microsporida) for mass mortalities (Dogiel *et al.*, 1958) among fish isolated in tide pools. The trematodes multiplied to numbers up to 1000 per fish; most of the fish died. Dogiel and Lutta (1937) studied an epizootic in the Aral Sea sturgeon. *Acipenser nudiventris* Lov., caused by the gill trematode, *Nitzchia sturionis* (Abilgaard). As a result of mortalities during 1936 the fishery, which previously had reached a peak of 400 metric tons per year, ceased to be of commercial significance for 20 years (Osmanov, 1959). Recent level of infestation in all conditions of salinity was reported at 50 to 75%. The epizootic in *A. nudiventris* was thought to have resulted from introduction of another sturgeon, *A. stellatus*, carrying the trematode on its gills. Even among sturgeons which serve as normal hosts, however, the parasite can cause extensive damage to gill tissue, hypertrophy of connective tissue, and loss of blood.

b. *Cestoda*

Adult cestodes are common and occasionally harmful parasites in the digestive tracts of fishes, but, as with the trematodes, larval stages are of greatest concern in the marine fishes. Larval tapeworms occur frequently in the viscera and flesh of marine and estuarine fishes. The definitive hosts of many of these parasites are elasmobranchs or fish-eating birds and mammals. Tapeworms which localize in the body muscles may occur in large numbers in individual hosts (Fig. 25). Linton (1907) described such an infestation in butterfish, *Poronotus triacanthus* (Peck), of the North American east coast, in which several thousand larvae could be found in individual fish. Encysted plerocercoids, less than 1 mm in diameter, were concentrated in the flesh adjacent to the vertebral column, and up to 75% of individuals in a sample were heavily infected. The parasite was identified as *Otobothrium crenacolle* Linton, which matures

Fig. 25. Larval tapeworms in the flesh of a rudderfish, *Seriola zonata* (Mitchill). (From Sindermann, 1966.)

in the spiral valve of certain shark species, particularly the hammerhead, *Sphyrna zygaena* (L.). Ripe, highly motile proglottids of the tapeworm are shed in the feces and are presumably ingested by butterfish and other teleosts, in which the embryos invade the musculature and encyst.

Other members of the cestode order Trypanorhyncha occur as adults in the digestive tract of elasmobranchs, and as larvae in the flesh and viscera of many teleost species (Fig. 26). Elongate larvae of *Poecilancistrium robustum* (Chandler), called "spaghetti worms," are very abundant in the flesh of drum, *Pogonius cromis* (L.), in the Gulf of Mexico. According to Chandler (1954) some municipal health departments have considered banning drum from markets because of frequent worm parasitization. Oppenheimer (1962) reported that spaghetti worms were common in the flesh of many other fishes from the Gulf of Mexico. Large spotted seatrout, *Cynoscion nebulosus* (Cuvier), harbored up to 100 larval worms, and as much as 44% of a sample were infested (Chandler, 1935a,b). Goldstein (1962, 1963) concluded from a reexamination of the genus *Poecilancistrium* that *P. robustum* is a synonym of *P. caryophyllum* (Diesing). A survey of the degree of infestation of sciaenid fishes from Texas coastal waters by trypanorhynchan larvae, carried out by Schlicht and McFarland (1967), revealed heavy infes-

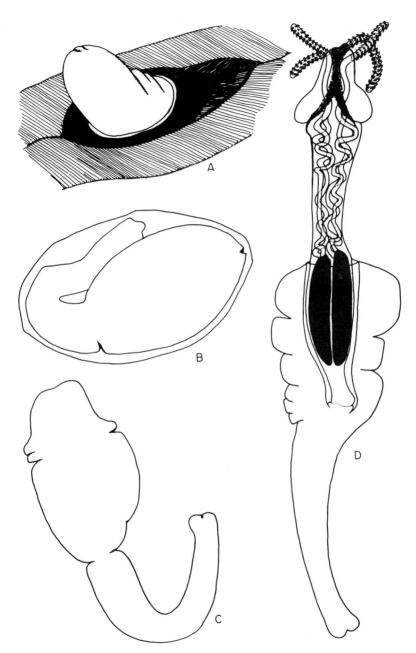

FIG. 26. Larval Trypanorhyncha. (A) Cyst in muscle of redfish, *Sebastes marinus;*
(B) orientation of larva within cyst; (C) larva freed from cyst membrane with
scolex retracted; (D) details of evaginated scolex. (Redrawn from Kahl, 1937.)

tations in several sciaenids, particularly *Bairdiella chrysura, Cynoscion nebulosus,* and *C. arenarus.* Most of the infestations were of *Poecilancistrium robustum,* and the infestations were age related (fish less than 1 year old were not parasitized). Differential mortality of older parasitized fish was suggested by decline in prevalence of larvae in fish more than 3 years old.

Many food fishes, such as herring, hake, and mackerel, have been reported to harbor other trypanorhynch larvae (Johnstone, 1912b; Linton, 1923; Ruszkowski, 1934; Kahl, 1937; R. T. Young, 1955; Rae, 1958). As an example, *Grillotia erinaceus* (van Beneden) is so common in many North Atlantic teleosts that an extensive literature on its occurrence existed in the nineteenth century. Pleroceroids of the cestode were described by Johnstone (1912b) as among the most abundant helminth parasites of Irish Sea fish; usually they occurred in mesenteries or the stomach wall, but in hake and halibut they were in the flesh adjacent to the vertebral column. The life cycle was elucidated by Ruszkowski (1934). Rae (1958), in a study of the cestode in halibut of the eastern North Atlantic, found the heaviest infestations in larger fish; 10 to 20% of catches from banks off the west coasts of Scotland and Ireland were infested. Wardle (1932, 1935) reported the worm from the Canadian Pacific coast. Linton (1924) described the adult stages of this and other Trypanorhyncha from sharks and skates, and Dollfus (1942) made an excellent critical examination of this interesting tapeworm group.

A larval cestode, *Pyramicocephalus phocarum* (Fabricius), causes extensive tissue destruction in livers of cod and other fishes (Polyanski, 1955). The parasite was widely distributed in Barents Sea cod, haddock, lumpfish, and *Myxocephalus scorpius;* the distribution paralleled that of arctic seals which are definitive hosts. The plerocercoids are large (3–4 cm) with characteristic sagittal scolices.

Adult cestodes may occur in significant numbers in the digestive tract of fishes, although their prevalence in marine teleosts is low in comparison with that of other helminths. Linton (1941) described many representatives from the western North Atlantic, and Wardle (1932, 1935) surveyed the Pacific coast fauna. The pseudophyllidean genus *Eubothrium* Bloch (*Abothrium* Lühe) is common in marine and freshwater fishes. Several species occur in the digestive tracts of cod, haddock, herring, and other sea fishes (Nybelin, 1922; Sprehn, 1934). Many other representatives of the Pseudophyllidea occur in teleost fishes (Wardle and McLeod, 1952), and the order Tetraphyllidea is well represented among the elasmobranchs (Woodland, 1927; Baer, 1948; H. H. Williams, 1958).

Adult cestodes can have severe effects on growth of the host fish.

Kändler (cited by Mann, 1954) reported disruption of growth as a result of tapeworm infestation of Baltic Sea turbot, *Rhombus maximus* (L.). Fish in their second year of life were most seriously parasitized, and complete recovery of normal growth rate took several years. Davey and Peachey (1968) reported infestation of turbot and brill, *Rhombus laevis* (L.), from the North Sea by presumably the same pseudophyllidean cestode, *Bothriocephalus scorpii* (Müller). Both species acquired infections before they were 1 year old; all the adult turbot were parasitized, often heavily, and half the brill were parasitized. Reported pathology was confined to reduction in size of epithelial cells and some connective tissue hypertrophy in the intestinal area adjacent to the scolex.

c. *Acanthocephala*

The "spiny-headed" worms are represented as adults and as larvae in marine fishes. A common parasite of North Atlantic species is the acanthocephalan, *Echinorhynchus gadi* Müller. It has been reported (Linton, 1900, 1901, 1914, 1933) from the digestive tract of 54 fish species in the Woods Hole, Massachusetts, region. The worm occurs in ocean pout, *Macrozoarces americanus*, in the western North Atlantic (Nigrelli, 1946) and in *Zoarces viviparus* (L.) from the English coast (Nicoll, 1907) and the Baltic (Markowski, 1939). It is circumpolar in distribution, having been found in diverse teleosts—particularly gadoids and salmonids—from northwestern Canada, Bering Sea, Kamchatka Peninsula, and Japan, as well as from the Baltic Sea, White Sea, Murman Coast, North Sea, and Gulf of Maine (Van Cleave, 1920; Dollfus, 1953). Heavy infestations of the digestive tract can cause weight loss and deterioration of condition. Zschokke and Heitz (1914) reported *E. gadi* as a common parasite of salmon, *Oncorhynchus nerka*, *O. keta*, and *O. tschawytscha*, from Kamchatkan waters, and Fujita (1920) found the parasite in *O. nerka* from Japan. Ekbaum (1938) observed it in a number of salmonids sampled in British Columbian waters; numbers were much larger in Chinook and coho salmon than in other species sampled. Ekbaum reported that the amphipod, *Cyphocaris challengeri*, was the normal intermediate host in the British Columbia area studied. Other amphipods serve as intermediate hosts in other areas (Nybelin, 1923, 1924).

Another member of the genus, *Echinorhynchus lageniformis*, is a common parasite of the starry flounder, *Platichthys stellatus* (Pallas), and to a lesser extent, the rock sole, *Lepidopsetta bilineata* (Ayres), from the Pacific coast of North America (Ekbaum, 1938; Prakash and

Adams, 1960). It was found in about one fourth of starry flounders sampled in British Columbia, and caused extensive intestinal pathology. The proboscis, particularly of the female, penetrates deeply into the intestinal wall, eventually forming a granulomatous polypoid protrusion of the wall or piercing it completely. H. L. Ward (1954) found other acanthocephalans in the bonito, *Euthynnus* sp., from Florida. Identified as *Nipporhynchus ornatus* (Van Cleave), the worms were very abundant in the intestine. Bonitos from other parts of the world harbor the same or a very similar acanthocephalan: *Euthynnus vagrans* (Lesson) from Japan and *Euthynnus alletteratus* (Rafinesque) from the Galapagos Islands. *Nipporhynchus ornatus* has also been reported from the skipjack tuna, *Katsuwonus pelamis,* from the Pacific (Van Cleave, 1940).

Another common acanthocephalan from the North American coast is *Telosentis tenuicornis* (Linton), found in a wide range of marine fish, including spot, *Leiostomus xanthurus* Lacépède (Huizinga and Haley, 1962); Atlantic croaker, *Micropogon undulatus,* and Atlantic threadfin, *Polydactylus octonemus* (Girard) (Chandler, 1935b); and the sand sea-trout, *Cynoscion arenarus* Ginsburg, and pigfish, *Orthropristis chrysopterus* (L.) (W. L. Bullock, 1957).

Pomphorhynchus laevis (Müller) is a common parasite of many European marine fishes, including gadoids, flatfishes, and eels. It may occur in great numbers in the gut or it may penetrate the gut wall and encyst in the viscera (Wurmbach, 1937; Shulman, 1959).

The mullet, *Mugil cephalus,* harbors an acanthocephalan of the family Neoechinorhynchidae, described by H. L. Ward (1953) as *Floridosentis elongatus.* Ward found the parasite in Biscayne Bay, Florida; W. L. Bullock (1957, 1960) found it in south Texas waters as well as southwest Florida; and Cable and Quick (1954) found it in white mullet, *Mugil curema,* from Puerto Rico. Machado-Filho (1951) had described *Atactorhynchus mugilis* from several Brazilian mullets. W. L. Bullock (1962) considered this species to be a member of Ward's genus *Floridosentis,* and suggested that *F. elongatus* is a synonym of *Floridosentis mugilis.*

Larval acanthocephala have not been reported in the massive numbers occasionally seen in freshwater fishes but are common in the viscera of many marine teleosts; for example, several species, including *Corynosoma semerme* (Forssell), *Corynosoma strumosum* (Rud.), and *Bolbosoma vasculosum* (Rud.), occur as adults in fish-eating birds and mammals and as larvae in mesenteries and viscera of many species of sea fishes (Lühe, 1911; Nybelin, 1923; A. Meyer, 1933). Ekbaum (1938) found *C. strumosum* encysted in liver, intestinal wall, and mesenteries of starry and two-lined flounders on the west coast of Canada. As many as 120 larvae were found in individual starry flounders, although numbers were usually much lower. Other encysted larval acanthocephala of the genus *Serrasentis* were reported from the viscera of numerous species of marine fishes at Woods Hole, Massachusetts, and Beaufort, North Carolina, by Linton (1889) and from Australia by Johnston and Deland (1929). Linton (1905) described the adult worm from the cobia, *Rachycentron canadus* (L.), taken at Beaufort, and H. L. Ward (1954) found it in permit, *Trachinotus falcatus* (L.), from Florida.

d. *Nematoda*

The nematodes, particularly as larvae, are very abundant in many marine fish. Larvae infest the flesh and viscera, reducing the commercial value of the host. An outstanding example is the codworm, *Porrocaecum decipiens* (Krabbe)—also known as *Terranova decipiens* or *Phocanema decipiens*. The definitive host is the harbor seal, *Phoca vitulina* L., according to D. M. Scott (1953), and larvae occur in the flesh of cod, smelt, plaice, ocean pout, and other species of inshore marine fish (Heller, 1949; D. M. Scott, 1950, 1954, 1955). Larvae may also pass from fish to fish if infected smaller individuals (for example, smelt) are eaten by cod. Olsen and Merriman (1946) reported ocean pout from New Brunswick to be heavily infested, some to the extent that the flesh had a porous appearance. A similar parasitization of ocean pout had been described from the same area 25 years previously (Clemens and Clemens, 1921). D. M. Scott and Martin (1957, 1959) found high prevalence but geographical variations in infestation of cod from the Canadian Atlantic coast; infestation decreased in deeper waters and increased with age of the host. A survey of *Porrocaecum* adults in seals (D. M. Scott and Fisher, 1958) did not disclose a direct distributional relationship with larvae in cod.

W. F. Templeman *et al.* (1957), in an extensive survey of groundfish in the Newfoundland fishing area, found larval *Porrocaecum* in cod, smelt, plaice, witch flounder, *Glyptocephalus cynoglossus* (L.), haddock, and redfish, *Sebastes marinus* L. Examination of more than 15,000 fish disclosed that over three fourths of all larval nematodes were *Porrocaecum;* the rest were other larval Anisakinae. Fishes such as halibut, pollock, *Pollachius virens* (L.), and sea raven, *Hemitripterus americanus* (Gmelin), living in the neighborhood of seal colonies also were infested. Marketing problems with worm-infested fillets were considered to be more serious with larvae of *Porrocaecum*, which are large and brown, than with those of other larval Anisakinae, which are small and white.

Studies of larval marine nematodes of the subfamily Anisakinae by a number of authors (Kahl, 1938a,b, 1939; Baylis, 1944; and others) have left us with some confusion about identification of larval *Porrocaecum*, because small specimens may lack the diagnostic intestinal cecum which separates this genus from others. Feeding studies with seals (D. M. Scott, 1953, 1956) established that most larval worms from cod, plaice, smelt, and eelpout of the western North Atlantic were actually *P. decipiens*. Other nematode genera represented by larvae in food fishes of the North Atlantic include *Eustoma* and *Anisakis* (Fig. 27). W. F. Templeman *et al.*

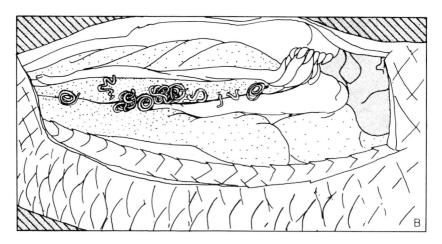

FIG. 27. Larval Anisakinae in viscera of adult Atlantic herring.

(1957) have summarized the problems inherent in specific identification of larval Heterocheilidae.

Porrocaecum larvae have been reported from 18 species of Pacific fishes, including the Pacific cod, *Gadus macrocephalus* Tilesius, by Yamaguti (1935). *Sebastodes alutus* from the Pacific coast of United States are often parasitized by larval *Porrocaecum* according to Liston and Hitz (1961). Smelt, cod, redfish, and other species from the North Sea also harbor this nematode (Martin, 1921; Kahl, 1936, 1939). Grainger (1959) identified as *Porrocaecum* larval nematodes in cod and other fishes from Greenland waters and the Barents Sea.

Infestation of cod livers by larval *Contracaecum aduncum* (Rud.), also of the subfamily Anisakinae, has been responsible for sizable economic losses in the Baltic Sea (Markowski, 1937; Shulman, 1948, 1959; Shulman and Shulman-Albova, 1953; Petrushevskii and Shulman, 1955; Getsevichyute, 1955). Numbers of worms per liver reached 100, and parasitized fish suffered loss of total weight and liver mass (Fig. 28). Larger, deeply penetrating worms were more harmful, and young or spawning fish showed less tolerance to infestation. Liver fat content and oil yield were seriously reduced by parasitization, and the fish lost weight. *Contracaecum* was also found in cod from the White and Murman Seas, but in lesser frequencies. Infestation increased with age of the host, and varied in intensity seasonally, with a peak in autumn.

Larval *Anisakis* and *Porrocaecum* also invade the liver of a number of marine fishes, and may produce pathological changes similar to those resulting from *Contracaecum* parasitization (Kahl, 1938b; Akhmerov, 1951; Petrushevskii and Kogteva, 1954; Mikhaylova *et al.*, 1964; Remotti, 1933a, 1933b). Cod, haddock, redfish, hake, and herring are some of the important commercial species so parasitized.

An interesting example of nematode parasitization that is of serious consequence to the host has been described by Janiszewska (1938). Flounders of the eastern Atlantic are often heavily parasitized by *Cucullanellus minutus* (Rud.). Larvae invade the intestinal wall, causing extensive pathological changes. After overwintering there, the worms reenter the lumen of the digestive tract and mature during early summer.

Extensive visceral adhesions are often serious concomitants of larval nematode and larval cestode parasitization. Best examples are probably seen in freshwater (e.g., larval cestodes such as *Proteocephalus* and *Triaenophorus*), but adhesions also occur as a result of larval nematode parasitization of anadromous salmonids. Visceral adhesions in sockeye and chum salmon, *Oncorhynchus nerka* and *O. keta*, from the Bering Sea and North Pacific Ocean result from parasitization by the larvae of the dracunculoid nematode *Philonema oncorhynchi* (French, 1965). Accord-

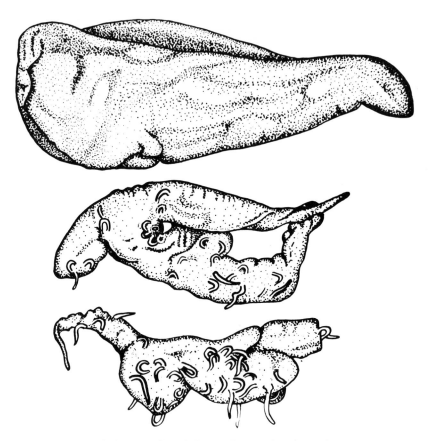

FIG. 28. Normal (top) and pathological livers of Baltic cod of equal size, the lower ones infested by larval *Contracaecum*. (Redrawn from Dogiel *et al.*, 1958.)

ing to French, "visceral elements were tightly compacted and joined to the body wall with mesenteric and peritoneal adhesions." Atlantic salmon, *Salmo salar*, are similarly affected by *Philonema agubernaculum* (M. C. Meyer, 1954, 1958, 1960). Infestation occurs in freshwater, but possible mortality in severe cases would occur during the high seas existence.

It can be seen readily from these examples that infestation of marine fishes by larval nematodes is a matter of serious concern in many parts of the world. Adult nematodes, usually inhabitants of the digestive tract, occur in many species of marine fish, but appear to do less damage to the host. Among those that might be mentioned, *Camellanus melanocephalus* (Rud.) occurs in the stomach and pyloric ceca of tuna and mackerel; *Ascarophis morrhuae* is found in cod (Fig. 29); and *Proleptus obtusus* Duj. occurs in sharks.

An adult dracunculoid nematode, *Philometra americana,* which parasitizes the fins and subcutaneous tissues, has been reported from the Pacific starry flounder, *Platichthys stellatus* (Pallas), the rock sole, *Lepidopsetta bilineata,* and several other fishes from Washington and British Columbia (Kuitunen-Ekbaum, 1933a,b). The parasites, known to fishermen as "bloodworms," are common in sport and commercial catches. The adult female worms carrying larvae are large and red, and form

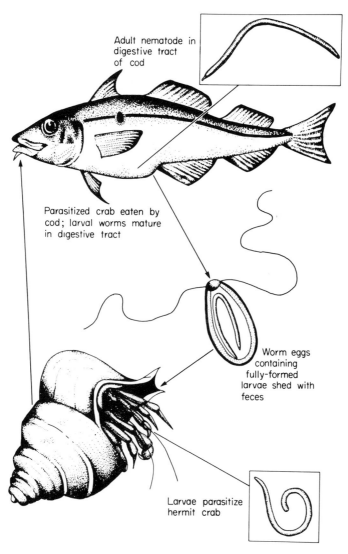

Adult nematode in digestive tract of cod

Parasitized crab eaten by cod; larval worms mature in digestive tract

Worm eggs containing fully-formed larvae shed with feces

Larvae parasitize hermit crab

FIG. 29. Life cycle of *Ascarophis morrhuae.* (Redrawn from Uspenskaya, 1953.)

unsightly nodules on the surface of the host, often causing rejection of parasitized fish. New infections are apparently acquired by the fish in autumn, presumably by ingestion of infested crustacean intermediate hosts. Female worms mature and release larvae the following summer. Recently Rasheed (1963) provisionally transferred *Philometra americana* to the new genus *Thwaitia*. The life cycle and morphology of several species of *Philometra* were outlined by Furuyama (1934). The genus is close to *Philonema*, some species of which may cause visceral adhesions and reproductive impairment in salmonids (M. C. Meyer, 1958, 1960). Another species of *Philometra* was reported by Annigeri (1962) to destroy the ovaries of the sciaenid *Otolithus argenteus* from the Indian Ocean, although the extent of parasitization of the host species was undetermined.

2. Parasitic Crustacea

a. *Copepoda*

Marine fishes are parasitized by a variety of copepods, of which several members of the families Lernaeoceridae, Pennellidae, and Sphyriidae are particularly injurious to the host (Fig. 30). Usually the adult females in these groups become highly modified and penetrate the flesh, often causing extensive ulceration.

Lernaeocera branchialis (L.) is a parasite of the gill region of gadoid fishes, particularly cod, whiting, pollock, and other species from both sides of the North Atlantic and from the Pacific (Dollfus, 1953; Shulman and Shulman-Albova, 1953; Kabata, 1961; Sherman and Wise, 1961; and others). *Lernaeocera branchialis* has been described as a heart parasite by Schuurmans-Stekhoven (1936) and Schuurmans-Stekhoven and Punt (1937), because the anterior end of the copepod sometimes penetrates the bulbus arteriosus of the host. It has been the subject of numerous studies, was reported in the scientific literature as early as 1762 by Strøm, and is considered one of the most harmful of the copepods parasitic on marine fishes. Intermediate hosts of the parasite include the lumpfish, *Cyclopterus lumpus*, and the flounder, *Pleuronectes flesus*, as well as several other pleuronectids. The adult female copepods, usually numbering one to three, but occasionally more, attach to the gill region of gadoids. The head sometimes penetrates to the heart or to the ventral aorta or branchial arteries, causing connective tissue hypertrophy and the formation of blood-filled lacunae. Invasion of the heart causes thickening of the walls and marked reduction in the lumen of the organ (Mann, 1954). Effects of parasitization can be divided into two phases: (1) invasion and attachment, resulting in destruction and dislocation of tissue, and (2) feeding, resulting in loss of blood (Kabata, 1958). Affected fish are almost always below average weight, and death of young cod can result from blood loss and pathological changes in the heart and aorta. Mann (1952) reported that infested cod were 20 to 30% underweight,

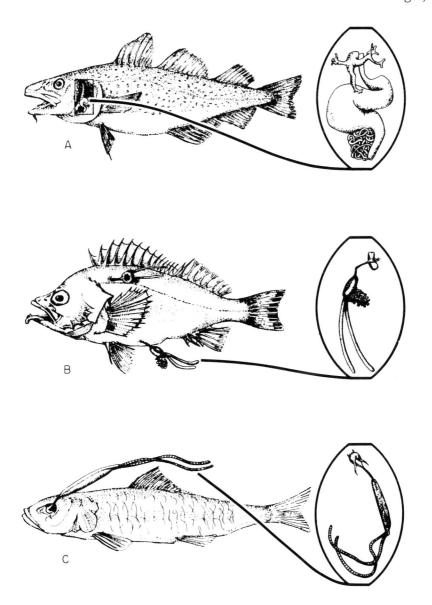

Fig. 30. Tissue-invading copepods. (A) *Lernaeocera branchialis* from cod; (B) *Sphyrion lumpi* from redfish; and (C) *Lernaeenicus sprattae* from the sardine.

and that the erythrocyte count and hemoglobin content of the blood were reduced. Extreme emaciation of whiting, *Gadus merlangus* L., was reported by A. Scott (1928) as the result of *L. branchialis* infestation. A second species, *L. obtusata,* has recently been distinguished by Kabata (1957a) as a parasite of the haddock. Separation was based on minor morphological variations in the adult females, site of penetration, and characteristics of the male. Severe impairment of infested haddock, in the form of anemia, loss of weight, loss of liver fat, and possible retardation of sexual development, was noted (Kabata, 1958). Walford (1958) cited results of a 2-year sampling in one English fishing port which disclosed *Lernaeocera* parasitization of 10% of haddock, 80% of whiting, and 20% of cod. Parasitized fish were as much as 23% below normal weight.

Mann (1965) also noted disturbances of fat metabolism in gobies, *Pomatoschistus minutus,* from the north German coast that were parasitized by *Lernaeocera minuta.* The normal fat content of 2.3 to 3.8% in uninfested fish was decreased to a low of 1.7% in infested fish. Similar reductions in fat content of gadoids parasitized by *L. obtusa* were observed by Kabata (1958). Mann (1960) found that once whiting were infested with *L. branchialis,* the quantity of fat decreased to half the normal level.

A second well-known tissue-invading copepod is *Sphyrion lumpi* (Krøyer), widely distributed in the North Atlantic on the redfish and several other species (Figs. 31 and 32). It has been reported from the Norwegian coast (Lüling, 1951), west Greenland and the Norwegian Sea (Hansen, 1923), Newfoundland (W. F. Templeman and Squires, 1960), and the Gulf of Maine (Herrington *et al.,* 1940; Nigrelli and Firth, 1939; Sindermann, 1961b). In the western North Atlantic *Sphyrion* is primarily a parasite of redfish, but to the eastward (Iceland and northwestern Europe) lumpfish and wolffish are more likely to be hosts. The parasite penetrates deeply into the flesh, where the anchor-like brown anterior extensions of the body are encapsulated in extensive host connective tissue. External ulcerations are also common. After death of the parasite the cysts persist in the flesh for a number of years as unsightly malodorous masses, often filled with brownish fluid. These cysts must be removed from fillets before marketing. Invasions by successive generations of parasites apparently continue throughout the life of the host; consequently the larger older fish are most likely to have more cysts.

An interesting and still unsolved aspect of *Sphyrion* infestation of redfish is its marked geographical variation in occurrence; major centers of abundance are in the Gulf of Maine and off the coast of Labrador, and minor centers are on the southeast part of the Grand Bank and in the southern Gulf of Saint Lawrence. The parasite is absent from other major fishing grounds of the western North Atlantic. Priebe (1963) found that 1 to 3% of redfish from the Norwegian coast, sampled in the Bremerhaven fish market, were parasitized by *Sphyrion*.

Members of the genus *Pennella* are among the largest of the tissue-invading copepods. *Pennella exocoeti* (Holten) from flying fish, *Parexocoetus brachypterus* (Richardson), and *Pennella filosa* (L.) from swordfish and ocean sunfish, *Mola mola* (L.), may reach a length of 20 cm. The adult female of this and other members of the genus may be found almost anywhere on the host's body; the head and neck are embedded in the host organs, where large hard cysts are formed (Gnanamuthu, 1957).

Another interesting parasitic copepod is *Lernaeenicus sprattae* (Sowerby) which occurs embedded in the eye or occasionally in the dorsal body muscles of sprat and sardines in Europe (Baudouin, 1904, 1905; Wilson, 1917). According to Baudouin, the parasite is called

FIG. 31. Redfish from Gulf of Maine infested with parasitic copepods, *Sphyrion lumpi*. Insert shows copepod removed from host to expose anchor-like anterior end.

"pavillon" by sardine fisherman, because it has three distinct body parts, showing the three colors of the French tricolor. The long thin body and egg cases of the parasite trail posteriorly as the host swims.

Parasitic copepods other than the tissue-invading forms may occasionally injure marine fish. Surface abrasions and lesions caused by the parasites can be of serious consequence to the fish host directly or as a route of entry for secondary invaders. Salmonids in the North Pacific and the North Atlantic are often parasitized by *Lepeophtheirus salmonis* (Krøyer), a caligid which causes severe skin erosion, and may even kill the fish host in heavy infestations (White, 1940, 1942; Margolis, 1958). The parasites, called "sea lice," drop off the fish soon after the anadromous hosts enter freshwater. Individual fish may carry hundreds of the copepods, each 3–12 mm long. White (1940), studying Atlantic salmon in Nova Scotia, observed that one of the results of heavy *Lepeophtheirus* infestation was extensive abrasion, with loosening and sloughing of the skin, particularly in the head region. It seems quite likely that this condition could result from secondary bacterial or even fungal infections, since White pointed out that before the skin sloughs there is a distinct white area over the abraded zones. A similar condition, called "white spot" disease, was described earlier from Atlantic salmon taken in Scotland (Calderwood, 1905) and in the Canadian Maritime Provinces (McGonigle, 1931). Gusev (1951) has found *L. salmonis* on *Salmo salar* from the White Sea and on pink salmon, *Oncorhynchus gorbuscha*, from the Okhotsk Sea. Margolis (1958) found the parasite on five species of Pacific salmon, particularly sockeye and pink salmon, from the west coast of North America.

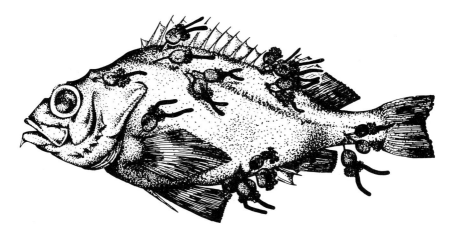

Fig. 32. Redfish heavily parasitized by *Sphyrion lumpi.*

Another member of the same caligid genus, *Lepeophtheirus pectoralis* Müller, is found, often in great numbers, on the pectoral fins and gills of flounders. Mann (1965) observed that the skin around the fins of flounders was damaged by the copepod and that the skin under the fins was inflamed. He pointed out the possibility of bacterial invasion as a consequence.

Lüling (1953) has described an instance of tissue damage in tuna, *Thunnus thynnus* (L.), caused by another caligid, *Elytrophora brachyptera*.

Several members of the lernaeopodid genus *Clavella*, parasitic on the fins and in the branchial and buccal cavities of gadoid fishes, may cause lesions and tumors (Poulsen, 1939; Nunes-Ruivo, 1957; Kabata, 1960, 1963b).

An aberrant parasitic group, generally considered to be copepods, but considered by some to be rhizocephalans, includes several species of the genus *Sarcotaces*. The parasites, male and female, live in cysts in the tissues of the fish host. Kuitunen-Ekbaum (1947) identified forms from the rasphead rockfish, *Sebastodes ruberrimus*, from British Columbia, as *Sarcotaces arcticus* Collett. Each infected fish contained one to three cysts containing live parasites, recognizable by external protuberances, or more commonly, by black fluid oozing from cysts. *Sarcotaces arcticus* was described and studied by Collett (1874) and Hjort (1895) from specimens taken from *Molva abyssorum* caught in Norway. Two other species, *S. verrucosus* and *S. pacificus*, have been described by Olsson (1872) and Komai (1923). *Sarcotaces verrucosus* has been found in *Iridio radiatus* caught at Martinique (Dollfus, 1928), and *S. arcticus* has been reported from *Molva abyssorum* landed in Scotland (Aitken, 1942), and from *Molva byrkelange* Walb. landed in Germany (Amlacher, 1958).

b. *Isopoda*

Isopods parasitic on fish include members of the Gnathiidae, parasitic in young stages only, and Cymothoidae, parasitic only as adults. Gnathiids attach to the fins and are blood feeders, whereas the cymothoids attach to gills or the inside of the mouth, or (in the genus *Ichthyoxenos*) form cavities in the skin.

Alperin (1966) found the isopod *Livoneca ovalis* attached inside the operculum of yearling striped bass, *Roccus saxatilis*, from Long Island, New York. This isopod has been found in the mouths and gill regions of a number of other Atlantic marine fish (Richardson, 1903): bluefish, *Pomatomus saltatrix* (L.), sawfish, *Pristis pectinatus* Latham, scup, *Stenotomus chrysops* (L.), weakfish, *Cynoscion regalis* (Bloch and

Schneider), ocean sunfish, *Mola mola* (L.), menhaden, *Brevoortia tyrannus* (Latrobe), and kingfish, *Menticirrhus saxatilis* (Bloch and Schneider). Effects of *L. ovalis* on condition and survival were not reported, but a related species, *Livoneca* (*Ichthyoxenos*) *amurensis*, which localizes in a depression under the pectoral fin, has been found to retard growth and cause deterioration in condition of the coregonid, *Leuciscus waleckii*, in the Amur River (Akhmerov, 1939, 1941; Krykhtin, 1951; Petrushevskii and Shulman, 1961). Krykhtin estimated that *L. amurensis* was fatal to 13% of infested fish before they reached market size. Another species, *Livoneca pontica*, was described by Borgea (1933) from the Black Sea clupeoids, *Alosa pontica* Eichw., *C. nordmani* Ant., and *Sardina pilchardus* Walb. Lodging in the branchial cavity, the isopod caused partial atrophy of the gills. Similar damage to gills of the host was reported by Bowman (1960) to result from parasitization of the Hawaiian moray eel, *Gymnothorax eurostus* (Abbott), by *Livoneca puhi.* Prevalences ranged from 15 to 70%. The isopods were found in either the right or left gill chamber, but not in both, since most of the hosts' gill filaments were missing on the parasitized side.

Menhaden (*Brevoortia tyrannus*, *B. patronus,* and *B. smithi*) from the Atlantic and Gulf coasts of the United States are often heavily infested with another cymothoid, *Olencira praegustator* (Latrobe, 1802; Goode, 1879, 1884; Richardson, 1905; Ellison, 1951; Hildebrand, 1963; Turner and Roe, 1967). This large isopod occupies much of the oral and branchial cavities and can cause deformation of the mouth, according to Hildebrand. Some gill erosion was noted by Turner and Roe, but general condition of the host did not seem to be affected.

D. GENETIC AND ENVIRONMENTALLY INDUCED ABNORMALITIES

In addition to abnormalities caused by particular disease-causing organisms, marine fishes offer numerous examples of physiological or structural defects, or conditions which may have genetic or other causes. A number of inherited abnormalities of fishes have been studied, including defective spinal columns, pigmented tumors, cataracts, kidney tumors, and association of certain pigment-producing genes with physiological disturbances (Gordon, 1954). On the basis of his review, Gordon felt that abundant evidence existed for genetic control of certain diseases and abnormalities of fishes despite the fact that the hereditary factors involved were usually complex.

Probably the most thorough studies have been made of the genetics of pigmented tumors (Gordon, 1948, 1950). Neoplastic growths in which pigmented cells play a dominant role are found in many animals, and such neoplasms can be among the most malignant tumors known. Among fishes, neoplasms developing from melanophores are the commonest type of pigment-cell tumor, whereas tumors arising from other chromatophores are rare. For example, Gordon (1948) found melanotic tumors in marine or freshwater representatives of 11 orders of teleosts and elasmobranchs. Takahashi (1929, 1934), in a 13-year survey of many types of tumors in 100,000 fish from the Sea of Japan, found three melanomas, one guanophoroma, and one allophoroma. Schmey (1911) reported a xanthoma from a single European shark and G. M. Smith (1934) an erythrophoroma from an American winter flounder.

Epidermoid carcinomas have been reported from several species of marine fishes. Johnstone (1924) reported an instance in whiting, G. Williams (1929) a case in pollock, and Beatti (1916) several examples in drum. Odontomas have been reported in a croaker, *Micropogon opercularis,* from South America (Roffo, 1925), and in a haddock from the Grand Bank (Thomas, 1926). Mesenchymal tumors have been found in cod by Johnstone (1920, 1924, 1926) and G. Williams (1929). Osteomas of the vertebrae were observed frequently in the red tai, *Pagrosomus major,* a Japanese food fish, by Takahashi (1929). Nerve-sheath tumors (neurilemmomas) are frequent in the snappers (Lutjanidae). Lucké (1942) estimated that up to 1% of the snappers found in Tortugas waters had such tumors; they were called "cancer fish" by fishermen. Thomas (1931), Schlumberger and Lucké (1948), and Lucké and Schlumberger (1949), who thoroughly reviewed the literature on tumors in fishes, found that more than 120 species were involved. On the basis of their review, the authors concluded that all the major varieties of tumors that occur in mammals and birds occur in cold-blooded vertebrates.

Goiter (thyroid hyperplasia) has been reported frequently from freshwater hatcheries (see, for example, Gaylord and Marsh, 1914), but occurs only rarely in marine fishes held in aquaria. Schlumberger (1955) observed goiter in a number of pilotfish, *Echeneis naucrates* L., held in the Philadelphia Aquarium for long periods. Other species held in the same low-iodine water did not develop goiter, suggesting species variability in metabolic need for iodine. Schlumberger observed that the few reported examples of thyroid tumors in marine fishes usually occurred in those kept in aquaria for long periods. Such tumors were especially characteristic of pilotfish and developed within a year after introduction of normal fish. Nigrelli (1952a) reported malignant thyroid tumors in both wild and captive marine fish.

Tumors and hyperplastic growths in fishes may have a number of causes other than genetic. Viral etiology for diseases such as lymphocystis has already been considered. Kudo (1924) and Nigrelli and Smith (1938, 1939) found Microsporida and Myxosporida associated with tissue hyperplasia in certain fishes. G. M. Smith (1935) reported papillomas of flounders possibly associated with invasion of larval trematodes, and Reichenbach-Klinke (1955b) cited several instances of fungi associated with tumors.

Increasing levels of pollution in the marine environment, in addition to killing fish and destroying habitats, may produce abnormalities. In an interesting comparison of marine fishes taken in polluted and unpolluted areas, P. H. Young (1964) described changes in consistency of flesh, reductions in weight, external lesions, exophthalmia, and papillomas as characteristic of fishes from grossly polluted waters off California. External lesions, similar to those found on trawled species, were produced experimentally on killifish by introducing sewer effluent diluted with seawater. The possible association of pollution with increased neoplasms in fishes had been mentioned previously. Lucké and Schlumberger (1941) noted the common occurrence of epitheliomas in brown bullheads, *Ictalurus nebulosus* (LeSueur), from the Delaware River, and Russell and Kotin (1957) reported on papillomas of white croakers, *Genyonemus lineatus* (Ayres), from the same area studied by P. H. Young (1964).

Abnormalities other than tumors have long attracted scientific attention also. An unusual condition described as "jellied" flesh, noted in several flatfish species, seems unrelated to a disease organism. W. F. Templeman and Andrews (1956) reported the condition in 40% of the catch of large American plaice, *Hippoglossoides platessoides* (Fabr.), caught in cold waters of the Grand Bank of Newfoundland. High water content and low protein content made fillets prepared from affected fish unsuitable for market. Most of the fish above 60 cm were jellied. The authors postulated that large fish in cold waters could not adequately meet protein demands of gonad development, tissue maintenance, and growth. Evidence was cited for similar conditions in other flatfish species, as well as in cod and haddock, that suggested a generalized condition of muscle-protein impoverishment under stresses of age, low temperature, and gonad development.

Abnormalities in morphology are abundantly described in the scientific literature. Gemmill (1912) published a book on teratology of fishes and Dawson (1964, 1966) has compiled a bibliography of fish anomalies which contains over 1000 references. Structural abnormalities in several skate species have been described recently by W. F. Templeman (1965a). Included were such conditions as separation of pectoral fins from the head, which has been observed repeatedly in the past in other parts of the North Atlantic; curvature of the vertebral column, a condition also found in many teleosts; and "blunt snout," caused by skeletal defects. Letaconnoux (1949), who reported on teratological studies of marine fishes landed in France, also noted malformations of the pectoral fins in skates, and described an interesting condition of pigmentation of the normally unpigmented blind side of plaice, often associated with incomplete eye migration. He also observed a common abnormality of "short tail," a definite abbreviation of the caudal region seen in many species of fishes, due to twisting, compression, or fusion of vertebrae. A similar shortening, torsion, and diminution of the caudal region has been observed frequently in immature Atlantic herring from the Gulf of Maine, especially in samples taken by bottom trawls rather than by conventional surface gear (Sindermann, 1959). Individuals of other species, such as haddock, have also been found with spinal abnormalities in the western North Atlantic. Although this condition may be due to a bone disease, it seems more likely that these and other structural abnormalities can be attributed to defective embryonic development.

"Pugheadedness" (*Mopsköpfe*), a shortening of the snout, was noted by Letaconnoux (1949) in several teleosts, particularly the gadoids. This condition has been reported by a number of other authors. Gudger (1930) and Raney (1952) described it in striped bass (Fig. 33), and Mann (1954) reported on the occurrence of pugheads (thought to be genetic, but possibly influenced during embryonic life) among the Baltic Sea pike. Such fish do not differ in weight from normal fish, but they are so often rejected by the European consumer that they are usually culled in advance. A pugheaded herring was described by Ford (1930), who also cited earlier evidence for the hereditary origin of the abnormality in fishes. Other clupeoids have since been found with this condition. Cheek (1965) and Goodwin and Vaughn (1968) reported pugheaded American shad, and Schwartz (1964–1965) a pugheaded menhaden.

Abnormal conditions in larval fishes, some undoubtedly genetic and some due to environmental variations, are most often seen in hatcheries, but structural defects are sometimes seen in larvae and postlarvae taken in plankton collections. Experimental variation of such single factors as temperature at time of hatching can drastically modify or inhibit formation of the jaws of larvae and can cause an increase in occurrence of other gross abnormalities. Volodin (1960), for example, found that exposures to low temperatures (0°–6°C.) during early incubation produced malformed larvae of bream, *Abramis ballerus* L., and pike (probably *Esox lucius* L.). Sharp changes in temperature during early development could also produce malformations or death. Physiological

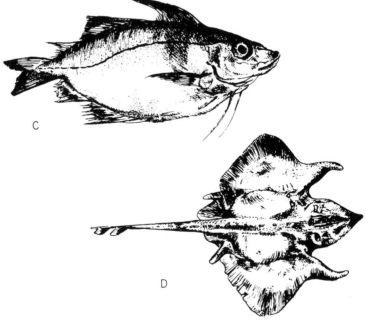

FIG. 33. Skeletal abnormalities in fish. (A) Pugheaded striped bass; (B) spinal curvature in sea herring; (C) short-tailed haddock; and (D) fin malformation in thorny skate.

abnormalities in larvae are less easily identified, except as they are reflected in lack of growth and death of individuals.

REFERENCES

Aitken, A. (1942). An undescribed stage of Sarcotaces. Nature 150, 180–181.
Akazawa, H. (1968). Bacterial disease of marine fishes. Bull. Japan. Soc. Sci. Fisheries 34, 271–272 (abstr.).
Akhmerov, A. K. (1939). On ecology of Livonica amurensis. (In Russian.) Vch. Zap. Leningr. Gos. Univ., Ser. Biol. Nauk 43, 11.
Akhmerov, A. K. (1941). Contributions to the study of fish parasites in Lake Bolkhash. (In Russian.) Vch. Zap. Leningr. Gos. Univ., Ser. Biol. Nauk 74, 18.
Akhmerov, A. K. (1951). Some data on the parasites of Alaskan pollack. (In Russian.) Izv. Tikhookean. Nauch. I-ssled. Inst. Rÿb. Khoz. Okeanogr., Vladivostok 30, 99–104.
Akhmerov, A. K. (1954). On the question of "sarannom" in coho salmon from Kamchatka. (In Russian.) Izv. Tikhookeans. Nauchn.-Issled. Inst. Rybn. Khoz. i Okeanogr. 41, 347–348.
Akhmerov, A. K. (1955). The parasite fauna of Kamchatka River fishes. (In Russian.) Izv. Tikhookeans. Nauchn.-Issled. Inst. Rybn. Khoz. i Okeanogr. 43, 99–137.
Aleem, A. A., Ruivo, M., and Théodoridès, J. (1953). Un cas de maladie à saprolegniale chez une Atherina des environs de Salses. Vie Milieu 3, 44–51.
Alexander, D. M. (1913). A review of piscine tubercle, with a description of an acid-fast bacillus found in the cod. Proc. Trans. Liverpool Biol. Soc. 27, 219–226.
Alexandrowicz, J. S. (1951). Lymphocystis tumours in the red mullet (Mullus surmuletus L.). J. Marine Biol. Assoc. U. K. 30, 315–332.
Allen, R. L., Meekin, T. K., Pauley, G. B., and Fujihara, M. P. (1968). Mortality among chinook salmon associated with the fungus Dermocystidium. J. Fisheries Res. Board Can. 25, 2467–2475.
Alperin, I. M. (1966). A new parasite of striped bass. N. Y. Fish Game J. 13, 121–123.
Altara, I. (1963). Symposium européen sur les maladies des poissons et l'inspection des produits de la pêche fluviale et maritime. Bull. Office Intern. Epizootics 59, 1–152.
Amlacher, E. (1958). Ein seltener und ein haufigerer parasitischer Krebs an Meeresfischen. Deut. Fischereiztg. 5, 75–77.
Amlacher, E. (1961). "Taschenbuch der Fischkrankheiten," 286 pp. Fischer, Jena.
Annenkova-Khlopina, N. P. (1920). Contribution to the study of parasitic diseases of Osmerus eperlanus. (In Russian.) Bull. Bur. Fisheries, Petrograd 1, 2.
Annigeri, G. G. (1962). A viviparous nematode, Philometra sp. in the ovaries of Otolithus argenteus (Cuvier). J. Mar. Biol. Assoc. India 3, 263–265.
Anonymous. (1951). Diseased stripers in Connecticut are safe to eat. Salt Water Sportsman June 22, p. 1.
Apstein, R. (1910). Cyclopterus lumpus, der Seehase. Mitt. Deut. Seafischeries ver. 26, 450–465.
Arai, Y., and Matsumoto, K. (1953). On a new Sporozoa, Hexacapsula neothunni gen. et sp. nov., from the muscle of yellowfin tuna, Neothunnus macropterus. Bull. Japan. Soc. Sci. Fisheries 18, 293–298.

Aronson, J. D. (1926). Spontaneous tuberculosis in salt water fish. *J. Infect. Diseases* **39**, 315–320.

Aronson, J. D. (1938). Tuberculosis of cold blooded animals. In "Tuberculosis and Leprosy, the Mycobacterial Diseases" (F. R. Moulton, ed.), A.A.A.S. Symp. Ser. 1, pp. 80–86. Am. Assoc. Advance. Sci., Washington, D. C.

Auerbach, M. (1906). Ein *Myxobolus* im Kopfe von *Gadus aeglefinus* L. *Zool. Anz.* **30**, 568–570.

Auerbach, M. (1912). Studien über Myxosporidien der norwegische Seefische und ihre Verbreitung. *Zool. Jahrb., Abt. I. Syst.* **34**, 1–50.

Awerinzew, S. (1911). Studien über parasitische Protozen. V. Einige neue Befunde aus der Entwicklungsgeschichte von *Lymphocystis johnstonei* Woodc. *Arch. Protistenk.* **22**, 179–196.

Baer, J. G. (1948). Contributions a l'étude des cestodes de sélaciens. I-IV. *Bull. Soc. Neuchâtel. Sci. Natur.* **71**, 1–122.

Bagge, J., and Bagge, O. (1956). *Vibrio anguillarum* som årsag til ulcus-sygdom hos torsk (*Gadus callarias* Linné). *Nord. Vetensk. Med.* **8**, 481–492.

Baudouin, M. (1904). Le *Lernaeenicus sprattae,* parasite de la sardine en Vendée. *Compt. Rend.* **139**, 998–1000.

Baudouin, M. (1905). Du mode de fixation dorsale du *Lernaeenicus sardinae* sur son hôte. *Compt. Rend.* **140**, 326–327.

Baylis, H. A. (1944). *Capsularia marina* and the Ascaridae of marine hosts. *Parasitology* **36**, 119–121.

Bazikalova, A. (1932). Additions to parasitology of Murmansk fishes. (In Russian.) *Fish Sci. Inv. Murmansk* pp. 136–153.

Beatti, M. (1916). Geschwülste bei Tieren, *Z. Krebsforsch.* **15**, 452–491.

Bergman, A. M. (1909). Die rote Beulenkrankheit des Aals. *Ber. Kgl. Bayer. Biol. Versuchsta. Muenchen* **2**, 10–54.

Bergman, A. M. (1912). Eine ansteckende Augenkrankheit, Keratomalacie, bei Dorschen an der Südküste Schwedens. *Zentr. Bakteriol., Parasitenk., Abt. I. Orig.* **62**, 200–212.

Bergman, A. M. (1922). Fiskarnas Sujukdomar. In "Sötvattensfiske och Fiskodling," 73 pp. Svenska Jordbrukets Bok, Stockholm.

Bespalyi, I. I. (1959). Coccidiosis of carp in the pond fisheries of the Ukrainian SSR. (In Russian.) *Tr. Soveshch. Bolez. Ryb., Ikhtiol. Komm. Akad. Nauk SSSR,* pp. 48–51.

Bogdanova, E. A. (1957). The microsporidian *Glugea hertwigi* Weissenberg in the stint (*Osmerus eperlanus* M. *spirinchus*) from Lake Ylyua-yarvi. In "Parasites and Diseases of Fish" (G. K. Petrushevskii, ed.), p. 328. (In Russian.) Izv. Vses. Nauchn.-Issled. Inst. Ozern. Rechn. Rybn. Khoz., Leningrad.

Bogdanova, E. A. (1960). Natural habitat of the myxosporidian *Myxosoma cerebralis* at Sakhalin, S. E. Russia. (In Russian.) *Tr. Akad. Nauk SSSR* **134**, 1501–1503.

Bond, F. F. (1937). A microsporidian infection of *Fundulus heteroclitus* (Linn.) *J. Parasitol.* **23**, 229–230.

Borgea, M. I. (1933). *Livoneca pontica* nov. sp., copépode parasite des aloses et sardines de la Mer Noire. *Bull. Museum Nat. Hist. Nat.* (*Paris*) [2] **5**, 128–129.

Bowman, T. E. (1960). Description and notes on the biology of *Lironeca puhi,* n. sp. (Isopoda: Cymothoidae), parasite of the Hawaiian moray eel, *Gymnothorax eurostus* (Abbott). *Crustaceana* **1**, 84–91.

Breed, R. S., Murray, E. G. D., and Smith, N. R. (1957). "Bergey's Manual of Determinative Bacteriology," 7th ed., 1094 pp. Williams & Wilkins, Baltimore, Maryland.

Breslauer, T. (1916). Zur Kenntnis der Epidermoidalgeschwülste von Kaltblütern. *Arch. Mikroskop. Anat. Entwicklungsmech.* **87**, 200–264.

Brown, E. M. (1951). *Cryptocaryon irritans* gen. et sp. n. *Proc. Zool. Soc. London* **120**, No. 11, 1–2 (agenda and abstr. sci. meetings).

Brumpt, E., and Lebailly, C. (1904). Description de quelques nouvelles espèces de trypanosomes et d'hémogrégarines parasites des téléostéens marins. *Compt. Rend.* **139**, 613–615.

Bruun, A. F., and Heiberg, B. (1932). The "Red Disease" of the eel in Danish waters. *Medd. Komm. Dan. Fisk.-og Havunders., Ser. Fiskeri* **9**, No. 6, 1–17.

Bruun, A. F., and Heiberg, B. (1935). Weitere Untersuchungen über die Rotseuche des Aals in den dänischen Gewässern. *Z. Fischerei* **33**, 379–381.

Bückmann, A. (1952). Infektion mit *Glugea stephani* und mit *Vibrio anguillarum* bei Schollen (*Pleuronectes platessa* L.). *Kurze Mitt. Fischereibiolog. Abt. Max-Planck Inst. Meeresbiol. Wilhelmshaven* No. 1, 1–7.

Bullock, G. L. (1961). A schematic outline for the presumptive identification of bacterial diseases of fish. *Progressive Fish Culturist* **23**, 147–151.

Bullock, G. L. (1964). Pseudomonadales as fish pathogens. *Develop. Ind. Microbiol.* **5**, 101–108.

Bullock, W. L. (1957). The acanthocephalan parasites of the fishes of the Texas coast. *Publ. Inst. Marine Sci., Univ. Texas* **4**, 278–283.

Bullock, W. L. (1960). Some acanthocephalan parasites of Florida fishes. *Bull. Marine Sci. Gulf Caribbean* **10**, 481–484.

Bullock, W. L. (1962). The status of the acanthocephalan genera *Floridosentis* Ward, 1953, and *Atactorhynchus* Chandler, 1935. *Proc. Helminthol. Soc. Wash., D. C.* **29**, 217–218.

Burton, P. (1956). Morphology of *Ascocotyle leighi* n. sp. (Heterophyidae), an avian trematode with metacercaria restricted to the conus arteriosus of the fish *Mollienesia latipinna* LeSueur. *J. Parasitol.* **42**, 540–543.

Bykhovskaya-Pavlovskaya, I. E., and Petrushevskii, G. K. (1959). Trematode larvae in fish of the USSR. (In Russian.) *Tr. Soveshch. Bolez. Ryb., Ikhtiol. Komm., Akad. Nauk SSSR* pp. 210–218.

Bykhovskii, B. E. (1957). "Trématodes monogènes, leur classification et leur phylogénie," 509 pp. Acad. Sci. U.R.S.S., Leningrad. (Transl. by W. J. Hargis and P. C. Oustinoff. Am. Inst. Biol. Sci., Washington, D. C., 1961.)

Cable, R. M., and Quick, L. A. (1954). Some Acanthocephala from Puerto Rico with the description of a new genus and three new species. *Trans. Am. Microscop. Soc.* **73**, 393–400.

Calderwood, W. L. (1905). "The White Spot" affecting salmon in the Island of Lewis. *Ann. Rept. Fishery Board Scot.* **24**, 77–79.

Canestrini, G. (1893). La malattia dominante della anguille. *Atti,Ist. Veneto Sci., Lettere Arti* [7] **4**, No. 6, 809–814. (Transl. by Bur. Comm. Fish., U. S. Dept. Interior, Seattle, Washington, 1966.)

Carini, A. (1932). Sobre uma hemogregarina de um peixe do mar do Brasil. *7th Reun. Soc. Argent. Patol. Reg. Norte* No. 2, pp. 902–921.

Chandler, A. C. (1935a). A new tetrarhynchid larva from Galveston Bay. *J. Parasitol.* **21**, 214–215.

Chandler, A. C. (1935b). Parasites of fishes in Galveston Bay. *Proc. U. S. Natl. Museum* **83**, 123–157.

Chandler, A. C. (1954). Cestoda. *U. S. Fish Wildlife Serv., Fishery Bull.* **55**, 351–353.

Cheek, R. P. (1965). Pugheadedness in an American shad. *Trans. Am. Fisheries Soc.* **94**, 97–98.

Christensen, N., and Roth, H. (1949). Investigations on internal parasites of dogs. *Kgl. Veterinaer-og Landbohøjsk. Aarsskr.* pp. 1–73.

Christiansen, M., and Jensen, A. (1950). On a recent and frequently occurring tumor disease in eel. *Rep. Dan. Biol. Sta.* **50,** 29–44.

Claussen, L. (1936). Mikrosporidieninfektion beim gefleckten Seewolf. *Deut. Tieraerztl. Wochschr.* **44,** 307.

Clem, L. W., Moewus, L., and Sigel, M. M. (1961). Studies with cells from marine fish in tissue culture. *Proc. Soc. Exptl. Biol. Med.* **108,** 762–765.

Clem, L. W., Sigel, M. M., and Friis, R. R. (1965). An orphan virus isolated in marine fish cell tissue culture. *Ann. N. Y. Acad. Sci.* **126,** 343–361.

Clemens, W. A., and Clemens, L. S. (1921). Contribution to the biology of the muttonfish, *Zoarces anguillaris. Contrib. Can. Biol. Fisheries* 1918–1920, 69–83.

Collett, R. (1874). *Sarcotaces arcticus,* en ny Art af en maerkelig Slaegt af Fiske-Parasiter. *Forhandl. Skand. Naturforsk. Mote* **11,** 387–389.

Colwell, R. R., and Liston, J. (1960). Taxonomic relationships among the pseudomonads. *J. Bacteriol.* **82,** 1–14.

Cox, P. (1916). Investigation of a disease of the herring (*Clupea harengus*) in the Gulf of St. Lawrence 1914. *Contrib. Can. Biol. Fisheries* 1914–1915, 81–85.

Dannevig, A., and Hansen, S. (1952). Faktorer av betydning for fiskeeggenes og fiskeynegelens oppvekst. *Fiskeridirektorat. Skrifter, Ser. Havunders.* **10,** 5–36.

Davey, J. T., and Peachey, J. E. (1968). *Bothriocephalus scorpii* (Cestoda: Pseudophyllidea) in turbot and brill from British coastal waters. *J. Marine Biol. Assoc. U. K.* **48,** 335–340.

Davies, R., and Beyers, E. (1947). A protozoal disease of South African trawled fish and its routine detection by fluorescence. *Nature* **159,** 714.

Davis, G. H. G., and Park, R. W. A. (1962). A taxonomic study of certain bacteria currently classified as *Vibrio* species. *J. Gen. Microbiol.* **27,** 101–119.

Davis, H. S. (1917). Myxosporidia of the Beaufort region, a systematic and biological study. *U. S. Bur. Fisheries, Bull.* **35,** 199–243.

Davis, H. S. (1922). A new bacterial disease of fresh water fishes. *U. S. Bur. Fisheries, Bull.* **38,** 261–280.

Davis, H. S. (1924). A new myxosporidian parasite, the cause of "wormy" halibut. *Rept. U. S. Comm. Fish.* Append. 8, 5 pp.

Davis, H. S. (1947). Studies on the protozoan parasites of fresh-water fishes. *U. S. Fish Wildlife Serv., Fishery Bull.* **51,** 1–29.

Davis, H. S. (1953). "Culture and Disease of Game Fishes," 332 pp. Univ. of California Press, Los Angeles, California.

Dawes, B. (1946). "The Trematoda with Special Reference to British and Other European Forms," 644 pp. Cambridge Univ. Press, London and New York.

Dawes, B. (1947). "The Trematoda of British Fishes," 364 pp. Ray Society, London.

Dawson, C. E. (1964). A bibliography of anomalies of fishes. *Gulf Res. Rept.* **1,** 308–399.

Dawson, C. E. (1966). A bibliography of anomalies of fishes—supplement 1. *Gulf Res. Rept.* **2,** 169–176.

De Mello, I. F., and Valles, C. T. (1936). *Haemogregarina thyrsoideae* n. sp. parasite of the Indian eel *Thyrsoidea macrurus* Bleeker. *Proc. Indian Acad. Sci.* **B4,** 403–404.

Dick, M. W. (1968). *Saprolegnia parasitica* Coker in estuaries. *Nature* **217,** 875.

Dogiel, V. A. (1936). Parasites of cod from the relic lake Mogilny. (In Russian.) *Vch. Zap. Leningr. Gos. Univ., Ser. Biol. Nauk* **7,** 123–133.

Dogiel, V. A. (1939). Coccidia of the testes of Clupeidae and their zoogeographical significance. (In Russian.) *Tr. Leningr. Obshch. Estestvoispyt.* **68**, 32–39.

Dogiel, V. A. (1945). Achievements in the field of the study of fish diseases in USSR and abroad. (In Russian.) *Tr. problem. i Temat. Soveschch. Akad. Nauk SSSR, Zool. Inst.* **4**, 11–17.

Dogiel, V. A. (1948). Parasitic protozoa of fishes from Peter the Great Bay. (In Russian.) *Trans. All-Union Sci. Res. Inst. Lake River Fish., Leningrad* **27**, 17–66.

Dogiel, V. A. (1955). The general character of the parasite fauna of animals inhabiting far-eastern seas. (In Russian.) *Tr. Zool. Inst., Akad. Nauk SSSR* **21**, 53–59.

Dogiel, V. A., and Bykhovskii, B. E. (1939). Parasites of Caspian Sea fishes. (In Russian.) *Tr. Kompleksn. Izuch. Kasp. Morya* **7**, 1–149.

Dogiel, V. A., and Lutta, A. S. (1937). Mortality among spiny sturgeon of the Aral Sea in 1936. (In Russian.) *Ryb. Khoz.* No. 12, 26–27 [Transl. Ser. No. 528, Fisheries Res. Board Can (1965)].

Dogiel, V. A., Petrushevskii, G. K., and Polyanski, Y. I., eds. (1958). "Parasitology of Fishes." (In Russian.) Leningrad Univ. Press, Leningrad. (Transl. by Z. Kabata. Oliver & Boyd, Edinburgh and London, 1961.)

Dollfus, R. P. (1928). Un hôte nouveau pour *Sarcotaces verrucosus* Olsson 1872 (Copepoda Paras.). *Bull. Museum Nat. Hist. Nat.* (*Paris*) [1] **5**, 341–345.

Dollfus, R. P. (1942). Etudes critiques sur les tétrarhynques du Muséum de Paris. *Arch. Museum Hist. Nat.* (*Paris*) [6] **19**, 1–466.

Dollfus, R. P. (1953). Parasites animaux de la morue Atlanto-Arctique. *Encyclopedie Biol.* **43**, 350–363.

Dollfus, R. P. (1955). Cnidosporidie chez un thon, *Thunnus thynnus* (L.) de l'Atlantique marocain. *Compt. Rend. Soc. Sci. Nat. Phys. Maroc* **5**, 92–95.

Dollfus, R. P. (1956). Liste des parasites animaux du hareng de l'Atlantique Nord et la Baltique. *J. Conseil, Conseil Perm. Intern. Exploration Mer* **22**, 58–65.

Dubinin, V. B. (1949). Relation between the distribution of larvae of parasitic helminths in the fishes of the Volga delta and changes in concentration of birds. (In Russian.) *Zool. Zh.* **28**, 2 (cited by Dogiel *et al.*, 1958).

Dunkerley, J. S. (1914). *Dermocystidium pusula* Perez, parasitic in *Trutta fario. Zool. Anz.* **44**, 179–182.

Earp, B. J., Ellis, C. H., and Ordal, E. J. (1953). Kidney disease in young salmon. *Wash. Dept. Fish., Spec. Sci. Rept.* No. 1, 74 pp.

Ekbaum, E. (1938). Notes on the occurrence of Acanthocephala in Pacific fishes. I. *Echinorhynchus gadi* (Zoega) Müller in salmon and *E. lageniformis* sp. nov. and *Corynosoma strumosum* (Rudolphi) in two species of flounder. *Parasitology* **30**, 267–274.

Ellison, W. A., Jr. (1951). The menhaden. *In* "Survey of Marine Fisheries of North Carolina" (H. F. Taylor, ed.), pp. 85–107. Univ. of North Carolina Press, Chapel Hill, North Carolina.

Engelbrecht, H. (1958). Untersuchungen über den Parasitenbefall der Nutzfische im Greifswalder Bodden und Kleinen Haff. *Z. Fisherei* [N.S.] **7**, 481–511.

Euzet, L. (1957). Recherches sur les Monogenoidea parasites de poissons marins. *Ann. Parasitol. Humaine Comparee* **32**, 469–481.

Euzet, L., and Oliver, G. (1967). Diplectanidae (Monogenea) de Téléostéens de la Méditerranée Occidentale. IV. Quelques *Lamellodiscus* Johnston et Tiegs, 1922, parasites de poissons du genre *Pagellus* Cuvier, 1829 (Sparidae). *Ann. Parasitol. Humaine Comparée* **42**, 407–425.

Fantham, H. B. (1919). Some parasitic Protozoa found in South African fishes and amphibians. I. *S. African J. Sci.* **15**, 337.

Fantham, H. B. (1930). Some parasitic Protozoa found in South Africa. XIII. S. African J. Sci. 27, 376–390.

Fantham, H. B., and Porter, A. (1912). Some effects of the occurrence of Myxosporidia in the gall bladder of fishes. Ann. Trop. Med. Parasitol. 5, 467–481.

Fantham, H. B., Porter, A., and Richardson, L. R. (1939). Some Myxosporidia found in certain freshwater fishes in Quebec Province, Canada. Parasitology 31, 1–77.

Fantham, H. B., Porter, A., and Richardson, L. R. (1941). Some Microsporidia found in certain fishes and insects in eastern Canada. Parasitology 33, 186–208.

Farrell, R. K., Lloyd, M. A., and Earp, B. J. (1964). Persistence of Neorickettsiae helminthoeca in an endoparasite of the Pacific salmon. Science 145, 162–163.

Feddersen, A. (1896a). En maerkelig Aal. Dansk Fiskeri foren. Medlemsblad 12 Nov.

Feddersen, A. (1896b). Den maerkelige Aal. Dansk Fiskeri foren. Medlemsblad 19 Nov.

Feddersen, A. (1897a). Rødsygen. Dansk Fiskeri foren. Medlemsblad 26 August.

Feddersen, A. (1897b). Rødsygen. Dansk Fiskeri foren. Medlemsblad 2 Dec.

Fiebiger, J. (1913). Studien über die Schwimmblasencoccidien der Gadusarten (Eimeria gadi n. sp.). Arch. Protistenk. 31, 95–137.

Fischthal, J. H. (1944). Observations on a sporozoan parasite of the eelpout, Zoarces anguillaris, with an evaluation of candling methods for its detection. J. Parasitol. 30, 35–36.

Fish, F. F. (1939). Observations on Henneguya salminicola Ward, a myxosporidian parasitic in Pacific salmon. J. Parasitol. 25, 169–172.

Fish, F. W. (1934). A fungus disease in fishes of the Gulf of Maine. Parasitology 26, 1–16.

Fletcher, L. I., Hodgkiss, W., and Shewan, J. M. (1951). The milkiness of Mauretanean hake and its probable cause. Fishing News, Aberdeen No. 2007, 11.

Ford, E. (1930). Some abnormal fishes received at the Plymouth laboratory. J. Marine Biol. Assoc. U. K. 17, 53–64.

Forrester, C. R. (1956). The relation of stock density to "milkiness" of lemon sole in Union Bay, B. C. Fisheries Res. Board Can., Progr. Rept. Pacific Coast Sta. No. 105, 11 pp.

França, C. (1908). Une hémogrégarine de l'anguille. Arch. Real. Inst. Bacteriol. (Lisboa) 2, 109–112.

French, R. F. (1965). Visceral adhesions in high-seas salmon. Trans. Am. Fisheries Soc. 94, 177–181.

Fujita, T. (1920). On the parasites of Japanese fishes. Dobutsugaku Zasshi 32, 275–281.

Fujita, T. (1934). Note on Eimeria of herring. Proc. 5th Pacific Sci. Congr. Pacific Sci. Assoc., Canada, 1933 Vol. 5, pp. 4135–4139.

Fujita, T. (1943). "Diseases of Fish and Shellfish," 227 pp. (In Japanese.) Koa Nippon Book Co., Tokyo.

Furuyama, T. (1934). On the morphology and life-history of Philometra fujimotoi Furuyama, 1932. Keijo J. Med. 5, 165–177.

Ganapati, P. N. (1936). A new species of myxosporidian from the heart of a marine fish Otolithus ruber. Current Sci. (India) 5, 204.

Ganapati, P. N. (1938). On a new myxosporidian, Henneguya otolithus. Proc. 20th. Indian Sci. Congr., 1937 p. 155 (abstr.).

Ganapati, P. N. (1941). On a new myxosporidian Henneguya otolithi n. sp., a tissue parasite from the bulbus arteriosus of two species of fish of the genus Otolithus. Proc. Indian Acad. Sci. B13, 135–150.

Garnjobst, L. (1945). *Cytophaga columnaris* (Davis) in pure culture: A myxobacterium pathogenic to fish. *J. Bacteriol.* **49**, 113–128.

Gaylord, H. R., and Marsh, M. C. (1914). Carcinoma of the thyroid in the salmonoid fishes. *Bull. U. S. Bur. Fisheries* **32**, 363–524.

Gemmill, J. F. (1912). "The Teratology of Fishes," 73 pp. James MacLehose & Sons, Glasgow.

Getsevichyute, S. I. (1955). Seasonal infestation of the liver of the Baltic cod with *Contracoecum aduncum*. (In Russian.) *Tr. Akad. Nauk Lit. SSR. Ser. Biol.* **2**, 38–39.

Ghittino, P. (1963). "Le Principali Malattie dei Pesci," 35 pp. Stab. Grafico Fratelli Lega, Faenza.

Gilchrist, J. D. F. (1924). A protozoal parasite (*Chloromyxum thyrsites*, sp. n.) of the Cape sea-fish, the "snoek" (*Thyrsites atun* Euphr.). *Trans. Roy. Soc. S. Africa* **11**, 263–273.

Gnanamuthu, C. P. (1957). Lernaeid copepods parasitic on flying fish. *Parasitology* **47**, 119–125.

Goldstein, R. J. (1962). The adult of *Poecilancistrium robustum* (Chandler, 1935). (Dollfus, 1943). *J. Parasitol.* **48**, Suppl., 46–47.

Goldstein, R. J. (1963). Note on the genus *Poecilancistrium* Dollfus, 1929 (Cestoda: Trypanorhyncha). *J. Parasitol.* **49**, 301–304.

Goode, G. B. (1879). The natural and economical history of the American menhaden. *Rept. U. S. Comm. Fish Fisheries, 1877* Part 5, Appendix A, pp. 1–529.

Goode, G. B. (1884). The menhadens. *In* "The Fisheries and Fishery Industries of the United States" (G. B. Goode, ed.), pp. 569–577, *U. S. Comm. Fish Fisheries* Sect. 1, Part 3, U. S. Govt. Printing Office.

Goodwin, W. F., and Vaughn, T. L. (1968). An adult pugheaded American shad *Alosa sapidissima*. *Trans. Am. Fisheries Soc.* **97**, 50.

Gordon, M., ed. (1948). "Biology of Melanomas," N. Y. Acad. Sci. Spec. Publ. Vol. 4, 466 pp.

Gordon, M. (1950). Heredity of pigmented tumors in fish. *Endeavour* **9**, 26–34.

Gordon, M. (1954). The genetics of fish diseases. *Trans. Am. Fisheries Soc.* **83**, 229–240.

Grainger, J. N. R. (1959). The identity of the larval nematodes found in the body muscles of the cod (*Gadus callarias* L.). *Parasitology* **49**, 121–131.

Griffith, A. S. (1930). Tuberculosis in cold-blooded animals. *In* "A System of Bacteriology in Relation to Medicine," Vol. 5, pp. 326–332. Med. Res. Council, London.

Gudger, E. W. (1930). Pug-headedness in the striped sea bass, *Roccus lineatus*, and in other related fishes. *Bull. Am. Museum Nat. Hist.* **61**, 1–19.

Guenther, R. W., Watson, S. W., and Rucker, R. R. (1959). Etiology of sockeye salmon "virus" disease. *U. S. Fish Wildlife Serv., Spec. Sci. Rept., Fisheries* **296**, 1–10.

Gusev, A. V. (1951). Parasitic copepods of several marine fish. (In Russian.) *Parazitol. Sb., Akad. Nauk SSSR, Zool. Inst.* **13**, 394–463.

Hagenmüller, M. (1899). Sur une nouvelle myxosporidie, *Nosema stephani*, parasite du *Flexus passer* Moreau. *Compt. Rend.* **129**, 836–839.

Hahn, C. W. (1918). On the sporozoon parasites of the fishes of Woods Hole and vicinity. III. On the *Chloromyxum clupeidae* of *Clupea harengus* (Young), *Pomolobus pseuoharengus* (Young) and *P. aestivalis* (Young). *J. Parasitol.* **4**, 13–20.

Haley, A. J. (1954). Microsporidian parasite, *Glugea hertwigi,* in American smelt from the Great Bay region, New Hampshire. *Trans. Am. Fisheries Soc.* **83,** 84–90.

Hall, D. L., and Iversen, E. S. (1967). *Henneguya lagodon,* a new species of myxosporidian, parasitizing the pinfish, *Lagodon rhomboides. Bull. Marine Sci.* **17,** 274–279.

Hansen, H. J. (1923). Crustacea Copepoda. II, Copepoda parasita. *Dansk Ingolf-Exped.* **3,** No. 7, 1–92.

Hardcastle, A. B. (1944). *Eimeria brevoortiana,* a new sporozoan parasite from menhaden (*Brevoortia tyrannus*), with observations on its life history. *J. Parasitol.* **30,** 60–68.

Hargis, W. J., Jr. (1954). Monogenetic trematodes of some Gulf of Mexico fishes. *Dissertation Abstr., Zool. Sect.* **14,** Publ. No. 8258, 1115–1116.

Hargis, W. J., Jr. (1957). The host specificity of monogenetic trematodes. *Exptl. Parasitol.* **6,** 610–625.

Hargis, W. J., Jr., and Dillon, W. A. (1965). Monogenetic trematodes from the southern Pacific Ocean. Part III. *Diplasiocotyle johnstoni* Sandars, 1944 from New Zealand and Australia, with a description of a new family. *Proc. Helminthol. Soc. Wash., D. C.* **32,** 220–224.

Heller, A. F. (1949). Parasites of cod and other marine fish from the Baie of Chaleur region. *Can. J. Res.* **27,** 243–264.

Henry, H. (1912). *Haemogregarina anarrhichadis* from *Anarrhicus lupus,* the catfish. *Parasitology* **5,** 190–196.

Henry, H. (1913). A summary of the blood parasites of British sea fish. *J. Pathol. Bacteriol.* **18,** 218.

Herrington, W. C., Bearse, H. M., and Firth, F. E. (1940). Observations on the life history, occurrence and distribution of the redfish parasite *Sphyrion lumpi. U. S. Fish Wildlife Serv., Spec. Sci. Rept.* **5,** 1–12.

Hildebrand, S. F. (1963). Family Clupeidae, genus *Brevoortia. In* "Fishes of the Western North Atlantic," Part 3, pp. 342–380. Sears Found. for Marine Res, Yale Univ., New Haven, Connecticut.

Hjort, J. (1895). Zur Anatomie und Entwicklungsgeschichte Einer im Fleisch von Fischen schmarotzenden Crustacée (*Sarcotaces arcticus* Collett). *Skrifter Videnskabsselsk. Christiania, Math.-Naturv. Kl.* **2,** 1–14.

Hodgkiss, W., and Shewan, J. M. (1950). *Pseudomonas* infection in a plaice. *J. Pathol. Bacteriol.* **62,** 655–657.

Hofer, B. (1904). "Handbuch der Fischkrankheiten," 395 pp. Verlag Allgem. Fischerei ztg., Muenchen.

Hoffman, G. L., and Sindermann, C. J. (1962). Common parasites of fishes. *U. S. Fish Wildlife Serv., Circ.* **144,** 1–17.

Hoffman, G. L., Dunbar, C. E., and Bradford, A. (1962). Whirling disease of trouts caused by *Myxosoma cerebralis* in the United States. *U. S. Fish Wildlife Serv., Spec. Sci. Rept., Fisheries* **427,** 1–15.

Honigberg, B. M., Balamuth, W., Bovee, E. C., Corliss, J. O., Gojdics, M., Hall, R. P., Kudo, R. R., Levine, N. D., Loeblich, A. R., Weiser, J., and Wenrich, D. H. (1964). A revised classification of the phylum Protozoa. *J. Protozool.* **11,** 7–20.

Honma, Y., and Kon, T. (1968). A case of the epidermal papilloma in the witch flounder from the Sea of Japan. *Bull. Japan. Soc. Sci. Fisheries* **34,** 1–5.

Hopkins, S. H. (1968). Personal communication.

Huizinga, H. W., and Haley, A. J. (1962). Occurrence of the acanthocephalan parasite *Telosentis tenuicornis* in the spot, *Leiostomus xanthurus*, in Chesapeake Bay. *Chesapeake Sci.* **3**, 35–42.

Inghilleri, F. (1903). On the etiology and pathogenesis of the 'red disease' ("peste rossa") of eels. *Atti Accad. Nazl. Lincei, Rend., Classe Sci. Fis., Mut. Nat.* [5] **12**, 13–21. (Transl. by I. Anderson, Scot. Home Dept., No. 582.)

Iversen, E. S. (1954). A new myxosporidian, *Myxosoma squamalis*, parasite of some salmonoid fishes. *J. Parasitol.* **40**, 397–404.

Iversen, E. S., and Van Meter, N. N. (1967). A new myxosporidian (Sporozoa) infecting the Spanish mackerel. *Bull. Marine Sci.* **17**, 268–273.

Iversen, E. S., and Yokel, B. (1963). A myxosporidian (sporozoan) parasite in the red drum, *Sciaenops ocellatus*. *Bull. Marine Sci. Gulf Caribbean* **13**, 449–453.

Jakowska, S., Nigrelli, R. F., and Alperin, I. (1954). A new *Henneguya* in the North Atlantic weakfish, *Cynoscion regalis*. *J. Protozool.* **1**, Suppl., 13 (abstr.).

Jameson, A. P. (1929). Myxosporidia from Californian fishes. *J. Parasitol.* **16**, 59–68.

Janiszewska, J. (1938). Studien über die Entwicklung und die Lebensweise der parasitischen Würmer in der Flunder (*Pleuronectes flesus* L.). *Mem. Acad. Polon. Sci., Classe Sci. Math. Nat.* **B14**, 1–68.

Jensen, M. H. (1963). Preparation of fish tissue cultures for virus research. *Bull. Office Intern. Epizooties* **59**, 131–134.

Johnson, T. W., Jr., and Sparrow, F. K., Jr. (1961). "Fungi in Oceans and Estuaries," 668 pp. Hafner, New York.

Johnston, T. H., and Cleland, J. B. (1910). The Haematozoa of Australian fish. I. *Proc. Roy. Soc. N. S. Wales* **44**, 406–415.

Johnston, T. H., and Deland, E. W. (1929). Australian Acanthocephala. No. 1. Census of recorded hosts and parasites. *Trans. Roy. Soc. S. Australia* **53**, 146–154.

Johnstone, J. (1901). Note on a sporozoan parasite of the plaice (*Pleuronectes platessa*). *Proc. Trans. Liverpool Biol. Soc.* **15**, 184–187.

Johnstone, J. (1906). On a myxosporidian infection of *Gadus esmarkii* (with a note on the identification of the parasite by H. M. Woodcock). *Proc. Trans. Liverpool Biol. Soc.* **20**, 304–308.

Johnstone, J. (1912a). Internal parasites and diseased conditions in fishes. *Proc. Trans. Liverpool Biol. Soc.* **26**, 103–104.

Johnstone, J. (1912b). *Tetrarhynchus erinaceus* van Benden. I. Structure of larva and adult worm. *Parasitology* **4**, 364–415.

Johnstone, J. (1913). Diseased conditions of fishes: A phycomycetous fungus in a mackerel (*Scomber scomber*). *Proc. Trans. Liverpool Biol. Soc.* **27**, 28–33.

Johnstone, J. (1920). On certain parasites, diseased and abnormal conditions of fishes. *Proc. Trans. Liverpool Biol. Soc.* **34**, 120–129.

Johnstone, J. (1924). Diseased conditions in fishes. *Proc. Trans. Liverpool Biol. Soc.* **38**, 183–213.

Johnstone, J. (1925). Malignant tumors in fishes. *Proc. Trans. Liverpool Biol. Soc.* **39**, 169–200.

Johnstone, J. (1926). Malignant and other tumours in marine fishes. *Proc. Trans. Liverpool Biol. Soc.* **40**, 75–98.

Johnstone, J. (1927). Diseased conditions of fishes. *Proc. Trans. Liverpool Biol. Soc.* **41**, 162–167.

Joseph, H. (1917). Über Lymphocystis einen fraglichen Protozischen Parasiten. *Verhandl. Zool.-Botan. Ges. Wien, Zool. Sekt.* p. 64.

Joseph, H. (1918). Untersuchungen über Lymphocystis Woodc. *Arch. Protistenk.* **38**, 155–249.

Kabata, Z. (1957a). Note on a new host of *Myxobolus aeglefini*. *Parasitology* **47**, 165–168.

Kabata, Z. (1957b). *Lernaeocera obtusa* sp. nov., a hitherto undescribed parasite of the haddock (*Gadus aeglefinus* L.). *J. Marine Biol. Assoc. U. K.* **36**, 569–592.

Kabata, Z. (1958). *Lernaeocera obtusa* n. sp. Its biology and its effects on the haddock. *Marine Res.* No. 3, 26 pp.

Kabata, Z. (1959). On two little-known Microsporidia of marine fishes. *Parasitology* **49**, 309–315.

Kabata, Z. (1960). Observations on *Clavella* (Copepoda) parasitic on some British gadoids. *Crustaceana* **1**, 342–352.

Kabata, Z. (1961). *Lernaeocera branchialis* (L.) a parasitic copepod from the European and the American shores of the Atlantic. *Crustaceana* **2**, 243–249.

Kabata, Z. (1963a). Incidence of coccidioses in Scottish herring, *Clupea harengus* L. *J. Conseil, Conseil Perm. Intern. Exploration Mer* **28**, 201–210.

Kabata, Z. (1963b). A new species of *Clavella* (Copepoda, Lernaeopodidae) from the South Atlantic. *Crustaceana* **5**, 257–262.

Kahl, A. (1934). Ciliata entocommensalia et parasitica. In "Die Tierwelt der Nord- und Ostsee" (G. Grimpe and E. Wagler, eds.), Vol. II, Chapter 4, pp. 84–107.

Kahl, A. (1935). Wimpertiere oder Ciliata (Infusoria). In "Die Tierwelt Deutschlands und der angrenzenden Meeresteile" (F. Dahl, ed.), Chapter 30, pp. 651–886. G. Fisher, Jena.

Kahl, W. (1936). Über den Befall des Stints mit Larven des Fadenwurmes *Porrocaecum decipiens*. *Fischmarkt* [N.S.] **4**, 177–181.

Kahl, W. (1937). Eine Tetrarhynchidenlarve aus der Muskulatur von *Sebastes marinus* L. *Z. Parasitenk.* **9**, 373–393.

Kahl, W. (1938a). Nematoden in Seefischen. I. Erhebungen über die durch Larven von *Porrocaecum decipiens* Krabbe in Fischwirten hervorgerufenen geweblichen Veränderungen und Kapselbildungen. *Z. Parasitenk.* **10**, 415–431.

Kahl, W. (1938b). Nematoden in Seefischen. II. Erhebungen über den Befall von Seefischen mit Larven von *Anacanthocheilus rotundatus* (Rudolf) und die durch diese Larven hervorgerufenen Reaktionen des Wirtsgewebes. *Z. Parasitenk.* **10**, 513–525.

Kahl, W. (1939). Nematoden in Seefischen. II$. Statistische Erhebungen über den Nematodenbefall von Seefischen. *Z. Parasitenk.* **11**, 16–41.

Kimura, I., Sugiyama, T., and Ito, Y. (1967). Papillomatous growth in sole from Wakasa Bay area. *Proc. Soc. Exptl. Biol. Med.* **125**, 175–177.

Kocylowski, B. (1963). Etat actuel des maladies des poissons, organization de l'inspection des poissons et de leurs produits de consommation en Pologne. *Bull. Office Intern. Epizooties* **59**, 89–109.

Kohl-Yakimoff, N., and Yakimoff, W. L. (1915). Hämogregarinen der Seefische. *Zentr. Bakteriol., Parasitenk., Abt. I. Orig.* **76**, 135–146.

Komai, T. (1923). Notes on *Sarcotaces pacificus*, n. sp., with remarks on its systematic position. *Mem. Coll. Sci., Kyoto Imp. Univ.*, **B1**, 265–271.

Koops, H., and Mann, H. (1966). The cauliflower disease of eels in Germany. *Bull. Office Intern. Epizooties* **65**, 991–998.

Krasilnikov, N. A. (1949). "Determination of Bacteria and Actinomycetes," 830 pp. (In Russian.) Inst. Microbiol. Akad. Nauk SSSR, Moscow-Leningrad.

Krykhtin, M. L. (1951). Some notes on the effects of the parasitic isopod *Livonica amurensis* on the stocks of *Leucisus waleckii* in the Amur. *Tr. Amursk. Ichtyol. Exped.* p. 11.

Kudo, R. R. (1920). Studies on Myxosporidia. A synopsis of genera and species of Myxosporidia. *Illinois Biol. Monographs* **5**, 1–265.

Kudo, R. R. (1924). A biologic and taxonomic study of the Microsporidia. *Illinois Biol. Monographs* **9**, 1–268.

Kudo, R. R. (1933). A taxonomic consideration of Myxosporidia. *Trans. Am. Microscop. Soc.* **52**, 195–216.

Kudo, R. R. (1966). "Protozoology," 5th ed., 1174 pp. C. C Thomas, Springfield, Ohio.

Kuitunen-Ekbaum, E. (1933a). *Philonema oncorhynchi* nov. gen. et spec. *Contrib. Can. Biol. Fisheries* [N.S.] **8**, 71–75.

Kuitunen-Ekbaum, E. (1933b). A case of dracontiasis in Pacific coastal fishes. *Contrib. Can. Biol. Fisheries* [N.S.] **8**, 162–168.

Kuitunen-Ekbaum, E. (1947). The occurrence of *Sarcotaces* in Canada. *J. Fisheries Res. Board Can.* **7**, 505–512.

Kusuda, R. (1968). Discussion. I. (Following a paper by S. Egusa on basic problems of the study of bacterial fish diseases.) *Bull. Japan. Soc. Sci. Fisheries* **34**, 277.

Labbé, A. (1893). Sur deux coccidies nouvelles, parasites des poissons. *Bull. Soc. Zool. France* **18**, 202–204.

Labbé, A. (1896). Recherches zoologiques, cytologiques et biologiques sur les coccidies. *Arch. Zool. Exptl. Gen.* [3] **4**, 517–654.

Laird, M. (1950). *Henneguya vitiensis* n. sp., a myxosporidian from a Fijian marine fish, *Leiognathus fasciatus* (Lacépède, 1803). *J. Parasitol.* **36**, 285–292.

Laird, M. (1951a). A contribution to the study of Fijian Hematozoa. *Zool. Publ. Victoria Univ.* No. 10, 15 pp.

Laird, M. (1951b). Studies on the trypanosomes of New Zealand fish. *Proc. Zool. Soc. London* **121**, 285–309.

Laird, M. (1952). New haemogregarines from New Zealand marine fishes. *Trans. Roy. Soc. New Zealand* **79**, 589–600.

Laird, M. (1953). The Protozoa of New Zealand intertidal zone fishes. *Trans. Roy. Soc. New Zealand* **81**, 79–143.

Laird, M. (1958). Parasites of South Pacific fishes. I. Introduction and Haematozoa. *Can. J. Zool.* **36**, 153–165.

Laird, M. (1961). Parasites from northern Canada. II. Haematozoa of fishes. *Can. J. Zool.* **39**, 541–548.

Latrobe, B. H. (1802). A drawing and description of the *Clupea tyrannus* and *Oniscus praegustator*. *Trans. Am. Phil. Soc.* **5**, 77–81.

Laveran, A. (1906). Sur une hémogrégarine de l'anguille. *Compt. Rend. Soc. Biol.* **60**, 457–458.

Laveran, A., and Mesnil, F. (1901). Deux hémogrégarines nouvelles des poissons. *Compt. Rend.* **133**, 572–577.

Laveran, A., and Mesnil, F. (1902a). Des trypanosomes des poissons. *Arch. Protistenk.* **1**, 475–498.

Laveran, A., and Mesnil, F. (1902b). Sur les Hématozoaires des poissons marins. *Compt. Rend.* **135**, 567–570.

Lebailly, C. (1904). Sur quelques hémoflagellés des téléostéens marins. *Compt. Rend.* **139**, 576–577.

Lebailly, C. (1905). Recherches sur les hématozoaires parasites des téléostéens marins. *Arch. Parasitol.* **10**, 348–404.

Lederer, G. (1936). Ichthyophonuskrankheit der Fische. *Wochschr. Aquar- u. Terrarienk.* **33**, 582–585.

Léger, L. (1906). Myxosporidies nouvelles parasites des poissons. *Ann. Univ. Grenoble* **18**, 267–272.

Léger, L. (1914). Sur un nouveau protiste du genre *Dermocystidium*, parasite de la truite. *Compt. Rend. Soc. Biol.* **158**, 807–809.

Léger, L., and Hollande, A. C. (1922). Coccidie de l'intestin de l'anguille. *Compt. Rend.* **175**, 999–1002.

Letaconnoux, R. (1949). Quelques cas tératologiques chez les poissons. *J. Conseil, Intern. Conseil Perm. Exploration Mer* **16**, 50–58.

Letaconnoux, R. (1960). Note sur la fréquence des cas de coccidiose par *Eimeria* (s. g. *Goussia* Labre 1896) *sardinae* (Thélohan 1890) chez la sardine de la region de la Rochelle. *Conseil Intern. Exploration Mer, Sardine Comm., Paper* No. 27, 3 pp. (mimeo.).

Liaiman, E. M. (1949). "A Course in Fish Diseases," 306 pp. (In Russian.) Food Ind. Publ., Moscow.

Liaiman, E. M. (1957). "Fish Diseases," 259 pp. (In Russian.) Food Ind. Publ., Moscow.

Linton, E. (1889). Notes on Entozoa of marine fishes. *Ann. Rept. U. S. Comm. Fish Fisheries, 1886* **14**, 453–511.

Linton, E. (1900). Fish parasites collected at Woods Hole in 1898. *Bull. U. S. Fish Comm.* **19**, 267–304.

Linton, E. (1901). Parasites of fishes of the Woods Hole region. *Bull. U. S. Fish Comm.* **19**, 405–492.

Linton, E. (1905). Parasites of fishes of Beaufort, North Carolina. *Bull. U. S. Bur. Fisheries* **24**, 321–428.

Linton, E. (1907). A cestode parasite in the flesh of the butterfish. *Bull. U. S. Bur. Fisheries* **26**, 111–132.

Linton, E. (1914). On the seasonal distribution of fish parasites. *Trans. Am. Fisheries Soc.* **44**, 48–56.

Linton, E. (1923). Notes on degenerating cestode cysts in mackerel. *J. Parasitol.* **9**, 176–178.

Linton, E. (1924). Notes on cestode parasites of sharks and skates. *Proc. U. S. Natl. Museum* **64**, 1–114.

Linton, E. (1933). On the occurrence of *Echinorhynchus gadi* in fishes of the Woods Hole region. *Trans. Am. Microscop. Soc.* **52**, 32–34.

Linton, E. (1941). Cestode parasites of teleost fishes of the Woods Hole region, Massachusetts. *Proc. U. S. Natl. Museum* **90**, 417–442.

Liston, J., and Hitz, C. R. (1961). Second survey of the occurrence of parasites and blemishes in Pacific Ocean perch, *Sebastodes alutus,* May–June, 1959. *U. S. Fish Wildlife Serv., Spec. Sci. Rept., Fisheries* **383**, 1–6.

Ljungberg, O. (1963). Report on fish diseases and inspection of fish products in Sweden. *Bull. Office Intern. Epizooties* **59**, 111–120.

Ljungberg, O., and Lange, J. (1968). Skin tumors of northern pike (*Esox lucius* L.). I. Sarcoma in a Baltic pike population. *Proc. 3rd Symp. Mond. Comm. Off. Intern. Epizoot. Etude Maladies Poissons, Separate* No. 16-I, 11 pp.

Lom, J. (1962). Trichodinid ciliates from fishes of the Rumanian Black Sea coast. *Parasitology* **52**, 49–61.

Lom, J. (1963). The ciliates of the family Urceolariidae inhabiting the gills of fishes (the Trichodinella-group). *Vestn. Cesk. Spolecnosti Zool.* **27**, 7–19.

Lowe, J. (1874). Fauna and Flora of Norfolk. Part IV. Fishes. *Trans. Norfolk Norwich Naturalists' Soc.* pp. 21–56.

Lucké, B. (1942). Tumors of the nerve sheaths in fish of the snapper family (Lutianidae). *A.M.A. Arch. Pathol.* **34,** 133–150.

Lucké, B., and Schlumberger, H. G. (1941). Transplantable epitheliomas of the lip and mouth of catfish. I. Pathology. Transplantation to anterior chamber of eye and into cornea. *J. Exptl. Med.* **74,** 397–408.

Lucké, B., and Schlumberger, H. G. (1949). Neoplasia in cold-blooded vertebrates. *Physiol. Rev.* **29,** 91–126.

Lühe, M. (1911). Acanthocephalen. Register der Acanthocephalen und parasitischen Plattwürmer geordnet nach ihren Wirten. *In* "Die Susswasserfauna Deutschlands," Chapter 16, pp. 1–116, A. Brauer, Jena.

Lühmann, M., and Mann, H. (1957). Beobachtungen über die Blumenkohlkrankheit der Aale. *Arch. Fischereiwiss.* **7,** 229–239.

Lüling, K. H. (1951). Neuere Untersuchungen über die Parasiten des Rotbarsches: *Sebastes marinus* (L.). *Z. Parasitenk.* **15,** 8–24.

Lüling, K. H. (1953). Gewebeschäden durch parasitäre Copepoden, besonders durch *Elytrophora brachyptera* (Gerstaecker). *Z. Parasitenk.* **16,** 84–92.

Lumsden, R. D. (1963). *Saccocoelioides sogandaresi* sp. n., a new haploporid trematode from the sailfin molly *Mollienisia latipinna* LeSueur in Texas. *J. Parasitol.* **49,** 281–284.

McGonigle, R. H. (1931). Pathological and other investigations. *Ann. Rept. Biol. Board Can.,* *1930* pp. 20–22.

McGonigle, R. H., and Leim, A. H. (1937). Jellied swordfish. *Fisheries Res. Board Can., Progr. Rept. Atlantic Coast Sta.* No. 19, 3–5.

McGregor, E. A. (1963). Publications on fish parasites and diseases, 330 BC-AD 1923. *U. S. Fish Wildlife Serv., Spec. Sci. Rept., Fisheries* **474,** 1–84.

Machado-Filho, D. A. (1951). Uma nova especie do genero *Atactorhynchus* Van Cleave 1935 (Acanthocephala, Neoechinorhynchidae). *Rev. Brasil. Biol.* **11,** 29–31.

McIntosh, W. C. (1885). Diseases of fishes. Multiple tumours in plaice and common flounders. *3rd Ann. Rept. Fishery Board Scot.,* *1884* pp. 66–67.

McIntosh, W. C. (1886). Diseases of fishes. Further remarks on the multiple tumours of common flounders, &c. *4th Ann. Rept. Fishery Board Scot.,* *1885* pp. 214–215.

Mackerras, I. M., and Mackerras, M. J. (1925). The Haematozoa of Australian marine Teleostei. *Proc. Linnean Soc. N. S. Wales* **50,** 359–366.

McMillen, S. (1960). *Mycobacterium fortuitum:* A mutant of *Mycobacterium marinum. Bacteriol. Proc.* p. 79.

McMillen, S., and Kishner, D. S. (1959). *Mycobacterium marinum* Aronson (1926). *Bacteriol. Proc.* p. 31.

Mann, H. (1952). *Lernaeocera branchialis* (Copepoda parasitica) und seine Schadewirkung bei einigen Gadiden. *Arch. Fischereiwiss.* **4,** 133–144.

Mann, H. (1954). Die wirtschaftliche Bedeutung von Krankheiten bei Seefischen. *Fischwirtshaft, Bremerhaven* **6,** 38–39.

Mann, H. (1960). Schadwirkung des parasitischen Copepoden *Lernaeocera branchialis* auf das Wachstum von Wittlingen. *Inform. Fischwirt.* **7,** 153–155.

Mann, H. (1965). The significance of the copepods as parasites on sea animals used economically. *Proc. Symp. Crustacea, Ernakolam, India, 1965* 10 pp. (mimeo.)

Mann, H. (1967). Occurrence and spreading of cauliflower disease in Europe. *Conseil Intern. Exploration Mer, Anadromous Catadromous Fish Comm.* 13 pp. (mimeo.)

Manter, H. W. (1934). Some digenetic trematodes from deep water fish of Tortugas, Florida. *Carnegie Inst. Wash. Publ.* **435**, 257–345.

Manter, H. W. (1940). Gasterostomes (Trematoda) of Tortugas, Florida. *Carnegie Inst. Wash. Publ.* **534**, 1–19.

Manter, H. W. (1947). The digenetic trematodes of marine fishes of Tortugas, Florida. *Am. Midland Naturalist* **38**, 257–416.

Manter, H. W. (1955). The zoogeography of trematodes of marine fishes. *Exptl. Parasitol.* **4**, 62–86.

Margolis, L. (1953). Milkiness in lemon sole fillets. *Fisheries Res. Board Can., Ann. Rept. Pacific Biol. Std. 1953* p. 158.

Margolis, L. (1958). The identity of the species of *Lepeophtheirus* (Copepoda) parasitic on Pacific salmon (Genus *Oncorhynchus*) and Atlantic salmon (*Salmo salar*). *Can. J. Zool.* **36**, 889–892.

Markowski, S. (1937). Über die Entwicklungsgeschichte und Biologie des Nematoden *Contracaecum aduncum* (Rudolphi 1802). *Bull. Acad. Polon. Sci. Ser. B, Sci. Natur. II* pp. 227–247.

Markowski, S. (1939). Über die Helminthenfauna der baltischen Aalmutter (*Zoarces viviparus* L.). *Zool. Polon.* **3**, 89–104.

Martin, O. (1921). Über Ascaridenlarven aus dem Fleische von Seefischen. *Z. Infektsionskrankh., Haustiere* **22**, 13–36.

Matsumoto, K. (1954). On the two new Myxosporidia, *Chloromyxum musculoliquefaciens* sp. nov. and *Neochloromyxum cruciformum* gen. et sp. nov., from the jellied muscle of swordfish, *Xiphias gladius* Linné, and common Japanese seabass, *Lateolabrax japonicus* (Temmink et Schlegel). *Bull. Japan. Soc. Sci. Fisheries* **20**, 469–478.

Mattheis, T. (1960). Das Aalsterben an der Ostseeküste zwischen Usedom und Wismar im Sommer 1959. *Deut. Fischerei Z. Radebeul, Berlin* **7**, 23–25.

Mavor, J. W. (1915). Studies on the Sporozoa of the fishes of the St. Andrew's region. *47th Ann. Rept. Dept. Marine Fish. Can.* Suppl., 25–38.

Meglitsch, P. A. (1947). Studies on Myxosporidia of the Beaufort region. I. Observations on *Chloromyxum renalis*, n. sp., and *Chloromyxum granulosum* Davis. *J. Parasitol.* **33**, 265–270.

Meglitsch, P. A. (1952). The myxosporidian fauna of some fresh water and marine fishes. *Proc. Iowa Acad. Sci.* **59**, 480–486.

Meyer, A. (1933). Acanthocephala. *In* "Klassen und Ordunungen des Tierreichs" (H. G. Bronn, ed.), Vol. 4, Sect. 2, Book 2, 582 pp. Leipzig.

Meyer, A. (1951). Keine Fischmarkierung, sondern ein Parasit. *Fischereiwelt* **2**, 76–77.

Meyer, A. (1952). Veränderung des Fleisches beim Katfisch. *Fischereiwelt* **4**, 57–58.

Meyer, M. C. (1954). The larger animal parasites of the fresh-water fishes of Maine. *Maine Dep. Inland Fish Game. Fish. Res. Manage. Div. Bull.* **1**, 1–92.

Meyer, M. C. (1958). Studies on *Philonema agubernaculum*, a dracunculoid nematode infecting salmonids. *J. Parasitol.* **44**, Suppl., 42 (abstr.).

Meyer, M. C. (1960). Notes on *Philonema agubernaculum* and other related dracunculoids infecting salmonids. *Libro Homenaje Dr. Eduardo Caballero y Caballero* pp. 487–492.

Mikhaylova, I. G., Prazdnikov, E. V., and Prusevich, T. O. (1964). Morphological changes in the fish tissue around the larvae of some parasitic worms. (In Russian.) *Trudy Murmansk. Morsk. Biol. Inst. Akad. Nauk SSSR* **5**, 251–264.

Millemann, R. E., Gebhardt, G. A., and Knapp, S. E. (1964). "Salmon poisoning" disease. I. Infection in a dog from marine salmonids. *J. Parasitol.* **50**, 588–589.

Moewus, L. (1963). Studies on a marine parasitic ciliate as a potential virus vector. *In* "Symposium on Marine Microbiology" (C. H. Oppenheimer, ed.), p. 366. Thomas, Springfield, Illinois.

Moewus-Kobb, L. (1965). Studies with IPN virus in marine hosts. *Ann. N. Y. Acad. Sci.* **126**, 328–342.

Nemeczek, A. (1911). Beiträge zur Kenntnis der Myxo- und Microsporidien der Fische. *Arch. Protistenk.* **22**, 143–169.

Neumann, R. O. (1909). Studien über protozoische Parasiten im Blut von Meeresfischen. *Z. Hyg. Infektionskrankh.* **64**, 1–112.

Nicoll, W. R. (1907). A contribution towards a knowledge of the Entozoa of British marine fishes. *Ann. Mag. Nat. Hist.* [7] **19**, 66–94.

Nicoll, W. R. (1910). On the Entozoa of fishes from the Firth of Clyde. *Parasitology* **3**, 322–359.

Nigrelli, R. F. (1938). Fish parasites and fish diseases. I. Tumors. *Trans. N. Y. Acad. Sci.* [2] **1**, 4–7.

Nigrelli, R. F. (1940). Mortality statistics for specimens in the New York Aquarium, 1939. *Zoologica* **25**, 525–552.

Nigrelli, R. F. (1946). Studies on the marine resources of southern New England. V. Parasites and diseases of the ocean pout, *Macrozoarces americanus*. *Bull. Bingham Oceanog. Collection* **9**, 187–202.

Nigrelli, R. F. (1952a). Spontaneous neoplasms in fish. VI. Thyroid tumors in marine fishes. *Zoologica* **37**, 185–189.

Nigrelli, R. F. (1952b). Virus and tumours in fishes. *Ann. N. Y. Acad. Sci.* **54**, 1076–1092.

Nigrelli, R. F., and Firth, F. E. (1939). On *Sphyrion lumpi* (Krøyer), a copepod parasite on the redfish, *Sebastes marinus* (Linnaeus), with special reference to the host parasite relationships. *Zoologica* **24**, 1–10.

Nigrelli, R. F., and Hutner, S. H. (1945). The presence of a myxobacterium *Chondrococcus columnaris* (Davis) Ordal and Rucker (1944) on *Fundulus heteroclitus* (Linn.). *Zoologica* **30**, 101–104.

Nigrelli, R. F., and Ruggieri, G. D. (1965). Studies on virus diseases of fishes. Spontaneous and experimentally-induced cellular hypertrophy (Lymphocystis disease) in fishes of the New York Aquarium, with a report of new cases and and annotated bibliography (1874–1965). *Zoologica* **50**, 83–96.

Nigrelli, R. F., and Smith, G. M. (1938). Tissue responses of *Cyprinodon variegatus* to the myxosporidian parasite *Myxobolus lintoni* Gurley. *Zoologica* **23**, 195–202.

Nigrelli, R. F., and Smith, G. M. (1939). Studies on lymphocystis disease in the orange filefish, *Ceratocanthus schoepfii* (Walbaum), from Sandy Hook Bay, N. J. *Zoologica* **24**, 255–262.

Nigrelli, R. F., and Stunkard, H. W. (1947). Studies on the genus *Hirudinella*, giant trematodes of scombriform fishes. *Zoologica* **31**, 185–196.

Nigrelli, R. F., and Vogel, H. (1963). Spontaneous tuberculosis in fishes and in other cold-blooded vertebrates with special reference to *Mycobacterium fortuitum* Cruz from fish and human lesions. *Zoologica* **48**, 131–144.

Nigrelli, R. F., Ketchen, K. S., and Ruggieri, G. D. (1965). Studies on virus diseases of fishes. Epizootiology of epithelial tumors in the skin of flatfishes of the Pacific coast, with special reference to the sand sole (*Psettichthys melanosticus*) from northern Hecate Strait, British Columbia, Canada. *Zoologica* **50**, 115–122.

Nordenberg, C. (1962). Das Vorkommen der Lymphocystiskrankheit bei Scholle und Flunder in Öresund. *Kgl. Fisiogr. Sallsk. Lund Forh.* **32**, 17–26.

Nũnes-Ruivo, L. P. (1957). Contribution a l'étude des variations morphologiques de *Clavella adunca* (H. Ström), copépode parasite de *Gadus callarias*. Considérations sur quelques *Clavella* parasites des Gadidae. *Rev. Fac. Cienc., Univ. Lisboa* **C5**, 229–252.

Nybelin, O. (1922). Anatomisch-systematischen Studien ueber Pseudophyllidien. *Goteborgs Vetenskaps-Vitterhetssamhales Handl.* **26**, 169–211.

Nybelin, O. (1923). Zur postembryonalen Entwicklungsgeschichte der Acanthocephalen. I. *Zool. Anz.* **58**, 32–36.

Nybelin, O. (1924). Zur postembryonalen Entwicklungsgeschichte der Acanthocephalen. II. *Zool. Anz.* **61**, 190–193.

Nybelin, O. (1935). Untersuchungen über den bei Fischen krankheitsenserregenden Spaltpilz *Vibrio anguillarum*. *Medd. Statens Unders. Forsogsanst. Sotvattenfisket* No. 8, 5–62.

Ojala, O. (1963). Fish diseases in Finland. *Bull. Office Intern. Epizooties* **59**, 31–42.

Olsen, Y. H., and Merriman, D. (1946). Studies on the marine resources of southern New England. IV. The biology and economic importance of the ocean pout, *Macrozoarces americanus* (Bloch and Schneider). *Bull. Bingham Oceanog. Collection* **9**, 132–184.

Olsson, P. (1872). Om *Sarcotaces* och *Acrobothrium*, två nya parasitslägten från fiskar. *Ofversigt af Kgl. Vetenskaps-Akad. Forhandl., Stockholm* No. 9, 37–44.

Oppenheimer, C. H. (1962). On marine fish diseases. *In* "Fish as Food" (G. Borgstrom, ed.), Vol. 2, p. 541. Academic Press, New York.

Oppenheimer, C. H., and Kesteven, G. L. (1953). Disease as a factor in natural mortality of marine fishes. *FAO Fisheries Bull.* **6**, 215–222.

Orlandini, C. (1957). Metacercariosi in *Mullus barbatus* (L.). e *Mullus surmuletus* (L.) del Mediterraneo. *Atti Soc. Ital. Sci. Vet.* **11**, 646–649.

Osmanov, S. O. (1959). Parasitofauna and parasitic diseases of fish of the Aral Sea. (In Russian.) *Proc. Conf. Fish Diseases, 1957* No. 9, 203–209. Akad. Nauk. SSSR, Moscow-Leningrad.

Pacheco, G. (1935). Diseases of fishes in Brazilian rivers. *Mem. Inst. Oswaldo Cruz* **40**, 349–371.

Padnos, M., and Nigrelli, R. F. (1942). *Trichodina spheroidesi* and *Trichodina halli* spp. nov. parasitic on the gills and skin of marine fishes, with special reference to the life-history of *T. spheroidesi*. *Zoologica* **27**, 65–72.

Parisi, B. (1912). Primo contributo alla distribusione geografica dei missosporidi in Italia. *Atti Soc. Ital. Sci. Nat. Museo Civico Storia Nat. Milano* **50**, 283–290.

Parisot, T. J. (1958). Tuberculosis of fish: A review of the literature with a description of the disease in salmonoid fish. *Bacteriol. Rev.* **22**, 240–245.

Parisot, T. J., and Pelnar, J. (1962). An interim report on Sacramento River chinook disease: A viruslike disease of chinook salmon. *Progressive Fish Culturist* **24**, 51–55.

Parisot, T. J., Yasutake, W. T., and Klontz, G. W. (1965). Virus diseases of the Salmonidae in western United States. I. Etiology and epizootiology. *Ann. N. Y. Acad. Sci.* **126**, 502–519.

Patashnik, A., and Groninger, H. S. (1964). Observations on the milky condition in some Pacific coast fishes. *J. Fisheries Res. Board Can.* **21**, 335–346.

Pavlovskii, E. N., ed. (1959). "Proceedings of the Conference on Fish Diseases," 224 pp. (In Russian.) Ikhtiol. Kom., Akad. Nauk SSSR, Moscow-Leningrad.

Pavlovskii, E. N., ed. (1962). "Key to Parasites of Freshwater Fish of the U.S.S.R.," 919 pp. (In Russian.) Akad. Nauks SSR Zool. Inst., Moscow-Leningrad.

Pellérdy, L. P. (1965). "Coccidia and Coccidiosis," 657 pp. Akademia Kiadó, Budapest.

Pérard, C. (1928). Sur une maladie du maquereau (Scomber scomber L.) due à une myxosporidie: Chloromyxum histolyticum n. sp. Compt. Rend. 186, 108–110.

Petrushevskii, G. K., ed. (1957). "Parasites and Diseases of Fish," 338 pp. (In Russian.) Izv. Vses. Nauchn.-Issled. Inst. Ozern. Rechn. Ryb. Khoz., Leningrad.

Petrushevskii, G. K., and Kogteva, E. P. (1954). Effect of parasitic diseases on condition of fish. (In Russian.) Zool. Zhurn. 33, 395–405.

Petrushevskii, G. K., and Shulman, S. S. (1955). Liver nematode infestations of the Baltic cod. (In Russian.) Tr. Akad. Nauk Lit. SSR, Ser. Biol. 2, 119–124.

Petrushevskii, G. K., and Shulman, S. S. (1961). The parasitic diseases of fishes in the natural waters of the USSR. In "Parasitology of Fishes" (In Russian.) (V. A. Dogiel et al., eds.), pp. 299–319. (Translation: Oliver & Boyd, Edinburgh and London.)

Pinto, J. S. (1956). Parasitic castration in males of Sardina pilchardus (Walb.) due to testicular infestation by the coccidia Eimeria sardinae (Thélohan). Rev. Fac. Cienc., Univ. Lisbon C5, 209–223.

Pinto, J. S., and Barraca, I. F. (1961). Parasitose testiculaire par Eimeria sardinae (Thél.). Conseil Intern. Exploration Mer, Sardine Comm. Paper No. 160, 4 pp. (mimeo.).

Pinto, J. S., Barraca, I. F., and Assis, M. E. (1961). Nouvelles observations sur la coccidiose par Eimeria sardinae (Thélohan), chez les sardines des environs de Lisbonne, en 1961. Notas Estud. Inst. Biol. Marine, Lisbon No. 23, 13 pp.

Plehn, M. (1924). "Praktikum der Fischkrankheiten," 179 pp. E. Schweizerbart'sche Verlagsbuchhandlung, Stuttgart.

Plehn, M., and Mulsow, K. (1911). Der Erreger der "Taumelkrankheit" der Salmoniden. Zentr. Bakteriol., Parasitenk., Abt. I. Orig. 59, 63–68.

Polyanski, Y. I. (1955). Contributions to the parasitology of fishes of the northern seas of the USSR. (In Russian.) Tr. Zool. Inst., Akad. Nauk SSSR 19, 5–170.

Post, G. (1965). A review of advances in the study of diseases of fish: 1954–64. Progr. Fish-Cult. 27, 3–12.

Poulsen, E. (1939). Investigations upon the parasitic copepod Clavella uncinata (O. F. Müller) in Danish waters. Vidensk. Medd. Dansk Naturhist. Foren. Kbh. 102, 223–244.

Prakash, A., and Adams, J. R. (1960). A histopathological study of the intestinal lesions induced by Echinorhynchus lageniformis (Acanthocephala-Echinorhynchidae) in the starry flounder. Can. J. Zool. 38, 895–897.

Precht, H. (1935). Epizoen der Kieler Bucht. Nova Acta Leopoldina [N.S.] 3, 405.

Prévot, A. R. (1961). "Traité de systématique bactérienne," 2 vols. Dunod, Paris.

Price, E. W. (1934). New digenetic trematodes from marine fishes. Smithsonian Inst. Misc. Collections 91, No. 7, 1–8.

Price, E. W. (1963). A new genus and species of monogenetic trematode from a shark, with a review of the family Microbothridae Price, 1936. Proc. Helminthol. Soc. Wash., D. C. 30, 213–218.

Priebe, K. (1963). Einige wenig bekannte parasitologische, lebensmittelhygienisch bedeutsame Befunde bei Meeresfischen. Arch. Lebensmittelhyg. 14, 257–260.

Putz, R. E., Hoffman, G. L., and Dunbar, C. E. (1965). Two new species of Plisto-

phora (Microsporidea) from North American fish with a synopsis of Microsporidea of freshwater and euryhaline fishes. *J. Protozool.* **12**, 228–236.

Rae, B. (1958). The occurrence of plerocercoid larvae of *Grillotia erinaceus* (van Beneden) in halibut. *Marine Res.* No. 4, 31 pp.

Raney, E. C. (1952). The life history of the striped bass, *Roccus saxatilis* (Walbaum). *Bull. Bingham Oceanog. Collection* **14**, 5–97.

Rasheed, S. (1963). A revision of the genus *Philometra* Costa 1845. *J. Helminthol.* **37**, 89–130.

Rašin, K. (1927). Příspěvek k pathogenesi *Lymphocystis johnstonei* Woodcock. I. *Biol. Spisy Vys. Sk. Zverolek.* **6**, 11–33.

Rašin, K. (1927). Příspěvek k pathogenesi *Lymphocystis johnstonei* Woodcock. I. *Biol. Spisy Vys. Sk. Zverolek.* **7**, 1–14.

Reichenbach-Klinke, H. H. (1954). Untersuchungen über die bei Fischen durch Parasiten hervorgerufenen Zysten und deren Wirkung auf den Wirtskorper. I. *Z. Fischerei* [N.S.] **3**, 565–636.

Reichenbach-Klinke, H. H. (1955a). Untersuchungen über die bei Fischen durch Parasiten hervorgerufenen Zysten und deren Wirkung auf den Wirtskorper. II. *Z. Fischerei* [N.S.] **4**, 1–54.

Reichenbach-Klinke, H. H. (1955b). Die Fischtuberkulose. *Z. Aquarien- u. Terrarienver.* **8**, 12.

Reichenbach-Klinke, H. H. (1955c). Pilze in Tumoren bei Fischen. *Verhandl. Deut. Zool. Ges. Tubingen* pp. 351–357.

Reichenbach-Klinke, H. H. (1956a). Augenschäden bei Meeresfischen durch den Pilz *Ichthyosporidium hoferi* (Plehn et Mulsow) und Bermerkungen zu seiner Verbreitung bei Mittelmeerfischen. *Pubbl. Sta. Zool. Napoli* **29**, 22–32.

Reichenbach-Klinke, H. H. (1956b). Über einige bisher unbekannte Hyphomyceten bei verschiedenen Süsswasser- und Meeresfischen. *Mycopathol. Mycol. Appl.* **7**, 333–347.

Reichenbach-Klinke, H. H. (1956c). Die Vermehrungsformen des zoophagen Pilzes *Ichthyosporidium hoferi* (Plehn & Mulsow) (Fungi, Phycomycetes) im Wirt. *Veroeffentl. Inst. Meeresforsch. Bremerhaven* **4**, 214–219.

Reichenbach-Klinke, H. H. (1956d). *Trichodina dohrni* n. sp., eine neue Fischpathogene Ciliatenart aus dem Golf von Neapel. *Z. Parasitenk.* **17**, 365–370.

Reichenbach-Klinke, H. H. (1958). Les parasites de la sardine (*Sardina pilchardus* Walb.) et de l'anchois *Engraulis encrasicholas* Rond.). *Rappt. Proces-Verbaux Reunions, Comm. Intern. Exploration Sci. Mer Mediter.* **14**, 351–353.

Reichenbach-Klinke, H. H. (1966). "Krankheiten und Schädigungen der Fische," 389 pp. Fischer, Stuttgart.

Reichenbach-Klinke, H. H., and Elkan, E. (1965). "The Principal Diseases of Lower Vertebrates," 600 pp. Academic Press, New York.

Reichenow, E. (1929). "Lehrbuch der Protozoenkunde," 5th ed. Fischer, Jena.

Remotti, E. (1933a). Sulla sistematica dell' *Ascaris capsularia* Rud. *Boll. Mus. Lab. Zool. Anat. Comp. R. Univ. Genova* **13**, No. 64, 1–26.

Remotti, E. (1933b). Ancora sull' *Ascaris capsularia* Rud. *Boll. Mus. Lab. Zool. Anat. Comp. R. Univ. Genova* **13**, No. 68, 1–15.

Richardson, H. (1903). Contributions to the natural history of the Isopoda. *Proc. U. S. Natl. Museum* **27**, 1–89.

Richardson, H. (1905). Monograph of the isopods of North America. *U. S. Natl. Museum, Bull.* **54**, 1–727.

Robin, C. (1879). Mémoire sur la structure et la réproduction de quelques infusoires tentaculés, suceurs et flagellés. *J. Anat. Physiol.* **15**, 529.

Roegner-Aust, S. (1953). Zur Fräge einer Virusätiologie bei verschiedenen Fischkrankheiten. *Muenchener Beitr. Abswasser Fisch.-Flussbiol.* 1, 120–145.

Roegner-Aust, S., and Schleich, F. (1951). Zur Ätiologie einiger Fischkrankheiten. *Z. Naturforsch.* 6B, 448–451.

Ross, A. J. (1960). *Mycobacterium salmoniphilum* sp. nov. from salmonoid fishes. *Am. Rev. Respirat. Diseases* 81, 241–250.

Ross, A. J., Earp, B. J., and Wood, J. W. (1959). Mycobacterial infections in adult salmon and steelhead trout returning to the Columbia River Basin and other areas in 1957. *U. S. Fish Wildlife Serv., Spec. Sci. Rept., Fisheries* 332, 1–34.

Ross, A. J., Pelnar, J., and Rucker, R. R. (1960). A virus-like disease of chinook salmon. *Trans. Am. Fisheries Soc.* 89, 160–163.

Roughley, T. C. (1951). "Fish and Fisheries of Australia," 343 pp. Angus & Robertson, Sydney, Australia.

Rowan, M. K. (1956). Fresh fish. 2. *Chloromyxum thyrsites* in various South African fishes. *Rept. Fishing Ind. Res. Inst., Cape Town* 9, 7–8.

Rucker, R. R. (1959). Vibrio infections among marine and fresh-water fish. *Progressive Fish Culturist* 21, 22–25.

Rucker, R. R., and Gustafson, P. V. (1953). An epizootic among rainbow trout. *Progressive Fish Culturist* 15, 179–181.

Rucker, R. R., Earp, B. J., and Ordal, E. J. (1954). Infectious diseases of Pacific salmon. *Trans. Am. Fisheries Soc.* 83, 297–312.

Russell, F. E., and Kotin, P. (1957). Squamous papilloma in the white croaker. *J. Natl. Cancer Inst.* 18, 857–861.

Ruszkowski, J. S. (1934). Études sur le cycle évolutif et sur la structure des cestodes marins. III. Le cycle évolutif du tetrarhynque *Grillotia erinaceus* (van Beneden 1858). *Mem. Acad. Polon. Sci., Classe Sci. Math. Nat.* B9, 6.

Sandeman, G. (1893). On the multiple tumours of plaice and flounders. *11th Ann. Rept. Fishery Res. Board Scot., 1892* pp. 391–392.

Sandholzer, L. A., Nostrand, T., and Young, L. (1945). Studies on an Ichthyosporidian-like parasite of ocean pout (*Zoarces anguillaris*). *U. S. Fish Wildlife Serv., Spec. Sci. Rept.* 31, 1–12.

Saunders, D. C. (1955). The occurrence of *Haemogregarina bigemina* Laveran and Mesnil and *H. achiri* n. sp. in marine fish from Florida. *J. Parasitol.* 41, 171–176.

Saunders, D. C. (1958a). The occurrence of *Haemogregarina bigemina* Laveran and Mesnil, and *H. dasyatis* n. sp. in marine fish from Bimini, Bahamas, B. W. I. *Trans. Amer. Microscop. Soc.* 77, 404–412.

Saunders, D. C. (1958b). Blood parasites of the marine fish of the Florida Keys. *Year Book, Amer. Phil. Soc.,* 261–266.

Saunders, D. C. (1959). *Trypanosoma balistes* n. sp. from *Balistes capriscus* Gmelin, the common triggerfish, from the Florida Keys. *J. Parasitol.* 45, 623–626.

Saunders, D. C. (1960). A survey of the blood parasites in the fishes of the Red Sea. *Trans. Am. Microscop. Soc.* 79, 239–252.

Saunders, D. C. (1964). Blood parasites of marine fish of southwest Florida, including a new haemogregarine from the menhaden, *Brevoortia tyrannus* (Latrobe). *Trans. Am. Microscop. Soc.* 83, 218–225.

Saunders, D. C. (1966). A survey of the blood parasites of the marine fishes of Puerto Rico. *Trans. Am. Microscop. Soc.* 85, 193–199.

Scattergood, L. W. (1948). A report on the appearance of the fungus *Ichthyosporidium hoferi* in the herring of the northwestern Atlantic. *U. S. Fish Wildlife Serv., Spec. Sci. Rept.* 58, 1–33.

Schäperclaus, W. (1927). Die Rotseuche des Aales im Bezirk von Rügen und Stralsund. Z. Fischerei 25, 99–128.

Schäperclaus, W. (1928). Die Hechtpest in Brandenburg und Rügen. Z. Fischerei 26, 343–366.

Schäperclaus, W. (1930). Pseudomonas punctata als Krankheitserreger bei Fischen. Z. Fischerei 28, 289–370.

Schäperclaus, W. (1934). Untersuchungen über die Aalseuchen in deutschen Binnen- und Küstengewässern 1930–1933. Z. Fischerei 32, 191–217.

Schäperclaus, W. (1953a). Fortpflanzung und Systematik von Ichthyophonus. Z. Aquarien- u. Terrarienver. 6, 177–182.

Schäperclaus, W. (1953b). Die Blumenkohlkrankheit der Aale und anderer Fische der Ostsee. Z. Fischerei [N.S.] 2, 105–124.

Schäperclaus, W. (1954). "Fischkrankheiten," 708 pp. Akademie Verlag, Berlin.

Schlicht, F. G., and McFarland, W. N. (1967). Incidence of trypanorhynchan plerocercoids in some Texas coast scianid fishes. Contrib. Marine Sci. Univ. Texas 12, 101–112.

Schlumberger, H. G. (1955). Spontaneous hyperplasia and neoplasia in the thyroid of animals. Brookhaven Symp. Biol. 7, 169–191.

Schlumberger, H. G., and Lucké, B. (1948). Tumors of fishes, amphibians and reptiles. Cancer Res. 8, 657–754.

Schmey, M. (1911). Über Neubildungen bei Fischen. Frankfurter Z. Pathol. 6, 230–252.

Scholes, R. B., and Shewan, J. M. (1964). The present status of some aspects of marine microbiology. Advan. Marine Biol. 2, 133–170.

Schrader, F. (1921). A microsporidian occurring in the smelt. J. Parasitol. 7, 151–153.

Schuurmans-Stekhoven, J. H. (1936). Beobachtungen zur Morphologie und Physiologie der Lernaeocera branchialis L. und der Lernaeocera lusci Bassett-Smith (Crustacea parasitica). Z. Parasitenk. 8, 659–696.

Schuurmans-Stekhoven, J. H., and Punt, A. (1937). Weitere Beiträge zur Morphologie und Physiologie der Lernaeocera branchialis L. Z. Parasitenk. 9, 648–668.

Schwartz, F. J. (1963). A new Ichthyosporidium parasite of the spot (Leiostomus xanthurus): A possible answer to recent oyster mortalities. Progressive Fish Culturist 25, 181–186.

Schwartz, F. J. (1964–1965). A pugheaded menhaden from Chesapeake Bay. Underwater Naturalist 2, 22–24.

Scott, A. (1928). The copepod parasites of Irish Sea fish. Proc. Trans. Liverpool Biol. Soc. 43, 81–119.

Scott, D. M. (1950). A preliminary report on the cod-worm investigation. Fisheries Res. Board Can., Progr. Rept. Atlantic Coast Sta. No. 48, 10–12.

Scott, D. M. (1953). Experiments with the harbour seal, Phoca vitulina, a definitive host of a marine nematode, Porrocaecum decipiens. J. Fisheries Res. Board Can. 10, 539–547.

Scott, D. M. (1954). Experimental infection of Atlantic cod with a larval nematode from smelt. J. Fisheries Res. Board Can. 11, 894–900.

Scott, D. M. (1955). On the early development of Porrocaecum decipiens. J. Parasitol. 41, 321–322.

Scott, D. M. (1956). On the specific identity of the larval Porrocaecum (Nematoda) in Atlantic cod. J. Fisheries Res. Board Can. 13, 343–356.

Scott, D. M., and Fisher, H. D. (1958). Incidence of the ascarid Porrocaecum *decipiens* in the stomachs of three species of seals along the southern Canadian Atlantic mainland. *J. Fisheries Res. Board Can.* **15**, 495–516.

Scott, D. M., and Martin, W. R. (1957). Variation in the incidence of larval nematodes in Atlantic cod fillets along the southern Canadian mainland. *J. Fisheries Res. Board Can.* **14**, 975–996.

Scott, D. M., and Martin, W. R. (1959). The incidence of nematodes in the fillets of small cod from Lockeport, Nova Scotia, and the southwestern Gulf of St. Lawrence. *J. Fisheries Res. Board Can.* **16**, 213–221.

Sherman, K., and Wise, J. P. (1961). Incidence of the cod parasite *Lernaeocera branchialis* L. in the New England area, and its possible use as an indicator of cod populations. *Limnol. Oceanog.* **6**, 61–67.

Shewan, J. M. (1961). The microbiology of sea-water fish. *In* "Fish as Food" (G. Borgstrom, ed.), Vol. 1, p. 487. Academic Press, New York.

Shewan, J. M. (1963). The differentiation of certain genera of Gram negative bacteria frequently encountered in marine environments. *In* "Symposium on Marine Microbiology" (C. H. Oppenheimer, ed.), p. 499. Thomas, Springfield, Illinois.

Shewan, J. M., Hodgkiss, W., and Liston, J. (1954). A method for the rapid differentiation of certain non-pathogenic, asporogenous bacilli. *Nature* **173**, 208–209.

Shewan, J. M., Floodgate, G. D., and Hayes, P. R. (1958). The national type culture collection of marine bacteria in Great Britain. *Intern. Bull. Bacteriol. Nomencl. Taxon.* **8**, 193–194.

Shewan, J. M., Hobbs, G., and Hodgkiss, W. (1960). A determinative scheme for the identification of certain genera of Gram-negative bacteria, with special reference to the Pseudomonadaceae. *J. Appl. Bacteriol.* **23**, 379–390.

Shulman, S. S. (1948). Helminth infection of a cod's liver. (In Russian.) *Ryb. Khoz. (Fish Ind.)* No. 4, 38–40.

Shulman, S. S. (1950). Parasites of fishes in the aquatories of the Latvian Republic. (In Russian.) *Tr. Gel'mintol. Lab., Akad. Nauk SSSR* **4** (Thesis abstr.).

Shulman, S. S. (1957). Pathogenicity of the myxosporidian *Myxobolus exiguus* and epizootics produced by it. *In* "Parasites and Diseases of Fish" (G. K. Petrushevskii, ed.), p. 42. *Izv. Vses. Nauchn.-Issled. Inst. Ozern. Rechn. Ryb. Khoz., Leningrad.* (Transl. by Natl. Sci. Found. and U. S. Dept. Interior, 1960.)

Shulman, S. S. (1959). Parasites of fish in the eastern part of the Baltic Sea. (In Russian.) *Proc. Conf. Fish Diseases, 1957* pp. 194–197. Akad. Nauk, SSSR, Moscow-Leningrad.

Shulman, S. S. (1966). "Myxosporidian Fauna of the USSR." (In Russian.) Acad. Sci. U.S.S.R., Zool. Inst., Sci. Publ., Moscow-Leningrad.

Shulman, S. S., and Shulman-Albova, R. E. (1953). "Parasites of Fishes of the White Sea," 192 pp. (In Russian.) Publ. Acad Sci. U.S.S.R., Moscow.

Sindermann, C. J. (1957). Diseases of fishes of the western North Atlantic. VI. Geographic discontinuity of myxosporidiosis in immature herring from the Gulf of Maine. *Maine Dept. Sea Shore Fish., Res. Bull. No. 29*, 1–20.

Sindermann, C. J. (1958). An epizootic in Gulf of Saint Lawrence fishes. *Trans. North Am. Wildlife Conf.* **23**, 349–360.

Sindermann, C. J. (1959). Unpublished data.

Sindermann, C. J. (1961a). Sporozoan parasites of sea herring. *J. Parasitol.* **47**, Suppl., 34 (abstr.).

Sindermann, C. J. (1961b). Parasitological tags for redfish of the western North

Atlantic. *Rappts. Proces-verbaux, Conseil Perm. Intern. Exploration Mer* **150**, 111–117.

Sindermann, C. J. (1963). Disease in marine populations. *Trans. North Am. Wildlife Conf.* **28**, 336–356.

Sindermann, C. J. (1965). Effects of environment on several diseases of herring from the western North Atlantic. *Spec. Publ. Intern. Comm. Northw. Atlantic Fish.* No. 6, 603–610.

Sindermann, C. J. (1966). Diseases of marine fishes. *Advan. Marine Biol.* **4**, 1–89.

Sindermann, C. J., and Rosenfield, A. (1954a). Diseases of fishes of the western North Atlantic. I. Diseases of the sea herring (*Clupea harengus*). *Maine Dept. Sea Shore Fish., Res. Bull.* No. 18, 23 pp.

Sindermann, C. J., and Rosenfield, A. (1954b). Diseases of fishes of the western North Atlantic. III. Mortalities of sea herring (*Clupea harengus*) caused by larval treatmode invasion. *Maine Dept. Sea Shore Fish., Res. Bull.* No. 21, 16 pp.

Sindermann, C. J., and Scattergood, L. W. (1954). Diseases of fishes of western North Atlantic. II. *Ichthyosporidium* disease of the sea herring (*Clupea harengus*). *Maine Dept. Sea Shore Fish., Res. Bull.* No. 19, 1–40.

Skrjabin, K. I., ed. (1947–1962). "Trematodes of Animals and Man," Vols. I–XX. (In Russian.) Tr. Akad. Nauk S.S.S.R., Moscow.

Smith, G. M. (1934). A cutaneous red pigmented tumor (erythrophoroma) with metastases in a flatfish (*Pseudopleuronectes americanus*). *Am. J. Cancer* **21**, 596–599.

Smith, G. M. (1935). A hyperplastic epidermal disease in the winter flounder infected with *Cryptocotyle lingua* (Creplin). *Am. J. Cancer* **25**, 108–112.

Smith, G. M., and Nigrelli, R. F. (1937). Lymphocystis disease in *Angelichthys*. *Zoologica* **22**, 293–296.

Smith, I. W. (1961). A disease of finnock due to *Vibrio anguillarum*. *J. Gen. Microbiol.* **24**, 247–252.

Snieszko, S. F. (1954). Research on fish diseases: A review of progress during the past 10 years. *Trans. Am. Fisheries Soc.* **83**, 219–349.

Snieszko, S. F. (1957). Suggestions for reduction of natural mortality in fish populations. *Trans. Am. Fisheries Soc.* **87**, 380–385.

Snieszko, S. F. (1964). Remarks on some facets of epizootiology of bacterial fish diseases. *Develop. Ind. Microbiol.* **5**, 97–100.

Snieszko, S. F., Bullock, G. L., Hollis, E., and Boone, J. G. (1964). *Pasteurella* sp. from an epizootic of white perch (*Roccus americanus*) in Chesapeake Bay tidewater areas. *J. Bacteriol.* **88**, 1814–1815.

Snieszko, S. F., Nigrelli, R. F., and Wolf, K. E. (Eds.) (1965). Viral diseases of poikilothermic vertebrates. *Ann. N. Y. Acad. Sci.* **126**, 1–680.

Sogandares-Bernal, F., and Bridgman, J. F. (1960). Three *Ascocotyle* complex trematodes (Heterophyidae) encysted in fishes from Louisiana, including the description of a new genus. *Tulane Studies Zool.* **8**, 31–39.

Sogandares-Bernal, F., and Lumsden, R. D. (1963). The generic status of the heterophyid trematodes of the *Ascocotyle* complex, including notes on the systematics and biology of *Ascocotyle angrense* Travassos 1916. *J. Parasitol.* **49**, 264–274.

Sogandares-Bernal, F., and Lumsden, R. D. (1964). The heterophyid trematode *Ascocotyle* (A.) *leighi* Burton, 1956, from the hearts of certain poeciliid and cyprinodont fishes. *Z. Parasitenk.* **24**, 3–12.

Sprague, V. (1965). *Ichthyosporidium* Caullery and Mesnil, 1905, the name of a genus of fungi or a genus of sporozoans? *Syst. Zool.* **14**, 110–114.

Sprague, V. (1966). *Ichthyosporidium* sp. Schwartz, 1963, parasite of the fish *Leiostomus xanthurus*, is a microsporidian. *J. Protozool.* **13**, 356–358.

Sprehn, C. (1934). Cestoidea. *In* "Tierwelt der Nord- und Ostsee" (G. Grimpe and E. Wagler, eds.), Vol. 4, p. 61. Leipzig.

Sproston, N. G. (1944). *Ichthyosporidium hoferi* (Plehn & Mulsow, 1911), an internal fungoid parasite of the mackerel. *J. Marine Biol. Assoc. U. K.* **26**, 72–98.

Sproston, N. G. (1946). A synopsis of the monogenetic trematodes. *Trans. Zool. Soc. London* **25**, 185–600.

Strøm, H. (1762). Physisk og Oeconomisk Beskrivelse over Fogderiet Søndiner, beliggende i Bergens Stift i Norge. Første Part. Copenhagen. (Cited by Kabata, 1957a.)

Stuart, M. R., and Fuller, H. T. (1968a). Mycological aspects of diseased Atlantic salmon. *Nature* **217**, 90–92.

Stuart, M. R., and Fuller, H. T. (1968b). *Saprolegnia parasitica* Coker in estuaries. *Nature* **217**, 1157–1158.

Stunkard, H. W. (1930). The life history of *Cryptocotyle lingua* (Creplin) with notes on the physiology of the metacercaria. *J. Morphol.* **50**, 143–191.

Stunkard, H. W., and Lux, F. E. (1965). A microsporidian infection of the digestive tract of the winter flounder, *Pseudopleuronectes americanus. Biol. Bull.* **129**, 371–387.

Sutherland, P. L. (1922). A tuberculosis-like disease in a salt-water fish (halibut) associated with the presence of an acid-fast tubercle-like bacillus. *J. Pathol. Bacteriol.* **25**, 31–35.

Takahashi, K. (1929). Studie über die Fischgeschwülste. *Z. Krebsforsch.* **29**, 1–73.

Takahashi, K. (1934). Studies on tumours of fishes from Japanese waters. *Proc. 5th Pacif. Sci. Congr. Pacific Sci. Assoc., Canada, 1933*, 4151–4155.

Templeman, W. F. (1948). The life history of the caplin (*Mallotus villosus* O. F. Müller) in Newfoundland waters. *Res. Bull. Newfoundland Govt. Lab.* No. 17, 151 pp.

Templeman, W. F. (1965a). Some abnormalities in skates (*Raja*) of the Newfoundland area. *J. Fisheries Res. Board Can.* **22**, 237–238.

Templeman, W. F. (1965b). Lymphocystis disease in American plaice of the eastern Grand Bank. *J. Fisheries Res. Board Can.* **22**, 1345–1356.

Templeman, W. F., and Andrews, G. L. (1956). Jellied condition in the American plaice, *Hippoglossoides platessoides* (Fabricius). *J. Fisheries Res. Board Can.* **13**, 147–182.

Templeman, W. F., and Squires, H. J. (1960). Incidence and distribution of infestation by *Sphyrion lumpi* (Krøyer) on the redfish, *Sebastes marinus* (L.) of the western North Atlantic. *J. Fisheries Res. Board Can.* **17**, 9–31.

Templeman, W. F., Squires, H., and Fleming, A. M. (1957). Nematodes in the fillets of cod and other fishes in Newfoundland and neighbouring areas. *J. Fisheries Res. Board Can.* **14**, 831–897.

Te Strake, D. (1959). Estuarine distribution and saline tolerance of some Saprolegniaceae. *Phyton* (*Buenos Aires*) **12**, 147–152.

Thélohan, P. (1890). Sur deux coccidies nouvelles, parasites de l'épinoche et de la sardine. *Compt. Rend. Soc. Biol.* (*Paris*) **42**, 345–348.

Thélohan, P. (1892). Sur quelques coccidies nouvelles parasites des poissons. *Compt. Rend. Soc. Biol.* (*Paris*) **44**, 12–14.

Thélohan, P. (1893). Nouvelles recherches sur les coccidies. *Compt. Rend.* **117**, 247–249.

Thélohan, P. (1895). Recherches sur les myxosporidies. *Bull. Sci. France Belg.* **26,** 100–394.

Thomas, L. (1926). Contribution a l'étude des lésions précancereuses chez les poissons. Les papillomas cutanées de la sole. *Bull. Assoc. Franc. Etude Cancer* **15,** 464–470.

Thomas, L. (1931). Les tumeurs des poissons (étude anatomique et pathogénique). *Bull. Assoc. Franc. Etude Cancer* **20,** 703–760.

Thompson, W. F. (1916). A note on a sporozoan parasite of the halibut. *Rept. Comm. Fisheries, Brit. Columbia* pp. 127–129.

Thomson, J. G., and Robertson, A. (1926). Fish as the source of certain Coccidia recently described as intestinal parasites of man. *Brit. Med. J.* **1,** 282–283.

Timon-David, J. (1961). Recherches sur la morphologie, le développement expérimental et la systématique d'une metacercaire du genre *Ascocotyle* Looss, 1899 (Trematoda, Digenea, Heterophyidae) parasite des branchies chez les tetards de *Rana esculenta* Linn. *Ann. Parasitol. Humaine Comparee* **36,** 737–751.

Torres, C. M., and Pacheco, G. (1934). Stomatite et inclusions cytoplasmiques chez *Geophagus brasiliensis,* expérimentalement infecté par le virus d'une épizootie des poissons au Brésil. *Compt. Rend. Soc. Biol. (Paris)* **117,** 508–510.

Tripathi, Y. R. (1948). A new species of ciliate, *Trichodina branchicola,* from some fishes at Plymouth. *J. Marine Biol. Assoc. U. K.* **27,** 440–450.

Turner, W. R., and Roe, R. B. (1967). Occurrence of the parasitic isopod *Olencira praegustator* (Latrobe) in the yellowfin menhaden, *Brevoortia smithi. Trans. Am. Fisheries Soc.* **96,** 357–359.

Tyzzer, E. E. (1900). Tumors and Sporozoa in fishes. *J. Boston Soc. Med. Sci.* **5,** 63–68.

Uspenskaya, A. V. (1953). The life cycles of the nematodes belonging to the genus *Ascarophis* van Beneden (Nematoda, Spirurata). (In Russian.) *Zool. Zh.* **32,** 828–832.

Van Cleave, H. J. (1920). Acanthocephala. *Rept. Can. Arctic Exped.* **9,** 1–11.

Van Cleave, H. J. (1940). The Acanthocephala collected by the Allan Hancock Expedition, 1934. *Allan Hancock Pacific Exped.* **2,** 501–527.

Vishniac, H. S., and Nigrelli, R. F. (1957). The ability of the Saprolegniacaea to parasitize platyfish. *Zoologica* **42,** 131–134.

Vogel, H. (1958). Mycobacteria from cold-blooded animals. *Am. Rev. Tuberc. Pulmonary Diseases* **77,** 823–838.

Volodin, V. M. (1960). Effect of temperature on the embryonic development of the pike, the blue bream (*Abramis ballerus* L.) and the white bream (*Blicca bjoerkna* L.). (In Russian.) *Tr. Inst. Biol. Vodokhranilishch, Akad. Nauk SSSR* **3,** 231–237.

Walford, L. A. (1958). "Living Resources of the Sea," 321 pp. Ronald Press, New York.

Walker, R. (1962). Fine structure of lymphocystis virus of fish. *Virology* **18,** 503–505.

Walker, R., and Wolf, K. E. (1962). Virus array in lymphocystis cells of sunfish. *Am. Zoologist* **2,** 566 (abstr.).

Ward, H. B. (1919). Notes on North American Myxosporidia. *J. Parasitol.* **6,** 49–64.

Ward, H. L. (1953). A new genus and species, *Floridosentis elongatus,* of Neo-echinorhynchidae (Acanthocephala). *J. Parasitol.* **39,** 392–394.

Ward, H. L. (1954). Parasites of marine fishes of the Miami region. *Bull. Marine Sci. Gulf Caribbean* **4,** 244–261.

Wardle, R. A. (1932). The Cestoda of Canadian fishes. I. The Pacific coast region. *Contrib. Can. Biol. Fisheries* [N.S.] **A7**, 221–243.

Wardle, R. A. (1935). The cestoda of Canadian fishes. III. Additions to the Pacific coastal fauna. *Contrib. Can. Biol. Fisheries* [N.S.] **A8**, 77–87.

Wardle, R. A., and McLeod, J. A. (1952). "The Zoology of Tapeworms," 780 pp. Univ. of Minnesota Press, Minneapolis, Minnesota.

Watson, S. W., Guenther, R. W., and Rucker, R. R. (1954). A virus disease of sockeye salmon: Interim report. *U. S. Fish Wildlife Serv., Spec. Sci. Rept., Fisheries* **138**, 1–36.

Weissenberg, R. (1909). Beiträge zur Kenntnis von *Glugea lophii* Doflein. I. Über den Sitz und die Verbreitung der Mikrosporidiencysten am Nervensystem von *Lophius piscatorius* und *budegassa*. *Sitzber. Berlin. Ges. Naturforsch. Freunde* pp. 557–565.

Weissenberg, R. (1911a). Beiträge zur Kenntnis von *Glugea lophii* Doflein. II. Über den Bau der Cysten und die Beziehungen zwischen Parasit und Wirtsgewebe. *Sitzber. Berlin. Ges. Naturforsch. Freunde* pp. 149–157.

Weissenberg, R. (1911b). Ueber einige Microsporiden aus Fischen. (*Nosema lophii* Doflein, *Glugea anomala* Moniez, *Glugea hertwigii* nov. spec.) *Sitzber. Berlin. Ges. Naturforsch. Freunde* pp. 344–351.

Weissenberg, R. (1911c). Über Mikrosporidien aus dem Nervensystem von Fischen (*Glugea lophii* Doflein) und die Hypertrophie der befallenen Ganglienzellen. *Arch. Mikroskop. Anat. Entwicklungsmech.* **78**, 383–421.

Weissenberg, R. (1913). Beiträge zur Kenntnis des Zeugungskreises der Microsporidien, *Glugea anomala* Moniez und *hertwigi* Weissenberg. *Arch. Mikroskop. Anat. Entwicklungsmech.* **82**, 81–163.

Weissenberg, R. (1914a). Über Bau und Entwicklung der Microsporidie "*Glugea anomala*" Moniez. *Proc. 9th Intern. Congr. Zool., Monaco, 1913* pp. 380–389.

Weissenberg, R. (1914b). Über infektiöse Zellhypertrophie bei Fischen (Lymphocystiserkrankung). *Sitzber. Preuss. Akad. Wiss. Berlin* **30**, 792–804.

Weissenberg, R. (1920). Lymphocystisstudien (Infektiöse Hypertrophie von Stützgewebzellen bei Fischen). I. Die reifen Geschwülste bei Kaulbarsch und Flunder. Lymphocystisgenese beim Kaulbarsch. *Arch. Mikroskop. Anat. Entwicklungsmech.* **94**, 55–134.

Weissenberg, R. (1921a). Lymphocystiskrankheit der Fischen. *In* "Handbuch der Pathogenen Protozoen" (S. V. Prowazek and W. Noller, eds.), Vol. 3, p. 1344, Barth, Leipzig.

Weissenberg, R. (1921b). Zur Wirtsgewebesabteilung des Plasmakörpers der *Glugea anomala*-Cysten. *Arch. Protistenk.* **42**, 400–421.

Weissenberg, R. (1938). Studies on virus diseases of fish. I. Lymphocystis disease of the orange filefish (*Aleutera schoepfii*). *Am. J. Hyg.* **28**, 455–462.

Weissenberg, R. (1939a). Studies on virus diseases of fish. II. Lymphocystis disease of *Fundulus heteroclitus*. *Biol. Bull.* **76**, 251–255.

Weissenberg, R. (1939b). Studies on virus diseases of fish. III. Morphological and experimental observations on the lymphocystis disease of the pike perch, *Stizostedion vitreum*. *Zoologica* **24**, 245–254.

Weissenberg, R. (1945). Studies on virus diseases of fish. IV. Lymphocystis disease in Centrarchidae. *Zoologica* **30**, 169–184.

Weissenberg, R. (1951a). Studies on lymphocystis tumor cells of fish. II. Granular structures of the inclusion substance as stages of the developmental cycle of the lymphocystis virus. *Cancer Res.* **11**, 608–613.

Weissenberg, R. (1951b). Some results of morphological studies on the developmental cycle of the lymphocystis virus of fish with reference to the experimental work of K. Rasin. *Anat. Record* 111, 289 (Abstr.).

Weissenberg, R. (1965). Fifty years of research on the lymphocystis virus disease of fishes (1914–1964). *Ann. N. Y. Acad. Sci.* 126, 362–374.

Weissenberg, R., Nigrelli, R. F., and Smith, G. M. (1937). Lymphocystis in the hogfish, *Lachnolaimus maximus*. *Zoologica* 22, 303–305.

Wellings, S. R., and Chuinard, R. G. (1964). Epidermal papillomas with virus-like particles in flathead sole, *Hippoglossoides elassodon*. *Science* 146, 932–934.

Wellings, S. R., Chuinard, R. G., Gourley, R. T., and Cooper, R. A. (1964). Epidermal papillomas in the flathead sole, *Hippoglossoides elassodon*, with notes on the occurrence of similar neoplasms in other pleuronectids. *J. Natl. Cancer Inst.* 33, 991–1004.

Wellings, S. R., Chuinard, R. G., and Bens, M. (1965). A comparative study of skin neoplasms in four species of pleuronectid fishes. *Ann. N. Y. Acad. Sci.* 126, 479–501.

Wellings, S. R., Chuinard, R. G., and Cooper, R. A. (1967). Ultrastructural studies of normal skin and epidermal papillomas of the flathead sole, *Hippoglossoides elassodon*. *Z. Zellforsch. Mikroskop. Anat.* 78, 370–387.

Wells, N. A., and ZoBell, C. W. (1934). *Achromobacter ichthyodermis*, n. sp., the etiological agent of an infectious dermatitis of certain marine fishes. *Proc. Natl. Acad. Sci. U. S.* 20, 123–126.

White, H. C. (1940). "Sea lice" (*Lepeophtheirus*) and death of salmon. *J. Fisheries Res. Board Can.* 5, 172–175.

White, H. C. (1942). Life history of *Lepeophtheirus salmonis*. *J. Fisheries Res. Board Can.* 6, 24–29.

Williams, G. (1929). Tumourous growths in fish. *Proc. Trans. Liverpool Biol. Soc.* 43, 120–148.

Williams, H. H. (1958). Some Phyllobothriidae (Cestoda: Tetraphyllidea) of elasmobranches from the western seaboard of the British Isles. *Ann. Mag. Nat. Hist.* [13] 1, 113–136.

Willis, A. G. (1949). On the vegetative forms and life history of *Chloromyxum thyrsites* Gilchrist and its doubtful systematic position. *Australian J. Sci. Res.* B2, 379–398.

Wilson, C. B. (1917). North American parasitic copepods belonging to the Lernaeidae with a revision of the entire family. *Proc. U. S. Natl. Museum* 53, 1–150.

Winqvist, G., Ljungberg, O., and Hellstroem, B. (1968). Skin tumors of northern pike (*Esox lucius* L.). II. Viral particles in epidermal proliferations. *Proc. 3rd Symp. Mond. Comm. Off. Intern. Epizoot. Etude Maladies Poissons, Separate* No. 16-II, 7 pp.

Wolf, K. (1962). Experimental propagation of lymphocystis disease of fishes. *Virology* 18, 249–256.

Wolf, K. (1964). Characteristics of viruses found in fish. *Develop. Ind. Microbiol.* 5, 140–148.

Wolf, K. (1966). The Fish Viruses. *Advan. Virus Res.* 12, 35–101.

Wolf, K., and Dunbar, C. E. (1957). Cultivation of adult teleost tissues *in vitro*. *Proc. Soc. Exptl. Biol. Med.* 95, 455–458.

Wolf, K., and Quimby, M. C. (1962). Established eurythermic line of fish cells *in vitro*. *Science* 135, 1065–1066.

Wolf, K., Snieszko, S. F., Dunbar, C. E., and Pyle, E. (1960). Virus nature of infectious pancreatic necrosis in trout. *Proc. Soc. Exptl. Biol. Med.* **104**, 105–108.

Wolfgang, R. W. (1954a). Studies of the trematode *Stephanostomum baccatum* (Nicoll, 1907). I. The distribution of the metacercaria in eastern Canadian flounders. *J. Fisheries Res. Board Can.* **11**, 954–962.

Wolfgang, R. W. (1954b). Studies of the trematode *Stephanostomum baccatum* (Nicoll, 1907). II. Biology, with special reference to the stages affecting the winter flounder. *J. Fisheries Res. Board Can.* **11**, 963–987.

Wolfgang, R. W. (1955a). Studies of the trematode *Stephanostomum baccatum* (Nicoll, 1907). III. Its life cycle. *Can. J. Zool.* **3**, 113–128.

Wolfgang, R. W. (1955b). Studies of the trematode *Stephanostomum baccatum* (Nicoll, 1907). IV. The variation of the adult morphology and the taxonomy of the genus. *Can. J. Zool.* **3**, 129–142.

Wolter, R. (1961). Die *Vibrio-anguillarum*-Seuche im Strelasund und Greifswalder Bodden. *Z. Fisherei* [N.S.] **9**, 763–770.

Wood, J. W., and Ordal, E. J. (1958). Tuberculosis in Pacific salmon and steelhead trout. *Fish Comm. Oregon, Contrib.* No. 25, 38 pp.

Woodcock, H. M. (1904a). On Myxosporidia in flatfish. *Proc. Trans. Liverpool Biol. Soc.* **18**, 42–46.

Woodcock, H. M. (1904b). Note on a remarkable parasite of plaice and flounders. *Proc. Trans. Liverpool Biol. Soc.* **18**, 143–152.

Woodland, W. N. F. (1927). A revised classification of the tetraphyllidean Cestoda, with descriptions of some Phyllobothriidae from Plymouth. *Proc. Zool. Soc. London* pp. 519–548.

Wurmbach, H. (1937). Zur krankheitserregenden Wirkung der Acanthocephalen. Die Kratzererkrankung der Barben in der Mosel. *Z. Fisherei* **35**, 217–232.

Yakimoff, W. L. (1929). Zur Frage über den Parasitismus der Süsswasserfische. IV. Coccidien beim Barsch (*Perca fluviatilis*). *Arch. Protistenk.* **67**, 501–508.

Yamaguti, S. (1934). Studies on the helminth fauna of Japan. Part 2. Trematodes of fishes. I. *Japan. J. Zool.* **5**, 249–541.

Yamaguti, S. (1935). Studies on the helminth fauna of Japan. Part 9. Nematodes of fishes. 1. *Japan. J. Zool.* **6**, 337–386.

Yamaguti, S. (1958–1963). "Systema Helminthum," Vols. I-V. Wiley (Interscience), New York.

Yasutake, W. T., Parisot, T. J., and Klontz, G. W. (1965). Virus diseases of the Salmonidae in western United States. II. Aspects of pathogenesis. *Ann. N. Y. Acad. Sci.* **126**, 520–530.

Yorke, W., and Maplestone, P. A. (1926). "The Nematode Parasites of Vertebrates," 536 pp. Churchill, London.

Young, P. H. (1964). Some effects of sewer effluent on marine life. *Calif. Fish Game* **50**, 33–41.

Young, R. T. (1955). Tetrarhynch (cestode) life histories. *Biol. Bull.* **109**, 354.

ZoBell, C. E., and Wells, N. A. (1934). An infectious dermatitis of certain marine fishes. *J. Infect. Diseases* **55**, 299–305.

Zschokke, F., and Heitz, F. A. (1914). Entoparasiten aus Salmoniden von Kamtschatka. *Rev. Suisse Zool.* **22**, 195–256.

III

Diseases of Shellfish

A. INTRODUCTION

As understanding of factors that influence the numbers of animals in the sea has expanded, it has become evident that disease, among other environmental variables, can drastically affect ·abundance. This fact has been clearly demonstrated in populations of sedentary inshore invertebrates, many of which are harvested in great numbers and constitute marine crops of high value. Some, such as mussels, oysters, clams, crabs, lobsters, and shrimps, occur in inshore or estuarine waters, and have been subjected to varying degrees of cultivation in different parts of the world. Under natural conditions or under cultivation, mass mortalities occasionally occur; here disease can be an important contributing factor.

The word "disease," as used in this chapter, includes abnormalities resulting from microbial pathogens or parasite invasion, tumors, genetically or environmentally induced abnormalities, and physiological disturbances. For each host group considered in this chapter, a sequence of diseases, beginning with those caused by bacteria [virus diseases, with but a single exception (Vago, 1966), have not been identified in marine invertebrates] and progressing to fungi, protozoans, and larger parasites, has been followed. Usually each host species is infected by several well-defined pathogens, as well as assorted parasites that have variable impact on the host population.

No general review of the literature on diseases of marine invertebrates has been made (Steinhaus, 1965), but particular groups, especially those of commercial importance, have received some attention. Sindermann and Rosenfield (1967) published a review of the principal diseases of commercially important marine bivalve Mollusca and Crustacea. Dollfus (1921a), Pelseneer (1928), Ranson (1936), Fischer (1951), and Cheng (1967) have summarized information about the parasites and diseases of mollusks, particularly oysters, and Hutton et al. (1959) reported on parasites and diseases of some of the commercial shrimps. Gordon (1966) summarized information on parasites and diseases of Crustacea, emphasizing freshwater representatives. Certain general aspects of invertebrate diseases, such as immune mechanisms, have been considered (Cantacuzène, 1923, 1928; Huff, 1940; Baer, 1944; Steinhaus, 1949; Stauber, 1961) and a few research groups, such as Frederik B. Bang and his associates at the Johns Hopkins University, Leslie A. Stauber and his associates at Rutgers University, Marennes R. Tripp and his associates at the University of Delaware, Albert K. Sparks and his associates at the University of Washington, and Sung Y. Feng of the University of Connecticut have been concerned with comparative pathology and immunology of marine invertebrates (Bang, 1956, 1961, 1962, 1967; Bang and Bang, 1962; Bang and Lemma, 1962; Levin and Bang, 1964; Rabin and Bang, 1964; Stauber, 1961; Tripp, 1958, 1960, 1963, 1966; Sparks and Pauley, 1964; Pauley et al., 1965; Feng, 1962, 1966, 1967). The former *Journal of Insect Pathology*, edited by E. A. Steinhaus, has recently been broadened in title (*Journal of Invertebrate Pathology*) and in content to include papers on diseases of all invertebrates.

Much of our knowledge about diseases of marine invertebrates concerns species of economic importance, particularly the crustacean and bivalve molluscan shellfish. Many diseases of marine invertebrates are inadequately characterized, and others probably have not even been recognized. Microbial pathogens that have been implicated in mass mortalities include bacteria, fungi, and protozoans. Several of the larger parasites have been found to be pathogenic under specific environmental conditions. Not included in this chapter are most of the parasites and diseases of noncommercial species—species that may be of great significance in the cycles of life in the sea, but which are not of significant direct importance as food for humans. Among the groups thus excluded are barnacles, copepods, and most of the smaller crabs. Also excluded are many diseases that have been incompletely described in the scientific literature.

Much published information about diseases of marine mollusks and crustaceans has accumulated, and at least a representative fraction of the available literature has been considered in this chapter. Preparation of a bibliography of molluscan shellfish diseases has been a continuing project of the Oxford (Maryland) Laboratory of the U. S. Bureau of

Commercial Fisheries for 6 years; this bibliography, as well as standard bibliographical and abstracting sources, has been used in preparing the manuscript. There is little representation of the Russian literature; this may be in part a reflection of the relative lack of emphasis placed on shellfish in Russian fisheries research, as well as the limited availability of translations of Russian literature. Some of the older European literature—particularly that on specific parasites of invertebrates—has not been considered in this chapter, but is accessible through references cited in more recent publications.

B. MOLLUSCA

1. Bivalve Mollusks

Most of the commercial bivalve mollusks occur in shallow inshore waters, often intertidally, where they are accessible to quantitative observation and evaluation. Unusual mortalities are more apparent here than in offshore populations. As a result, literature on mass mortalities of species such as oysters and mussels is voluminous. Disease has sometimes been demonstrated to be the cause of deaths; when the cause has not been determined, disease has been strongly suspected. Within the past decade knowledge about molluscan shellfish diseases has been increasing at a greatly accelerated pace, largely because of concern about mortalities which have occurred in widely scattered populations. Literature on oyster diseases is most abundant; that on mussel and clam diseases is less voluminous.

a. *Oysters*

The twentieth century has been a difficult and troublesome period for oysters (family Ostreidae) in many parts of the world (Orton, 1924a; Roughley, 1926; Gross and Smyth, 1946; Logie, 1956; Mackin, 1961; Sindermann, 1966a, 1968). Decline in abundance of oysters actually started in the nineteenth century, probably caused in large part by indiscriminate harvesting and destruction of beds. Extensive mortalities from unknown causes also contributed to decreased oyster production. The rate of decline on the North American east coast and in other geographical areas has recently increased because of large-scale mortalities, several of which have been caused by disease. Largely because of their worldwide economic importance, oysters are among the most thoroughly studied of marine animals—especially their diseases and parasites. Many unsolved problems remain, but the body of literature is large and growing rapidly.

Among the important diseases of oysters are those caused by bacteria, fungi, protozoans, trematodes, cestodes, and parasitic crustaceans.

(1) MICROBIAL DISEASES

(a) BACTERIA. Reports of mass mortalities of Pacific oysters, *Crassostrea gigas* (Thunberg), have been published recently in Japan (Fujita *et al.*, 1953; 1955; Takeuchi *et al.*, 1960; Ogasawara *et al.*, 1962; Imai *et al.*, 1965; Kan-no *et al.*, 1965; K. Mori *et al.*, 1965a,b; Numachi *et al.*, 1965; Tamate *et al.*, 1965). Takeuchi *et al.* (1960) implicated a gram-negative, motile, 1 to 3 μ bacillus, probably an *Achromobacter*, in large-scale mortalities in Pacific oyster culture areas of Hiroshima Bay since 1946. Experimental infections were achieved with cultured bacteria, but the organisms could be isolated from healthy as well as sick oysters, and from seawater. Moribund oysters had diffuse cell infiltration, massive increase in bacterial numbers, and tissue necrosis.

Numachi *et al.* (1965) found up to 20% infection with gram-positive bacteria (not further identified) in oysters during mass mortalities in Matsushima Bay, Japan, in the early 1960's. The disease was called "multiple abscesses," but the authors did not think that a causal relation existed between bacteria and mortalities. A similar disease was found in 1965 by staff members of the Bureau of Commercial Fisheries Biological Laboratory, Oxford, Maryland, in seed oysters (less than 1 year old) imported to the United States west coast from Matsushima Bay, and in adult oysters from Willapa Bay, Washington. The disease has been labeled "focal necrosis" (Fig. 34). Studies of the etiological agent and its pathogenicity are incomplete. The disease affects seed oysters as young as 6 months, as well as adults. The necrotic foci or multiple abscesses may represent the resistant or arrested disease state, and the active, fulminating phase may have already killed susceptible members of the population.

Several bacterial pathogens of bivalve larvae have been isolated (Guillard, 1959; Tubiash *et al.*, 1965). Identified only as *Aeromonas* sp. or *Vibrio* sp., the organisms killed larvae and juveniles of five bivalve species tested, including American oysters, *Crassostrea virginica* (Gmelin), and European oysters, *Ostrea edulis* L., but did not affect adults.

(b) FUNGI. Oysters have several fungus diseases, some of serious consequence. Identification of fungus pathogens, especially in the early literature, has often been tentative, and only a few adequate characterizations of etiological agents have been made.

A relatively well-known fungus infecting oysters from the Atlantic and Gulf coasts of the United States is *Dermocystidium marinum*. First described by Mackin *et al.* (1950), the pathogen has been the subject of much research. A useful diagnostic technique, based on a fluid thioglycollate medium fortified with an antibiotic, was devised by Ray (1952, 1966b) during attempts to culture the organism. A number of authors

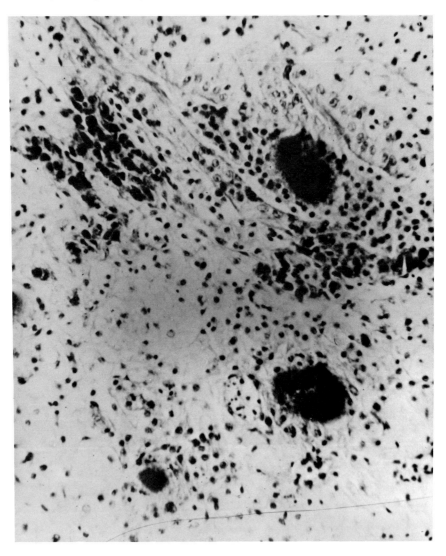

FIG. 34. Focal necrosis in connective tissue of Pacific oyster from Willapa Bay, Washington, surrounded by extensive leukocyte infiltration. (From Sindermann and Rosenfield, 1967.)

have shown that *D. marinum* causes oyster mortalities (Mackin *et al.*, 1950; Andrews and Hewatt, 1954; Hewatt and Andrews, 1954; Mackin, 1953; Ray, 1954a,b,c). Pathological changes in infected oysters were described by Mackin (1951). Invasion takes place through the gut epithelium and possibly through the mantle. The epithelium is destroyed; the parasite lyses the basement membrane and is distributed by the blood to all parts of the body (Fig. 35). All tissues are invaded and damaged, and multiple abscesses are formed. Normal gonad development is inhibited, infected oysters become severely emaciated (Ray *et al.*, 1953; Ray, 1954b), and growth is retarded (Menzel and Hopkins, 1955b).

Temperature is important in the epizootiology of *Dermocystidium* disease (Hewatt and Andrews, 1956). Infections and associated mortalities rise during the warm months and decline during colder periods. Mortalities decline in winter, probably because of reduced parasite metabolism, rather than elimination of the organism. Failure to find *D. marinum* consistently north of Chesapeake Bay suggests that prolonged low temperature may be a significant limiting factor. Andrews (1965) found that *D. marinum* proliferates readily only at temperatures above 25°C., and overwinters as subpatent infections. His further observation that the partial destruction of oyster populations by a protozoan disease resulted in decreased prevalence of the fungus organism suggests that *Dermocystidium* depends upon direct transmission from one oyster to another. Other evidence for direct transmission was provided by Ray and Mackin (1955).

Infections and resulting mortalities are reduced in salinities below 15‰. Ray (1954b) showed that low salinity retarded development of terminal infections in laboratory populations. Ray and Chandler (1955) suggested that excessively high salinities may also be unfavorable for *Dermocystidium*. Mackin (1956) found a positive correlation between high salinity and high incidence of the fungus, but observed in experimental studies that the salinity tolerance range was wide. Dilution of infective elements by inflow of freshwater was suggested as an important limiting factor and a possible control measure.

Dermocystidium marinum is abundant in waters of the southern United States. Ray (1966a), who surveyed the occurrence of the fungus in the Gulf of Mexico in 1961 and 1962, found infections in 35 of 39 oyster samples, and prevalences as high as 100%. Hoese (1964) was able to find *D. marinum* in the digestive tracts and feces of fish, oyster drills, and crabs that had fed on dying and dead infected oysters. He speculated that transmission of the fungus might be furthered by scavengers, and that scavengers may release the parasite from host tissue.

Dermocystidium marinum is common in oysters from most high

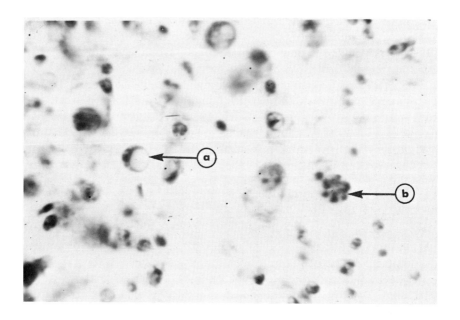

FIG. 35. Characteristic life-cycle stages of the fungus *Dermocystidium marinum* in the oyster: (a) hypnospore and (b) rosette. (From Sindermann and Rosenfield, 1967.)

salinity areas of the South Atlantic and Gulf of Mexico coasts of the United States, but is absent in a few such areas. Hoese (1963) attempted assays of water samples from different coastal locations in one section of the Texas coast, to determine whether seawater from some areas inhibited development of fungus hypnospores. Although results were not conclusive, water samples from certain localities apparently stopped hypnospore development. Hoese speculated that the absence of *D. marinum* may be related to the presence of *Spartina* salt marsh where consistently high salinities occur. It should be noted, however, that *Spartina* also predominates in some low-salinity, high-*Dermocystidium* areas.

In addition to its common occurrence in *C. virginica*, *Dermocystidium* has been found in other species. Ray (1954b) reported it in the leafy oyster, *Ostrea frons* L., from Florida and in horse oysters, *Ostrea equestris* Say, from Texas. The organism was not found, however, in mangrove oysters, *Crassostrea rhizophorae* (Guilding) from Puerto Rico, in *Ostrea edulis* from Holland, or in the rock oyster, *Crassostrea commercialis* (Iredale and Roughley), from Australia. The Olympia oyster, *Ostrea lurida* (Carpenter), was experimentally infected by exposure to infected *C. virginica. Dermocystidium*-like organisms have also been seen in other mollusks and annelids. Andrews (1955) found what he termed "*Dermocystidium*-like" organisms in 12 of 16 mollusk species from the Chesapeake Bay area.

This important fungus pathogen of oysters continues to be the subject of much research. Knowledge of its biology has been summarized by Ray (1954b), Ray and Chandler (1955), Andrews and Hewatt (1957), and Mackin (1962). Mackin and Boswell (1956) proposed a life cycle for *D. marinum* that included a saprophytic stage leading to production of an infective spore. Recently, Perkins and Menzel (1966) described motile biflagellate stages that were also postulated to be infective to oysters. Mackin and Ray (1966) grew the organism on beef-serum agar plates, and suggested that it belongs in the genus *Labyrinthomyxa,* a member of the Labyrinthulales. The change in generic name does not seem justified on the basis of the evidence presented, and in view of the confused state of classification of this protistan group. Culture of a *Dermocystidium* similar to *D. marinum* in chemically defined medium (Goldstein *et al.,* 1965) should make possible the study of isolates from many areas to determine whether one species or a species complex exists, and should permit more precise determination of the taxonomic affinities of the *Dermocystidium* group of protistan parasites.

Korringa (1947, 1951b,c) reported that mortalities of the European oyster in Holland, beginning in 1930, were caused by a fungus disease characterized by formation of green or brown pustules on the inner shell surfaces. Activity of the fungus varied directly with temperature, and the outbreak was said to be intensified by widespread use of cockle shells as spat collectors. Thin parts of oyster shells were perforated by the disease agent, which proliferated after reaching the interior surfaces. The fungus had been identified earlier as a species of *Monilia* by Voisin (1931), who found the infection, called "shell disease," in 40% of oysters imported into France from Holland in 1931. Cole (1950) and Cole and Waugh (1956) reported infections in the European oyster from Brittany, and in Portuguese oysters, *Crassostrea angulata* (Lamarck), grown in England. Infections were common in beds where old shells were abundant. Cole and Hancock (1956) found the disease in almost all beds of native European oysters in England, and described two distinct forms: the typical one which was characterized by greenish rubbery warts and knobs on the inside of the shell, particularly in the region of the muscle attachment; and an atypical form in which young oysters had thickened shells with numerous white patches but had no deformation of the muscle attachment area.

Another disease of the European oyster, which may be identical to shell disease, has been misnamed "foot disease" or "*maladie du pied*" (Dollfus, 1921a). It has long been known on the coast of France; Giard (1894) described its etiological agent as a bacterium, *Myotomus ostrearum*, but further definitive studies of the causative organism are needed. The disease is localized in the shell under the attachment of the adductor muscle, where it causes roughening and blistering of the shell and degeneration of adjacent muscle tissue. The muscle may become detached as irregular cysts are formed. Major mortalities occurred on oyster beds at Arcachon, France, in 1877 (Hornell, 1910; Orton, 1937). The cause was not determined, but some evidence of foot disease was found. Galtsoff (1964) reported the rare occurrence of the disease in the American oyster from the southern United States, but did not consider it a serious threat to oyster populations. Durve and Bal (1960) reported the rare occurrence of a shell disease which they considered to be *maladie du pied* in the backwater oyster, *Crassostrea gryphoides* (Schlotheim), from India.

A recent study by Alderman and Jones (1967) indicates that shell disease and *maladie du pied* are the same, and that both are associated with presence in the shell of a phycomycetous fungus, possibly a member of the Saprolegniaceae. The shell disease in this latest report occurred in native *Ostrea edulis* in England and Ireland.

Davis *et al.* (1954) isolated a fungus, later described as *Sirolpidium zoophthorum* (Vishniac, 1955), from hatchery-produced oyster and clam larvae. The infections were rare, but produced occasional epizootics that killed most of the cultured larval population in 2 to 4 days. Juvenile as well as larval bivalves were infected; growth ceased and death followed soon after infection. Infected cultures of bivalve larvae contained large numbers of motile biflagellate zoospores of the fungus. The authors speculated that an epizootic of the fungus could occur among lamellibranch larvae in nature.

There are several inconclusive reports of organisms resembling actinomycetes in oysters. Eyre (1924) reported *Cladothrix dichotoma* from oysters examined during the great mortalities of 1919–1923 in western Europe. The isolate was not pathogenic in experimental studies. Dollfus (1921a) stated that Eyre's isolate was a species of *Nocardia*. Pettit (1921) also identified a *Nocardia* from *Ostrea edulis*, but Dollfus (1921b) considered the condition presumed to have been caused by *Nocardia* to be merely normal cell reticulum of the oyster. Mackin (1962) described a "mycelial" disease of *Crassostrea virginica* which he thought might be caused by an actinomycete. An organism similar to that described by Mackin has been seen recently in *Crassostrea angulata* from France (Sindermann and Rosenfield, 1967).

(c) Protozoa. A variety of Protozoa parasitize oysters (Rosenfield, 1964; Sindermann, 1966b) and certain Sporozoa are serious pathogens. Two haplosporidans, *Minchinia costalis* (Wood and Andrews) and *M. nelsoni* Haskin, Stauber, and Mackin, have caused oyster mortalities on the North American east coast within the past decade.

Minchinia costalis (sometimes referred to as SSO or "seaside organism") is found in seaside bays of Maryland and Virginia, along the lower eastern shore of Virginia, and in Delaware Bay (Andrews *et al.*, 1962; Wood and Andrews, 1962; Sprague, 1963; Haskin *et al.*, 1966; Couch, 1967). First recognized in moribund and dead oysters from Hog Island Bay, Virginia, by Wood and Andrews (1962), *M. costalis* was held responsible, on the basis of epizootiological evidence, for sharp peaks of mortality in May and June. Striking characteristics of the disease are the sudden onset of mortalities in May, and the abrupt termination of mortalities about mid-June. The pathogen and mortalities caused by it continue to characterize Maryland and Virginia seaside oyster populations (Couch, 1967; Couch and Rosenfield, 1968).

The second haplosporidan species, *Minchinia nelsoni* (sometimes referred to as MSX), has a wider distribution, from Connecticut to North Carolina. It has caused extensive mortalities and drastic decline of the oyster fishery in Delaware Bay beginning about 1957, and in lower Chesapeake Bay beginning in 1959 (Haskin, 1961; Mackin, 1960; Engle and Rosenfield, 1963; Andrews, 1964). In each affected area, mortalities have exceeded 95% for several years. Because of the severe impact of the *M. nelsoni* epizootic on oyster stocks of the Middle Atlantic States, a number of research groups—university, state, and federal—have participated in scientific studies since the late 1950's, and significant papers have been published recently. Haskin *et al.* (1966) named the plasmodial stage of the parasite as *Minchinia nelsoni;* Couch *et al.* (1966) associated the plasmodium with spore and prespore stages (Fig. 36); and Barrow and Taylor (1966) confirmed, with immunological techniques, the association of plasmodium and spore. Andrews (1964, 1966, 1968) described aspects of the epizootiology of the disease in Virginia waters, and Haskin *et al.* (1965) briefly summarized the epizootiology in Delaware Bay. Farley (1965, 1968), after completing a 5-year histopathological study of Chesapeake Bay oysters, categorized natural infections according to extent of invasion and nature of host response. He found that initial infections occurred in epithelia of gills and palps. The pathogen spread into adjacent connective tissue, provoking infiltration of hyaline hemocytes. In intermediate infections the haplosporidan plasmodia (Fig. 37) invaded connective tissue adjacent to the digestive tract and gonad, and advanced infections were recognized by generalized invasion and infiltration of connective tissue by hyaline hemocytes. Terminal infections

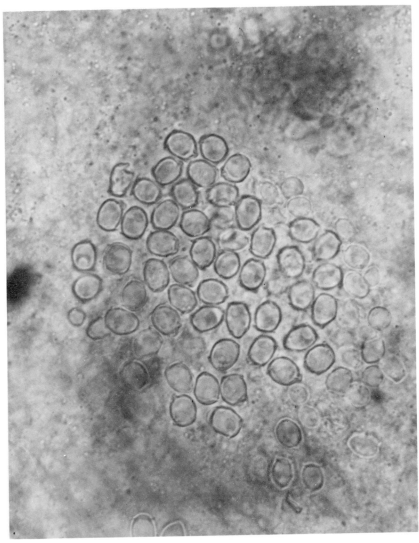

FIG. 36. Spores of the haplosporidan oyster pathogen *Minchinia nelsoni*.

were characterized histologically by pyknosis of nuclei and tissue necrosis even before gross signs of death were apparent. Farley also recognized a stage of the disease termed "remission," identified by diminished intensity of infection and cell infiltration, localization of parasites near external epithelia, increased pigment cell formation, diapedesis, deposition of necrotic tissue and moribund parasites against the shell, and conchio-linous encapsulation (Fig. 38). Death from *M. nelsoni* infection was at-tributed to combined action of seasonal environmental or physiological stresses on oysters weakened by effects of the disease.

Farley (1967) has also proposed a detailed life cycle of *Minchinia nelsoni* in the oyster, based on the study of over 1000 natural infections over a 5-year period. Multinucleate plasmodia develop from uninucleate infective stages, then reproduce by plasmotomy. Gametic nuclei fuse within large plasmodia and undergo sporogonic divisions. Sporoblasts differentiate into spores in the epithelium of digestive diverticula. Sea-sonal variations in occurrence of particular life cycle stages were noted: initial infections were most common from April to September; parasite activity decreased during the colder months (December through March); and sporogony occurred in midsummer.

As an example of the effects of *M. nelsoni* on the United States oyster fishery, landings in New Jersey waters of Delaware Bay in the late 1940's and early 1950's had fluctuated around 6 million pounds of shucked meats. Disease decimated the stocks beginning in the mid-1950's. Land-

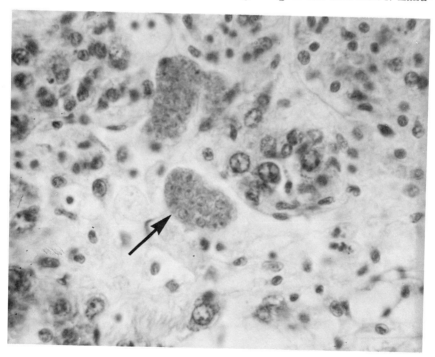

FIG. 37. Plasmodia of *Minchinia nelsoni* in oyster tissues.

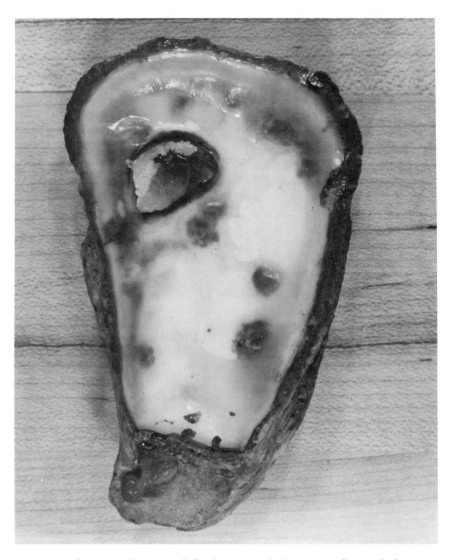

Fig. 38. Blisters on the inner shell of oysters, which are actually conchiolinous encapsulations of necrotic cells and the haplosporidan *Minchinia nelsoni.*

ings fell precipitously to a low of 167,000 pounds in 1960, and have not recovered significantly (Fig. 39). Comparable effects have been felt in the high salinity waters of lower Chesapeake Bay, another major oyster-producing area. The grim story of the effects of "Delaware Bay disease" in Chesapeake Bay has been summarized by Andrews and Wood (1967):

". . . 1960 was the year of reckoning for the industry. Late winter losses were followed by near decimation in early summer of plantings made before June 1959. In 1960 the last commercial plantings were made in lower Chesapeake Bay and oysters were decimated in a vast area. By June 1961, all plantings worth salvaging had been marketed, regardless of age. Millions of dollars worth of oysters were lost in 1960. . . ."

Thus far, one alleviating influence seems to be salinity. *M. nelsoni* occurs in waters whose salinity consistently exceeds 15‰; during the recent years (1963–1965) of drought along the Atlantic coast, the pathogen invaded areas of middle Chesapeake Bay formerly free of the disease (Rosenfield and Sindermann, 1966). Probably the clearest observational evidence for the decisive role of salinity in the epizootiology of the disease was presented by Andrews (1964). Simultaneous examinations of salinity regimes, disease prevalence, and mortalities in the James River seed beds of Virginia disclosed that infections disappeared from areas of marginal disease occurrence during low seasonal salinities and during several years of high rainfall. The importation of infective agents from high salinity

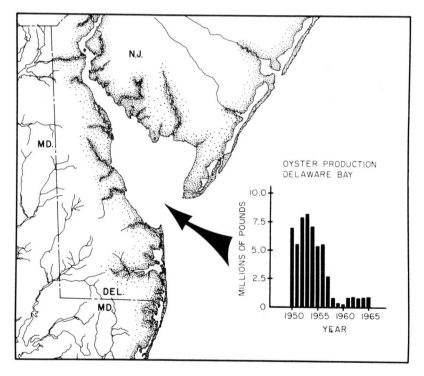

Fig. 39. Decline in production of oysters in New Jersey waters of Delaware Bay that resulted from an epizootic of the haplosporidan *Minchinia nelsoni*.

areas of the lower estuary of the James River was postulated to explain the persistence of the disease in marginal salinity zones.

Temperature may also be an important factor in the epizootiology of *M. nelsoni*. Andrews (1966) found that in Virginia infections persisted through the winter; death rates decreased with decreasing temperature in autumn but rose again in February and March. Infection of new hosts and mortality peaks occurred primarily during the warm season.

Proximity of oysters does not seem to be a significant epizootiological factor in Delaware Bay disease. Andrews (1966, 1967b) found continued high levels of disease activity in lower Chesapeake Bay, even after oyster populations had been drastically reduced. This phenomenon suggests strongly that a reservoir host exists, although surveys have thus far failed to disclose it.

Whether the disease was newly introduced into waters of the Middle Atlantic States, or was enzootic in oyster populations of the area, remains unresolved. Circumstantial evidence favors the view that *M. nelsoni* was present years before the epizootic (Andrews and Wood, 1967; Andrews, 1968) and that some change in the pathogen or the host population permitted an outbreak to occur. It is perhaps pertinent that similar organisms have been reported as rare parasites of Pacific oysters in Washington and Taiwan (Pereyra, 1964; Sindermann and Rosenfield, 1967).

Although several life-history stages have been recognized for both species of *Minchinia,* and concurrent infections have been described (Couch, 1967), routes of infection and methods of transmission are still unknown, and Koch's postulates have not been fully satisfied. Experimental studies have been further hampered by inability to maintain infections in oysters under experimental conditions for extended periods. Because several research groups are actively concerned with oyster diseases on the United States east coast, particularly with *M. nelsoni,* increased understanding of this and other pathogens should develop rapidly. One example of continuing scientific interest in *M. nelsoni* is the fact that the most recent volume (1968) of *Proceedings of the National Shellfisheries Association* contains four abstracts and two major papers concerned with aspects of Delaware Bay disease. Andrews' (1968) presented a thought-provoking review of evidence and hypotheses concerned with the epizootiology of *M. nelsoni,* and announced findings indicating that seed oysters could be successfully planted in epizootic areas, if this were done at a very early age. Couch and Rosenfield (1968) summarized a well-conceived and executed study of the fate of disease-free oysters introduced into an epizootic area.

Léger and Hollande (1917) described another haplosporidan, *Chy-*

tridiopsis ovicola, infecting the eggs of European oysters taken at Marennes, France. The parasite was relatively rare and occurred only in certain ovarian follicles of parasitized oysters.

Nematopsis ostrearum Prytherch, a gregarine parasite of the American oyster, was held by Prytherch (1938, 1940) to be the cause of extensive mortalities in Virginia and Louisiania. Later studies (Sprague, 1949; Sprague and Orr, 1955) indicated, however, that *Nematopsis* did not cause deaths of oysters and suggested that *Dermocystidium* infections may have complicated earlier results. Owen *et al.* (1952) found no correlation between *Nematopsis* infections and oyster mortalities in Louisiana. Sprague and Orr (1953, 1955) demonstrated that *N. ostrearum,* as described by Prytherch, was actually two species, which they designated *N. ostrearum* (emended) and *N. prytherchi.* Spores of *N. prytherchi* are larger and more elongate, localize in the gills rather than in the mantle, and have reproductive stages only in the crab *Menippe mercenaria* (Say). The life cycle of *N. ostrearum* includes a mud crab host, *Panopeus herbstii* Milne Edwards, *Eurypanopeus depressus* (Smith), or *Eurytium limosum* (Say). In many growing areas most oysters are infected, although infections are rarely heavy. Mackin (1962) has pointed out the lack of tissue reaction to the parasite, and the lack of evidence for existence of lysins or toxins. Feng (1958) found that a dynamic equilibrium existed between acquisition by the oyster of new parasites and elimination of spores. Oysters eliminated *Nematopsis* infections rapidly in the absence of crabs and continued reinfection.

Nematopsis was shown to be widely distributed on the Atlantic and Gulf coasts of the United States by Landau and Galtsoff (1951). Infections were heavy in oysters from certain localities, such as the mouth of Chesapeake Bay, but relations with other ecological factors such as abundance of crabs were not apparent. The intensity of infection was cumulative and increased with age of the host. No evidence was obtained to indicate that *Nematopsis* infection killed oysters or reduced the quality of the meats.

While the weight of evidence seems to indicate lack of lethality of *Nematopsis* infections, their possible pathogenicity is not easily dismissed. Sprague and Orr (1955) pointed out that heavy infections by *N. prytherchi* can clog gill blood vessels. I have observed massive infections by *N. ostrearum* in which extensive areas of the oyster were occupied by spores. Such mechanical interference with host physiology must have some harmful effects.

A flagellate protozoan, recently redescribed as *Hexamita nelsoni* by Schlicht and Mackin (1968), occurs frequently in the digestive tract of oysters, but its parasitic or saprozoic role has not been adequately determined. First described by Certes (1882) as a commensal in European oysters, the flagellate was later held responsible for oyster mortalities from "pit disease" in Holland (Mackin *et al.*, 1952). Clear evidence of pathological effects was not obtained, and heavy bacterial infections complicated the study. *Hexamita* was also blamed for mortalities of Olympia oysters, *Ostrea lurida*, in Washington (Stein *et al.*, 1961), but again clear evidence of pathogenicity was not presented. Scheltema (1962), who examined the relation between *Hexamita and* American oysters from Delaware Bay, concluded that the organism did not contribute significantly to deaths of oysters. He suggested, as did Stein *et al.* (1961), that *Hexamita* may act as a pathogen during periods of low environmental temperatures and low host metabolism, but that prevalence declines at higher temperatures because the processes in oysters which act to remove the trophozoites exceed the reproductive rate of the flagellate.

An excellent experimental study of hexamitiasis in oysters was published by Feng and Stauber (1968). Their results showed that survival of the infected host was influenced by temperature, and that the course of infection could be altered by the physiological condition of the host, the size of inoculum, and the route of entry. The authors believed that further studies were still needed to answer the question of whether *Hexamita* is a true pathogen, since the invasive power of the organism has not been conclusively demonstrated and the role of associated bacteria has not been elucidated.

Several ciliate parasites have been described from American oysters. A member of the genus *Sphenophrya* was reported by the Bureau of Commercial Fisheries Biological Laboratory, Oxford, Maryland (Anonymous, 1965), as the cause of an oyster disease characterized by formation of large cysts on the gills. Richardson (1939)* and Laird (1961) identified ciliates in the gut of *C. virginica* from Prince Edward Island, Canada, as *Orchitophrya stellarum* Cépède. Prevalence was low, but infections were heavy and the intestinal epithelium had been invaded. *Orchitophrya stellarum* is known as a serious pathogen of starfish, in which it causes gonad destruction (Cépède, 1911; Smith, 1936; Vevers, 1951). Laird speculated that the organism may be a regular and possibly harmful parasite of oysters and that starfish may become infected from them. Further examination of the specific identification of this

---

* Data provided in Fisheries Research Board of Canada, Manuscript Report Series (Biology), mimeographed, unnumbered, 1939, "Report on the studies of eastern coast oysters during the season of 1939," by L. R. Richardson.

oyster parasite is needed, since other closely related ciliates seem to be quite host-specific.

Mackin (1962) mentioned a ciliate parasite of oysters from the Atlantic and Gulf coasts of the United States, which he considered to be *Ancistrocoma pelseneeri,* a well-known parasite of mussels. The ciliates were abundant in the digestive tracts of oysters infected with *Dermocystidium marinum,* but Mackin did not believe that they were pathogenic to the oyster host.

Two amoebas are known from American oysters. Hogue (1914, 1921) described *Vahlkampfia calkensi* and *V. patuxent,* which are parasitic in the digestive tract. She distinguished the two species on the basis of differences in the cyst wall. No evidence of pathogenicity was found, nor were these forms demonstrated to be other than saprozoic. Bovee (1965) removed both species to the genus *Flabellula.* Additional amoeboid organisms isolated from American oysters were reported briefly by Sawyer (1966).

(2) Diseases Caused by Other Animal Parasites

(a) Helminths. *i. Trematoda.* European and American oysters are parasitized by larval trematodes of the provisional larval genus *Bucephalus* (Fig. 40). *Bucephalus haimeanus* was first reported by Lacaze-Duthiers (1854) from European oysters in the Mediterranean Sea, and *B. cuculus* was described by McCrady (1874) in American oysters from South Carolina. Sporocysts occur in the gonads and digestive gland of the oyster (Fig. 41), and sterilize the host. In advanced infections sporocysts spread to gills, mantle, and even the adductor muscle. The tentative life cycle of the parasite as proposed by Tennent (1906), included silverside minnows, *Menidia menidia,* as second intermediate hosts, and gars, *Strongylura marina* (Walbaum) and *Lepisosteus spatula* Lacépède, as definitive hosts. Hopkins (1954a) found bucephalid metacercariae in striped mullet, *Mugil cephalus* L., and white mullet, *M. curema* Cuv. and Val. He attempted to resolve some of the confusion about names of bucephalids, and concluded that in the absence of further experimental evidence, the correct name of the American oyster bucephalid is *Bucephalus cuculus.* Hopkins (1954a, 1957b) reported parasitization of more than one third of the oyster population in localized areas of the United States, although prevalence generally was much lower, particularly in open waters. Menzel and Hopkins (1955a,b) suggested that early infections temporarily stimulate growth of the oyster, but that older infections retard growth. Hopkins (1957b) made the interesting, if somewhat facetious, observation that *Bucephalus* might be considered a gastronomically

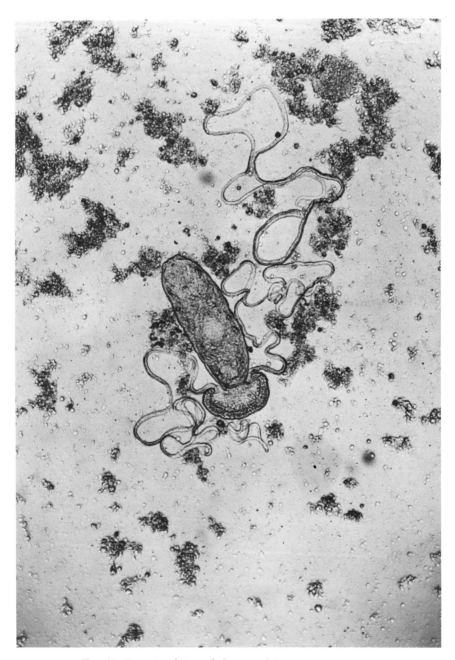

Fig. 40. Cercaria of *Bucephalus* teased from oyster tissue.

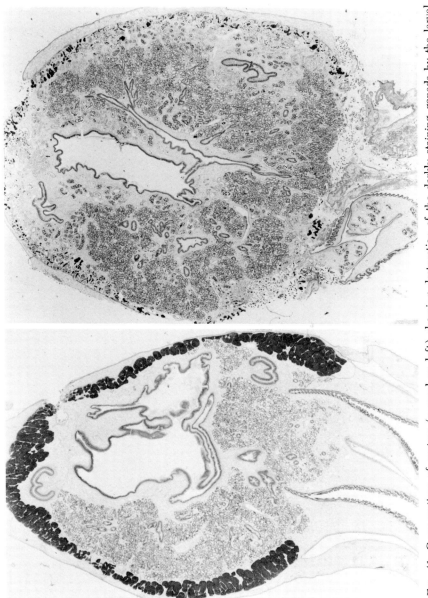

FIG. 41. Cross-sections of oysters (normal on left) showing destruction of the darkly staining gonads by the larval trematode *Bucephalus*.

beneficial parasite in southern waters, since infected oysters have an excellent flavor and are fat-looking and glycogen-rich throughout the year, whereas normal oysters are spawned out, thin, and relatively taste-less during part of the year. Recently, Cheng (1965) and Cheng and Burton (1965a) used histochemical methods to examine the host-para-site relationship of the American oyster and the larval trematode, *Bucephalus* sp. Parasitization caused marked changes in the distribution of fats.

Larval trematodes of the family Bucephalidae occur in New Zealand oysters, *Ostrea lutaria* Hutton. Millar (1963) reported that oysters im-ported from New Zealand and maintained for breeding studies in Scot-land were frequently parasitized and that the percentage mortality was much higher among parasitized individuals than among normal ones. Howell (1966) experimentally completed most of the important features of the life cycle of *Bucephalus longicornutus* from *O. lutaria*. Cercariae encysted in fins, skin, and muscles of several genera of experimental intermediate hosts. Adult worms were recovered from the intestine of the scarpee, *Scorpaena cardinalis* Richardson, after experimental feedings with metacercariae. Adult *B. longicornutus* were also recovered from monkfish, *Kathetostoma giganteum* Haast, from Cook Strait, New Zealand. In a later paper Howell (1967) suggested that an observed decline in abundance of oysters on particular New Zealand beds was largely due to high prevalence of *B. longicornutus*.

Sindermann and Rosenfield (1967) recently found Pacific oysters from Taiwan to be infected with larval *Bucephalus*.

Hyperparasitization of sporocysts of *Bucephalus* in American oysters from the Gulf of Mexico was reported by Mackin and Loesch (1955). This hyperparasitization produced blackish discoloration of oyster man-tle and viscera, and destruction of sporocysts, followed by release of the haplosporidan spores into host oyster tissue. Pronounced cellular reac-tion was elicited in the localized areas where spores were found in oyster tissue; the authors described some abnormal development of the hyperparasite in such tissue. The hyperparasite was not named, but it was considered on the basis of spore morphology to be a haplosporidan distinct from the parasite *Urosporidium pelseneeri* (Caullery and Chap-pellier) found in clams of the genus *Donax*. Howell (1967) described *Urosporidium constantae* from *Bucephalus longicornutus* parasitizing *Ostrea lutaria*. The haplosporidan completely destroyed embryonic cercariae within the sporocyst system. Howell proposed (with reserva-tions) that the hyperparasite might be used as a biological control meas-ure in areas of high trematode prevalence.

Sprague (1964) described a microsporidan hyperparasite, *Nosema dollfusi,* of *Bucephalus* and speculated that escape of the protozoan into the tissues of the oyster could contribute to the death of the molluscan host. Shuster and Hillman (1963) and Cheng (1964) made a similar speculation about haplosporidan hyperparasites of oysters.

Other larval trematodes occur on and in oysters. Fujita (1925, 1943) described *Gymnophalloides tokiensis,* a metacercaria which encysts, often in great numbers, on the mantle and gills. The host's physiology is disturbed, growth is halted, and reproduction is inhibited (Hoshina and Ogino, 1951). Marine birds are definitive hosts for the parasite. Metacercariae of *Proctoeces ostreae* Fujita are also found in Japanese oysters. About 10% of the oysters in Hiroshima Bay were infected by the larval trematode, which localizes in gonad tissue. European oysters harbor the related *Proctoeces maculatus* (Looss). Definitive hosts are labrid fishes in Europe, and snappers, *Pagrosomus major,* and red groupers, *Epinephelus akaara,* in Japan.

Massive invasion of American oysters from the southern tip of Texas by metacercariae was reported recently by Little *et al.* (1966). Feeding experiments showed that the trematodes were *Acanthoparyphium spinulosum* (Johnston), which matures in the intestine of shore birds. Most of the oysters examined had metacercariae in the mantle; the number averaged 45 worms per oyster.

ii. Cestoda. Oysters in several regions of the world are parasitized by larval cestodes usually, but possibly incorrectly, considered to be members of the genus *Tylocephalum.* These parasites are Lecanicephaloidea that occur as adults in the digestive tracts of elasmobranchs. Sparks (1963) reported heavy infections of *Tylocephalum* in American oysters introduced in Hawaii. In an addendum, Sparks noted that oysters from Florida had been reported by the Bureau of Commercial Fisheries Biological Laboratory, Oxford, Maryland, to harbor similar larval cestodes (Fig. 42). Similar larvae have been found in oysters from Georgia and North Carolina (Sindermann and Rosenfield, 1967). The coracidium of *Tylocephalum* was recently reported in the stomach and gills of American oysters collected at Pearl Harbor, Hawaii (Cheng, 1966). Penetration of gill or digestive epithelium was postulated from study of histological sections. The pronounced cellular reaction in the subepithelial tissues, including encapsulation of the larvae, was described. Larval cestodes, probably *Tylocephalum,* have been found in Pacific oysters from Japan and Taiwan by staff members of the Bureau of Commercial Fisheries Biological Laboratory, Oxford, Maryland. Members of this tapeworm group are known as parasites of pearl oysters in the Far East and were held to be the cause of pearl formation (Herdman, 1904; Herdman and Hornell, 1906; Shipley and Hornell, 1904, 1906;

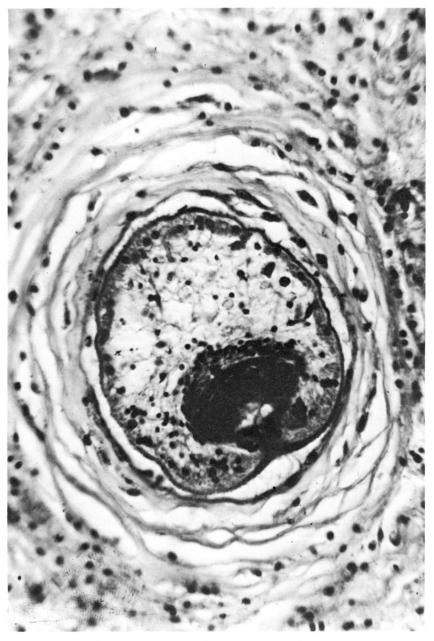

Fig. 42. Larval tapeworm *Tylocephalum* in the tissues of the American oyster.

Southwell, 1924). Jameson (1912) presented convincing evidence, however, that invasion by larval trematodes, rather than larval cestodes, was more important in pearl development. Pearl formation around trematode and cestode larvae which invade the mantle and die appears to follow a similar pattern of host responses in bivalve mollusks (Wright, 1966).

(b) PARASITIC GASTROPODA. One family of gastropods, the Pyramidellidae, contains members ectoparasitic on commercial marine bivalves—oysters, mussels, clams, and scallops—as well as on other marine invertebrates. These very small snails feed on the body fluids of their hosts, and in so doing, produce morphological and physiological changes. Several species of the genus *Odostomia* parasitize oysters. *Odostomia bisuturalis* and *O. eulimoides* cause severe damage to the oyster hosts. Loosanoff (1956) observed that damage to the mantle edge of *Crassostrea virginica* caused by activity of *O. bisuturalis* resulted in deformed shells (deeply cupped with thickened margins). Cole and Hancock (1955) noted that *Ostrea edulis* parasitized by *O. eulimoides* also had irregular thickened margins, often with multiple edges. These authors also felt that *Odostomia* parasitization interfered with the normal physiology of the oyster. Retraction of the mantle eventually led to atrophy of the adductor muscle and death. Another species, *O. impressa*, has also been reported from American oysters (Hopkins, 1956a; Allen, 1958; Wells, 1959a).

(c) PARASITIC CRUSTACEA. A parasitic copepod, *Mytilicola orientalis* (Fig. 43A), was described from the digestive tract of the Pacific oyster from Japan by T. Mori (1935). The parasite was transferred to the United States west coast with imports of seed oysters from Japan, and was described as *Mytilicola ostrea* by Wilson (1938), who was apparently unaware of Mori's report. Odlaug (1946) stated that Olympia oysters infected with even small numbers of *M. orientalis* had a lower condition index than uninfected oysters. Chew *et al.* (1965) found a similar relation in Pacific oysters, and Sparks (1962) demonstrated pathological changes in gut epithelium and underlying tissues of Pacific oysters infected with the copepod. Mori and Odlaug reported *M. orientalis* as a parasite of mussels (*Mytilus crassitesta* Lischke and *M. edulis* L.) as well as oysters, in both Japanese and United States waters. Another species, *Mytilicola intestinalis*, first described by Steuer (1902, 1903), has been blamed by Korringa (1950, 1959) and others for widespread mortalities, stunting of growth, and poor condition of sea mussels, *Mytilus edulis*, in Europe, but is found only rarely in European oysters (Baird *et al.*, 1950; Hepper, 1953, 1955), and has not been reported to

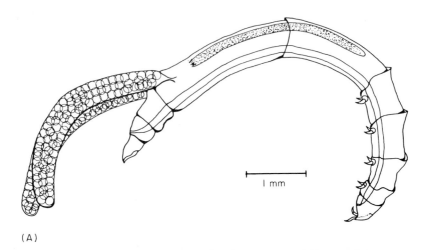

(A)

(B)

Fig. 43. (A) Parasitic copepod, *Mytilicola orientalis,* from Pacific oysters; (B) "mud blisters" caused by *Polydora* in Pacific oysters from Taiwan.

cause significant mortalities. A small specimen, identified as *Mytilicola intestinalis,* was found by Pearse and Wharton (1938) in an American oyster from the Florida coast. Humes (1954) believed that this copepod was probably *M. porrecta,* which he described from mussels and clams from Louisiana.

Crabs of the genus *Pinnotheres* occasionally inhabit the shell cavity of oysters, where their activities and effects suggest that they are parasites rather than commensals (Christensen and McDermott, 1958; Haven, 1959). Stauber (1945) studied a sudden increase in abundance of the oyster crab, *Pinnotheres ostreum* (Say), in American oysters of Delaware Bay in 1941. He observed that the crabs robbed the oyster of food and injured the gills, resulting in a weakened condition of the host. Stauber found in 1941 that 90% of the oysters of Delaware Bay harbored 4 to 6 crabs in the first parasitic stage. He ascribed unusual mortalities in certain oyster populations to debilitation caused by high abundance of crabs. In 1942, abundance of crabs dropped to 25–30%, and continued to decline in the following years. Sandoz and Hopkins (1947) observed that "normal" crab parasitization of *Crassostrea virginica* (one female per host) caused a decline in condition in Virginia, where as many as 80% of the oysters in particular beds were parasitized.

Another *Pinnotheres* was described from Madagascar oysters, *Ostrea vitrifacta* Sowerby, by Poisson (1946); infestation was accompanied by development of a characteristic irritating flavor in the parasitized oyster. He speculated that this flavor might be traced in some way to the coelenterate *Sertularia*, which often grows on shells of oysters that contain *Pinnotheres*. Korringa (1952a) pointed out the striking similarity of this observation with the popular belief in Holland that eating mussels parasitized by *P. pisum* causes "nettle rash."

(3) Tumors and Other Abnormalities

The literature on tumors of mollusks and other invertebrates has been reviewed by Scharrer and Lockhead (1950). Ryder (1887) published the earliest report of a tumor in oysters, describing a nodular growth over 3 cm in greatest dimension in the pericardial cavity of *C. virginica*. The tumor seemed to originate from connective tissue surrounding the rectum or from the pericardial membranes. Smith (1934) described a stalked mesenchymal tumor arising from the outer surface of the pericardium in the same species, which he considered to be similar to that reported by Ryder. Another stalked mesenchymal tumor in *C. gigas* was reported by Sparks and Pauley (1963, 1964) and Sparks et al., (1964). The growth was located posterior to the rectum and appeared to originate from the mantle in the region of the rectum. Still another stalked mesenchymal tumor originating from the body mass was reported by Pauley et al. (1965). The neoplasm was elongate, ovoid, and had an irregular nodular surface. Other tumorous growths on Pacific oysters, one apparently originating from the adductor muscle, were described by Pauley and Sayce (1968). An internal fibrous tumor, considered to originate from undifferentiated gonad cells or from muscle, was described by Pauley and Sayce (1968). The lesion consisted of a stroma of elongate fibrous connective tissue with a hollow center. The tumor margin was well defined and non-invasive, and no mitotic figures were seen.

Polypoid growths in the intestines of European oysters, *Ostrea edulis*, grown in California, were reported by Katkansky (1968).

Certain shell abnormalities in oysters and other bivalves may result from activities of boring animals. Outstanding in this respect are annelids of the genus *Polydora* and sponges of the genus *Cliona*. *Polydora* causes the formation of "mud blisters" (Fig. 43B) on the inner shell of oysters in many parts of the world (Haswell, 1885; Leloup, 1937; Kavanagh, 1940; Lunz, 1940; Medcof, 1946; and others). The worms penetrate to the inner wall of the oyster, where they are sealed off by a nacreous layer. If penetration occurs in the region of the adductor muscle, the oyster may be rendered more vulnerable to predators such as crabs or starfish. Boring sponges have long been known as destructive pests of oysters. Giard (1881) reported that *Cliona* was known to oystermen of France in the form of "spice bread disease" which was claimed to destroy entire beds of oysters. Often oyster shells are so completely riddled that they crumble with the slightest touch. An extensive literature on boring sponges exists (Giard, 1881; Old, 1941; Hopkins, 1956a,b, 1962; Wells, 1959b; and others).

b. *Mussels*

Marine mussels, particularly the sea mussel, *Mytilus edulis*, are abundant and palatable. They are grown by highly developed culture methods, especially in western Europe. Culture of a single species, however, often under crowded conditions, increases vulnerability to disease. As with cultivated oysters, extensive and repeated mortalities, presumably caused by disease, have occurred in mussel beds. The parasitic copepod, *Mytilicola*, is the only specific pathogen that has been shown to cause mortalities in European mussels, although other parasites, particularly haplosporidan Protozoa and larval trematodes, have been reported.

(1) MICROBIAL DISEASES

Eggs of the sea mussel from the western North Atlantic are occasionally infected with a haplosporidan, *Chytridiopsis mytilovum*. Field (1923) first described the parasite and several of its life-history stages; Sprague (1965) redescribed the life-history stages in more detail. The parasite had a high prevalence in some samples, although the proportion of infected eggs to normal eggs in any individual was low. De Vincentiis and Renzoni (1963) recognized what seems to be the same organism in eggs of the Mediterranean edible mussel, *Mytilus galloprovincialis* L., from the Gulf of Naples. A similar parasite, *Chytridiopsis ovicola*, has been reported from eggs of the European oyster (Léger and Hollande, 1917).

Taylor (1966) described a disease of California mussels, *Mytilus californianus* Conrad, caused by another haplosporidan, *Haplosporidium tumefacientis*. The disease, characterized by tumefactions of the digestive gland, was found in 23 of 1114 individuals examined. The gross enlargement of the gland was apparently due to plasmodia of the parasite; no necrosis was reported. Samples of sea mussels collected simultaneously from the California coast by Taylor were not parasitized by the haplosporidan.

A gregarine, *Nematopsis schneideri*, was described by Léger (1903) in the gills of sea mussels from the French coast, while another species, *N. legeri*, was reported from the Mediterranean edible mussel (Léger, 1905; Léger and Duboscq, 1925; Hatt, 1931).

Sea mussels from the Baltic were found by Raabe (1934, 1936, 1938, 1949) to harbor a number of ciliates, including *Ancistrocoma pelseneeri* Chatton and Lwoff, *Kidderia mytili* (DeMorgan), *Ancistruma mytili* (Quennerstedt), and *Hypocomides mytili* (Chatton and Lwoff). The same species of ciliates have also been identified from *Mytilus* sampled in other geographical areas (Kidder, 1933; Chatton and Lwoff, 1934; Kozloff, 1946). Although many ciliates occur in bivalve Mollusca (Fenchel, 1965), a parasitic role has not been adequately determined for most of them.

(2) Diseases Caused by Helminths

Invasion of mussels by larval trematodes is thought to be responsible in part for pearl formation. Jameson (1902) believed that most mussel pearls resulted from encystment of metacercariae and encapsulation by the host. Herdman (1904), who studied sea mussels in England, found pearls very common near Piel and attributed them to invasion by larvae of *Distomum* (*Gymnophallus*) *somateriae*.

The literature on trematode-induced pearl formation in mussels has been reviewed by Stunkard and Uzmann (1958). The relation between pearls in European sea mussels and trematode parasites was first described by Garner (1872), and later by Dubois 1901a,b, 1903, 1907a,b, 1909), who proposed the name *Distomum margaritarum* (=*Gymnophallus margaritarum*) for parasites found in reddish-brown spots which served as foci for pearl formation in mussels from the French coast. Jameson (1902) stated that the larval trematodes resembled *D. somateriae*, which had been described as an adult from the intestine of the eider duck, *Somateria mollissima*, by Levinsen (1881). Jameson referred the parasite to the genus *Lecithodendrium* Looss, and described the process of pearl formation by the mantle of the mussel around the metacercariae. Giard (1903, 1907) confirmed these observations on pearl formation. Odhner (1905) designated the larvae causing pearl formation in mussels as *Gymnophallus bursicola*. Similar metacercariae were found by Stafford (1912) in mussels from the Gulf of Saint Lawrence. Jameson and Nicoll (1913) reviewed pearl formation in mussels and concluded that several gymnophallid larvae were involved. Since then other gymnophallid cercariae have been associated with metacercariae in mussels (Palombi, 1924; Cole, 1935; Rees, 1939). Stunkard and Uzmann (1958) fed mussels from Long Island to newly hatched eider ducks and recovered adult gymnophallids, probably *G. bursicola*.

Other larval trematodes have been described from mussels. Cole (1935) reported "orange sickness" of sea mussels at Conway in Wales. The color was due to masses of orange-pigmented trematode sporocysts in the mantle and throughout the body; the tailless cercariae they contained were described as *Cercaria tenuans*. A similar condition had been noted previously by Atkins (1931). Cole also described a second larval trematode infestation caused by *Bucephalus mytili*. Uzmann (1953) found microcercous trematode larvae in sea mussels from Long Island and Connecticut that had a similar orange coloration. Described as *Cercaria milfordensis*, the larvae were primarily parasites of the blood vascular system of the host and had foci in the blood vessels of the mantle. Sporocyst development precluded normal gametogenesis in mussels; infected mussels held in aquaria had unusually high mortalities. Uzmann suggested that *C. milfordensis* infections are probably lethal to the host under unfavorable environmental conditions. Stunkard and Uzmann (1959) later identified progenetic stages of the worm in the mussel as *Proctoeces maculatus* (Looss). A very similar trematode was reported by Hopkins (1954b) from the hooked mussel, *Brachidontes recurvus*, from Louisiana; cercariae developed in orange-pigmented sporocysts which completely destroyed the gonad of the mussel. Yamaguti (1938) identified as *Proctoeces* larval trematodes from the mussel *Brachidontes senhausi* from Japan. Freeman and Llewellyn (1958) found adult trematodes which they identified as *Proctoeces subtenuis* in the bivalve *Scrobicularia plana* from England, but at present there seems to be no adequate basis for separation of *P. maculatus* and *P. subtenuis*.

(3) Diseases Caused by Parasitic Crustacea

A well documented example of the effects of disease on mussel populations is that of the invasion of the north European sea mussel

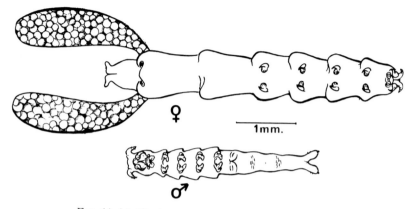

FIG. 44. *Mytilicola intestinalis* from the sea mussel.

stocks by the copepod *Mytilicola intestinalis* (Fig. 44). A fascinating body of literature has accumulated about this parasite and its effects on mussels; only a sampling of the many published papers is cited here. An excellent review, with full literature citations, has been published by Korringa (1968). Steuer (1902) first described the parasite from the intestines of Mediterranean edible mussels, *Mytilus galloprovincialis* L., and Pesta (1907) outlined the life history. Korringa (1950, 1959) described the relatively sudden appearance of *Mytilicola* in sea mussel stocks of the Netherlands in 1949, and its subsequent spread to many mussel beds during the following decade. The organism is known to have occurred in Mediterranean mussels since the beginning of the twentieth century (Monod and Dollfus, 1932), and in 1938 was found near Cuxhaven, Germany, from whence it was assumed to have spread westward to the Netherlands. Korringa and others believed that distribution was aided by mussel-encrusted ships, by movement of planktonic larvae, and by transfer of seed mussels from infested areas. *Mytilicola* was also very abundant in localized areas of the English coast in 1946. Korringa stated that the condition of mussels was generally correlated with intensity of parasitization; mussels with less than 5 copepods were still healthy, those with 5 to 10 were visibly thinner, and those more heavily infested suffered serious mortalities. According to Meyer-Waarden and Mann (1954b) and Mann (1956), gonad weights of infested individuals were 10–30% less than those of nonparasitized mussels.

There is some indication, however, that *M. intestinalis* exerts a less severe effect on populations of *Mytilus galloprovincialis* than on those of *M. edulis,* possibly because of longer association and consequent better adaptation of host and parasite, as was pointed out by Fleury *et al.* (1951). Hrs-Brenko (1964), for example, found no difference in condition index of parasitized and unparasitized mussels (*M. gallo-*

provincialis) on the Yugoslav Adriatic coast, and Genovese (1959) made similar findings on the Italian coast.

Infestation of sea mussels (*M. edulis*) led to poor growth, thin meats (Cole and Savage, 1951; Mann, 1951), cream-colored rather than dark brown liver, failure of byssal development, and a dirty red-brown color. Reproduction of the parasite was accelerated by warm water, and the many young parasites present in the summer invaded and killed mussels. Deaths occurred among mussels of all sizes, including "seed." Mussels fell from culture racks and died during transport to markets (Brienne, 1964). Density of mussel beds was believed to directly influence survival and multiplication of the parasite. Infestations were light in areas where the mussels were thinly scattered and near the surface of the water. Because of the continued spread of *Mytilicola* in the Netherlands, an extensive scheme of repeated dredging of natural beds, transfer of lightly infested stocks, and destruction of heavily infested stocks was outlined by Korringa (1959) to create a barrier to further invasion.

Mytilicola in mussel populations (*M. edulis*) grown on floats in Spain was studied by Andreu (1963). He found the infestation to be greatest near shore where tidal currents were weak. Vertical distribution of the parasite in cultured mussels grown on 6-meter ropes was uniform in areas of strong currents, but increased with depth where currents were weak. Such findings agree well with those of Hepper (1955) who concluded from field observations that mussels raised from the bottom, or in fast-moving water at either end of an estuary, were less heavily infested with *Mytilicola* than those on the bottom, in slow-moving water, or in the mid-regions of estuaries. Hepper felt that control of the copepod was possible by using off-bottom culture or by locating culture beds in fast-moving water or at the brackish-water ends of estuaries.

Except for one doubtful North American record (Pearse and Wharton, 1938), *M. intestinalis* is known only from Europe, where it has been reported from a number of areas: Germany (Caspers, 1939; Meyer and Mann, 1950, 1952a,b; Meyer-Waarden and Mann, 1956), the Netherlands (Korringa, 1951a, 1952b, 1953, 1967), Belgium (Leloup, 1951, 1960), Scotland, England, and Ireland (Ellenby, 1947; Grainger, 1951; Hockley, 1952; Thomas, 1953; Bolster, 1954; G. D. Waugh, 1954), the north coast of France (Dollfus, 1914, 1927b; Monod and Dollfus, 1932; Brienne, 1964), the northwest coast of Spain (Andreu, 1960, 1961, 1963), the Mediterranean Sea (Bassedas, 1950; Meyer-Waarden and Mann, 1954b), and the Adriatic Sea (Steuer, 1902; Pesta, 1907; Meyer-Waarden and Mann, 1954b). D. Waugh (1966) has mapped the recent distribution of the parasite in northern Europe.

The proceedings of a conference held in Paris to review and discuss problems of parasitization by *Mytilicola* were published in 1951 (Cole, 1951; Dollfus, 1951; Havinga, 1951; Heldt, 1951; Korringa, 1951d; Korringa and Lambert, 1951; Lambert, 1951a,b; Leloup, 1951; Meyer and Mann, 1951). It was agreed that *Mytilicola* constituted a severe threat to the mussel industry of Europe, but the question as to whether the copepod was a direct or indirect cause of death was left undecided. Continuing mortalities associated with the presence of *Mytilicola* (Brienne, 1964; Korringa, 1968), however, indicate a causal relationship, possibly influenced by stresses of spawning, high temperatures, and inadequate food supply. Korringa believes that there is little chance of eradicating *Mytilicola* once it invades an area; that it has been a new intruder in many coastal areas; and that man (rather than other factors) has been responsible for much of the spread of the parasite since 1950.

Another species, *Mytilicola porrecta* Humes, occurs in ribbed and recurved mussels (*Modiolus demissus* Sowerby and *Brachydontes recurvus* Rafinesque) in the Gulf of Mexico. Humes (1954) found as many as 15 individuals per mussel, but no pathology or mortality was indicated. A third species, *Mytilicola orientalis,* known to occur in *Mytilus edulis* and *M. crassitesta,* was recently reported from the California mussel by Chew *et al.* (1964).

Pinnotherid crabs of several species, best known as parasites of oysters, also occur in mussels. McDermott (1962) found that *Pinnotheres ostreum* and *P. maculatus* cause gill damage and palp erosion in *Mytilus edulis.* Earlier Atkins (1931) described similar palp abnormalities in mussels from England.

c. *Clams*

Many species of bivalves called by the general term "clam" are harvested throughout the world. Some species constitute a significant commercial crop in many coastal areas; other species are fished for sport or are ignored. Changes in clam abundance have been documented, although mass mortalities comparable to those in oysters and mussels have not been reported. Mass deaths may pass unnoticed in sediment-hidden clams; it may be for this reason that information on diseases of clams is scarce. Among the diseases and parasites that are known in clams are several protistan organisms, larval trematodes, larval cestodes, parasitic copepods, and tumors.

(1) MICROBIAL DISEASES

Coe's study (1955) of population fluctuations of the California bean clam, *Donax gouldi* Dall, included a description of a possible fungus parasite "apparently similar to *Dermocystidium marinum*" as a cause of mass mortalities during the summer. Moribund clams of all ages were heavily infected with "irregularly spherical or ovoid cells, 2 to 6 microns in diameter." The identity of the pathogen was not further determined, however, and the information presented is insufficient to identify it as a *Dermocystidium*.

Much earlier, Léger (1897) found a coccidian, *Hyaloklossia pelseneeri*, in kidneys of *Donax* sp. and *Tellina* sp. in Europe, and Léger and Duboscq (1917) described another coccidian, *Pseudoklossia glomerata*, parasitic in *Tapes floridus* L. and *T. virgineus* L. from the Mediterranean Sea.

A gregarine, described only as *Nematopsis* sp. (Schneider, 1892) was reported from the mantle of razor clams, *Solen vagina*, from France. Spores of *Nematopsis schneideri* were found in the gills of *Cardium edule, Mactra solida, Donax vittatus* and other bivalves from France (Léger, 1903; Léger and Duboscq, 1913).

Ciliate parasites have been described from soft-shell clams, *Mya arenaria* L., by Uzmann and Stickney (1954). The peritrich, *Trichodina myicola* Uzmann and Stickney, was found, often in large numbers, on the palps. These infections were often accompanied by the nonpathogenic thigmotrich, *Ancistrocoma myae* (Kofoid and Busch). *Ancistrocoma myae* had been described earlier from *M. arenaria* sampled in California (Kofoid and Busch, 1936; Kozloff, 1946) and in Massachusetts (Chatton and Lwoff, 1950). Kozloff considered the ciliate identical to *A. pelseneeri*, a common parasite of sea mussels. Fenchel (1965) also found *A. myae* in nearly 100% of *M. arenaria* sampled from two locations in Denmark.

(2) Diseases Caused by Helminths

Several life-history stages of diverse trematodes occur in the soft-shell clam. Uzmann (1952) reported sporocysts and cercariae (*Cercaria myae*) from gonads and digestive gland of this clam from Massachusetts, and held that parasitization resulted in a condition known as "water belly." [Subsequent observations, summarized by Dow and Wallace (1961), suggest that this condition may be a general sign of physiological disturbance.] Uzmann considered *Cercaria myae* to be the same species as that reported by Stafford (1912) from the soft-shell clam in the Gulf of Saint Lawrence. Hutton (1953) believed that the larvae were members of the genus *Gymnophallus*. Stunkard and Uzmann (1958) discussed gymnophallid sporocysts and cercariae from the soft-shell clam, and Stunkard (1960) found echinostome metacercariae of the genus *Himasthla* in palps and gills of clams from the Maine coast. Three species were recognized. Earlier, Stunkard (1938) had demonstrated experimentally that cercariae of *Himasthla* would penetrate and encyst in the gills of *Mya arenaria* and a number of other bivalves, and Uzmann (1951) had reported natural occurrence of *Himasthla quissetensis* (Miller and Northrup) in *M. arenaria*. Susceptibility and response of a number of marine pelecypods, including four species of clams, to cercariae of *H. quissetensis* were tested experimentally by Cheng *et al.* (1966). Metacercariae were found in all clams and mussels, but were not found in oysters used in the study.

Several larval trematodes have been reported from clams of the genus *Donax*. Giard (1897, 1907) identified bucephalid and gymnophallid cercariae. Rees (1939) found gymnophallid metacercariae, and Young (1953) described the life cycle of a monorchid, *Postmonorchis donacis*, whose larvae occur in the California bean clam, *Donax gouldi*. Hopkins (1958) identified sporocysts and cercariae of three species and metacercariae of two species in coquina clams, *Donax variabilis* Say, from the Texas coast. Infections by larval trematodes were considered by Pelseneer (1896, 1906, 1928) to be responsible for reduced abundance of *Donax vittatus* in France, and Coe (1946) held that trematode parasites (probably *Postmonorchis donacis*) were important in controlling population size in California *Donax gouldi*.

Fujita (1906, 1907a, 1943) has described two larval trematode parasites of asari clams, *Tapes phillippinarum* Adams and Reeve, from Japan. Parasitic castration of the hosts was observed.

Hopkins (1957a), in a brief but excellent exposition of the role of parasitism in marine communities, referred to an interesting interrelationship of host, parasite, and hyperparasite in the case of *Donax trunculus* parasitized by trematodes, which in turn were parasitized by the haplosporidan *Urosporidium pelseneeri* (Caullery and Chappellier). The often severe fluctuations in abundance of this clam have been attributed to shifts of balance in this tripartite relationship (Caullery and Chappellier, 1906; Cépède, 1911). Other haplosporidan and microsporidan hyperparasites of *Donax* have also been described (Guyénot *et al.*, 1925; Dollfus, 1946; Mackin and Loesch, 1955).

MacGinitie and MacGinitie (1949), who surveyed a number of species of clams from the Pacific coast of the United States for parasitization by larval tapeworms, found encysted larvae of the cestode genus *Anabothrium*, occasionally in large numbers, in the foot muscles of the gaper clam, *Schizothaerus nuttallii* Conrad. They identified the definitive host as the bat stingray, *Myliobatis californicus*.

Sparks and Chew (1966) described remarkable levels of parasitization of littleneck clams, *Venerupis staminea*, from Humboldt Bay, California, by larval tetraphyllidean cestodes of the genus *Echeneibothrium*. Cysts of the worm were closely packed throughout the tissue of the clams, which were abnormally exposed on the surface of gravel beds. Adult *Echeneibothrium*, with bothridia similar to those of larvae in clams, were found in bat stingrays caught in the same area.

(3) DISEASES CAUSED BY PARASITIC CRUSTACEA

Clams, like certain other bivalves, harbor parasitic copepods. Hoshina and Kuwabara (1959) described *Mytilicola mactrae* from Japanese *Mactra veneriformis* Reeve. About half the clams in a sample of 69 were infested. Yamaguti (1939) described another species of *Mytilicola* from *Brachidontes senhausi* (Reeve), and Humes (1954) found *M. porrecta* in a single hard clam, *Mercenaria mercenaria* (L.), from the Gulf of Mexico.

Pinnotherid crabs live within the mantle cavities of clams and other bivalves. Rathbun (1918) and Sakai (1965) listed a number of clams as hosts for several genera of the Pinnotheridae.

(4) TUMORS AND OTHER ABNORMALITIES

Hueper (1963) reported cauliflower-like papillary tumors at the anterior end of soft-shell clams collected from Chesapeake Bay. He termed the condition "endemic" and reported it in about 2% of clams collected from certain bay areas. Hyperplastic polypoid and papillary lesions were reported by Taylor and Smith (1966) from the foot of the gaper clam, *Tresus nuttalli*. One such fleshy growth measured 4×7 mm. Histologically, the area was characterized by intense inflammatory reaction with infiltration of leukocytes and fibroblasts. A polypoid tumor of the foot of the butter clam, *Saxidomus giganteus*, was reported by Pauley (1967). The growth was composed primarily of histologically normal muscle tissue covered by convoluted columnar epithelium, without mitotic figures or inflammatory response.

As in marine fish, a number of abnormalities, other than those resulting from activities of pathogens and parasites, have been observed and reported in shellfish. Some of these seem to be of genetic origin, and others may be environmentally induced. Among the Mollusca, shell and siphon abnormalities have been reported. Shell malformations of unknown origin have been recorded from several species of clams (Morse, 1923; Blake, 1929; Fisher, 1932; Clench, 1948; Shuster, 1966). Supernumerary siphons, either functional or nonfunctional, were reported in quahaugs, *Mercenaria mercenaria*, and soft-shell clams, *Mya arenaria*, by Tubiash *et al.* (1968). Causes were unknown, but developmental aberrations or abnormal regeneration after injury were suggested.

d. *Other Bivalve Mollusks of Commercial Importance*

Some information on diseases and parasites is available for two other groups of commercially important bivalve mollusks, scallops and pearl oysters. Mass mortalities caused by disease have not been reported in either group. Scallops are infected by protozoan and trematode parasites, and occasionally are affected by a shell disease. Pearl oysters harbor a number of larval trematode parasites.

(1) SCALLOPS

Although major mortalities have occurred in scallop populations (Dickie and Medcof, 1963; Medcof and Bourne, 1964; Merrill and Posgay, 1964; Sanders, 1966), none has been definitely associated with disease. In fact, only a few diseases and parasites are known, and their effects on the hosts are slight. A coccidian, *Pseudoklossia pectinis*, was described as a rare parasite in the kidney tubules of *Aequipecten maximus* at Roscoff, France, by Léger and Duboscq (1915). They found usually light infections with no extensive pathology. Spores of the gregarine *Nematopsis duorari* were found in the bay scallop, *Aequipecten irradians*, and certain other bivalves from the Florida coast by Kruse (1966). Sporocysts and fork-tailed cercariae of a trematode (not further identified) were found by Linton (1915) in large bay scallops from Woods Hole, Massachusetts. Infections were rare.

A larval nematode, *Paranisakis pectinis*, was described from the bay scallop at Beaufort, North Carolina (Cobb, 1930; Gutsell, 1930). The same, or a similar, worm was seen in the calico scallop, *A. gibbus*, from the east coast of Florida, and was redescribed as *Porrocaecum pectinis* by Hutton (1964). Encysted larvae produce areas of brownish discoloration in the adductor muscle (Sindermann, 1969).

The parasitic pyramidellid snail, *Odostomia seminuda*, has been reported from bay scallops and calico scallops from the east coast of the United States (Adams, 1839; Hackney, 1944; Wells and Wells, 1961). Merrill and Boss (1964) found that the proboscis of the snail was able to pierce the mantle and visceral mass of the host. Other members of the genus reported to parasitize scallops are *O. scalaris* from *Chlamys opercularis* in Denmark (Ankel and Christensen, 1963) and *O. eulimoides* from several genera of scallops.

An abnormal brown discoloration of meats was studied by Medcof (1949) in sea scallops off the south coast of Nova Scotia, Canada. He considered the condition to result from extensive invasion of the shell by a boring sponge. In advanced stages, the shell was completely honeycombed, causing excessive inner shell deposition and producing weak, shrunken individuals which, Medcof assumed, eventually died from effects of the shell disease. Meat yields from heavily infected scallops were less than half those of normal individuals, but only the larger scallops (8 or 9 years old) were infected.

The shell of the scallop, like that of other molluscs, is secreted by the mantle, and can be modified by abnormal mantle activity. Probably the best example of this was observed and reported by Merrill (1967). Extreme shell deformity in the sea scallop, *Placopecten magellanicus* (Gmelin), was produced by overgrowth of the growing edge by the colonial hydrozoan *Hydractinia echinata* (Fleming). Zooids of the coelenterate, armed with nematocysts, cause the mantle to retract. To resume growth, the scallop must successfully overgrow the hydroid colony; it does so by secreting an entirely new shell margin (Fig. 45). Sometimes the process of retraction and successful new growth is repeated several times, producing a grossly abnormal shell. Also, if the hydroid colony is confined to only one area of the shell, distortions in symmetry result because growth is inhibited along only part of the shell margin.

(2) PEARL OYSTERS

Pearl-producing bivalves of the family Pteriidae, called "pearl oysters" but taxonomically remote from edible oysters of the family Ostreidae,

FIG. 45. Gross deformity of scallop shell caused by growth of the coelenterate *Hydractinia*.

occur in many parts of the world (Sivalingam, 1962). Interest in parasites of pearl oysters has naturally centered on the larval worms considered responsible for pearl formation (Jameson, 1902, 1912; Wright, 1966), but a few other parasites and diseases have been recognized.

Parasites of the pearl oysters of Ceylon, *Margaritifera* (*Pinctada*) *vulgaris* Schum., were studied by Shipley and Hornell (1904) and Southwell (1911, 1912), particularly with regard to the role of parasitic worms in pearl formation. These authors described several stages of cestode larvae, some clearly trypanorhynchid, from the liver and gills of the pearl oyster. The worms occurred, often in great numbers, in fibrous capsules. Several larval trematodes were also found, but only one, described as *Muttua margaritiferae*, was abundant. Metacercariae localized in the gills. Other metacercariae, described as *Musalia herdmani*, were found in the muscles, mantle, and foot. An aspidobothrid trematode, *Aspidogaster margaritiferae*, occurred in the pericardial cavity, and several species of encysted larval nematodes were seen in the gonads, stomach walls, and adductor muscles.

Pearl oysters of Japan, *Pinctada martensii*, are commonly infested with sporocysts and cercariae of a bucephalid trematode described as *Bucephalus margaritae* by Ozaki and Ishibashi (1934). Experimental infections of several species of small fishes with cercariae from pearl oysters (Sakaguchi, 1962, 1966a) produced metacercariae morphologically the same as those identified as *B. varicus* by Manter (1940). Adult trematodes were found in the digestive tracts of carangid fishes, *Caranx sexfasciatus* and *C. ignobilis*, which were abundant in the waters near oyster farms where pearl oysters were heavily infested (Sakaguchi, 1966b). The life-cycle stages were completed when Sakaguchi (1967) obtained adult *Bucephalus varicus* from *Caranx sexfasciatus*, *C. ignobilus*, and *C. equula* which had been fed metacercariae grown in the forage fish, *Rudarius ercodes*, by experimental infections with cercariae from pearl oysters. Marked decline in condition of pearl oysters resulted from invasion by larval trematodes. Sporocysts were found to overwinter in the host, and production of cercariae began again when water temperatures rose in spring (Sakaguchi, 1965). Pearl oysters infected in the preceding year suffered high mortalities after insertion of pearl cores, and high percentages of pearls produced by infected individuals were of low quality (Sakaguchi, 1964).

2. Gastropoda

Marine snails are of direct but relatively minor economic importance as food in many parts of the world. Examples are the abalones, periwinkles, limpets, and other edible snails. Negative economic roles that result in losses to human utilization of marine products are played by the many snails, especially shell-boring ones, which prey on bivalves. Drills are common in most high salinity areas where bivalves are found. Some marine snails harbor larval stages of avian schistosomes which can invade the human skin, causing dermatitis. Many other snails are of greatest significance as intermediate hosts of trematodes that damage marine fish. Effects of larval trematodes on molluscan intermediate hosts are severe; they include sterilization and inhibition of normal migrations of the snail. Included here, then, are examples of diseases and parasites of gastropods that have direct economic significance. Some references to the almost limitless literature on larval trematode parasites of noncommercial gastropods are included also, and additional information can be found in Fretter and Graham (1949).

A possible biological control measure for the oyster drill, *Urosalpinx cinerea*, was examined by Ganaros (1957). A fungus was observed parasitic on ova within egg cases in laboratory holding tanks. Tentatively identified as a species of *Sirolpidum*, the fungus was found experimentally to be infective to several stages of living *Urosalpinx* larvae but not to later developmental stages (protoconchs). Ganaros seemed unnecessarily pessimistic about the possible use of the fungus for biological control of drills, on the basis of doubtful practicability of creating environmental conditions conducive to infection and dissemination. He did believe, however, that if the snails themselves could spread the pathogen it might prove an effective control method. A very interesting facet of the study was that an isolate of *Sirolpidium* sent to England was able to infect eggs of the oyster pea crab, *Pinnotheres;* in this way it resembled a fungus pathogen of crustacean eggs, *Plectospira dubia*, described by Atkins (1954). Apparently, and unfortunately, no further work was done with this disease agent from *Urosalpinx* eggs. It is to be hoped that the pathogen can be reisolated for further drill control studies.

Gregarines are known as parasites of gastropods. Hatt (1927) first pointed out that *Nematopsis galloprovincialis*, which was described from mussels in France by Léger (1903), also occurred in a number of snails of the family Trochidae. Spores were massed in blood sinuses of the gills, and some individuals were heavily infected. Experimental infections were achieved in a number of crabs, and invasion of the snail host was direct, by penetration of the gill epithelium.

Larval trematode parasitization was examined as a possible method of biological control of the southern oyster drill, *Thais haemostoma*, by Cooley (1958, 1962). Normal infection levels in natural populations of *Thais* were about 2% in Florida, 3.4% in Mississippi, and less than 1% in Texas. Infected individuals were sterilized by massive invasion of the gonads (Hopkins, 1957a). Cooley (1962), on concluding the study, was not optimistic about use of the trematode *Parorchis* as a biological control measure because (1) prevalence of adult worms in gulls (the definitive hosts) was low; (2) heavy infections of drills by experimental exposures were not obtained; and (3) drills not near gull feeding grounds were uninfected or very lightly infected. Cooley also reported the presence of rare larval nematodes and larval tetraphyllidean cestodes in *Thais* from the north coast of the Gulf of Mexico. Larval stages of other unidentified trematodes that caused gonad damage were seen previously in the southern oyster drill (Schechter, 1943; Butler, 1953). *Parorchis acanthus* has also been reported to cause sterilization of the most significant oyster drill of the Atlantic coastal states, *Urosalpinx cinerea* (Carriker, 1955), and has been found in another muricid, *Purpura* (*Thais*) *lapillus* (Stunkard and Shaw, 1931; Stunkard and Cable, 1932). Rees (1937, 1939, 1940) also found *P. acanthus* in *P. lapillus* from England. Biological control of drills has been discussed by Carriker (1955) and Cole (1935).

The pervasive and, at times, severe effects of larval trematode infection on abundance and reproduction of marine snails and snail populations must not be underestimated. Such parasitization almost invariably sterilizes the host, inhibits its seasonal migrations, and often leads to its early death. Infections vary seasonally and geographically (Sindermann, 1960, 1965; Sindermann and Farrin, 1962) but may at times involve a significant part of the snail population. Sindermann and Farrin found, for example, a general average of 52% of the *Littorina littorea* population at a New England study site infected, whereas a coastwide sampling of the species in the Gulf of Maine disclosed an average mid-tide zone prevalence of 11%. Seasonal peaks of infection were different in different tide zones, partly because infected snails did not participate in normal spring and autumn migrations. Infected individuals remained behind in the harsh winter high tide zone environment of the northern New England coast.

Larval avian schistosomes, which can produce dermatitis in humans, parasitize some marine snails, and, like certain other trematodes, cause sterilization and inhibition of migration. Known only since 1942 (Penner, 1942, 1950), larval avian schistosomes from marine snails have been described from both coasts of the United States and elsewhere (Hutton, 1952; Stunkard and Hinchcliffe, 1952; Sindermann and Gibbs, 1953; Chu and Cutress, 1954; Grodhaus and Keh, 1958; Hutton, 1960; Sindermann, 1960; and others). One such trematode, *Austrobilharzia variglandis*, parasitizes *Nassarius obsoletus* and a number of migratory birds on the United States east coast. Infections are highest in the high tide zone (Sindermann, 1960) with a peak in autumn, due in part to inhibition of normal offshore migration at that time of year. The highest prevalence found was 27%. Greatest cercarial emergence, hence greatest risk of human infection, occurred at intermediate salinities (15–25%). Emergence was inhibited at temperatures below 10°C. The same larval trematode has been reported from *Littorina planaxis* and from introduced *Nassarius obsoletus* in California (Penner, 1950; Grodhaus and Keh, 1958), from *Littorina pintado* in Hawaii (Chu and Cutress, 1954), and from *Haminoea antillarum guadalupensis* in Florida (Hutton, 1952).

The pink abalone, *Haliotis corrugata*, from California harbors an encysted larval nematode, *Echinocephalus pseudouncinatus*, of the family Gnathostomidae (Millemann, 1951). Heavy infestations of older specimens were found; the worms encysted in the ventral part of the foot, producing external vesicles. The presence of blisters, and the burrowing of the larvae were considered by Millemann to weaken the foot as a holdfast organ. The disease was known to commercial divers by gross appearance and ease of removal of parasitized animals from rocks. The green abalone from the same area can also be infested, according to reports from processors and divers. The larval worms average about 18 mm in length, and have six anterior rows of 40 to 50 hooks around the head bulb. Adult *E. pseudouncinatus* were found by Millemann (1963) in the horned shark, *Heterodontus francisci*, and the bat stingray, *Myliobatis californicus*, from the Gulf of California. Recovery of early juvenile stages of the nematode from teleost fishes (Shipley and Hornell, 1904; Johnston and Mawson, 1945) indicates that elasmobranchs may become infected by ingestion of molluscan intermediate hosts or teleost transport hosts.

A copepod parasite of gastropods of the family Trochidae was described from the French coast by Dollfus (1914). Described as *Trochicola enterica*, the copepod localized in the digestive tract, extending almost to the rectum, with egg cases projecting into the pallial cavity of the host. Dollfus found similarities of *T. enterica* with *Mytilicola intestinalis*, parasitic in European mussels.

Growth anomalies in the shells of gastropods are sometimes seen. Duplication of the siphonal canal is one such anomaly (Clench and Merrill, 1963); and reversal of normal coiling is another (De Lagoda, 1868; Robertson and Merrill, 1963).

3. Cephalopoda

Squids and other cephalopods are eaten as delicacies in many parts of the world, and are commercially important mollusks in many countries, particularly in the Orient. Although little is known about factors that affect population abundance of cephalopods, some of their parasites, particularly ciliates, Mesozoa, and larval helminths have been examined.

Ciliates have been described from the kidneys of several squids. Dobell (1909) described *Chromadina elegans* and *C. coronata* from *Illex coindeti*. Jepps (1931) found *C. elegans* in *Spirula spirula*.

A discussion of parasites of cephalopods would not be complete without consideration of the dicyemid Mesozoa, a small systematically isolated group parasitic in the kidney. The source of infection and life-cycle stages other than those in the cephalopod are unknown, but an intermediate host is probably involved (Bresciani and Fenchel, 1965). Nouvel (1947, 1948), who studied the biology of certain dicyemids, reported that they do not damage host tissues, but absorb nutrients present in the nephridial fluid of cephalopod hosts. Their phagocytic somatic cells may, however, ingest particulate matter such as host sperm cells, which are also found in this fluid.

Larval cestodes, particularly those that mature in elasmobranch fishes, are probably the most common parasites of cephalopods. Cestodes dominated the list of parasites reported by Clarke (1966), who summarized information on parasites of oceanic squids, particularly the ommastrephids. MacGinitie and MacGinitie (1949) found jumbo squid, *Dosidicus gigas,* to be heavily infested with larval tetraphyllidean cestodes. Larvae occurred in the liver and digestive tract. Other larval tapeworms of the genus *Tetrarhynchus* were found in the tissues of the same squids. Larvae of the cestode family Tetrarhynchidae (order Trypanorhyncha) were also found in the mantle cavity of an octopus (*Octopus* sp.) from the Indian Ocean by Adam (1938), and Dollfus (1923, 1927a, 1929) has reported members of the same group in a variety of cephalopods, including five species of squids and *Octopus vulgaris*. Dollfus (1958) has published an extensive list of copepod, isopod, and helminth parasites of cephalopods from the Mediterranean and Atlantic. Larval cestodes, particularly trypanorhynchids were most abundantly represented. Cestode larvae have also been found in cephalopods by Squires (1957) and Clarke and Maul (1962).

Squids also harbor larval nematodes. Squires (1957) and Clarke and Maul (1962) found larval anisakid worms in *Illex illecebrosus* and *Lepidoteuthis grimaldii.*

A few tumors have been recognized and reported in squids. Jullien (1928) described as tumors certain protuberances and inflammations in the mouths of two squids, *Sepia officinalis* L. Later, Jullien and Jullien (1951) found two other squids with extensive benign tumors on the ventral side of the visceral mass. In each case the lesions were characterized by leukocytic infiltration, disruption of the epidermis, and lack of vascularization at the center of the tumor. They were considered to be of connective tissue origin.

C. CRUSTACEA

Crustacea such as crabs, lobsters, and shrimps are among the most valuable of marine crops in many parts of the world. Large populations of crustaceans occur on the continental shelves, and often part or all of the life cycle is spent· in estuarine or inshore waters. Here individuals may be observed and studied in natural habitats as well as in the landed catches. These studies have disclosed certain parasites and diseased conditions. Disease may have severe effects on survival, particularly when crabs and lobsters are impounded before sale. Diseases exist in natural populations of Crustacea as well, although effects are less apparent than in captives or in more sedentary marine animals. No widespread epizootic is known for marine Crustacea that would be comparable to "krebspest," a microbial disease caused by the fungus *Aphanomyces astaci* that swept through populations of freshwater crayfishes of Europe (Schikora, 1906, 1926; Schäperclaus, 1935; Nybelin, 1935; Mannsfield, 1942; Unestam, 1965; Gordon, 1966).

1. Crabs

Many species of crabs have great commercial value in various parts of the world. Consequently, diseases and parasites have been included in studies of factors which affect abundance. Among the microbial diseases of crabs are those caused by a virus, a bacterium, several fungi, and a variety of protozoans. Helminth infestations include larval trematodes and cestodes, as well as nemerteans and leeches. Parasitic crustaceans—rhizocephalans, isopods, and copepods—also infest crabs.

a. *Microbial Diseases*

(1) VIRUSES

Virus diseases have not been reported from marine invertebrates, with the single exception described recently, and only very briefly, by Vago (1966), in crabs, *Portunus depurator* (L.), from the French Mediterranean coast. Gross disease signs included the slow development of paralysis, and sometimes a slight darkening (presumably of the exoskeleton) in later phases of the disease. Virus particles were seen with the electron microscope; inoculation of blood from infected animals produced disease signs in healthy crabs; and infections were obtained with ultrafiltrates and ultracentrifugates of homogenized tissues from sick crabs. No indication of disease prevalence was given by Vago.

(2) Bacteria

King crabs, *Paralithodes camtschatica* (Tilesius) and *P. platypus* Brandt, from the eastern North Pacific are occasionally affected by "rust disease," which seems to result from action of chitin-destroying bacteria on the exoskeleton. Microorganisms of this type are common in the sea (ZoBell and Rittenberg, 1938; Hock, 1940, 1941; Lear, 1963) but usually degrade the exoskeletons of dead animals and do not affect living individuals. Over 30 species of chitin-destroying bacteria are known, of which half have been isolated from shells of crustaceans.

Bright *et al.* (1960),[*] described observations of rust disease in landed catches of king crabs from Kachemak Bay, Cook Inlet, Alaska, as well as experimental studies of the bacteria involved. The disease was characterized by progressive darkening and softening of the exoskeleton, particularly on the ventral surfaces. Underlying living tissues were unaffected. Natural infections reached 11% in larger, older crabs in 1957 but were much lower in 1958 and 1959. Shell abrasions and injuries served as foci of the disease, which developed experimentally within 2 weeks. The disease was not carried over to the new exoskeleton after molting, but recently shed crabs were highly susceptible because the new shell was easily punctured or abraded. Chitin-destroying bacteria were isolated from infected crabs, and cultured organisms produced the disease experimentally in normal crabs. Similar bacteria were also isolated from seawater in Kachemak Bay. The authors concluded that the disease would not affect the commercial fishery seriously unless the catch of crabs was substantially less than annual recruitment, since larger individuals, which do not molt annually, were more frequently infected.

A condition known as "Brandfleckenkrankheit" or "burn spot disease" occurs in European edible crabs, *Cancer pagurus* (Schäfer, 1954; Gordon, 1966). Although it is thought by some to be of fungal etiology, others believe that it may be due to chitinivorous bacteria. Gross pathology

---

[*] Data furnished from unpublished contract report, "King crab investigations of Cook Inlet, Alaska," by Donald B. Bright, Floyd E. Durham, and Jens W. Knudsen of the Allan Hancock Foundation, University of Southern California, Los Angeles, to U. S. Bureau of Commercial Fisheries Biological Laboratory, Auke Bay, Alaska, June 1960. (Cited with permission of Laboratory Director, U. S. Bureau of Commercial Fisheries Biological Laboratory, Auke Bay, Alaska.)

consists of dark brown to black spots with red margins on the carapace and appendages, particularly the chelipeds. The chitin in the center of the spots becomes friable, and may be destroyed, exposing the underlying musculature. Gordon reported that in 1956 many diseased crabs from waters to the southwest of England and from the North Sea reached the market. A similar disease is known in European freshwater crayfish and river crabs, from which three fungi have been isolated and described (Mann and Pieplow, 1938; Mann, 1939).

Another problematic disease, probably caused by chitin-destroying microorganisms, was described from blue crabs in Maryland by Rosen (1967). Chitinoclastic bacteria were isolated from characteristic brown depressed areas of chitin destruction. The disease was progressive and was evident in 3% of crabs examined. It is important to note that the crabs had been crowded together in shedding tanks for an extended period. A similar disease has been seen in blue crabs from Galveston Bay, Texas (Hopkins, 1968).

(3) FUNGI

Eggs of blue crabs from lower Chesapeake Bay were found to be parasitized by a fungus, *Lagenidium callinectes* Couch (Couch, 1942; Sandoz *et al.*, 1944; Sandoz and Rogers, 1944; Newcombe and Rogers, 1947; Rogers-Talbert, 1948). Infected eggs either failed to hatch, or gave rise to abnormal zoea larvae. Up to 90% of a sample of ovigerous female crabs were infected, and up to 25% of the eggs in a "sponge" (egg mass) were invaded. Penetration of the egg mass was slow and did not exceed 3 mm. This fact, combined with the short (2-week) incubation time, permitted normal development of much of the egg mass internal to the infection. Experimentally, the fungus developed normally in salinities from 5 to 30%₀. The fungus was transmitted experimentally to the eggs of two other species of crabs (the oyster crab and the mud crab, *Neopanope texiana* Rathbun) inhabiting the same bay area.

Pea crabs (*Pinnotheres*) taken from the sea mussel at Plymouth, England, were parasitized by the fungus *Leptolegnia marina* (Atkins, 1929, 1954a). The mycelium was usually found in the gills but penetrated other body organs and appendages as well. Zoosporangia developed in the appendages, and large numbers of zoospores were released upon the death of the host. No further growth of the fungus took place in dead crabs, and no external development, beyond papillae of zoospore exit tubes, was seen. Atkins (1954b, 1955) described two other fungi, *Plectospira dubia* and *Pythium thalassium*, which infect eggs of pea crabs and other Crustacea. *Plectospira dubia* was less pathogenic for prezoeal and zoeal stages than for earlier stages of egg development.

An interesting and aberrant group of parasitic or commensal fungi are the Trichomycetes or Eccrinides which may occur on the lining of the gut or on the exoskeleton of Crustacea, particularly amphipods and isopods. A number of species have been described from various crabs, especially the hermit crabs. These fungi require a chitinous substrate, and exhibit specificity, not only for particular host species, but for location in the host as well. Furthermore, spore formation in some instances seems linked with molting of the host. Dubosq *et al.* (1949) and Manier (1950) have summarized information about the group.

(4) PROTOZOA

Gregarines are common parasites of many Crustacea, and an extensive and at times confusing literature has accumulated. Many members of the group have been reported from crabs. For example, species of the genus *Cephaloidophora* occur in spider and fiddler crabs of the United States east coast (Watson, 1915, 1916a,b; Watson-Kamm, 1922), in the striped shore crab, *Pachygrapsus crassipes,* of the Pacific coast, and in the Mediterranean "flat crab," *Pachygrapsus marmoratus* (Ball, 1938; Théodorides, 1961, 1962). As mentioned in the discussion of oyster diseases, several representatives of the genus *Nematopsis* occur in Atlantic species of mud crabs (Prytherch, 1940; Ball, 1951; Sprague and Orr, 1955).

Although the gregarines are not usually considered serious pathogens of Crustacea, masses of the parasites may occlude the lumen of the intestinal caeca and may damage the epithelium. Ball (1938) found that the lumen of the intestinal caeca of the crab *Pachygrapsus marmoratus* may be practically occluded by *Carcinoecetes conformis,* and that a thinning and even sloughing of the epithelium occurred. A similar sloughing was noted in *Panopeus occidentalis* and *P. herbstii* due to activities of *Nematopsis panopei* (Ball, 1951).

The Haplosporida are rapidly becoming known as significant parasites of mollusks, but only one species has been described thus far from decapod crustaceans. *Minchinia louisiana* was described by Sprague (1963) from the mud crab, *Panopeus herbstii,* taken on the Louisiana coast. Life-cycle stages, including definitive spores, were identified from heavy infection of the entire gut wall.

Several microsporidans are parasites of crabs. Sprague (1965) described a species of *Nosema* parasitic in muscles of the blue crab. Infected muscles became opaque with a coarse fibrous texture, and heavy infections caused lysis of myofibrils. Sprague, who considered the parasite to be common and widespread in Chesapeake Bay, believed it might be a significant factor in crab mortality. Sprague (1966) also described

Plistophora cargoi from the skeletal and cardiac muscles of a single blue crab from the Patuxent River, Maryland. Earlier, Pérez (1905a,b) reported *Nosema pulvis* in the muscles of the green crab, *Carcinus maenas* (L.), and Pérez (1907) also described ovarian infections with a microsporidan, *Thelohania maenadis,* in green crabs from Arcachon, France. The parasite was normally in the body muscles.

Ciliates are also significant parasites and epibionts of crabs. Molting blue crabs from Chesapeake Bay suffered serious mortalities in the summers of 1965 and 1966. Their gills had a massive infestation of peritrichous ciliates (Fig. 46) of the genera *Lagenophrys* and *Epistylus* (Couch, 1966, 1967). Mortalities were most severe among crabs in holding tanks just before or after molting, but wild crabs were also heavily infested, and fishermen reported mortalities. Infestations of gills frequently seemed heavy enough to interfere with respiration. Although these gill ciliates are not technically parasitic, in that they do not derive nourishment directly from the host, they are of obvious detriment to the crab.

Another ciliate, *Anophrys sarcophaga* Cohn, is found in the blood of green crabs. Originally described as a free-living form (Cohn, 1866), it was first seen in the blood of crabs by Cattaneo (1888). Poisson (1930) described the active and encysted forms of the parasite in great detail, and cultured the organism. *Anophrys* apparently ingests large numbers of host amoebocytes, and multiplies until the blood becomes a dense "soup" of motile parasites. The disease, though often fatal once infection has occurred, was relatively rare on the French coast. Experimental infections, achieved by injecting the ciliates, killed crabs in 2 to 7 days. Certain individual crabs seemed resistant to infection, but no antibody response was detected. Effects on the parasites included inhibition of reproduction, immobilization, and eventual death.

Other parasitic ciliates occur in the blood of crustaceans. Gordon (1966) mentioned the genera *Hematodinium* in *Macropipus* and *Carcinus,* and *Paradinium* and *Syndinium* in copepods of the genus *Calanus. Syndinium* destroys the host's gonads, whereas *Paradinium* colors the copepod a deep red (a host response produced by larval trematode parasitization also).

Sprague and Beckett (1966) published a preliminary note on a disease of soft-shell and molting blue crabs, *Callinectes sapidus* Rathbun. The disease, of undetermined etiology, was called "gray crab disease" because of a characteristic grayish or translucent appearance of the ventral side of body and appendages. It occurred in crabs from seaside bays of Maryland and Virginia, where it caused deaths among captive crabs. Sick individuals were sluggish, and died a few minutes after removal from sea water. One processor reported that 20–30% of crabs in shedding tanks

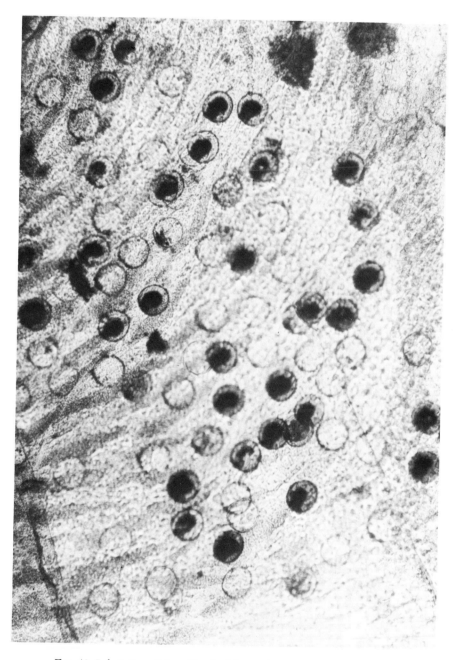

FIG. 46. Infestation of the gills of a blue crab by the ciliate *Lagenophrys*.

died with signs of the disease. Smears of body fluids contained enormous numbers of amoeboid cells 5 to 15 μ in diameter, each containing two nucleus like basophilic bodies with different morphology. Identification of the parasite was not attempted, but a subsequent note (Sprague and Beckett, 1968) identified the amoeboid cells as *Paramoeba* sp.

b. *Diseases Caused by Helminths*

Trematode metacercariae are common in several species of crabs. Larvae of *Microphallus* (*Spelotrema*) *nicolli*, encysted in body muscles of blue crabs, were described by Cable and Hunninen (1940). Adult trematodes occur in young herring gulls, *Larus argentatus*, and sporocyst generations in the snail *Bittium alternatum* (Say). A haplosporidan hyperparasite, *Urosporidium crescens* [DeTurk] has been found in metacercariae of *Microphallus nicolli* from blue crabs caught in North Carolina (De Turk, 1940). One third of the crabs contained metacercariae, but the extent of hyperparasitization was not determined. The host metacercarial tissue was often completely destroyed, leaving little more than a sack of protozoan spores. Invasion of *Urosporidium* was thought to occur before encystment of cercariae. Masses of dark pigmented spores in the destroyed metacercaria produce a black spot, which has led to the application of the descriptive colloquial term "pepper crab" to hyperparasitized individuals. "Pepper spots" occur most commonly in fat bodies, digestive gland, and muscles of the crab.

Metacercariae of *Microphallus* (*Spelotrema*) *carcini* Lebour were reported from the hepatopancreas of green crabs from the English Channel (Guyenot *et al.*, 1925), the Mediterranean (Timon-David, 1949), and elsewhere. Hyperparasitization of metacercariae by the microsporidan, *Nosema* (*Plistophora*) *spelotremae*, was reported by Guyenot *et al.* (1925). Metacercariae of *Microphallus similis* (Jägerskiöld) occur in the hepatopancreas of the green crab of the western North Atlantic (Stunkard, 1957). Young green crabs were killed in 10 to 20 days by massive experimental exposures to cercariae of *M. similis*.

Larval diphyllidean cestodes (*Echinobothrium affine* Diesing) have been reported by Dollfus (1964a,b) from green crabs sampled at Roscoff on the coast of France.

Some polyclad Turbellaria are ectoparasitic on crabs. Gordon (1966) mentioned *Coleophora chinonoecetis* on the eggs of the spider crab *Chionoectes*, and *Paraclistus oofagus* on the crab *Hyas*.

Juvenile nemerteans, *Carcinonemertes carcinophila* (Kölliker), encyst on the gills of the blue crab. After the female crab spawns, the worms excyst and migrate to the egg mass, where they mature, lay eggs, then return to the gills (Davis, 1965). Hargis (1959) has cited this parasite as an indicator of host physiology, since Hopkins (1947) has pointed out that increased size and more noticeable color are characteristic of reencysted worms after the host has spawned. This and other nemerteans have been described from a number of crabs, including the green crab, of Europe (Coe, 1902a,b; Humes, 1942; Gordon, 1966).

Nematodes occur as commensals in egg masses of crabs, or as internal parasites. *Rhabdochona uca* parasitizes the digestive tract of *Uca mani*, and *Carcinus* and *Pagurus* are intermediate hosts of nematodes that mature in elasmobranch fishes (Gordon, 1966).

A localized mortality of blue crabs, thought to be caused by parasitization by leeches, *Myzobdella lugubris* Leidy, was reported from a Florida river by Hutton and Sogandares-Bernal (1959). A sample of 7 crabs had 32 leeches attached near the base of the legs and near perforations in the exoskeleton. The parasite is known from the Atlantic and Gulf coasts of the United States, but had not previously been considered to cause mortalities (Moore, 1946).

Other leeches occur on crabs. Oka (1927) described *Carcinobdella kanibir* from Japanese edible crabs, *Chionoectes opilio*. Egg cases and adults of the leech *Notostomobdella cyclostoma* (Johansson) are common on Alaskan king crabs, particularly during summer (Moore and Meyer, 1951; Bright *et al.*, 1960). Undescribed worms, probably leeches, were seen by MacKay (1942) on the abdomens of female Dungeness crabs, *Cancer magister* Dana, from British Columbia. The worms were much larger on egg-bearing crabs, and were found chiefly among the eggs.

c. *Diseases Caused by Parasitic Crustaceans*

Many species of crabs, in many parts of the world, are parasitized by rhizocephalan Cirripedia (Pérez, 1903, 1931c; Boschma, 1928, 1963; Shiino, 1931, 1943; Reinhard 1942, 1956). These parasites invade the host's body and cause degeneration of the gonads (Reinhard, 1956). The tumor-like body of the rhizocephalan ramifies throughout much of the crab, causing extensive morphological changes. The crab is usually sterilized, secondary sex characters are modified, and molting is often inhibited (Giard, 1888; Potts, 1906, 1915; Smith, 1906; Cantacuzène, 1925; Reinhard, 1950; Ichikawa and Yamagunachi, 1957).

Brachyuran or true crabs are parasitized by members of the rhizocephalan family Sacculinidae. In United States waters, crabs most frequently parasitized are the green crab of the Atlantic coast and the masking crab, *Loxorhynchus grandis*, the kelp crab, *Pugettia producta*

(Randall), and the black-clawed crab, *Lophopanoepeus bellus* (Stimpson) of the Pacific coast. Green crabs and swimming crabs, *Macropipus* (*Portunus*) *holsatus* (Fabricius), from the English coast are parasitized by *Sacculina carcini* Thompson (Delage, 1884; Day, 1935; Foxon, 1940). Blue crabs from the Texas coast are parasitized by the rhizocephalan, *Loxothylacus texanus* (Reinhard, 1950; Hopkins, 1957). Mud crabs, *Eurypanopeus depressus* (Smith), from lower Chesapeake Bay (Virginia) were discovered by Van Engel *et al.* (1966) to harbor high incidences of the sacculinid, *Loxothylacus panopaei* (Gissler). The localized nature of the infestations suggested that the parasite had been introduced with its hosts in shipments of oysters from the Gulf of Mexico.

Many species of anomuran crabs may be parasitized by rhizocephalans. King crabs, *Paralithodes platypus*, from Alaskan waters are occasionally invaded, probably by a species of *Peltogaster* (Kirkwood, 1967). Hermit crabs are also frequently invaded by members of the family Peltogastridae. Reinhard (1942), who examined 3092 *Pagurus pubescens* Krøyer from the Maine coast of the United States, found 13.7% parasitized by *Peltogaster paguri* Rathke. The same rhizocephalan occurs on the coast of France, where its host is *Pagurus bernhardus* (L.) (Pérez, 1927, 1928, 1931a,b,c), and in Japan, where it parasitizes four species of hermit crabs (Shiino, 1943). Infestation can have significant effects on crab populations, since parasitization usually causes degeneration of host gonads. Pérez (1929, 1931a), however, found interesting evidence for sterilization and mortalities of *Peltogaster paguri* because of hyperparasitization by an epicaridean isopod of the family Cryptoniscidae, *Liriopsis pygmaea* (Rathke); in some samples from northern France, most of the rhizocephalans were parasitized. Pérez believed that this parasitization was an important control for *Peltogaster* populations. *Liriopsis* has an effect on *Peltogaster* that is similar to that of *Peltogaster* on *Pagurus*—gonadal degeneration.

Epicaridean isopods can also be significant parasites of crabs. Two families are important: the Bopyridae, which live principally in the gill chambers, and the Entoniscidae, which invade the hemocoele. Morphological modification for parasitic existence is similar in some entoniscids to that which occurs in rhizocephalans (Veillet, 1945; Nicol, 1967). Effects on the crab host often include sterilization and changes in secondary sexual characteristics (Tucker, 1930; Reverberi, 1943, 1952; Reinhard and Buckeridge, 1950). Parasitization of crabs by female entoniscids causes internal deformities, including reduction in size of organs (Atkins, 1933; Reinhard, 1945) and changes in the nervous system (Matsumoto, 1953).

Detailed studies of Epicaridea of crabs have been carried out in several parts of the world. Shiino (1942b), for example, examined the entoniscids parasitizing littoral crabs in the Seto area of Japan. He described seven new species, including *Entoniscus japonicus,* parasitic on the porcellanid *Petrolisthes japonicus* deHaan. This was the fifth parasitic crustacean described from *P. japonicus* in the Seto area; Shiino (1933) had previously identified two bopyrids, and Boschma (1935), two rhizocephalans. Shiino (1942b) described the entoniscid *Portunion flavidus* as a common parasite of the crab *Pachygrapsus crassipes,* which was also parasitized by two species of *Sacculina.* Shiino (1933, 1934, 1936, 1937, 1939a,b, 1949, 1958, 1964a) has described bopyrids from Japanese crabs, as well as those from Palau, California and Chile (1942a, 1964b,c).

The Bopyridae are only moderately modified for parasitic existence in the branchial chamber of the host, whereas the Entoniscidae are highly modified, and live in the hemocoele of the host, within a sac formed by invagination of host integument. Modification is limited to females; the dwarf male retains typical isopod characters.

Copepods are known as parasites of crab eggs. Connolly (1929) described *Choniosphaera cancrorum* from the egg masses of two American rock crabs, *Cancer borealis* and *C. irroratus.* Later, Gnanamuthu (1954) described *Choniosphaera indica* from gills and egg masses of an Indian edible crab, *Neptunus sanguinolentus.* Copepod larvae were found between the crab's gill lamellae, probably feeding on tissue fluids; adults apparently suck out the fluids of the crab eggs. Many other species of copepods, particularly of the family Choniostomatidae, are parasitic on Crustacea (Hansen, 1897, 1904, 1923).

An extensive and fascinating body of literature on rhizocephalan, epicaridean, and other crustacean parasites and hyperparasites of Crustacea has accumulated (Giard and Bonnier, 1887, 1895; Smith, 1906; Shiino, 1942a,b; Veillet, 1945; Reinhard, 1944, 1956; Baer, 1951; Nicol, 1967; Hartnoll, 1967).

2. Lobsters

Lobsters, because of their great economic importance in North America and Europe, have been subjects of many scientific studies, including some concerned with diseases and parasites. Because of the practice of holding lobsters in pounds and live cars, occasionally for extended periods and frequently under crowded conditions, mortalities have been observed and causes examined. Two bacterial diseases have significant effects on impounded lobsters. Among the known larger parasites are trematodes, nematodes, acanthocephalans, annelid worms, and copepods.

a. *Microbial Diseases*

A bacterial disease, caused by gram-positive, tetrad-forming encapsulated cocci, described as *Gaffkya homari* Hitchner and Snieszko, is known from wild and impounded populations of American lobsters, *Homarus americanus* (Milne-Edwards). The disease (gaffkaemia) was first noted on the Maine coast in 1946 (Hitchner and Snieszko, 1947; Snieszko and Taylor, 1947; Getchell, 1949). "Red-tail" disease, as it was originally called, is characterized by a variable pink coloration of the ventral abdomen, pink blood, prolonged clotting time, and drastic reduction in blood phagocytes. Infected lobsters become progressively weaker, and mortalities may reach 50% after short periods of storage. Mortalities increase sharply if water temperature exceeds 15°C. Moribund lobsters move to shoal water and die in a "spread-eagle" position.

Goggins and Hurst (1960)[*] have provided information about two epizootics of gaffkaemia along the entire Maine coast, one in 1946–1947, and another in 1959–1960, with losses as great as 58% of impounded populations. They found that the pathogen could live and multiply outside the lobster, in the slime on lobster cars, crates, tanks, and live wells. *Gaffkya* was also isolated from mud of tidal pounds and from seawater several miles from infected pounds. The disease was transmitted directly by allowing presumably healthy lobsters to feed on infected individuals or by holding healthy lobsters in seawater containing the pathogen. Incubation time was 14 to 21 days, although the animals possibly were already gaffkaemic before the start of the experiments. Treatment of tidal pounds with calcium hypochlorite reduced populations of the pathogen in bottom mud, and reduced subsequent losses of impounded lobsters.

The disease organism is often present in wild populations. Stewart and MacDonald (1962) and Stewart *et al.* (1966) isolated *Gaffkya* from 96 of 2035 recently caught lobsters in Canada and found the disease to be widespread in the Canadian Atlantic region. Cornick and Stewart (1966) recovered, from presumptive tests for *Gaffkya* in Canadian lobsters, several other kinds of bacteria, including *Micrococcus, Pseudomonas, Achromobacter,* and *Brevibacterium,* none of which was considered to be pathogenic. Rabin (1965) found a *Gaffkya*-like organism in lobsters from Woods Hole, Massachusetts; and Wood (1965a,b) isolated *Gaffkya*-like organisms from two North Sea lobsters, *Homarus vulgaris* Edwards. Wood observed mortalities in storage tanks in southern England in 1962, and

---

[*] Data provided in unpublished mimeographed report of the Department of Sea and Shore Fisheries, Augusta, Maine, "Progress report on lobster gaffkyaremia (Red Tail)," by P. L. Goggins and J. W. Hurst, 1960.

recovered *Gaffkya* with cultural and biochemical characteristics similar to Canadian and United States isolates. Epizootics of gaffkaemia have been reported from European lobsters in Ireland (Gibson, 1961), and Norway and the Netherlands (Roskam, 1957). Gibson noted that diseased lobsters were also infected with the "gill maggot," *Nicothoë astaci* Audouin and Milne Edwards, which was absent from uninfected individuals.

The taxonomy of *Gaffkya* is still unsettled. Deibel and Niven (1960) examined various cocci from cured meat, oral cocci isolated from humans, tetrad-forming cocci from meat-curing brines, and *G. homari*. They found them sufficiently similar to one another and to members of the genus *Pediococcus* in morphology and physiology to justify placing them in a single species of *Pediococcus* which they designated *P. homari* nov. comb. Aaronson (1956) had reviewed the genus *Gaffkya* earlier, and suggested that it might be abandoned. Despite these studies, the generic name *Gaffkya* persists in recent literature.

Experimental studies of host-parasite relationships showed that lobsters became infected and died a few days after inoculation with *G. homari* (Rabin, 1965). Prior inoculation with *Vibrio* endotoxin did not enhance the infection and prior inoculation of heat-killed *Gaffkya* did not alter the course of infection. Lobster serum stimulated *in vitro* growth of *G. homari* in almost every test, but growth of *Vibrio* was sometimes inhibited. Studies of possible defense mechanisms of lobsters against *G. homari* have also been carried out at the Halifax (Nova Scotia) and Saint Andrews (New Brunswick) stations of the Fisheries Research Board of Canada (Fisheries Research Board of Canada, 1966). Lobster serum, as indicated by Rabin's work, had no bactericidal activity against the pathogen, but instead promoted its growth.

A preliminary note by Bell and Hoskins (1966) described experimental transmission of *G. homari* to Dungeness crabs, *Cancer magister* Dana, and spot shrimps, *Pandalus platyceros*. Infection was achieved by intramuscular inoculation, but not by ingestion or contact. Mortalities were produced in both species.

Cornick and Stewart (1968a) have published an extensive study of the natural defense mechanisms of the lobster against *G. homari* and other bacteria. Experimental infection with *Gaffkya* was almost invariably fatal; even at doses approximating only five organisms per lobster, 90% of the experimental animals were killed in 17 days. This indicates lack of effective defense against the pathogen. Using four different bacteria, one of which was *G. homari*, Cornick and Stewart found lobster serum *in vitro* to be bactericidal or bacteriostatic for all but *G. homari*, whose growth was stimulated. Lobster serum also agglutinated *in vitro* eight different bacteria, but not *G. homari*. Fluorescent-labeled pathogens were found to be actively phagocytized *in vivo*. Phagocyte numbers were markedly reduced after injections of bacteria, but returned to normal in a few hours. Some evidence for possible inactivation of *G. homari* was seen in the formation of nodules in the gills containing tightly clumped reddish-brown tissue cells containing the pathogens. That this defense mechanism is not effective is indicated by the fact that low dosages are able to establish fatal infection. The Atlantic rock crab, *Cancer irroratus,* was found to be susceptible to *Gaffkya homari* by Cornick and Stewart (1968b). Moderate to heavy infections were produced experimentally. The mean time to death was 6 weeks, as opposed to less than 3 weeks for lobsters. The authors believed that the activity of serum agglutinins of the crab might account in part for the milder infection, and suggested that crabs might serve as reservoirs of infection for lobsters. A related study by Stewart and Dingle (1968), comparing sera of the crabs *Cancer irroratus, C. borealis,* and *Hyas coarctatus,* disclosed no differences that would exclude *G. homari* as a potential pathogen for *C. borealis* or *H. coarcticus.*

A second bacterial disease of lobsters, known as "shell disease" (Hess, 1937), is caused by chitin-destroying, gram-negative bacilli. Hess isolated chitin-degrading bacteria from live lobsters impounded at Yarmouth, Nova Scotia, but collected from various parts of the Canadian Maritime provinces. This was the first report of attacks by such microorganisms on living Crustacea. The disease was characterized by a pitting and sculpturing of the exoskeleton (Fig. 47); although it was first seen in impounded lobsters, similar conditions were later observed in freshly caught lobsters from several widely separated Canadian fishing grounds. Initial lesions occurred on the walking legs, and were distinguished by white outer margins, from which the bacteria were most readily isolated. Hess found the disease relatively rare in natural populations but noted severe shell erosion and weakening of lobsters stored in pounds over the winter. Microorganisms isolated were biochemically and physiologically similar to *Bacillus chitinovorous* type II and type XIV of Benton (1935). All isolates were able to decompose pure chitin in saline solution containing no other nitrogen or carbon source. None of Hess' isolates—nor, for that matter, isolates prepared in subsequent work—was reported to reproduce the disease experimentally.

Significant mortalities of lobsters accompanied the shell disease; Taylor (1948) found that 71% of infected captive lobsters died from the disease, but observed no correlation between mortality and intensity of external shell erosion. Contraction of the disease by healthy lobsters placed in seawater tanks with infected individuals indicated direct transmission. The disease developed slowly, requiring at least 3 months before

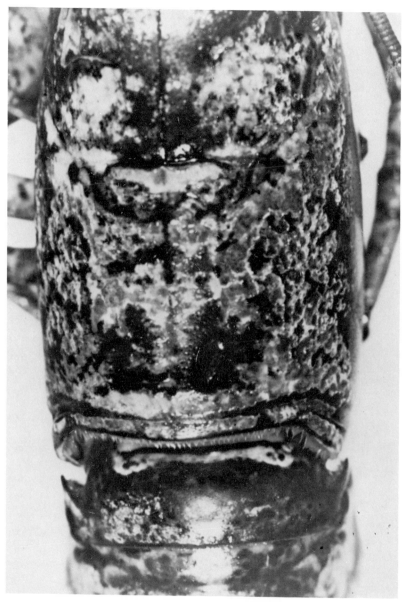

Fig. 47. Shell disease of lobsters caused by chitin-destroying bacteria.

the advanced stages were reached. Progress of chitin destruction was directly temperature-dependent and new shell laid down after molting was not affected, except by reinfection.

Sawyer and Taylor (1949) observed that shell disease produced thickening or complete destruction of the chitinous layer of the gill filaments. No living gill tissue was attacked, but the authors postulated respiratory impairment as an important consequence of the disease. The infection appeared to be entirely external, confined to the exoskeleton; it did not invade living tissues nor was it transmitted internally. Sawyer and Taylor also reported the disease to be present on the Maine coast as well as in Canada, and considered it a potential threat to the lobster industry, in view of the ease of transmission and the observed mortalities of captive individuals. The method of infection of lobsters is unknown; lodging of bacteria in pores and ducts of the shell was proposed by Sawyer and Taylor as a route of invasion.

Another recently recognized disease of lobsters from the Maine coast, probably of fungus etiology, is called "mottling disease." Characterized by yellowish splotches in an otherwise dark green exoskeleton (Fig. 48), the condition has been known for many years as a color variation. Affected individuals are called "leopard lobsters" (Herrick, 1895, 1911). The shell condition and color result from progressive growth of areas of necrosis in underlying tissues and, in advanced cases, even blisters of the shell. The areas of necrosis expand slowly in lobsters held in seawater tanks. Our histological examination of diseased tissues disclosed numerous Schiff-positive, subspherical, heavy-walled bodies, 30–60 μ in diameter. Tentatively, the organism is considered a chytrid fungus. Preliminary attempts at culture and transmission have been unsuccessful. The disease occurs infrequently in Gulf of Maine lobster populations and has not been reported from other areas.

Dannevig (1928, 1939) in a report on Norwegian lobster hatcheries, described infection and destruction of eggs on the female by the suctorian *Ephelota gemmipara* Hertwig. The protozoan was found on newly caught individuals, and increased tremendously on lobsters in hatching boxes. Dannevig attributed substantial (90%) decreases in production of larvae to the effects of the parasite. The organism was abundant only in certain years.

The gregarine protozoan, *Porospora gigantea* (Van Beneden), has been reported as parasitic in the digestive tract of the European lobster (Hatt, 1928, 1931), and was found in all of 202 American lobsters from the Magdalen Islands, Gulf of Saint Lawrence, Canada, by Montreuil (1954). *Porospora nephropis* has been described from the Norway lobster, *Nephrops norvegicus* L., by Léger and Duboscq (1915) and Tuzet and Ormières (1961).

Fig. 48. Mottling disease of the lobster caused by a presumed fungus pathogen.

Spiny lobsters (family Palinuridae) are of economic importance in many parts of the world, but little is known about their diseases (Sims, 1966). One fatal and apparently infectious disease of *Panulirus argus* (Latreille) from Florida waters was observed by Sims (1967). Affected individuals became disoriented and their abdomens were "milky"—a condition reminiscent of microsporidan infections of shrimps (Sprague, 1950a) and freshwater crayfishes (Sprague, 1950b; Sogandares-Bernal, 1962), as was pointed out by Sims. A fungus disease of *Palinurus vulgaris* and *Homarus vulgaris* was associated with mortalities in the Aquarium of Livorno in Italy (Sordi, 1958). Two fungi, *Ramularia branchialis* and *Didymaria palinuri*, both members of Fungi Imperfecti, were isolated from extensive gill lesions, but *R. branchialis* was considered the principal pathogen.

b. *Diseases Caused by Helminths*

Immature aspidobothrid trematodes, *Stichocotyle nephropis* Cunningham, encyst in the stomach and intestinal walls of lobsters, *Nephrops norvegicus* and *Homarus americanus*, from Europe and North America (Cunningham, 1887; Nickerson, 1894; Herrick, 1895; Odhner, 1910; Montreuil, 1954; MacKenzie, 1963). Montreuil found the parasite in lobsters taken near the mouth of the Bay of Fundy in the Gulf of Maine but not in more than 500 lobsters examined from the Gulf of Saint Lawrence. Adult *S. nephropis* parasitize several species of skates and rays (Odhner, 1898; Linton, 1940).

A larval nematode, tentatively assigned to the genus *Ascarophis* Van Beneden, has been recognized from lobsters taken off northeastern United States (Anonymous, 1966; Uzmann, 1967a). Adults of the genus occur in fishes, particularly gadoids (Uspenskaya, 1963). Larvae occurred commonly in lobsters from Georges Bank and several canyons along the edge of the Continental Shelf south of Cape Cod, Massachusetts, but were absent in lobsters from near the coast. The larvae were encysted in the rectal wall of 25% of the offshore lobsters examined by Uzmann, who speculated that larvae from lobsters reach maturity in abundant cod (*Gadus morhua* L.) and haddock, *Melanogrammus aeglefinus* (L.), populations of Georges Bank.

A larval acanthocephalan, probably of the genus *Corynosoma*, was identified in American lobsters from the Gulf of Saint Lawrence and elsewhere in the Canadian Maritime Provinces by Montreuil (1954). The worms were usually encysted in the thin wall of the intestine, although some had apparently perforated the gut and encysted in the heart and body muscles. Montreuil believed that accidental gut perforation may provide a route of entry for secondary invaders, and account for appreciable mortality. Feeding experiments with cats and seals suggested that the stage of *Corynosoma* in the lobster is not infective to mammals.

Havinga (1921), in a discussion of artificial lobster rearing, described the attachment of a small green annelid worm, *Histriobdella homari* Van Beneden, to the eggs and to all parts of the bodies of larval and adult lobsters in Norway. He attributed poor success in production of larvae to effects of the worm. The same parasite had been observed earlier (Sund, 1914, 1915) in massive numbers on eggs of lobsters held in floating boxes at Korshavn, Norway, where it was held responsible for destruction of the brood. Every female lobster was infested with thousands of worms, and they also occurred on lobster larvae. Although *H. homari* had not been reported previously from American lobsters, Uzmann (1967b) has recently found it to be widely distributed on the gills of lobsters from New England coastal waters (Maine to Connecticut) and from Georges Bank.

Copepods have been reported as parasites of lobsters. *Nicothoë astaci,* known as the "gill maggot," and a member of the family Choniostomatidae, occurs on the gills of the European lobster, *Homarus vulgaris,* and a harpaticid, *Unicaleuthes,* occurs on the exoskeleton of the American lobster. A copepod "related to *Anchorella*" was reported by Gordon (1966) to occur in the vas deferens of *Nephrops norvegicus;* this may be the same parasite reported earlier (but not identified) by Thomson (1896) from the vas deferens of *Nephrops norvegicus*. The parasite reached a length of 4 cm, and was considered to cause occlusion and degeneration of the duct. Recently Kabata (1966, 1967) described three other copepods from *Nephrops: Nicothoë analata* from *Nephrops sinensis* taken in the South China Sea; *N. brucei* from *Nephrops sagamiensis* Parisi from Japan and *Nephrops andamanicus* Wood-Mason from South Africa; and *N. simplex* from *Nephrops japonicus* Tapparone-Canefri from Japan.

c. *Tumors and Other Abnormalities*

One of the earliest observations of neoplasms in invertebrates, according to Scharrer and Lockhead (1950), was made by McIntosh and reported by Prince (1897). A lobster tumor originated in the stomach wall, pushed through the carapace behind the eyes, became enlarged, and finally killed the lobster.

Color and structural abnormalities are well known in Crustacea. Particularly numerous are reports of partial albinism and absence of certain pigments in crabs and lobsters. White American lobsters, *Homarus americanus,* were reported by Templeman (1948). He also noted a bicolored condition seen earlier by Herrick (1895, 1911). A similar bicolored condition has been seen repeatedly in the European lobster, *Homarus vulgaris* (Schaanning, 1929; Dexter, 1959). Lobsters with this condition have an exact dividing line in the center of the cephalothorax and abdomen, with normal pigmentation on one side and red, blue, or white on the other. Some individuals had other combinations of colors, but the exact dividing line suggests modification in color-producing genes in the earliest division of the egg. Still other individuals have abnormal coloration confined to certain appendages, or certain parts of the body. Chace and Moore (1959) even found a bicolored lobster which was also a gynandromorph, again suggesting genetic change in the first egg division. Color variations in blue crabs, *Callinectes sapidus,* have been described (Rathbun, 1930; Newcombe, 1945; Haefner, 1961; Sims and Joyce, 1965). Often partial albinism, especially in the appendages, is seen. Complete albinism, especially in the appendages, is seen. Complete albinism is less common, but several examples have been reported.

Abnormal chelipeds in lobsters and crabs have received some attention in the literature. Herrick (1895), Emmel (1907), and Templeman (1948) all observed lobsters with two crusher claws, and more rarely two biting claws. Cole (1910) found a double extra claw on the cheliped of a lobster, and he was one of many who have noted extra processes on the claws of crabs (Faxon, 1881; Leavitt, 1909; Verrill, 1908). The spectrum of claw anomalies in decapods has been well illustrated by Shuster *et al.* (1963). They pointed out that such anomalies occur most frequently in the chelipeds, which have the greatest capacity for regeneration, and that they probably are most often produced by injury while the exoskeleton is soft. The authors also pointed out, however, that some abnormalities persist through molting.

3. Shrimps

Many shrimps, particularly those of the families Penaeidae and Pandalidae, are of worldwide commercial significance. Shrimps are the most valuable fishery resource in the United States (Lyles, 1966). Parasites and diseases that may have adverse effects on shrimp stocks have been studied, particularly in the Gulf of Mexico. Several diseases caused by Microsporida are known, and larval helminths—trematodes, cestodes, and nematodes—have been reported. Isopods and rhizocephalans have also been observed.

a. Microbial Diseases

The only scientific report of virus disease in marine invertebrates is a very incomplete one concerning a disease of European edible crabs (Vago, 1966) considered earlier, although Hall (1966) made fleeting reference to a nonpathogenic virus in shrimps from the east coast of Africa. The report, without substantiating evidence, merely stated that the virus occurs frequently in *Penaeus indicus* in the Rufiji Delta, its presence being indicated by a "whitish blotchy disfigurement dorsally under the integument." Further study might disclose other causes for the condition; the report is mentioned here only because of the extreme paucity of information about viruses in marine invertebrates.

A disease of possible bacterial etiology in English prawns, *Palaemon serratus*, was described briefly by Anderson and Conroy (1968). Labeled "brown spot disease" and characterized by erosion and destruction of the exoskeleton, the disease was particularly evident in crowded culture tanks. Although the etiology was undetermined, the authors observed an association between the occurrence of spots and the presence of myxobacteria, and also alluded to other similar crustacean diseases caused by chitinivorous bacteria.

A mycosis affecting English prawns was also described in some detail by Anderson and Conroy (1968). The disease seemed to be associated with damage to the exoskeleton, and was characterized by massive fungal invasion of the hemocoel, muscles, and sometimes the gonads. The course of infection was rapid, and mortalities occurred in culture tanks. Isolates were tentatively identified as *Pythium sp.*, and transmission was effected by inoculation and feeding.

The only other fungus disease known to affect shrimps was reported by Uzmann and Haynes (1969) from the pandalid, *Dichelopandalus leptocerus* (Smith), trawled on the continental shelf off the northeast coast of the United States. The chytrid-like parasite invaded the gills, producing a dark brown discoloration. Diseased shrimp were found at 79 of 126 sampling locations from southern Nova Scotia to Long Island, and prevalence in individual samples reached 96%. The authors suggested that the infection could have serious effects on the respiratory efficiency of diseased individuals, and that it could be an important mortality factor in this and other species of shrimps.

Protozoan parasites have been shown to be of significance to commercial shrimp populations of the Gulf of Mexico. Several microsporidan protozoa cause a condition known as "cottony" or "milky" shrimps. *Nosema nelsoni* was described by Sprague (1950a) from the brown shrimp, *Penaeus aztecus* Ives. Affected body muscles had an opaque white discoloration, and black pigment spots occurred externally. The disease was common in bait shrimps as well as in those processed as food. Infected individuals did not survive well in bait tanks, and were also discarded in processing plants, thus representing significant losses to the industry (Woodburn et al., 1957; Hutton et al., 1959b). Sprague (1950a) found microsporidan spores in the gonads of the white shrimp, Penaeus setiferus (L.), some of which he described as Thelohania penaei. Earlier, Viosca (1945) reported that "about 90%" of white shrimp in Louisiana waters were infected in 1919 by a protozoan disease (not further identified) which destroyed the reproductive organs. If the disease was caused by T. penaei, the microsporidan may play a role in fluctuations of the host species when present at epizootic levels. Iversen and Manning (1959) described still another microsporidan, Thelohania duorara, from the musculature of pink shrimp, Penaeus duorarum Burkenroad, of the Gulf of Mexico. Infected individuals were relatively rare, however, in landed catches. Brazilian brown shrimp, Penaeus brasiliensis, also harbor the same parasite (Iversen and Van Meter, 1964). Other species of Thelohania have been reported from the body muscles of European shrimps (Henneguy and Thélohan, 1892; Gurley, 1893).

Several gregarine Protozoa also occur in shrimps. Sprague (1954) tentatively identified as Nematopsis penaeus a gregarine from the digestive tract of brown shrimp from Louisiana, and mentioned the possibility of extensive damage to the intestinal epithelium of heavily infected individuals. The same parasite was observed by Kruse (1959a, 1959b) and Hutton et al. (1959b) in several species of shrimps from Florida. Another species, Nematopsis duorari, was recently identified and described by Kruse (1966) from the digestive tract of Florida pink shrimp. Kruse demonstrated by infection experiments that shrimp become infected by eating mucus strings from bivalve molluscs in which the spore stages occur.

Kruse (1959a,b) erected a new genus, Cephalolobus, for a gregarine, C. penaeus, from the chitinous lining of the stomach of pink and brown shrimps of the northern Gulf coast of Florida. Another member of the genus, C. petiti, infects commercial shrimp, Solenocera membranacea (Risso) from the French Mediterranean coast (Théodoridès, 1964).

Ciliates also occur as parasites and epibionts of shrimps. The peritrich, Lagenophrys lunatus, was described from Leander squilla in Japan by Imamura (1940). The apostome, Terebrospira lenticularis, an ectoparasite which perforates the exoskeleton of Palaemon varians, was identified and studied by Debaisieux (1960). A complex life cycle, intimately related to molting of the host, was capable of producing heavy parasitization in restricted environments.

b. Diseases Caused by Helminths

Shrimps occasionally harbor larval helminths. Metacercariae of the trematode *Opecoeloides fimbriatus* (Linton) were found by Hutton *et al.* (1959b) and Sogandares-Bernal and Hutton (1959) in several Florida species. Larval *Microphallus* sp. have been reported from the body muscles and hepatopancreas of pink shrimp (Hutton *et al.*, 1959a,b).

Several larval cestodes of the order Trypanorhyncha have been found in the digestive gland and other organs of shrimps. Larval *Prochristianella penaei* Kruse were identified from four species of shrimps—brown, pink, white, and humpback (*Trachypeneus constrictus* (Stimpson))— from the Florida coast (Sparks and Mackin, 1957; Woodburn *et al.*, 1957; Hutton *et al.*, 1959b; Kruse, 1959a,b). Aldrich (1965) found the same cestode larvae in *Penaeus aztecus* and *P. setiferus* from the Texas coast. The adult worm was identified from the Atlantic stingray *Dasyatis sabina* LeSueur. Another trypanorhynch larvae, unidentified was seen by Ward (1962) in great numbers in the abdominal muscles, gills, and pericardium of white shrimp from the Gulf of Mexico.

Typanorhynch larvae have been found in commercial shrimps from other parts of the world. Yamaguti (1934) reported larvae, probably *Tetrarhynchus rubromaculatus* Diesing, in *Penaeopsis* sp. from Japan. Heldt (1949) took a larval cestode resembling *Eutetrarhynchus ruficollis* (Eysenhardt) from *Penaeus trisulcatus* Leach from the North African coast.

A large endoparasitic turbellarian, *Kronborgia caridicola*, has been found in North Atlantic shrimps from Greenland by Kanneworff and Christensen (1966). The parasitic female lies tightly coiled and occupying much of the body cavity of the host, rendering the shrimp sterile, and probably killing it before the mature worm leaves to secrete a cocoon and deposit egg capsules. Many cocoons were collected from level shrimp bottoms. Infected shrimps of three species, *Lebbeus polaris*, *Eualus machilenta*, and *Paciphaea tarda*, were taken by commercial shrimp trawlers.

Larval nematodes of the genus *Contracaecum* were found in Florida shrimps by Woodburn *et al.* (1957), Hutton *et al.* (1959b), and Kruse (1959b). Margolis and Butler (1954) observed adult nematodes, *C. aduncum*, in a single specimen of northern pink shrimp, *Pandalus borealis* Krøyer, from British Columbia, Canada.

c. Diseases Caused by Parasitic Crustacea

Epicaridean isopods are well-known parasites of Crustacea, and several genera occur on shrimps (Fig. 49). Baer (1951), for example, stated

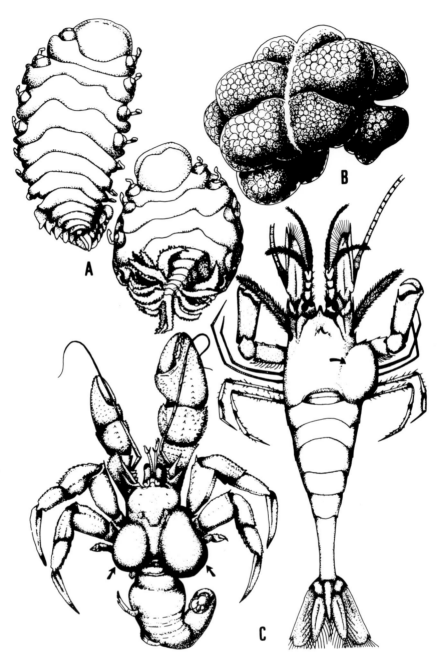

Fig. 49. Parasitic isopods and their effects. (A) Bopyrid isopods; (B) gravid female Entoniscid isopod; (C) host abnormalities (arrows) resulting from isopod parasitization. (Redrawn from Shiino, 1965; Baer, 1951; Waterman, 1960, 1961; Williams, 1965.)

that the epicaridean, *Hemiarthrus abdominalis* (Krøyer), had been recovered from 20 species of shrimps belonging to the genera *Pandalus* and *Spirontocaris*. Uzmann (1967c) has found *H. abdominalis* on northern pink shrimp from the Gulf of Maine. The parasite has also been reported on *P. borealis* from Greenland (Horsted and Smidt, 1956) but not from Norway or England (Dahl, 1949; Allen, 1966). *Bopyrus fougerouxi* parasitizes the prawn, *Palaemon serratus* (Brian and Parenzan, 1967; Nicol, 1967), causing suppression of breeding characters.

Ricketts and Calvin (1962) described the occurrence of the bopyrid isopod *Argeia pugettensis*, which caused unilateral protuberances of the carapace of the black-tailed shrimp, *Crago nigricauda* (Stimpson), from the Pacific coast of the United States. Infestation was estimated at 3–5%. Japanese "red prawns," *Penaeopsis akayebi* Rathbun, are frequently (up to 70%) infested with another bopyrid *Epipenaeon japonicus* Thielemann. Hiraiwa and Sato (1939) found the gonads of parasitized individuals reduced or, in some males, completely atrophied. Presence of the branchial parasite, *Bopyrus squillarum*, on the shrimp, *Leander serrifer*, causes suppression of the ovaries and the breeding characters of the pleopods (Yoshida, 1952).

Several rhizocephalans have been reported as parasites of shrimps. Potts (1912) described *Mycetomorpha vancouverensis* from *Crago communis* Rathbun, and Calman (1898) described *Sylon hippolytes* from the dock shrimp, *Pandalus danae* Stimpson, both from Puget Sound, Washington.

REFERENCES—MOLLUSCA

Adam, W. (1938). Sur la présence d'une larve de cestode (Tetrarhynchidae) dans la cavité palléale d'un *Octopus* des Iles Andamans. *Bull. Musee Roy. Hist. Nat. Belg.* (*Brussels*) 14, No. 35, 1–4.

Adams, C. B. (1839). Observations on some species of the marine shells of Massachusetts, with descriptions of five new species. *Boston J. Nat. Hist.* 2, 262–289.

Alderman, D. J., and Jones, E. B. G. (1967). Shell diseases of *Ostrea edulis* L. *Nature* 216, 797–798.

Allen, J. F. (1958). Feeding habits of two species of *Odostomia. Nautilus* 72, 11–15.

Andreu, B. (1960). Dispersión de *Mytilicola intestinalis* Steuer en el mejillón de cultivo a flote de la rías de Arosa y Vigo (N.W. de España). *4th Reunion Prod. Pesquerias, Barcelona, 1960* pp. 115–118.

Andreu, B. (1961). Un parásito del mejillón. Propagación del copépodo parásito *Mytilicola intestinalis* en el mejillón de la rías bajas. *Rev. Econ. Galicia, Vigo* 17–18, 12–18.

Andreu, B. (1963). Propagación del copépodo parásito *Mytilicola intestinalis* en el mejillón cultivado de la rías gallegas (N.W. de España). *Invest. Pesquera* 24, 3–20.

Andrews, J. D. (1955). Notes on fungus parasites of bivalve mollusks in Chesapeake Bay. *Proc. Natl. Shellfisheries Assoc.* **45**, 157–163.

Andrews, J. D. (1964). Oyster mortality studies in Virginia. IV. MSX in James River public seed beds. *Proc. Natl. Shellfisheries Assoc.* **53**, 65–84.

Andrews, J. D. (1965). Infection experiments in nature with *Dermocystidium marinum* in Chesapeake Bay. *Chesapeake Sci.* **6**, 60–67.

Andrews, J. D. (1966). Oyster mortality studies in Virginia. V. Epizootiology of MSX, protistan pathogen of oysters. *Ecology* **47**, 19–31.

Andrews, J. D. (1967a). Oyster mortality studies in Virginia. VI. History and distribution of *Minchinia nelsoni,* a pathogen of oysters, in Virginia. *Chesapeake Sci.* **8**, 1–13.

Andrews, J. D. (1967b). Interaction of two diseases of oysters in natural waters. *Proc. Natl. Shellfisheries Assoc.* **57**, 38–49.

Andrews, J. D. (1968). Oyster mortality studies in Virginia. VII. Review of epizootiology and origin of *Minchinia nelsoni. Proc. Natl. Shellfisheries Assoc.* **58**, 23–36.

Andrews, J. D., and Hewatt, W. G. (1954). Incidence of *Dermocystidium marinum,* Mackin, Collier, and Owen, a fungus disease of oysters, in Virginia. *Conv. Add. Natl. Shellfisheries Assoc., 1953* p. 79 (abstr.).

Andrews, J. D., and Hewatt, W. G. (1957). Oyster mortality studies in Virginia. II. The fungus disease caused by *Dermocystidium marinum* in oysters of Chesapeake Bay. *Ecol. Monographs* **27**, 1–26.

Andrews, J. D., and Wood, J. L. (1967). Oyster mortality studies in Virginia. VI. History and distribution of *Minchinia nelsoni,* a pathogen of oysters, in Virginia. *Chesapeake Sci.* **8**, 1–13.

Andrews, J. D., Wood, J. L., and Hoese, H. D. (1962). Oyster mortality studies in Virginia. III. Epizootiology of a disease caused by *Haplosporidium costale* Wood and Andrews. *J. Insect Pathol.* **4**, 327–343.

Ankel, F., and Christensen, A. M. (1963). Non-specificity in host selection by *Odostomia scalaris* MacGillivary. *Vidensk. Medd. Dansk Naturh. Foren.* **125**, 321–325.

Anonymous (C. A. Farley). (1965). New parasite disease under study. *Com. Fisheries Rev.* **27**, No. 1, 44.

Atkins, D. (1931). On abnormal conditions of the gills in *Mytilus edulis.* II. Structural abnormalities, with a note on the method of division of the mantle cavity in normal individuals. *J. Marine Biol. Assoc. U. K.* **17**, 489–543.

Atkins, D. (1954). A marine fungus *Plectospira dubia* n. sp. (Saprolegniaceae), infecting crustacean eggs and small Crustacea. *J. Marine Biol. Assoc. U. K.* **33**, 721–732.

Baer, J. G. (1944). Immunité et réactions immunitaires chez les invertébrés. *Schweiz. Z. Allgem. Pathol. Bakteriol.* **7**, 442–462.

Baird, R. H., Bolster, G. C., and Cole, H. A. (1950). *Mytilicola intestinalis* Steuer in the European flat oyster (*Ostrea edulis*). *Nature* **168**, 560.

Bang, F. B. (1961). Reaction to injury in the oyster (*Crassostrea virginica*). *Biol. Bull.* **121**, 57–68.

Bang, F. B. (1962). Serological aspects of immunity in invertebrates. *Nature* **196**, 88–89.

Bang, F. B. (1967). Serological responses among invertebrates other than insects. *Federation Proc.* **26**, 1680–1684.

Bang, F. B., and Bang, B. G. (1962). Studies on sipunculid blood: Immunologic properties of coelomic fluid and morphology of "urn cells." *Cahiers Biol. Marine* **3**, 363–374.

Bang, F. B., and Lemma, A. (1962). Bacterial infection and reaction to injury in some echinoderms. *J. Insect Pathol.* **4**, 401–414.

Barrow, J. H., Jr., and Taylor, B. C. (1966). Fluorescent-antibody studies of haplosporidian parasites of oysters in Chesapeake and Delaware Bays. *Science* **153**, 1531–1533.

Bassedas, M. (1950). Sobre la presencia de *Mytilicola intestinalis* Steuer en Barcelona. *Publ. Inst. Biol. Apl. (Barcelona)* **7**, 153–154.

Blake, J. H. (1929). An abnormal clam. *Nautilus* **38**, 89–90.

Bolster, G. C. (1954). The biology and dispersal of *Mytilicola intestinalis* Steuer, a copepod parasite of mussels. *Min. Agr. Fish, Fish. Invest., London* [2] **18**, No. 6, 1–30.

Bovee, E. C. (1965). An emendation of the ameba genus *Flabellula* and a description of *Vannella* gen. nov. *Trans. Amer. Microscop. Soc.* **84**, 217–227.

Bresciani, J., and Fenchel, T. (1965). Studies on dicyemid Mesozoa. I. The fine structure of the adult (the nematogen and rhombogen stage). *Vidensk. Medd. Dansk Naturh. Foren.* **128**, 85–92.

Brienne, H. (1964). Observations sur l'infestation des moules de pertuis Breton par *Mytilicola intestinalis* Steuer. *Rev. Trav. Inst. Peches Maritimes* **28**, 205–230.

Butler, P. A. (1953). The southern oyster drill. *Proc. Natl. Shellfieries Assoc.* **44**, 67–75.

Cantacuzène, J. (1923). Le problème de l'immunité chez les invertebrés. *Compt. Rend. Soc. Biol. (75th ann.)* 48–119.

Cantacuzène, J. (1928). Recherches sur les réactions d'immunité chez les invertebrés. I. Réactions d'immunité chez *Sipunculus nudus*. *Exptl. Microbiol.* **1**, 7–80.

Carriker, M. R. (1955). Critical review of biology and control of oyster drills *Urosalpinx* and *Eupleura*. *U. S. Fish Wildlife Serv., Spec. Sci. Rept. Fisheries* **148**, 1–150.

Caspers, H. (1939). Über Vorkommen und Metamorphose von *Mytilicola intestinalis* Steuer (Copepoda parasitica) in der südlichen Nordsee. *Zool. Anz.* **126**, Nos. 7/8, 161–171.

Caullery, M., and Chappellier, A. (1906). *Anurosporidium pelseneeri*, n. g. n. sp., haplosporidie infectant les sporocysts d'un trématode parasite de *Donax trunculus* L. *Compt. Rend. Soc. Biol.* **60**, 325–328.

Cépède, C. (1911). Le cycle évolutif et les affinités systématiques de l'haplosporidie des *Donax*. *Compt. Rend.* **153**, 507–509.

Certes, A. (1882). Note sur les parasites et les commensaux de l'huître. *Bull. Soc. Zool. France* **7**, 347–353.

Chatton, E., and Lwoff, A. (1934). Sur un cilié thigmotriche nouveau: *Gargarius gargarius* n. gen., n. sp., de *Mytilus edulis*. *Bull. Soc. Zool. France* **39**, 375–376.

Chatton, E., and Lwoff, A. (1950). Recherches sur les ciliés thigmotriches. II. *Arch. Zool. Exptl. Gen.* **86**, 393–485.

Cheng, T. C. (1964). "The Biology of Animal Parasites." Saunders, Philadelphia, Pennsylvania.

Cheng, T. C. (1965). Histochemical observations on changes in the lipid composition of the American oyster, *Crassostrea virginica* (Gmelin), parasitized by the trematode *Bucephalus* sp. *J. Invertebrate Pathol.* **7**, 398–407.

Cheng, T. C. (1966). The coracidium of the cestode *Tylocephalum* and the migration and fate of this parasite in the American oyster, *Crassostrea virginica*. *Trans. Am. Microscop. Soc.* **85**, 246–255.

Cheng, T. C. (1967). Marine molluscs as hosts for symbioses with a review of known parasites of commercially important species. *Advan. Marine Biol.* **5**, 1–424.

Cheng, T. C., and Burton, R. W. (1965a). Relationships between *Bucephalus* sp. and *Crassostrea virginica:* Histopathology and sites of infection, *Chesapeake Sci.* **6**, 3–16.

Cheng, T. C., and Burton, R. W. (1965b). Relationships between *Bucephalus* sp. and *Crassostrea virginica:* A histochemical study of some carbohydrates and carbohydrate complexes occurring in the host and parasite. *Parasitology* **56**, 111–122.

Cheng, T. C., Shuster, C. N., Jr., and Anderson, A. H. (1966). A comparative study of the susceptibility and response of eight species of marine pelecypods to the trematode *Himasthla quissetensis. Trans. Am. Microscop. Soc.* **85**, 284–295.

Chew, K. K., Sparks, A. K., and Katkansky, S. C. (1964). First record of *Mytilicola orientalis* Mori in the California mussel *Mytilus californianus* Conrad. *J. Fisheries Res. Board Can.* **21**, 205–207.

Chew, K. K., Sparks, A. K., and Katkansky, S. C. (1965). Preliminary results on the seasonal size distribution of *Mytilicola orientalis* and the effect of this parasite on the condition of the Pacific oyster, *Crassostrea gigas. J. Fisheries Res. Board Can.* **22**, 1099–1101.

Christensen, A. M., and McDermott, J. J. (1958). Life history and biology of the oyster crab, *Pinnotheres ostreum* Say. *Biol. Bull.* **114**, 146–179.

Chu, G. W. T. C., and Cutress, C. E. (1954). *Austrobilharzia variglandis* (Miller and Northrup, 1926) Penner, 1953 (Trematoda: Schistosomatidae) in Hawaii with notes on its biology. *J. Parasitol.* **40**, 515–523.

Clarke, M. R. (1966). A review of the systematics and ecology of the oceanic squids. *Advan. Marine Biol.* **4**, 91–300.

Clarke, M. R., and Maul, G. E. (1962). A description of the "scaled" squid *Lepidoteuthis grimaldi* Joubin 1895. *Proc. Zool. Soc. London* **139**, 97–118.

Clench, W. J. (1948). A remarkable malformed specimen of *Venus campechiensis* Gmelin. *Rev. Soc. Malacol.* **6**, 10.

Clench, W. J., and Merrill, A. S. (1963). Some shell malformations. *Shells and their Neighbors* No. **16**, 1–2.

Cobb, N. A. (1930). A nemic parasite of *Pecten. J. Parasitol.* **17**, 104–105.

Coe, W. R. (1946). A resurgent population of the California bay-mussel (*Mytilus edulis diegensis*). *J. Morphol.* **78**, 85–103.

Coe, W. R. (1955). Ecology of the bean clam *Donax gouldi* on the coast of southern California. *Ecology* **36**, 512–515.

Cole, H. A. (1935). On some larval trematode parasites of the mussel (*Mytilus edulis*) and the cockle (*Cardium edule*). *Parasitology* **27**, 276–280.

Cole, H. A. (1950). Shell disease in re-laid French oysters. *Nature* **166**, 19–20.

Cole, H. A. (1951). Le *Mytilicola* en Angleterre. *Rev. Trav. Office Sci. Tech. Peches Maritimes* **17**, 59–61.

Cole, H. A., and Hancock, D. A. (1955). *Odostomia* as a pest of oysters and mussels. *J. Marine Biol. Assoc. U. K.* **34**, 25–31.

Cole, H. A., and Hancock, D. A. (1956). Progress in oyster research in Britain 1949–1954, with special reference to the control of pests and diseases. *Rapport.*

Proces-Verbaux Reunions, Conseil Perm. Intern. Exploration Mer **140**, No. 3, 24–29.

Cole, H. A., and Savage, R. E. (1951). The effect of the parasitic copepod, *Mytilicola intestinalis* (Steuer) upon the condition of mussels. *Parasitology* **41**, 156–161.

Cole, H. A., and Waugh, G. D. (1956). Shell disease in Portuguese oysters. *Nature* **178**, 422.

Cooley, N. R. (1958). Incidence and life history of *Parorchis acanthus,* a digenetic trematode, in the southern oyster drill, *Thais haemastoma. Proc. Natl. Shellfisheries Assoc.* **48**, 174–188.

Cooley, N. R. (1962). Studies on *Parorchis acanthus* (Trematoda: Digenea) as a biological control for the southern oyster drill, *Thais haemastoma. U. S. Fish Wildlife Serv., Fishery Bull.* **62**, 77–91.

Couch, J. A. (1967). Concurrent haplosporidian infections of the oyster, *Crassostrea virginica* (Gmelin). *J. Parasitol.* **53**, 248–253.

Couch, J. A., and Rosenfield, A. (1968). Epizootiology of *Minchinia costalis* and *Minchinia nelsoni* in oysters introduced into Chincoteague Bay, Virginia. *Proc. Natl. Shellfisheries Assoc.* **58**, 51–59.

Couch, J. A., Farley, C. A., and Rosenfield, A. (1966). Sporulation of *Minchinia nelsoni* (Haplosporida, Haplosporidiidae) in *Crassostrea virginica* (Gmelin). *Science* **153**, 1529–1531.

Davis, H. C., Loosanoff, V. L., Weston, W. H., and Martin, C. (1954). A fungus disease in clam and oyster larvae. *Science* **120**, 36–38.

De Lagoda, A. (1868). Note sur une variété anormale du *Torinia variegata,* Lamarck. *J. Conchyliol.* **16**, 264–265.

de Vincentiis, M., and Renzoni, A. (1963). Sulla presenza di uno sporozoo in ovociti di *Mytilus galloprovincialis* Lam. *Arch. Zool. Ital.* **47**, 21–26.

Dickie, L. M., and Medcof, J. C. (1963). Causes of mass mortalities of scallops (*Placopecten magellanicus*) in the southwestern Gulf of Saint Lawrence. *J. Fisheries Res. Board Can.* **20**, 451–482.

Dobell, C. C. (1909). Some observations on the Infusoria parasitic in Cephalopoda. *Quart. J. Microscop. Sci.* **53**, 183–199.

Dollfus, R. P. (1914). *Trochicola enterica* nov. gen. nov. sp., eucopépode parasite de l'intestin des troques. *Compt. Rend.* **158**, 1528–1531.

Dollfus, R. P. (1921a). Résumé de nos principales connaissance pratiques sur les maladies et les ennemis de l'huître. *Notes Mem. Office Sci. Tech. Peches Maritimes* **7**, 1–46.

Dollfus, R. P. (1921b). Sur les cellules a mucus de l'huître (*Ostrea edulis* L.) et la mycose de Pettit. *Compt. Rend. Soc. Biol.* **85**, 449–452.

Dollfus, R. P. (1923). Énumération des cestodes du plancton et des invertébrés marins. II. Mollusques céphalopodes et crustacés. *Ann. Parasitol. Humaine Comparee* **1**, 363–394.

Dollfus, R. P. (1927a). Sur une métacercaire progénétique d'Hémiuridae (Trematoda: Digenea). *Bull. Biol. France Belg.* **61**, 49–58.

Dollfus, R. P. (1927b). Notules sur des copépodes parasites de la faune française. (I-III). *Bull. Soc. Zool. France* **52**, 119–121.

Dollfus, R. P. (1929). Addendum a mon "Énumération des cestodes du plancton et des invertébrés marins." *Ann. Parasitol. Humaine Comparee* **7**, 325–347.

Dollfus, R. P. (1946). Parasites des helminths, *Encycl. Biol.* **27**, 1–482.

Dollfus, R. P. (1951). Le copépode *Mytilicola intestinalis* A. Steuer peut-il être la cause d'une maladie épidémique des moules? *Rev. Trav. Office Sci. Tech. Peches Maritimes* **17**, 81–84.

Dollfus, R. P. (1958). Copépodes, isopodes et helminthes parasites de céphalopodes de la Méditerranée et de l'Atlantique Européen. *Faune Mar. Pyrenees-Orientales* No. 1, 61–72.

Dow, R. L., and Wallace, D. E. (1961). The soft-shell clam industry of Maine. *U. S. Fish Wildlife Serv., Circ.* **110**, 1–36.

Dubois, R. (1901a). Sur la mécanisme de la formation des perles fines dans le *Mytilus edulis. Compt. Rend.* **133**, 603–605.

Dubois, R. (1901b). Sur le mode de formation des perles dans *Mytilus edulis* L. *Compt. Rend. Assoc. Franc. Advan. Sci.* **1**, 149–150.

Dubois, R. (1903). L'origine des perles chez le *Mytilus gallo-provincialis. Compt. Rend.* **136**, 178–179.

Dubois, R. (1907a). Sur un sporozoaire parasite de l'huître perlière, *Margaritifera vulgaris* Jam., son rôle dans la formation des perles fines. *Compt. Rend. Soc. Biol.* **62**, 310–311.

Dubois, R. (1907b). Sur les métamorphoses du distome parasite des *Mytilus* perliers. *Compt. Rend. Soc. Biol.* **63**, 334–336.

Dubois, R. (1909). Contribution a l'étude des perles fines de la nacre et des animaux qui les produisent. *Ann. Univ. Lyon* [N.S.] **29**, 1–126.

Durve, V. S., and Bal, D. V. (1960). Shell disease in *Crassostrea gryphoides* (Schlotheim). *Current Sci. (India)* **29**, 489–490.

Ellenby, C. (1947). A copepod parasite of the mussel new to the British fauna. *Nature* **159**, 645–646.

Engle, J. B., and Rosenfield, A. (1963). Progress in oyster mortality studies. *Proc. Gulf Carib. Fish. Inst., 15th. Ann. Sess.* pp. 116–124.

Eyre, J. W. H. (1924). An account of investigations into the cause or causes of the unusual mortality among oysters in English oyster beds during 1920 and 1921. Part II. Appendix D. Final bacteriological report. *Min. Agr. Fish., Fish. Invest., London* [2] **6**, No. 4, 29–39.

Farley, C. A. (1965). Pathologic responses of the oyster, *Crassostrea virginica* (Gmelin), to infection by the protistan parasite, MSX. *Am. Malacol. Un., Bull.* **32**, 23–24 (abstr.).

Farley, C. A. (1967). A proposed life cycle of *Minchinia nelsoni* (Haplosporida, Haplosporidiidae) in the American oyster *Crassostrea virginica. J. Protozool.* **14**, 616–625.

Farley, C. A. (1968). *Minchinia nelsoni* (Haplosporida, Haplosporidiidae) disease syndrome in the American oyster, *Crassostrea virginica. J. Protozool.* **15**, 585–599.

Fenchel, T. (1965). Ciliates from Scandinavian molluscs. *Ophelia* **2**, 71–174.

Fenchel, T. (1966). On the ciliated Protozoa inhabiting the mantle cavity of lamellibranchs. *Malacologia* **5**, 35–36.

Feng, S. Y. (1958). Observations on distribution and elimination of spores of *Nematopsis ostrearum* in oysters. *Proc. Natl. Shellfisheries Assoc.* **48**, 162–173.

Feng, S. Y. (1962). The response of oysters to the introduction of soluble and particulate materials and the factors modifying the response. Ph.D. Thesis, Rutgers University.

Feng, S. Y. (1966). Experimental bacterial infections in the oyster *Crassostrea virginica. J. Invertebrate Pathol.* **8**, 505–511.

Feng, S. Y. (1967). Responses of molluscs to foreign bodies, with special reference to the oyster. *Federation Proc.* **26**, 1685–1692.

Feng, S. Y., and Stauber, L. A. (1968). Experimental hexamitiasis in the oyster *Crassostrea virginica. J. Invertebrate Pathol.* 10, 94–110.

Field, I. A. (1923). Biology and economic value of the sea mussel *Mytilus edulis. U. S. Bur. Fisheries, Bull.* 38, 127–259.

Fischer, P. H. (1951). Causes de déstruction des mollusques: Maladies et mort. *J. Conchyliol.* 91, 29–59.

Fisher, N. (1932). Malformation in *Mya arenaria* L. *J. Conchol.* 19, 270.

Fleury, G., Lubet, P., and Ledantec, J. (1951). Note sur la *Mytilicola intestinalis* Steuer. *Ann. Pharmacol. Franc.* 9, 569–574.

Freeman, R. F. H., and Llewellyn, J. (1958). An adult digenetic trematode from an invertebrate host: *Proctoeces subtenuis* (Linton) from the lamellibranch *Scrobicularia plana* (da Costa). *J. Marine Biol. Assoc. U. K.* 37, 435–457.

Fretter, V., and Graham, A. (1949). The structure and mode of life of the Pyramidellidae, parasitic opisthobranchs. *J. Marine Biol. Assoc. U. K.* 28, 493–532.

Fujita, T. (1906). Two species of cercariae from *Paphia* (*Amygdala*) *philippinarum.* (In Japanese.) *Dobutsugaku Zasshi* 18, 197–202.

Fujita, T. (1907a). The specific name of the cercaria found in *Paphia* (*Amygdala*) *philippinarum.* (In Japanese.) *Dobutsugaku Zasshi* 19, 281–282.

Fujita, T. (1907b). Sur les trematodes margaritigènes du Pas-de-Calaise. *Compt. Rend. Soc. Biol.* 63, 416–420.

Fujita, T. (1925). Études sur les parasites de l'huître comestible du Japon *Ostrea gigas* Thunberg. Traduction accompagnée de notes, de diagnoses et d'une bibliographie, par Robert Ph. Dollfus. *Ann. Parasitol. Humaine Comparee* 3, 37–59.

Fujita, T. (1943). "Diseases of Fish and Shellfish." (In Japanese.) Koa Nippon Book Co., Tokyo.

Fujita, T., Matsubara, T., Hirokawa, H., and Araki, F. (1953). On the inflammatorious changes of the *Ostrea gigas* in Hiroshima Bay. (In Japanese with English summary.) *Bull. Japan. Soc. Sci. Fisheries* 19, 766–770.

Fujita, T., Matsubara, T., Hirokawa, H., and Araki, F. (1955). On the inflammatorious changes of the *Ostrea gigas* in Hiroshima Bay. II. (In Japanese with English summary.) *Bull. Japan. Soc. Sci. Fisheries* 20, 1063–1065.

Galtsoff, P. S. (1964). The American oyster *Crassostrea virginica* Gmelin. *U. S. Bur. Fisheries, Bull.* 64, 1–480.

Ganaros, A. E. (1957). Marine fungus infecting eggs and embryos of *Urosalpinx cinerea. Science* 125, 1194.

Garner, R. (1872). On the formation of British pearls and their possible improvement. *J. Linnean Soc. London* 11, 426–428.

Genovese, S. (1959). Sulla presenza de *Mytilicola intestinalis* Steuer (Copepoda Parasitica) nel lago de Ganzirri. *Atti Soc. Peloritana Sci. Fis. Mat. Nat.* 5, 47–53

Giard, A. (1881). Fragments biologiques. II. Deux ennemis de l'ostreiculture. *Bull. Sci. Dept. Nord, 4th Ann.* pp. 70–73.

Giard, A. (1894). Sur une affection parasitaire de l'huître (*Ostrea edulis* L.) connue sous le nom de *maladie du pied. Compt. Rend. Soc. Biol.* 46, 401–403.

Giard, A. (1897). Sur un cercaire sétigère (*Cercaria lutea*) parasite des pélécypodes. *Compt. Rend. Soc. Biol.* 49, 954–956.

Giard, A. (1903). Sur la production volontaire des perles fines, ou margarose artificielle. *Compt. Rend. Soc. Biol.* 55, 1225–1226.

Giard, A. (1907). Sur les trématodes margaritigènes du Pas-de-Calais (*Gymnophallus somateriae* Levinsen et *G. bursicola* Odhner). *Compt. Rend. Soc. Biol.* 63, 416–420.

Goldstein, S., Belsky, M., and Chasak, R. (1965). Cultivation of a new marine *Dermocystidium* in complex and chemically defined media. *Bacteriol. Proc.* p. 22.

Grainger, J. N. R. (1951). Notes on the biology of the copepod *Mytilicola intestinalis* Steuer. *Parasitology* **41**, 135–142.

Grodhaus, G., and Keh, B. (1958). The marine dermatitis-producing cercaria of *Austrobilharzia variglandis* in California (Trematoda: Schistosomatidae). *J. Parasitol.* **44**, 633–638.

Gross, F., and Smyth, J. C. (1946). The decline of oyster populations. *Nature* **157**, 540–542.

Guillard, R. R. L. (1959). Further evidence of the destruction of bivalve larvae by bacteria. *Biol. Bull.* **117**, 258–266.

Gutsell, J. S. (1930). Natural history of the bay scallop. *Bull. U. S. Bur. Fish. Wash. D. C.* **46**, 569–631.

Guyénot, E., Naville, A., and Ponse, K. (1925). Deux microsporidies parasites de trématodes. *Rev. Suisse Zool.* **31**, 399–421.

Hackney, A. G. (1944). List of mollusca from around Beaufort, N. Carolina, with notes on *Tethys*. *Nautilus* **58**, 56–64.

Haskin, H. H. (1961). Delaware Bay oyster mortalities. *Proc. Gulf Carib. Fish. Inst., 13th Ann. Sess.* p. 109 (abstr.).

Haskin, H. H., Canzonier, W. J., and Myhre, J. L. (1965). The history of "MSX" on Delaware Bay oyster grounds, 1957–1965. *Am. Malacol. Un., Bull.* **32**, 20–21 (abstr.).

Haskin, H. H., Stauber, L. A., and Mackin, J. G. (1966). *Minchinia nelsoni* n. sp. (Haplosporida, Haplosporidiidae) causative agent of the Delaware Bay oyster epizootic. *Science* **153**, 1414–1416.

Haswell, W. A. (1885). On a destructive parasite of the rock oyster. *Proc. Linnean Soc. N. S. Wales* **10**, 273–275.

Hatt, P. (1927). Spores de *Porospora* (*Nematopsis*) chez les gastéropodes. *Compt. Rend. Soc. Biol.* **96**, 90–91.

Hatt, P. (1931). L'évolution des porosporides chez les mollusques. *Compt. Rend. Soc. Biol.* **98**, 647–649.

Haven, D. (1959). Effects of pea crabs *Pinnotheres ostreum* on oysters *Crassostrea virginica*. *Proc. Natl. Shellfisheries Assoc.* **49**, 77–86.

Havinga, B. (1951). *Mytilicola intestinalis* in relation to other invasions of aquatic animals. *Rev. Trav. Office Sci. Tech. Peches Maritimes* **17**, No. 2, 77–80.

Heldt, J. H. (1951). Observations sur *Mytilicola intestinalis* Steuer parasite des moules. *Rev. Trav. Office Sci. Tech. Peches Maritimes* **17**, No. 2, 33–40.

Hepper, B. T. (1953). Artificial infection of various molluscs with *Mytilicola intestinalis* Steuer. *Nature* **172**, 250.

Hepper, B. T. (1955). Environmental factors governing the infection of mussels *Mytilus edulis* by *Mytilicola intestinalis*. *Min. Agr. Fish. Food, Fish. Invest., London* [2] **20**, No. 3, 1–21.

Herdman, W. A. (1904). Recent investigations on pearls in shellfish. *Proc. Trans. Liverpool Biol. Soc.* **17**, 88–97.

Herdman, W. A., and Hornell, J. (1906). Pearl production. *In* "Report to the Government of Ceylon on the Pearl Oyster Fisheries of the Gulf of Manaar" (W. A. Herdman *et al.*, eds.), Part V., pp. 1–42. Roy. Soc., London.

Hewatt, W. G., and Andrews, J. D. (1954). Oyster mortality studies in Virginia. I. Mortalities of oysters in trays at Gloucester Point, York River. *Texas J. Sci.* **6**, 121–133.

Hewatt, W. G., and Andrews, J. D. (1956). Temperature control experiments on the fungus disease, *Dermocystidium marinum,* of oysters. *Proc. Natl. Shellfisheries Assoc.* **46,** 129–133.

Hockley, A. R. (1952). On the biology of *Mytilicola intestinalis* (Steuer). *J. Marine Biol. Assoc. U. K.* **30,** 223–232.

Hoese, H. D. (1963). Absence of *Dermocystidium marinum* at Port Aransas, Texas, with notes on an apparent inhibitor. *Texas J. Sci.* **15,** 98–103.

Hoese, H. D. (1964). Studies on oyster scavengers and their relation to the fungus *Dermocystidium marinum. Proc. Natl. Shellfisheries Assoc.* **53,** 161–174.

Hogue, M. J. (1914). Studies in the life history of an amoeba of the Limax group, *Vahlkampfia calkensi. Arch. Protistenk.* **35,** 153–163.

Hogue, M. J. (1921). Studies on the life history of *Vahlkampfia patuxent* n. sp., parasitic in the oyster, with experiments regarding its pathogenicity. *Am. J. Hyg.* **1,** 321–345.

Hopkins, S. H. (1954a). The American species of trematode confused with *Bucephalus* (*Bucephalopsis*) *haimeanus. Parasitology* **44,** 353–370.

Hopkins, S. H. (1954b). *Cercaria brachidontis* n. sp. from the hooked mussel in Louisiana. *J. Parasitol.* **40,** 29–31.

Hopkins, S. H. (1956a). *Odostomia impressa* parasitizing southern oysters. *Science* **124,** 628–629.

Hopkins, S. H. (1956b). Notes on the boring sponges in Gulf Coast estuaries and their relation to salinity. *Bull. Marine Sci. Gulf Caribbean* **6,** 44–58.

Hopkins, S. H. (1956c). The boring sponges which attack South Carolina oysters, with notes on some associated organisms. *Contrib. Bears Bluff Labs.* (*S. Carolina*) No. 23, 1–30.

Hopkins, S. H. (1957a). Interrelations of organisms. B. Parasitism. *In* "Treatise on Marine Ecology and Paleoecology" (J. W. Hedgpeth, ed.), Vol. 1, Chapter 15. Geol. Soc. Am., New York.

Hopkins, S. H. (1957b). Our present knowledge of the oyster parasite "*Bucephalus.*" *Proc. Natl. Shellfisheries Assoc.* **47,** 58–61.

Hopkins, S. H. (1958). Trematode parasites of *Donax variabilis* at Mustang Island, Texas. *Publ. Inst. Marine Sci. Univ. Texas* **5,** 301–311.

Hopkins, S. H. (1962). Distribution of species of *Cliona* (boring sponge) on the eastern shore of Virginia in relation to salinity. *Chesapeake Sci.* **3,** 121–124.

Hopkins, S. H. (1968). Personal communication.

Hornell, J. (1910). The practice of oyster culture at Arcachon and its lessons for India. *Madras Fisheries Bull.* **2,** No. 5, 1–90.

Hoshina, T., and Kuwabara, R. (1959). On a new commensal copepod, *Mytilicola mactrae* n. sp. obtained from the intestine of *Mactra veneriformis* Reeve. *J. Tokyo Univ. Fisheries* **45,** 33–35.

Hoshina, T., and Ogino, C. (1951). Studien ueber *Gymnophalloides tokiensis* Fujita, 1925. I. Ueber die Einwirkung der larvalen Trematoda auf die chemische Komponente und das Wachstum von *Ostrea gigas* Thunberg. *J. Tokyo Univ. Fisheries* **38,** 355–350.

Howell, M. (1966). A contribution to the life history of *Bucephalus longicornutus* (Manter, 1954). *Zool. Publ. Victoria Univ. New Zealand* No. 40, 42 pp.

Howell, M. (1967). The trematode, *Bucephalus longicornutus* (Manter, 1954) in the New Zealand mud-oyster, *Ostrea lutaria. Trans. Roy. Soc. New Zealand* **8,** 221–237.

Hrs-Brenko, M. (1964). *Mytilicola intestinalis* Steuer as a parasite of mussels in natural beds and artificial rearing places of the eastern Adriatic. *Acta Adriat.* **11**, No. 21, 161–165.

Hueper, W. C. (1963). Environmental carcinogenesis in man and animals. *Ann. N. Y. Acad. Sci.* **108**, 963–1038.

Huff, C. G. (1940). Immunity in invertebrates. *Physiol. Rev.* **20**, 68–88.

Humes, A. G. (1954). *Mytilicola porrecta* n. sp. (Copepoda: Cyclopoida) from the intestine of marine pelecypods. *J. Parasitol.* **40**, 186–194.

Hutton, R. F. (1952). Schistosome cercariae as the probable cause of seabather's eruption. *Bull. Marine Sci. Gulf Caribbean* **2**, 346–359.

Hutton, R. F. (1953). *Cercaria reesi* n. sp., a new furcocercous larva from Plymouth. *J. Marine Biol. Assoc. U. K.* **31**, 581–585.

Hutton, R. F. (1960). Marine dermatosis. Notes on "seabather's eruption" with *Creseis acicula* Rang (Mollusca: Pteropoda) as the cause of a particular type of sea sting along the west coast of Florida. *Arch. Dermatol.* **82**, 951–956.

Hutton, R. F. (1964). A second list of parasites from marine and coastal animals of Florida. *Trans. Am. Microscop. Soc.* **83**, 439–447.

Imai, T., Numachi, K., Oizumi, J., and Sato, S. (1965). Studies on the mass mortality of the oyster in Matsushima Bay. II. Search for the cause of mass mortality and the possibility to prevent it by transplantation experiment. (In Japanese with English summary.) *Bull. Tohoku Regional Fisheries Res. Lab.* **25**, 27–38.

Jameson, H. L. (1902). On the origin of pearls. *Proc. Zool. Soc. London* pp. 140–165.

Jameson, H. L. (1912). Studies on pearl oysters and pearls. (1) The structure of the shell and pearls of the Ceylon pearl oyster (*Margaritifera vulgaris* Schumacher) with an examination of the cestode theory of pearl formation. *Proc. Zool. Soc. London* pp. 260–358.

Jameson, H. L., and Nicoll, W. R. (1913). On some parasites of the scoter duck (*Oedemia nigra*) and their relation to the pearl-inducing trematode in the edible mussel (*Mytilus edulis*). *Proc. Zool. Soc. London* pp. 53–63.

Jepps, M. W. (1931). On a parasitic ciliate from *Spirula. Oceanog. Rept. 'Dana' Exped. 1920–22* No. 8, pp. 35–36.

Johnston, T. H., and Mawson, P. M. (1945). Some parasitic nematodes from South Australian marine fish. *Trans. Roy. Soc. S. Australia* **69**, 114–117.

Jullien, A. (1928). De certaines tumeurs et inflammations du manteau de la seiche. *Arch. Zool. Exptl. Gen.* **67**, 139–158.

Jullien, A., and Jullien, A. P. (1951). Sur un type de tumeur non provoquée expérimentalement et observée chez la seiche. *Compt. Rend.* **233**, 1322–1324.

Kan-no, H., Sasaki, M., Sakurai, Y., Watanabe, T., and Suzuki, K. (1965). Studies on the mass mortality of the oyster in Matsushima Bay. I. General aspects of the mass mortality of the oyster in Matsushima Bay and its environmental conditions. (In Japanese with English summary.) *Bull. Tohoku Regional Fisheries Res. Lab.* **25**, 1–26.

Katkansky, S. C. (1968). Intestinal growths in the European flat oyster, *Ostrea edulis. Calif. Fish Game* **54**, 203–206.

Kavanagh, L. D. (1940). Mud blisters in Japanese oysters imported to Louisiana. *Louisiana Conserv. Rev. Autumn, 1940* pp. 31–34.

Kidder, G. W. (1933). Studies on *Conchophthirus mytili* De Morgan. *Arch. Protistenk.* **79**, 25–49.

Kofoid, C. A., and Busch, M. (1936). The life cycle of *Parachaenia myae* gen. nov., sp. nov., a ciliate parasitic in *Mya arenaria* Linn. from the San Francisco Bay, California. *Bull. Musee Roy. Hist. Nat. Belg.* (*Brussels*) 12, 1–15.

Korringa, P. (1947). Les vicissitudes de l'ostréiculture hollandaise élucidées par la science ostréicole moderne. *Ostreicult. Cult. Mar. Paris* 16, 3–9.

Korringa, P. (1950). De aanval van de parasiet *Mytilicola intestinalis* op de Zeeuwse mosselcultuur. *Visserijnieuws* 3, No. 7, 1–7. (Transl. by S. H. Hopkins, Texas A & M Res. Found. 1951, mimeo.)

Korringa, P. (1951a). Over *Mytilicola intestinalis* (Copepoda parasitica) en enkele andere ongewenste vreemdelingen in onze wateren. *Vakbl. Biol.* 31, 63–74.

Korringa, P. (1951b). On the nature and function of "chalky" deposits in the shell of *Ostrea edulis* Linnaeus. *Proc. Calif. Acad. Sci.* [4] 27, No. 5, 133–158.

Korringa, P. (1951c). Investigations on shell-disease in the oyster, *Ostrea edulis* L. *Rappt. Proces-Verbaux Reunions Conseil Perm. Intern. Exploration Mer* 128, No. 2, 50–54.

Korringa, P. (1951d). Le *Mytilicola intestinalis* Steuer (Copepoda parasitica) menace l'industrie moulière en Zelande. *Rev. Trav. Office Sci. Tech. Peches Maritimes* 17, No. 2, 9–13.

Korringa, P. (1952a). Recent advances in oyster biology. *Quart. Rev. Biol.* 27, 266–308 and 339–365.

Korringa, P. (1952b). Epidemiological observations on the mussel parasite *Mytilicola intestinalis* Steuer, carried out in the Netherlands 1951. *Ann. Biol., Conseil Perm. Exploration Mer* 8, 182–185.

Korringa, P. (1953). Epidemiological observations on the mussel parasite *Mytilicola intestinalis* Steuer carried out in The Netherlands 1952. *Ann. Biol., Conseil Perm. Exploration Mer* 9, 219–224.

Korringa, P. (1957). Epidemiological observations on the mussel parasite *Mytilicola intestinalis* Steuer, undertaken in the Netherlands in 1955. *Ann. Biol., Conseil Perm. Exploration Mer* 12, 230–231.

Korringa, P. (1959). Checking *Mytilicola's* advance in the Dutch Waddensea. *Conseil Perm. Intern. Exploration Mer, 45th Meeting, 1959, Shellfish Comm. Rept. No.* 87, 1–3 (mimeo.).

Korringa, P. (1968). On the ecology and distribution of the parasitic copepod *Mytilicola intestinalis* Steuer. *Bijdr. Dierk.* 38, 47–57.

Korringa, P., and Lambert, L. (1951). Quelques observations sur la fréquence de *Mytilicola intestinalis* Steuer (Copepoda parasitica) dans les moules du littoral mediterraneen français avec une note sur la présence de *Pseudomyicola spinosus* (Raff. & Mont.) (Copepoda parasitica). *Rev. Trav. Office Sci. Tech. Peches Maritimes* 17, No. 2, 15–29.

Kozloff, E. N. (1946). Studies on ciliates of the family Ancistrocomidae Chatton and Lwoff (order Holotricha, suborder Thigmotricha). I. *Hypocomina tegularum* sp. nov. and *Crebricoma* gen. nov. *Biol. Bull.* 90, 200–209.

Lacaze-Duthiers, F. J. H. (1854). Mémoire sur le bucephale Haime (*Bucephalus haimeanus*) helminthe parasite des huîtres et des bucardes. *Ann. Sci. Nat. Zool.* [4] 1, 294–302.

Laird, M. (1961). Microecological factors in oyster epizootics. *Can. J. Zool.* 39, 449–485.

Lambert, L. (1951a). Renseignements pouvant aider à la reconnaissance de *Mytilicola* et de ses larves et description des méthodes d'examen d'échantillons de moules. *Rev. Trav. Office Sci. Tech. Peches Maritimes* 17, No. 2, 41–46.

Lambert, L. (1951b). Le Cop Rouge (*Mytilicola intestinalis* Steuer) sur les côtes de France. *Rev. Trav. Office Sci. Tech. Peches Maritimes* **17**, No. 2, 51–56.

Landau, H., and Galtsoff, P. S. (1951). Distribution of *Nematopsis* infection on the oyster grounds of the Chesapeake Bay and in other waters of the Atlantic and Gulf States. *Texas J. Sci.* **3**, 115–130.

Léger, L. (1897). Sur la présence des coccidies chez les mollusques lamellibranches. *Compt. Rend. Soc. Biol.* **49**, 987–988.

Léger, L. (1903). Sporozoaire parasite des moules et autres lamellibranches comestibles. *Compt. Rend.* **137**, 1003–1006.

Léger, L. 1905. Un nouveau *Nematopsis* parasite des moules de la Mediterranée. *Bull. Mem. Ass. Franc. Advanc. Sci.* (*Paris*) **9**, 331.

Léger, L., and Duboscq, O. 1913. Le cycle évolutif de *Porospora portunidarum* Frenzel. *Compt. Rend.* **156**, 1932–1934.

Léger, L., and Duboscq, O. (1915). *Pseudoklossia pectinis* n. sp. et l'origine des adéleidées. *Arch. Zool. Exptl. Gen.* **55**, 88–94.

Léger, L., and Duboscq, O. (1917). *Pseudoklossia glomerata* n. g. n. sp., coccidie de lamellibranches. *Arch. Zool. Exptl. Gen.* **56**, 7–16.

Léger, L., and Duboscq, O. 1925. Les porosporides et leur évolution *Trav. Sta. Zool. Wimereux* **9**, 126–139.

Léger, L., and Hollande, A. C. (1917). Sur un nouveau protiste à facies de *Chytridiopsis*, parasite des ovules de l'huître. *Compt. Rend. Soc. Biol.* **80**, 61–64.

Leloup, E. (1937). Contributions à l'étude de la faune Belge. VIII. Les dégats causés par le ver polychete *Polydora ciliata* (Johnston) dans les coquilles des bigorneaux et des huîtres. *Bull. Musee Roy. Hist. Nat. Belg.* (*Brussels*) **13**, 1–4.

Leloup, E. (1951). Sur la présence de *Mytilicola intestinalis* Steuer le long de la côte de Belgique. *Rev. Trav. Office Sci. Tech. Peches Maritimes* **17**, No. 2 57–58.

Leloup, E. (1960). Recherches sur la repartition de *Mytilicola intestinalis* Steuer, 1905, le long de la côte Belge (1950–1958). *Inst. Roy. Sci. Nat. Belg., Bull.* **36**, No. 4, 1–12.

Levinsen, G. M. R. (1881). Bidrag til Kundstab om Grønlands Trematodfauna. *Overs. Danske Videnskab. Selskab. Forth.* **23**, 52–84.

Linton, E. (1915). Note on trematode sporocysts and cercariae in marine mollusks of the Woods Hole region. *Biol. Bull.* **28**, 198–209.

Little, J. W., Hopkins, S. H., and Schlicht, F. G. (1966). *Acanthoparyphium spinulosum* (Trematoda: Echinostomatidae) in oysters at Port Isabel, Texas. *J. Parasitol.* **52**, 663.

Logie, R. R. (1956). Oyster mortalities, old and new, in the Maritimes. *Fisheries Res. Board Can., Progr. Rept. Atlantic Coast Sta.* No. 65, 3–11.

Loosanoff, V. L. (1956). Two obscure oyster enemies in New England waters. *Science* **123**, 1119–1120.

Lunz, G. R. (1940). The annelid worm, *Polydora*, as an oyster pest, *Science* **92**, 310.

McDermott, J. J. (1962). The incidence and host-parasite relations of pinnotherid crabs (Decapoda, Pinnotheridae). *Proc. 1st Natl. Coastal Shallow Water Res. Conf., NSF-ONR, Baltimore, Md. 1961* pp. 162–164.

MacGinitie, G. E., and MacGinitie, N. (1949). "Natural History of Marine Animals." McGraw-Hill, New York.

McGrady, J. (1874). Observations on the food and reproductive organs of *Ostrea virginica*, with some account of *Bucephalus cuculus* nov. sp. *Proc. Boston Soc. Nat. Hist.* **16**, 170–192.

Mackin, J. G. (1951). Histopathology of infection of *Crassostrea virginica* (Gmelin) by *Dermocystidium marinum* Mackin, Owen, and Collier. *Bull. Marine Sci. Gulf Caribbean* 1, 72–87.

Mackin, J. G. (1953). Incidence of infection of oysters by *Dermocy.tidium* in the Barataria Bay area of Louisiana. *Conv. Add. Natl. Shellfisheries Assoc., 1951* pp. 22–35.

Mackin, J. G. (1956). *Dermocystidium marinum* and salinity. *Proc. Natl. Shellfisheries Assoc.* 46, 116–128.

Mackin, J. G. (1960). Status of researches on oyster diseases in North America. *Proc. Gulf Carib. Fish. Inst., 13th Annu. Sess.* pp. 98–113.

Mackin, J. G. (1961). Mortalities of oysters. *Proc. Natl. Shellfisheries Assoc.* 51, 21–40.

Mackin, J. G. (1962). Oyster disease caused by *Dermocystidium marinum* and other microorganisms in Louisiana. *Publ. Inst. Marine Sci. Univ. Texas* 7, 132–229.

Mackin, J. G., and Boswell, J. L. (1956). The life cycle and relationships of *Dermocystidium marinum*. *Proc. Natl. Shellfisheries Assoc.* 46, 112–115.

Mackin, J. G., and Loesch, H. (1955). A haplosporidian hyperparasite of oysters. *Proc. Natl. Shellfisheries Assoc.* 45, 182–183.

Mackin, J. G., and Ray, S. M. (1966). The taxonomic relationships of *Dermocystidium marinum*, Mackin, Owen, and Collier. *J. Invertebrate Pathol.* 8, 544–545.

Mackin, J. G., Owen, H. M., and Collier, A. (1950). Preliminary note on the occurrence of a new protistan parasite, *Dermocystidium marinum* n. sp. in *Crassostrea virginica* (Gmelin). *Science* 111, 328–329.

Mackin, J. G., Korringa, P., and Hopkins, S. H. (1952). Hexamitiasis of *Ostrea edulis* L. and *Crassostrea virginica* (Gmelin). *Bull. Marine Sci. Gulf Caribbean* 1, 266–277.

Mann, H. (1951). Qualitätsverminderung der Fleisches der Miesmuscheln durch den Befall mit *Mytilicola intestinalis*. *Fischereiwelt* 3, No. 8, 121–122.

Mann, H. (1956). The influence of *Mytilicola intestinalis* (Copepoda parasitica) on the development of the gonads of *Mytilus edulis*. *Rappt. Proces-Verbaux Reunions, Conseil Perm. Intern. Exploration Mer* 140, No. 3, 57–58.

Manter, H. W. (1940). Gasterostomes (Trematoda) of Tortugas, Florida. *Carnegie Inst. Wash. Publ.* 534, 1–19.

Medcof, J. C. (1946). The mud-blister worm, *Polydora*, in Canadian oysters. *J. Fisheries Res. Board Can.* 6, 498–565.

Medcof, J. C. (1949). Dark-meat and the shell disease of scallops. *Fisheries Res. Board Can., Progr. Rept. Atlantic Coast Sta.* No. 45, 3–6.

Medcof, J. C., and Bourne, N. (1964). Causes of mortality of the sea scallop, *Placopecten magellanicus*. *Proc. Natl. Shellfisheries Assoc.* 53, 33–50.

Menzel, R. W., and Hopkins, S. H. (1955a). Effects of two parasites on the growth of oysters. *Proc. Natl. Shellfisheries Assoc.* 45, 184–186.

Menzel, R. W., and Hopkins, S. H. (1955b). The growth of oysters parasitized by the fungus *Dermocystidium marinum* and by the trematode *Bucephalus cuculus*. *J. Parasitol.* 41, 333–342.

Merrill, A. S. (1967). Shell deformity of mollusks attributable to the hydroid, *Hydractinia echinata*. *U. S. Fish Wildlife Serv., Fishery Bull.* 66, 273–279.

Merrill, A. S., and Boss, K. J. (1964). Reactions of hosts to proboscis penetration by *Odostomia seminuda* (Pyramidellidae). *Nautilus* 78, 42–45.

Merrill, A. S., and Posgay, J. A. (1964). Estimating the natural mortality rate of the sea scallop (*Placopecten magellanicus*). *Intern. Comm. N.W. Atlantic Fishery, Res. Bull.* No. 1, 88–106.

Meyer, P. F., and Mann, H. (1950). Beiträge zur Epidemiologie und Physiologie des parasitischen Copepoden *Mytilicola intestinalis. Arch. Fishereiwiss.* 2, 120–134.

Meyer, P. F., and Mann, H. (1951). Recherches allemandes relatives au "*Mytilicola*," copépode parasite de la moule, existant dans les watten allemandes 1950/51. *Rev. Trav. Office Sci. Tech. Peches Maritimes* 17, No. 2, 63–74.

Meyer, P. F., and Mann, H. (1952a). *Mytilicola*-Epidemie 1951–52. *Fishereiwelt* 4, 136.

Meyer, P. F., and Mann, H. (1952b). Ein weiterer Beitrag zur Epidemiologie von *Mytilicola intestinalis. Arch. Fishereiwiss.* 5, 26–34.

Meyer-Waarden, P. F., and Mann, H. (1954a). Der Befall von *Mytilus edulis* durch *Mytilicola intestinalis* in den deutschen Wattengebeiten 1950–1953. *Ber. Deut. Komm. Meeresforsch.* 13, 347–362.

Meyer-Waarden, P. F., and Mann, H. (1954b). Untersuchungen über die Bestände von *Mytilus galloprovincialis* an der italienischen Küste auf ihren Befall mit *Mytilicola intestinalis* (Copepoda parasitica). *Boll. Pesca, Piscicolt. Idrobiol.* [N.S.] 8, 5–24.

Meyer-Waarden, P. F., and Mann, H. (1956). German investigations with respect to *Mytilicola intestinalis* in *Mytilus edulis* in 1953. *Rappt. Proces-Verbaux Reunions, Conseil Perm. Intern. Exploration Mer* 140, No. 3, 54–56.

Millar, R. H. (1963). Oysters killed by trematode parasites. *Nature* 197, 616.

Millemann, R. E. (1951). *Echinocephalus pseudouncinatus* n. sp., a nematode parasite of the abalone. *J. Parasitol.* 37, 435–439.

Millemann, R. E. (1963). Studies on the taxonomy and life history of echinocephalid worms (Nematoda: Spiruroidea) with a complete description of *Echinocephalus pseudouncinatus* Millemann 1951. *J. Parasitol.* 49, 754–764.

Monod, T., and Dollfus, R. P. (1932). Les copépodes parasites de mollusques. *Ann. Parasitol. Humaine Comparee* 10, 129–204.

Mori, K., Imai, T., Toyoshima, K., and Usuki, I. (1965a). Studies on the mass mortality of the oyster in Matsushima Bay. IV. Changes in the physiological activity and the glycogen content of the oyster during the stages of sexual maturation and spawning. (In Japanese with English summary.) *Bull. Tohoku Regional Fisheries Res. Lab.* 25, 49–64.

Mori, K., Tamate, H., Imai, T., and Itikawa, O. (1965b). Studies on the mass mortality of the oyster in Matsushima Bay. V. Changes in the metabolism of lipids and glycogen of the oyster during the stages of sexual maturation and spawning. (In Japanese with English summary.) *Bull. Tohoku Regional Fisheries Res. Lab.* 25, 66–88.

Mori, T. (1935). *Mytilicola orientalis*, a new species of parasitic Copepoda. (In Japanese with English summary). *Dobutsugaku Zasshi* 47, 687–693.

Morse, E. S. (1923). An abnormal shell of *Mya arenaria. Nautilus* 36, 28–30.

Nouvel, H. (1947). Les dicyémides. I. *Arch. Biol.* (*Liege*) 58, 54–220.

Nouvel, H. (1948). Les dicyémides. II. *Arch. Biol.* (*Liege*) 59, 147–223.

Numachi, K., Oizumi, J., Sato, S., and Imai, T. (1965). Studies on the mass mortality of the oyster in Matsushima Bay. III. The pathological changes of the oyster caused by gram-positive bacteria and the frequency of their infection. (In Japanese with English summary.) *Bull. Tohoku Regional Fisheries Res. Lab.* 25, 39–48.

Odhner, T. (1905). Die Trematoden des arktischen Gebietes. *In* "Fauna Artica" (F. Romer and F. R. Schaudinn, eds.), Vol. 4, p. 291. Fischer, Jena.

Odlaug, T. O. (1946). The effect of the copepod, *Mytilicola orientalis*, upon the Olympia oyster, *Ostrea lurida*. *Trans. Am. Microscop. Soc.* **65**, 311–317.

Ogasawara, Y., Kobayashi, U., Okamoto, R., Furukawa, A., Hisaoka, M., and Nogami, K. (1962). The use of the hardened seed oyster in the culture of the food oyster and its significance to the oyster culture industry. (In Japanese with English summary.) *Bull. Naikai Regional Fisheries Res. Lab.* **19**, 1–153.

Old, M. C. (1941). The taxonomy and distribution of the boring sponges (Clinoidae) along the Atlantic coast of North America. *Chesapeake Biol. Lab. Publ.* No. 44, 1–30.

Orton, J. H. (1924a). An account of investigations into the cause or causes of the unusual mortality among oysters in English oyster beds during 1920 and 1921. Part I. *Min. Agr. Fish, Fish. Invest., London* [2] **6**, No. 3, 1–199.

Orton, J. H. (1924b). An account of the investigations into the cause or causes of the unusual mortality among oysters in English oyster beds during 1920 and 1921. Part II. Appendix A. Interim report on oyster mortality investigations, 1920. *Min. Agr. Fish, Fish. Invest., London* [2] **6**, No. 4, 3–14.

Orton, J. H. (1937). "Oyster Biology and Oyster Culture," Buckland Lectures for 1935. Arnold, London.

Owen, H. M., Walters, L. L., and Bregan, L. A. (1952). Etiological studies on oyster mortality. I. *Nematopsis ostrearum* Prytherch 1940 (Sporozoa: Porosporidae). *J. Marine Res.* **10**, 82–90.

Ozaki, Y., and Ishibashi, C. (1934). Notes on the cercariae of the pearl oyster. *Proc. Imp. Acad. (Tokyo)* **10**, 439–441.

Palombi, A. (1924). Le cercarie del genere *Gymnophallus* Odhner dei mitili. *Pubbl. Sta. Zool. Napoli* **5**, 137–152.

Pauley, G. B. (1967). A butter clam (*Saxidomus giganteus*) with a polypoid tumor on the foot. *J. Invertebrate Pathol.* **9**, 577–579.

Pauley, G. B., and Sayce, C. S. (1968). An internal fibrous tumor in a Pacific oyster, *Crassostrea gigas*. *J. Invertebrate Pathol.* **10**, 1–8.

Pauley, G. B., Sparks, A. K., and Chew, K. K. (1965). Studies in oyster pathology. Research in Fisheries, 1964. *Univ. Wash., Coll. Fisheries, Contrib.* No. 184, 53–54.

Pearse, A. S., and Wharton, G. W. (1938). The oyster "leech" *Stylochus inimicus* Palombi, associated with oysters on the coasts of Florida. *Ecol. Monographs* **8**, 605–655.

Pelseneer, P. (1896). Un trématode produisant la castration parasitaire chez *Donax trunculus*. *Bull. Sci. France Belg.* [4] **27**, 357–363.

Pelseneer, P. (1906). Trématodes parasites de mollusques marins. *Bull. Sci. France Belg.* [4] **40**, 161–186. (Transl. by M. Alden, No. 1229, Dept. Agr. Fish. Scot., Marine Lab., Aberdeen.)

Pelseneer, P. (1928). Les parasites des mollusques et les mollusques parasites. *Bull. Soc. Zool. France* **53**, 158–189.

Penner, L. R. (1942). Studies on dermatitis-producing schistosomes in Eastern Massachusetts, with emphasis on the status of *Schistosomatium pathlocopticum* Tanabe, 1923. *J. Parasitol.* **28**, 103–116.

Penner, L. R. (1950). *Cercaria littorinalinae* sp. nov., a dermatitis-producing schistosome larva from the marine snail, *Littorina planaxis* Philippi. *J. Parasitol.* **36**, 466–472.

Pereyra, W. T. (1964). Mortality of Pacific oysters, *Crassostrea gigas* (Thunberg), in various exposure situations in Washington. *Proc. Natl. Shellfisheries Assoc.* **53**, 51–63.

Perkins, F. O., and Menzel, R. W. (1966). Morphological and cultural studies of a motile stage in the life cycle of *Dermocystidium marinum*. *Proc. Natl. Shellfisheries Assoc.* **56**, 23–30.

Pesta, O. (1907). Die Metamorphose von *Mytilicola intestinalis* Steuer. *Z. Wiss. Zool.* **88**, 77–98.

Pettit, A. (1921). [Observations a propos de la note de R. Dollfus.] *Compt. Rend. Soc. Biol.* **85**, 451–452.

Poisson, H. (1946). Huîtres et ostréiculture à Madagascar. Étude zoologique et economique. *Trav. Sect. Oceanog. Appl. Soc. Amis Parc Botan. Zool. Tananariva* **3**, 1–37.

Prytherch, H. F. (1938). Life-cycle of a sporozoan parasite of the oyster. *Science* **88**, 451–452.

Prytherch, H. F. (1940). The life cycle and morphology of *Nematopsis ostrearum*, sp. nov., a gregarine parasite of the mud crab and oyster. *J. Morphol.* **66**, 39–65.

Raabe, Z. (1934). Über einige an den Kiemen von *Mytilus edulis* L. und *Macoma balthica* (L.) parasitierende Ciliaten-Arten. *Ann. Musei Zool. Polon.* **10**, No. 15, 289–303.

Raabe, Z. (1936). Weitere Untersuchungen an parasitischen Ciliaten aus dem polnischen Teil der Ostsee. I. *Ciliata thigmotricha* aus den Familien: Thigmophryidae, Conchophthiridae und Ancistrumidae. *Ann. Musei Zool. Polon.* **11**, No. 26, 419–442.

Raabe, Z. (1938). Weitere Untersuchungen an parasitischen Ciliaten aus dem polnischen Teil der Ostsee. II. *Ciliata thigmotricha* aus den Familien: Hypocomidae Bütschli und Sphaenophryidae Ch. & Lw. *Ann. Musei Zool. Polon.* **13**, No. 6, 41–75.

Raabe, Z. (1949). Remarks on protozoan parasitocenose of some representatives of genus *Mytilus*. *Ann. Univ. Mariae Curie-Sklodowska, Lublin-Polonia* C4, No. 1, 1–16.

Rabin, H., and Bang, F. B. (1964). *In vitro* studies of the antibacterial activity of *Goldfingia gouldii* (Pourtalés) coelomic fluid. *J. Insect Pathol.* **6**, 457–465.

Ranson, G. (1936). Sur quelques maladies des huîtres. *Rev. Pathol. Comp. Hyg. Gen.* No. 475, 506–526.

Rathbun, M. J. (1918). The grapsoid crabs of America. *Bull. U. S. Natl. Museum* **97**, 1–461.

Ray, S. M. (1952). A culture technique for diagnosis of infections with *Dermocystidium marinum* Mackin, Owen, and Collier in oysters. *Science* **116**, 360–361.

Ray, S. M. (1954a). Experimental studies on the transmission and pathogenicity of *Dermocystidium marinum*, a fungus disease of oysters. *J. Parasitol.* **40**, 235.

Ray, S. M. (1954b). Biological studies of *Dermocystidium marinum*, a fungus parasite of oysters. *Rice Inst. Pam., Spec. Issue, Nov. 1954, Monograph Biol.* 114 pp.

Ray, S. M. (1954c). Studies on the occurrence of *Dermocystidium marinum* in young oysters. *Conv. Add. Natl. Shellfisheries Assoc., 1953*, pp. 80–92.

Ray, S. M. (1966a). Notes on the occurrence of *Dermocystidium marinum* on the Gulf of Mexico coast during 1961 and 1962. *Proc. Natl. Shellfisheries Assoc.* **54**, 45–54.

Ray, S. M. (1966b). A review of the culture method for detecting *Dermocystidium marinum*, with suggested modifications and precautions. *Proc. Natl. Shellfisheries Assoc.* **54**, 55–69.

Ray, S. M., and Chandler, A. C. (1955). *Dermocystidium marinum,* a parasite of oysters. *Exptl. Parasitol.* 4, 172–200.

Ray, S. M., and Mackin, J. G. (1955). Studies of pathogenesis of *Dermocystidium marinum. Proc. Natl. Shellfisheries Assoc.* 45, 164–167.

Ray, S. M., Mackin, J. G., and Boswell, J. L. (1953). Quantitative measurement of the effect on oysters of disease caused by *Dermocystidium marinum. Bull. Marine Sci. Gulf Caribbean* 3, 6–33.

Rees, F. G. (1937). The anatomy and encystment of *Cercaria purpurae* Lebour, 1911. *Proc. Zool. Soc. London* B107, 65–73.

Rees, F. G. (1939). *Cercaria strigata* Lebour from *Cardium edule* and *Tellina tenuis. Parasitology* 31, 458–463.

Rees, F. G. (1940). Studies on the germ-cell cycle of the digenetic trematode *Parorchis acanthus* Nicoll. Part II. Structure of the miracidium and germinal development in the larval stages. *Parasitology* 32, 372–391.

Richardson, L. R. (1939). Report on the studies of eastern coast oysters during the season of 1939. *Fisheries Res. Board Can., Ms. Rept. Ser. Biol.* 4 pp. (mimeo. unnumbered).

Robertson, R., and Merrill, A. S. (1963). Abnormal dextral hyperstrophy of post-larval *Heliacus* (Gastropoda: Architectonicidae). *Veliger* 6, 76–79.

Rosenfield, A. (1964). Studies of oyster microparasites. *U. S. Fish Wildlife Serv., Circ.* 200, 30–37.

Rosenfield, A., and Sindermann, C. J. (1966). The distribution of "MSX" in middle Chesapeake Bay. *Proc. Natl. Shellfisheries Assoc.* 56, 6 (abstr.).

Roughley, T. C. (1926). An investigation of the cause of an oyster mortality on the George's River, New South Wales, 1924–5. *Proc. Linnean Soc. N. S. Wales* 51, 446–491.

Ryder, J. A. (1887). On a tumor in oyster. *Proc. Natl. Acad. Sci.* 44, 25–27.

Sakaguchi, S. (1962). Studies on a trematode parasitic on pearl oysters. I. On the encystation of cercaria, *Bucephalus margaritae.* (In Japanese.) *Bull. Natl. Pearl Res. Lab.* 8, 1060–1063.

Sakaguchi, S. (1964). Studies on a trematode parasite of pearl oyster. II. Its effects on pearl oyster as the first intermediate host. (In Japanese with English summary.) *Bull. Natl. Pearl Res. Lab.* 9, 1161–1169.

Sakaguchi, S. (1965). Studies on a trematode parasite on the pearl oyster (*Pinctada martensii*). V. Development of its cercaria in the first intermediate host. (In Japanese with English summary.) *Bull. Natl. Pearl Res. Lab.* 10, 1244–1253.

Sakaguchi, S. (1966a). Studies on a trematode parasite of the pearl oyster *Pinctada martensii.* III. The metacercaria obtained from the second intermediate host artificially infected with the cercaria, *Bucephalus margaritae.* (In Japanese with English summary.) *Bull. Japan. Soc. Sci. Fisheries* 32, 312–315.

Sakaguchi, S. (1966b). Studies on a trematode parasite of the pearl oyster, *Pinctada martensii.* IV. On the Trematoda of genus *Bucephalus* found in the fishes, *Caranx sexfasciatus* and *C. ignobilis.* (In Japanese with English summary.) *Bull. Japan. Soc. Sci. Fisheries* 32, 316–321.

Sakaguchi, S. (1967). Studies on a trematode parasite of the pearl oyster, *Pinctada martensii.* VI. Artificial infection with the encysted metacercaria to the final host. (In Japanese with English summary.) *Bull. Natl. Pearl Res. Lab.* 12, 1445–1454.

Sakai, T. (1965). "The Crabs of Sagami Bay." East-West Center Press, Honolulu.

Sanders, M. J. (1966). Victorian offshore scallop explorations. *Australian Fishery Newsletter* 25, 11 and 13.

Sandoz, M., and Hopkins, S. H. (1947). Early life history of the oyster crab, *Pinnotheres ostreum* (Say). *Biol. Bull.* **93**, 250–258.

Sawyer, T. K. (1966). Observations on the taxonomic status of ameboid organisms from the American oyster, *Crassostrea virginica. J. Protozool.* **13**, Suppl., 23 (abstr.).

Scharrer, B., and Lochhead, M. S. (1950). Tumors in the invertebrates: A review. *Cancer Res.* **10**, 403–419.

Schechter, V. (1943). Two flatworms from the oyster-drilling snail *Thais floridana haysae* Clench. *J. Parasitol.* **29**, 362.

Scheltema, R. S. (1962). The relationship between the flagellate protozoon *Hexamita* and the oyster *Crassostrea virginica. J. Parasitol.* **48**, 137–141.

Schlicht, F. G., and Mackin, J. G. (1968). *Hexamita nelsoni* sp. n. (Polymastigina: Hexamitidae) parasitic in oysters. *J. Invertebrate Pathol.* **11**, 35–39.

Schneider, A. 1892. Signalement d'un nouveau Sporozoaire. *Tabl. Zool.* **2**, 209–210.

Shipley, A. E., and Hornell, J. (1904). The parasites of the pearl oyster. *In* "Report to the Government of Ceylon on the Pearl Oyster Fisheries of the Gulf of Manaar" (W. A. Herdman *et al.*, eds.), Part II, p. 77–106. Roy. Soc., London.

Shipley, A. E., and Hornell, J. (1906). Report on the cestode and nematode parasites from the marine fishes of Ceylon. *In* "Report to the Government of Ceylon on the Pearl Oyster Fisheries of the Gulf of Manaar" (W. A. Herdman *et al.*, eds.), Part V, p. 43–96. Roy. Soc., London.

Shuster, C. N., Jr. (1966). A uniquely shaped quahog. *Maritimes* **10**, 14.

Shuster, C. N. Jr., and Hillman, R. E. (1963). Comments on "Microecological factors in oyster epizootics" by Marshall Laird. *Chesapeake Sci.* **4**, 101–103.

Sindermann, C. J. (1960). Ecological studies of marine dermatitis-producing schistosome larvae in northern New England. *Ecology* **41**, 785–790.

Sindermann, C. J. (1965). Effects of environment on several diseases of herring from the western North Atlantic. *Intern. Comm. N. W. Atlantic Fish., Spec. Publ.* No. 6, 603–610.

Sindermann, C. J. (1966a). Parasites of oysters, *Crassostrea virginica*, from the east coast of North America. *Proc. 1st Intern, Congr. Parasitol., Rome, 1964* Vol. 1, pp. 585–586. Pergamon Press, Oxford.

Sindermann, C. J. (1966b). Epizootics in oyster populations. *Proc. 11th Pacific Sci. Congr. Pacific Sci. Assoc., (Tokyo) 1966* Vol. 7, p. 9. *Research Council of Japan.*

Sindermann, C. J. (1968). Oyster mortalities, with particular reference to Chesapeake Bay and the Atlantic coast of North America. *U. S. Fish Widlife Serv., Spec. Sci. Rept., Fisheries No.* **569**, 1–10.

Sindermann, C. J. (1969). Unpublished observations.

Sindermann, C. J., and Farrin, A. E. (1962). Ecological studies of *Cryptocotyle lingua* (Trematoda: Heterophyidae) whose larvae cause "pigment spots of marine fish. *Ecology* **43**, 69–75.

Sindermann, C. J., and Gibbs, R. F. (1953). A dermatitis-producing schistosome which causes "clam diggers' itch" along the central Maine coast. *Maine Dept. Sea Shore Fish., Res. Bull.* **12**, 1–20.

Sindermann, C. J., and Rosenfield, A. (1967). Principal disease of commercially important marine bivalve Mollusca and Crustacea. *U. S. Fish Wildlife Serv., Fishery Bull.* **66**, 335–385.

Sivalingam, S. (1962). Bibliography on pearl oysters. *Fish. Res. Sta., Dept. Fish., Ceylon* No. 13, 1–21.

Smith, G. M. (1934). A mesenchymal tumor in an oyster (*Ostrea virginica*). *Am. J. Cancer* **22**, 838–841.

Smith, G. F. M. (1936). A gonad parasite of the starfish. *Science* **84**, 157.

Southwell, T. (1911). Some notes on the Ceylon pearl-inducing worm. *Spolia Zeylan.* **7**, 124–134.

Southwell, T. (1912). The Ceylon pearl inducing worm. *Parasitology* **5**, 27–36.

Southwell, T. (1924). The pearl-inducing worm in the Ceylon pearl oyster. *Ann. Trop. Med. Parasitol.* **18**, 37–53.

Sparks, A. K. (1962). Metaplasia of the gut of the oyster *Crassostrea gigas* (Thunberg) caused by infection with the copepod *Mytilicola orientalis* Mori. *J. Insect Pathol.* **4**, 57–62.

Sparks, A. K. (1963). Infection of *Crassostrea virginica* (Gmelin) from Hawaii with a larval tapeworm, *Tylocephalum*. *J. Insect Pathol.* **5**, 284–288.

Sparks, A. K., and Chew, K. K. (1966). Gross infestation of the little neck clam, *Venerupis staminea*, with a larval cestode (*Echeneibothrium* sp.). *J. Invertebrate Pathol.* **8**, 413–416.

Sparks. A. K., and Pauley, G. B. (1963). Studies in oyster pathology. Research in Fisheries, 1962. *Univ. Wash., Coll. Fisheries, Contrib.* No. 147, 51–53.

Sparks, A. K., and Pauley, G. B. (1964). Studies in oyster pathology. Research in Fisheries, 1963. *Univ. Wash., Coll. Fisheries, Contrib.* No. 166, 59–60.

Sparks, A. K., Pauley, G. B., Bates, R. R., and Sayce, C. S. (1964). A mesenchymal tumor in a Pacific oyster, *Crassostrea gigas* (Thunberg). *J. Insect. Pathol.* **6**, 448–452.

Sprague, V. (1949). Species of *Nematopsis* in *Ostrea virginica*. *J. Parasitol.* **35**, Suppl., 42 (abstr.).

Sprague, V. (1963). Revision of genus *Haplosporidium* and restoration of genus *Minchinia* (Haplosporia, Haplosporidiidae). *J. Protozool.* **10**, 263–266.

Sprague, V. (1964). *Nosema dollfusi* n. sp. (Microsporidia, Nosematidae), a hyperparasite of *Bucephalus cuculus* in *Crassostrea virginica*. *J. Protozool.* **11**, 381–385.

Sprague, V. (1965). Observations on *Chytridiopsis mytilovum* (Field), formerly *Haplosporidium mytilovum* Field (Microsporida?). *J. Protozool.* **12**, 385–389.

Sprague, V., and Orr, P. E., Jr. (1953). Studies on *Nematopsis*. III. *N. ostrearum* and *N. prytherchi* with special references to host-parasite relation. *Conv. Add. Natl. Shellfisheries Assoc., 1952*, pp. 26–43.

Sprague, V., and Orr, P. E. Jr. (1955). *Nematopsis ostrearum* and *N. prytherchi* (Eugregarinina: Porosporidae) with special reference to the host-parasite relations. *J. Parasitol.* **41**, 89–104.

Squires, H. J. (1957). Squid, *Illex illecebrosus* (LeSueur) in the Newfoundland fishing area. *J. Fisheries Res. Board Can.* **14**, 693–728.

Stafford, J. (1912). On the fauna of the Atlantic coast of Canada. Third Report—Gaspe, 1905–1906. *Contrib. Can. Biol. Fisheries 1906–12*, pp. 45–67.

Stauber, L. A. (1945). *Pinnotheres ostreum*, parasite on the American oyster, *Ostrea* (*Gryphaea*) *virginica*. *Biol. Bull.* **88**, 269–291.

Stauber, L. A. (1961). Immunity in invertebrates, with special reference to the oyster. *Proc. Natl. Shellfisheries Assoc.* **50**, 7–20.

Stein, J. E., Denison, J. G., and Mackin, J. G. (1961). *Hexamita* sp. and an infectious disease in the commercial oyster *Ostrea lurida*. *Proc. Natl. Shellfisheries Assoc.* **50**, 67–81.

Steinhaus, E. A. (1949). "Principles of Insect Pathology." McGraw Hill, New York.

Steinhaus, E. A. (1965). Symposium on microbial insecticides. IV. Diseases of invertebrates other than insects. *Bacteriol. Rev.* **29**, 388–396.

Steuer, A. (1902). *Mytilicola intestinalis* n. gen. n. sp. aus dem Darme von *Mytilus galloprovincialis* Lam. *Zool. Anz.* **25**, 635–637.

Steuer, A. (1903). *Mytilicola intestinalis* n. gen. n. sp. *Arb. Zool. Inst. Univ. Wien.* **15**, 1–45.

Stunkard, H. W. (1938). The morphology and life history of the trematode *Himasthla quissetensis* (Miller and Northup, 1926). *Biol. Bull.* **75**, 145–164.

Stunkard, H. W. (1960). Further studies on the trematode genus *Himasthla* with descriptions of *H. mcintoshi* n. sp., *H. piscicola* n. sp., and stages in the life-history of *H. compacta* n. sp. *Biol. Bull.* **119**, 529–549.

Stunkard, H. W., and Cable, R. M. (1932). The life history of *Parorchis avitus* (Linton), a trematode from the cloaca of the gull. *Biol. Bull.* **62**, 328–338.

Stunkard, H. W., and Hinchliffe, M. C. (1952). The morphology and life history of *Microbilharzia variglandis* (Miller and Northup, 1926) Stunkard and Hinchliffe, 1951, avian blood flukes whose larvae cause "swimmer's itch" of ocean beaches. *J. Parasitol.* **38**, 248–265.

Stunkard, H. W., and Shaw, C. R. (1931). The effect of dilution of sea water on the activity and longevity of certain marine cercariae with descriptions of two new species. *Biol. Bull.* **61**, 242–271.

Stunkard, H. W., and Uzmann, J. R. (1958). Studies on digenetic trematodes of the genera *Gymnophallus and Parvatrema. Biol. Bull.* **115**, 276–302.

Stunkard, H. W., and Uzmann, J. R. (1959). The life cycle of the digenetic trematode, *Proctoeces maculatus* (Looss, 1901) Odhner, 1911 (syn. *P. subtenuis* (Linton 1907) Hanson, 1950), and description of *Cercaria adranocerca* n. sp. *Biol. Bull.* **116**, 184–193.

Takeuchi, T., Takemoto, Y., and Matsubara, T. (1960). Haematological study of bacteria affected oysters. *Rept. Hiroshima Prefect. Fish. Expt. Sta.* **22**, No. 1, 1–7. (Transl. by U. S. Joint Publ. Res. Serv. for Transl. Program, Bur. Comm. Fish., Milford, Conn., 1965).

Tamate, H., Numachi, K., Mori, K., Itikawa, O., and Imai, T. (1965). Studies on the mass mortality of the oyster in Matsushima Bay. VI. Pathological studies. (In Japanese with English summary.) *Bull. Tohoku Regional Fisheries Res. Lab.* **25**, 89–104.

Taylor, R. L. (1966). *Haplosporidium tumefacientis* sp. n., the etiologic agent of a disease of the California sea mussel, *Mytilus californianus* Conrad. *J. Invertebrate Pathol.* **8**, 109–121.

Taylor, R. L., and Smith, A. C. (1966). Polypoid and papillary lesions in the foot of the gaper clam, *Tresus nuttalli. J. Invertebrate Pathol.* **8**, 264–266.

Tennent, D. H. (1906). A study of the life history of *Bucephalus haimeanus;* a parasite of the oyster. *Quart. J. Microscop. Sci.* **49**, 635–690.

Thomas, H. J. (1953). *Mytilicola intestinalis* Steuer in England and Wales. Progress Report 1953. *Conseil Perm. Intern. Exploration Mer, Rept. Shellfisheries Comm.* pp. 1–2.

Tripp, M. R. (1958). Studies on the defense mechanisms of the oyster, *Crassostrea virginica. J. Parasitol.* **44**, Suppl., 35–36 (abstr.).

Tripp, M. R. (1960). Mechanisms of removal of injected microorganisms from the American oyster, *Crassostrea virginica* (Gmelin). *Biol. Bull.* **119**, 273–282.

Tripp, M. R. (1963). Cellular responses of mollusks. *Ann. N. Y. Acad. Sci.* **113**, 467–474.

Tripp, M. R. (1966). Oyster amebocytes *in vitro*. *J. Invertebrate Pathol.* **8**, 137–140.

Tubiash, H. S., Chanley, P. E., and Leifson, E. (1965). Bacillary necrosis, a disease of larval and juvenile bivalve mollusks. I. Etiology and epizootiology. *J. Bacteriol.* **90**, 1036–1044.

Tubiash, H. S., Schuster, C. N., Jr., and Couch, J. A. (1968). Anomalous siphons in two species of bivalve mollusks. *Nautilus* **81**, 120–125.

Uzmann, J. R. (1951). Record of the larval trematode *Himasthla quissetensis* (Miller and Northup, 1926) Stunkard, 1934 in the clam, *Mya arenaria*. *J. Parasitol.* **37**, 327–328.

Uzmann, J. R. (1952). *Cercaria myae* sp. nov., a fork-tailed larva from the marine bivalve, *Mya arenaria*. *J. Parasitol.* **38**, 161–164.

Uzmann, J. R. (1953). *Cercaria milfordensis* nov. sp., a microcercous trematode larva from the marine bivalve, *Mytilus edulis* L. with special reference to its effect on the host. *J. Parasitol.* **39**, 445–451.

Uzmann, J. R., and Stickney, A. P. (1954). *Trichodina myicola* n. sp., a peritrichous ciliate from the marine bivalve *Mya arenaria* L. *J. Protozool.* **1**, 149–155.

Vevers, H. G. (1951). The biology of *Asterias rubens* L. II. Parasitization of the gonads by the ciliate *Orchitophrys stellarum* Cépède. *J. Marine Biol. Assoc. U. K.* **29**, 619–624.

Vishniac, H. S. (1955). The morphology and nutrition of a new species of *Sirolpidium*. *Mycologia* **47**, 633–645.

Voisin, P. (1931). Biologie ostréicole. La maladie des huîtres de Zélande. *Rev. Trav. Office Sci. Tech. Peches Maritimes* **4**, 221–222.

Waugh, G. D. (1954). The occurrence of *Mytilicola intestinalis* (Steuer) on the east coast of England. *J. Animal Ecol.* **23**, 364–367.

Waugh, G. D. (1966). Protecting British shellfisheries. *Min. Agr. Fish. Food, Fish. Lab., Burnham on Crouch, Leafl.* [N.S.] **10**, 1–8.

Wells, H. W. (1959a). Notes on *Odostomia impressa* (Say). *Nautilus* **72**, 140–144.

Wells, H. W. (1959b). Boring sponges (Clionidae) of Newport River, North Carolina. *J. Elisha Mitchell Sci. Soc.* **75**, 168–173.

Wells, H. W., and Wells, M. J. (1961). Three species of *Odostomia* from North Carolina, with description of new species. *Nautilus* **74**, 149–157.

Wilson, C. B. (1938). A new copepod from Japanese oysters transplanted to the Pacific coast of the United States. *J. Wash. Acad. Sci.* **28**, 284–288.

Wood, J. L., and Andrews, J. D. (1962). *Haplosporidium costale* (Sporozoa) associated with a disease of Virginia oysters. *Science* **136**, 710–711.

Wright, C. A. (1966). The pathogenesis of helminths in the Mollusca. *Helminthol. Abstr.* **35**, 207–224.

Yamaguti, S. (1938). Studies on the helminth fauna of Japan. Part 21. "Trematodes of Fishes," Vol. IV, pp. 1–139. Kyoto, Japan.

Yamaguti, S. (1939). A new commensal copepod from *Brachidontes senhausi* (Reeve). *Trans. Am. Microscop. Soc.* **58**, 371–373.

Young, R. T. (1953). *Postmonorchis donacis*, a new species of monorchid trematode from the Pacific coast, and its life history. *J. Wash. Acad. Sci.* **43**, 88–93.

REFERENCES—CRUSTACEA

Aaronson, S. (1956). A biochemical-taxonomic study of a marine micrococcus, *Gaffkya homari*, and a terrestrial counterpart. *J. Gen. Microbiol.* **15**, 478–484.

Aldrich, D. V. (1965). Observations on the ecology and life cycle of *Prochristianella penaei* Kruse (Cestoda: Trypanorhyncha). *J. Parasitol.* **51**, 370–376.

Allen, J. A. (1966). Notes on the relationship of the bopyrid parasite *Hemiarthrus abdominalis* (Krøyer) with its hosts. *Crustaceana* 10, 1–6.

Anderson, J. I. W., and Conroy, D. A. (1968). The significance of disease in preliminary attempts to raise Crustacea in sea water. *Proc. 3rd Symp. Mond. Comm. Office Intern. Epizoot. Etude Maladies Poissons Stockholm,* (1968) *Separate* No. 3, 8 pp.

Anonymous (Uzmann, J. R.). (1966). Boothbay studies parasite of ocean lobster. *U. S. Fish Wildlife Serv., Fish Wildlife Rept., Feb.-Mar.* p. 21.

Atkins, D. (1929). On a fungus allied to the Saprolegniaceae found in the pea-crab *Pinnotheres. J. Marine Biol. Assoc. U. K.* 16, 203–219.

Atkins, D. (1963). *Pinnotherion vermiforme* Giard and Bonnier, an entoniscid infecting *Pinnotheres pisum. Proc. Zool. Soc. London* pp. 319–363.

Atkins, D. (1954a). Further notes on a marine member of the Saprolegniaceae, *Leptolegnia marina* n. sp., infecting certain invertebrates. *J. Marine Biol. Assoc. U. K.* 33, 613–625.

Atkins, D. (1954b). A marine fungus *Plectospira dubia* n. sp. (Saprolegniaceae), infecting crustacean eggs and small Crustacea. *J. Marine Biol. Assoc. U. K.* 33, 721–732.

Atkins, D. (1955). *Pythium thalassium* n. sp. infecting the egg-mass of the pea-crab *Pinnotheres pisum. Brit. Mycol. Soc. Trans.* 38, 31–46.

Baer, J. G. (1951). "Ecology of Animal Parasites." Univ. of Illinois Press, Urbana, Illinois.

Ball, G. H. (1938). The life history of *Carcinoectes hesperus* n. gen., n. sp., a gregarine parasite of the striped shore crab, *Pachygrapsus crassipes,* with observations on related forms. *Arch. Protistenk.* 90, 299–319.

Ball, G. H. (1951). Gregarines from Bermuda marine crustaceans. *Univ. Calif. (Berkeley) Publ. Zool.* 47, 351–368.

Bang, F. B. (1956). A bacterial disease of *Limulus polyphemus. Bull. Johns Hopkins Hosp.* 98, 325–351.

Bell, G. R., and Hoskins, G. E. (1966). Experimental transmission of the lobster pathogen, *Gaffkya homari,* to Pacific crabs and prawns. *16th Ann. Meeting, Can. Soc. Microbiol., Saskatoon* 1 p. (abstr., unnumbered).

Benton, A. G. (1935). Chitinovorous bacteria. A preliminary survey. *J. Bacteriol.* 29, 449–463.

Boschma, H. (1928). Rhizocephala of the North Atlantic region. *Dan. Ingolf-Exped.* 3, No. 10, 1–49.

Boschma, H. (1935). Notes on Japanese Rhizocephala, with description of two new species. *Zool. Meded. Leiden* 18, 151–160.

Boschma, H. (1963). A rhizocephalan parasite of the crab *Charybdis callianassa* (Herbst). *Koninkl. Ned. Akad. Wetenschap. Proc.* C66, 132–138.

Brian, A., and Parenzan, P. (1967). Nota sull'epicarideo *Bopyrus squillarum* Lam. parassita de Palaemonidae. *Thalassia Salentina* 2, 37–41.

Bright, D. B., Durham, F. E., and Knudsen, J. W. (1960). King crab investigations of Cook Inlet, Alaska. *U. S. Bur. Comm. Fisheries Biol. Lab., Auke Bay, Alaska, Contract Rept.* pp. 149–154 (unpublished).

Cable, R. M., and Hunninen, A. V. (1940). Studies on the life-history of *Spelotrema nicolli* (Trematoda: Microphallidae) with the description of a new microphallid cercaria. *Biol. Bull.* 78, 136–157.

Calman, W. T. (1898). On a collection of Crustacea from Puget Sound. *Ann. N. Y. Acad. Sci.* 11, 259–292.

Cantacuzène, J. (1925). Réactions de crabe sacculine vis à vis d'une infection expérimentale de la sacculine. *Compt. Rend. Soc. Biol.* 93, 1417–1419.

Cattaneo, G. (1888). Su di un infusorio ciliato, parassito del sangue del *Carcinus maenas. Zool. Anz.* 11, 456–459.

Chace, F. A., Jr., and Moore, G. M. (1959). A bicolored gynandromorph of the lobster, *Homarus americanus. Biol. Bull.* 116, 226–231.

Coe, W. R. (1902a). The nemertean parasites of crabs. *Am. Naturalist* 36, 431–450.

Coe, W. R. (1902b). The genus *Carcinonemertes. Zool. Anz.* 25, 409–414.

Cohen, F. (1866). Neue Infusorien im Seeaquarium. *Z. Wiss. Zool.* 16, 253–302.

Cole, L. J. (1910). Description of an abnormal lobster cheliped. *Biol. Bull.* 18, 252–268.

Connolly, C. J. (1929). A new copepod parasite *Choniosphaera cancrorum*, gen. et sp. n., representing a new genus, and its larval development. *Proc. Zool. Soc. London* Part 3, pp. 415–427.

Cornick, J. W., and Stewart, J. E. (1966). Microorganisms isolated from the hemolymph of the lobster (*Homarus americanus*). *J. Fisheries Res. Board Can.* 23, 1451–1454.

Cornick, J. W., and Stewart, J. E. (1968a). Interaction of the pathogen *Gaffkya homari* with natural defense mechanisms of *Homarus americanus. J. Fisheries Res. Board Can.* 25, 695–709.

Cornick, J. W., and Stewart, J. E. (1968b). Pathogenicity of *Gaffkya homari* for the crab *Cancer irroratus. J. Fisheries Res. Board Can.* 25, 795–799.

Couch, J. A. (1966). Two peritrichous ciliates from the gills of the blue crab. *Chesapeake Sci.* 7, 171–176.

Couch, J. A. (1967). A new species of *Lagenophrys* (Ciliata: Peritrichida: Lagenophryidae) from a marine crab, *Callinectes sapidus. Trans. Am. Microscop. Soc.* 86, 204–211.

Couch, J. N. (1942). A new fungus on crab eggs. *J. Elisha·Mitchell Sci. Soc.* 58, 158–162.

Cunningham, J. T. (1887). On *Stichocotyle nephropis*, a new trematode. *Trans. Roy. Soc. Edinburgh* 32, 273–280.

Dahl, E. (1949). Epicaridea and Rhizocephala from northern Norway with a discussion on the bathymetrical distribution of Rhizocephala. *Tromso Museums Aarrsh.* 69, 1–44.

Dannevig, A. (1928). Beretning om Flødevigens utklekningsanstalt for 1926–1927. *Aarsberetn. Norg. Fisk.* pp. 150–156.

Dannevig, A. (1939). Beretning for Flødevigens utklekningsanstalt 1936–37. *Aarsberetn. Norg. Fisk.* pp. 70–75.

Davis, C. C. (1965). A study of the hatching process in aquatic invertebrates. XX. The blue crab, *Callinectes sapidus*, Rathbun. XXI. The nemertean *Carcinonemertes carcinophila* (Kölliker). *Chesapeake Sci.* 6, 201–208.

Day, J. H. (1935). The life history of *Sacculina. Quart. J. Microscop. Sci.* 77, 549–583.

Debaisieux, P. (1960). Ciliates apostomes parasites de *Palaemon. La Cellule* 60, 333–352.

Deibel, R. H., and Niven, C. F., Jr. (1960). Comparative study of *Gaffkya homari*, *Aerococcus viridans*, tetrad-forming cocci from meat-curing brines, and the genus *Pediococcus. J. Bacteriol.* 79, 175–180.

Delage, M. Y. (1884). Evolution de la sacculine (*Sacculina carcini* Thomps.)

crustacé endoparasite de l'ordre nouveau des kentrogonides. *Arch. Zool. Exptl. Gen.* [2] **2**, 417–738.

De Turk, W. E. (1940). The occurrence and development of a hyperparasite *Urosporidium crescens* sp. nov. (Sporozoa, Haplosporidia), which infests the metacercariae of *Spelotrema nicolli,* parasitic in *Callinectes sapidus. J. Eli,ha Mitchell Sci. Soc.* **56**, 231–232.

Dexter, R. W. (1959). Blue lobsters. *Estuarine Bull.* **4**, No. 2, 6–7.

Dollfus, R. P. (1964a). Sur le cycle évolutif d'un cestode diphyllide. Identification de la larve chez *Carcinus maenas* (L. 1758) hôte intermédiare. *Ann. Parasitol. Humaine Comparee* **39**, 235–241.

Dollfus, R. P. (1964b). Énumeration des cestodes du plancton et des invertébrés marins. *Ann. Parasitol. Humaine Comparee* **39**, 329–379.

Duboscq, O. Léger, L., and Tuzet, O. (1949). Contribution à la connaissance des éccrinides. Les trichomycètes. *Arch. Zool. Exptl. Gen.* **86**, 29–144.

Emmel, V. E. (1907). Regenerated and abnormal appendages in the lobster. *37th Ann. Rept. Comm. Inland Fisheries, Rhode Island* pp. 99–152.

Faxon, W. (1881). On some crustacean deformities. *Bull. Museum Comp. Zool. Harvard Coll.* **8**, No. 13, 257–274.

Fisheries Research Board of Canada. (1966). "Review of the Fisheries Research Board of Canada, 1964." The Queen's Printer, Ottawa.

Foxon, G. E. H. (1940). Notes on the life history of *Sacculina carcini* Thompson. *J. Marine Biol. Assoc. U. K.* **24**, 253–264.

Getchell, J. S. (1949). A study of abnormal shrinkage of Maine lobsters ("red tail") with observations and recommendation. *Maine Dept. Sea Shore Fisheries Bull.,* 6 pp.

Giard, A. (1888). La castration parasitaire, nouvelles recherches. *Bull. Sci. France Belg.* [3] **19**, 12–45.

Giard, A., and Bonnier, J. (1887). Contributions à l'étude des bopyriens. *Trav. Sta. Zool. Wimereux* **5**, 1–252.

Giard, A., and Bonnier, J. (1895). Contributions à l'étude des épicarides. XX. Sur les épicarides parasites des arthrostaces et sur quelques copépods symbiotes de cas épicarides. *Bull. Sci. France Belg.* [4] **25**, 417–493.

Gibson, F. A. (1961). Gaffkaemia in stored lobsters. *Conseil Perm. Exploration Mer, Shellfish Comm.* No. 58, 1 p. (mimeo.)

Gnanamuthu, C. P. (1954). *Choniosphaera indica,* a copepod parasitic on the crab *Neptunus* sp. *Parasitology* **44**, 371–378.

Goggins, P. L., and Hurst, J. W., Jr. (1960). Progress report on lobster gaffkyaremia (red tail). *Maine Dept. Sea Shore Fisheries* 9 pp. (mimeo., unpublished).

Gordon, I. (1966). Parasites and diseases of Crustacea. *Mem. Inst. Fondam. Afrique Noire* No. 77, 27–86.

Gurley, R. R. (1893). On the classification of the Myxosporidia, a group of protozoan parasites infesting fishes. *Bull. U. S. Fish. Comm.* **11**, 407–420.

Guyenot, E., Naville, A., and Ponse, K. (1925). Deux microsporidies parasites de trématodes. *Rev. Suisse Zool.* **31**, 399–421.

Haefner, P. A., Jr. (1961). A blue blue crab. *Estuarine Bull.* **6**, Nos. 3/4, 3–5.

Hall, D. N. F. (1966). Penaeidae of the east coast of Africa. *Mem. Inst. Fondam. Afrique Noire* No. 77, 87–97.

Hansen, H. J. (1897). "The Choniostomatide. A Family of Copepoda, Parasites on Crustacea Malacostraca." Andr. Fred Høst & Son, Copenhagen.

Hansen, H. J. (1904). Two new forms of Choniostomatidae: Copepoda parasitic on Crustacea Malacostraca and Ostrocoda. *Quart. J. Microscop. Sci.* **48**, 347–358.

Hansen, H. J. (1923). Crustacea Copepoda. II. Copepoda parasita and hemiparasita. *Dan. Ingolf-Exped.* 3, 1–92.

Hargis, W. J., Jr. (1959). Parasites and fishery problems. *Proc. Gulf Caribbean Fish. Inst., 11th Ann. Sess.* pp. 70–75.

Hartnoll, R. G. (1967). The effects of sacculinid parasites on two Jamaican crabs. *J. Linnean Soc. London, Zool.* 46, 275–295.

Hatt, P. (1928). L'évolution de la grégarine du homard (*Porospora gigantea* E. V. Bened.) chez les mollusques. *Compt. Rend. Soc. Biol.* 98, 647–649.

Hatt, P. (1931). L'évolution des porosporides chez les mollusques. *Arch. Zool. Exptl. Gen.* 72, 341–415.

Havinga, B. (1921). Rapport over de kreeftenvisserij in Zeeland en de kunstmatige kreeftenteelt. *Meded. Visscherijinsp., Amsterdam* No. 30, 1–51.

Heldt, J. H. (1949). Notes sur la présence d'une plérocercoide de tetrarhynque dans l'hepatopancreas de la crevette caramote *Penaeus trisulcatus* Leach. *Bull. Soc. Sci. Nat. Tunisie* 2, 13.

Henneguy, G., and Thélohan, P. (1892). Sur une sporozoaire parasite des muscles des crustacés décapodes. *Compt. Rend. Soc. Biol.* 4, 585–588.

Herrick, F. H. (1895). The American lobster; a study of its habits and development. *Bull. U. S. Fish Comm.* 15, 1–252.

Herrick, F. H. (1911). Natural history of the American lobster. *U. S. Bur. Fisheries. Bull.* 29, 149–408.

Hess, E. (1937). A shell disease in lobsters (*Homarus americanus*) caused by chitinovorous bacteria. *J. Biol. Board Can.* 3, 358–362.

Hiraiwa, Y. K., and Sato, M. (1939). On the effect of parasitic Isopoda on a prawn, *Penaeopsis akayebi* Rathbun, with a consideration of the effect of parasitization on the higher Crustacea in general. *J. Sci. Hiroshima Univ.* B7, Art. 6, 105–124.

Hitchner, E. R., and Snieszko, S. F. (1947). A study of a microorganism causing a bacterial disease of lobster. *J. Bacteriol.* 54, 48 (abstr.).

Hock, C. W. (1940). Decomposition of chitin by marine bacteria. *Biol. Bull.* 79, 199–206.

Hock, C. W. (1941). Marine chitin-decomposing bacteria. *J. Marine Res.* 4, 99–106.

Hopkins, S. H. (1947). The nemertean *Carcinonemertes* as an indicator of the spawning history of the host, *Callinectes sapidus*. *J. Parasitol.* 33, 146–150.

Hopkins, S. H. (1957). Interrelations of organisms. B. Parasitism. *In* "Treatise on Marine Ecology and Paleoecology" (J. W. Hedgpeth, ed.) Vol. 1, Chapter 15. Geol. Soc. Am., New York.

Hopkins, S. H. (1968). Personal communication.

Horsted, S. A., and Smidt, E. (1956). The deep sea prawn (*Pandalus borealis* Kr.) in Greenland waters. *Medd. Komm. Havundersog, Kjobenhaven* [N.S.] 1, No. 11, 1–118.

Humes, A. G. (1942). The morphology, taxonomy, and bionomics of the nemertean genus *Carcinonemertes*. *Illinois Biol. Monographs* 18, No. 4, 1–105.

Hutton, R. F., and Sogandares-Bernal, F. (1959). Notes on the distribution of the leech, *Myzobdella lugubris* Leidy, and its association with the mortality of the blue crab, *Callinectes sapidus* Rathbun. *J. Parasitol.* 45, 384, 404, and 430.

Hutton, R. F., Sogandares-Bernal, F., and Eldred, B. (1959a). Another species of *Microphallus* Ward, 1901, from the pink shrimp, *Penaeus duorarum* Burkenroad. *J. Parasitol.* 45, 490.

Hutton, R. F., Sogandares-Bernal, F., Eldred, B., Ingle, R. M., and Woodburn, K. D. (1959b). Investigations on the parasites and diseases of saltwater shrimps

(Penaeidae) of sports and commercial importance to Florida. (Preliminary report.) *Florida State Board Conserv., Tech. Ser.* **26**, 1–38.

Ichikawa, A., and Yamagunachi, R. (1957). The sexual nature of a rhizocephalan, *Peltogasterella socialis. J. Fac. Sci., Hokkaido Univ., Ser. VI* **13**, 384–389.

Imamura, T. (1940). Two species of *Lagenophrys* from Sapporo. *Annotationes Zool. Japon.* **19**, 267–270.

Iversen, E. S., and Manning, R. B. (1959). A new microsporidian parasite from the pink shrimp (*Penaeus duorarum*). *Trans. Am. Fisheries Soc.* **88**, 130–132.

Iversen, E. S., and Van Meter, N. N. (1964). A record of the microsporidian, *Thelohania duorara*, parasitizing the shrimp *Penaeus brasiliensis. Bull. Marine Sci. Gulf Caribbean* **14**, 549–553.

Kabata, Z. (1966). *Nicothoe analata* sp. nov., a parasitic copepod from the south China Sea. *Crustaceana* **11**, 10–16.

Kabata, Z. (1967). *Nicothoe* Audouin & H. Milne-Edwards, 1826 (Crustacea, Copepoda), a genus parasitic on *Nephrops* Leach, 1816 (Crustacea, Decapoda). *Zool. Meded.* **42**, No. 15, 147–161.

Kanneworff, B., and Christensen, A. M. (1966). *Kronborgia caridicola* sp. nov., an endoparasitic turbellarian from North Atlantic shrimps. *Ophelia* **3**, 65–80.

Kirkwood, J. B. (1967). Personal communication.

Kruse, D. N. (1959a). Parasites of commercial shrimp. *Assoc. S.E. Biol. Bull.* **6**, No. 2, 28.

Kruse, D. N. (1959b). A study of the taxonomy, morphology, incidence and biology of the parasites of the commercial shrimp, *Penaeus aztecus* Ives, *P. duorarum* Burkenroad and *P. setiferus* Linnaeus. Master's Thesis Florida State University.

Kruse, D. N. (1959c). Parasites of the commercial shrimps, *Penaeus aztecus* Ives, *P. duorarum* Burkenroad and *P. setiferus* (Linnaeus). *Tulane Studies Zool.* **7**, 123–144.

Kruse, D. N. (1966). Life cycle studies on *Nematopsis duorari* n. sp. (Gregarina Porosporidae) a parasite of the pink shrimp (*Penaeus duorarum*) and pelecypod molluscs. *Diss. Abstr.* **27B**, 2919-B.

Lear, D. W., Jr. (1963). Occurrence and significance of chitinoclastic bacteria in pelagic waters and zooplankton. *In* "Symposium on Marine Microbiology" (C. Oppenheimer, ed.), pp. 594–610. Thomas, Springfield, Illinois.

Leavitt, R. G. (1909). An interesting crab's claw. *Guide to Nature* **3**, No. 3, 89–91.

Léger, L., and Duboscq, O. (1915). *Porospora nephropis* n. sp. *Compt. Rend. Soc. Biol.* **78**, 368–371.

Levin, J., and Bang, F. B. (1964). The role of gram-negative endotoxin in the extracellular coagulation of *Limulus* blood. *Bull. Johns Hopkins Hosp.* **115**, 265–274.

Linton, E. (1940). Trematodes from fishes mainly from the Woods Hole region, Massachusetts. *Proc. U. S. Natl. Museum.* **88**, 1–172.

Lyles, C. H. (1966). Fishery statistics of the United States, 1964. *U. S. Fish Wildlife Serv., Statist. Dig.* **58**, 541 pp.

MacKay, D. C. (1942). The Pacific edible crab, *Cancer magister. Fisheries Res. Board Can., Bull.* **62**, 1–32.

MacKenzie, K. (1963). *Stichocotyle nephropis* Cunningham, 1887 (Trematoda) in Scottish waters. *Ann. Mag. Nat. Hist.* [13] **6**, 505–506.

Manier, J. F. (1950). Recherches sur les trichomycètes. *Ann. Sci. Nat. Botan. Biol. Vegetale* [11] **11**, 53–162.

Mann, H. (1939). Die Brandfleckenkrankheit beim Sumpfkrebs (*Potamobius leptodactylus* Eschh.). *Z. Parasitenk.* **11**, 430–432.

Mann, H., and Pieplow, U. (1938). Die Brandfleckenkrankheit bei Krebsen und ihre Erreger. Z. Fischerei 36, 225–240.

Mannsfield, W. (1942). Die Krebspest im Generalbezirk Lettland in den Jahren 1924–1938. Z. Fischerei 40, 395–417.

Margolis, L., and Butler, T. H. (1954). An unusual and heavy infection of a prawn, Pandalus borealis Krøyer, by a nematode, Contracaecum sp. J. Parasitol. 40, 649–655.

Matsumoto, K. (1953). On the epicaridization of the fresh-water crab Eriocheir japonicus. (In Japanese with English summary.) Dobutsugaku Zasshi 62, 354–361.

Montreuil, P. (1954). Parasitological investigations. Rappt. Ann. Sta. Biol. Mar. Dept. Pech., 1953, Quebec, Contrib. No. 50, Appen. 5, 69–73.

Moore, J. P. (1946). The anatomy and systematic position of Myzobdella lugubris Leidy (Hirudinea). Notulae Natur. (Acad. Nat. Sci. Phila.) 184, 1–12.

Moore, J. P., and Meyer, M. C. (1951). Leeches (Hirudinea) from Alaskan and adjacent waters. Wasmann J. Biol. 9, 11–77.

Newcombe, C. L. (1945). The biology and conservation of the blue crab Callinectes sapidus Rathbun. Virginia Fish. Lab., Ed. Ser. 4, 1–39.

Newcombe, C. L., and Rogers, M. R. (1947). Studies of a fungus parasite that infects blue crab eggs. Turtox News 25, No. 9, 1–7.

Nickerson, W. S. (1894). On Stichocotyle nephropis Cunningham, a parasite of the American lobster. Zool. Jahrb., Abt. Anat. 8, 447–480.

Nicol, J. A. C. (1967). "The Biology of Marine Animals." Pitman, New York.

Nybelin, O. (1935). Über die Ursache der Krebspest in Schweden. Fischereiztg., Neudamm 38, 21.

Odhner, T. (1898). Uber die geschlechtsreife Form von Stichocotyle nephropis Cunningham. Zool. Anz. 21, 509–513.

Odhner, T. (1910). Stichocotyle nephropis J. T. Cunningham ein aberranter Trematode der Digenenfamilie Aspidogastridae. Kgl. Svenska Vetenskapsakad. Handl. 45, No. 3, 1–16.

Oka, A. (1927). Sur la morphologie externe de Carcinobdella kanibir. Proc. Imp. Acad. (Tokyo) 3, 171–174.

Pérez, C. (1903). Sur un isopode parasite d'une sacculine. Proc. Verbaux Seances Soc. Sci. Phys. Nat. Bordeaux pp. 109–110.

Pérez, C. (1905a). Microsporidies parasites des crabes d'Arcachon. Note préliminaire. Trav. Lab. Soc. Sci. Arcachon 8, 15–36.

Pérez, C. (1905b). Sur une nouvelle glugéidée parasite du Carcinus maenas. Compt. Rend. Soc. Biol. 58, 146–151.

Pérez, C. (1907). Sur un cas d'envahissement de l'ovaire par Thelohania maenadis. Compt. Rend. Soc. Biol. 60, 1091–1092.

Pérez, C. (1927). Notes sur les épicarides et les rhizocéphales des côtes de France. I. Sur l' "Eupagurus bernhardus" et sur quelques-uns de ses parasites. Bull. Soc. Zool. France 52, 99–104.

Pérez, C. (1928). Notes sur les épicarides et les rhizocéphales des côtes de France. II. Nouvelles observations sur les parasites de l'Eupagurus bernhardus. III. L'Eupagurus cuanensis et ses parasites. Bull. Soc. Zool. France 53, 523–526.

Pérez, C. (1929). Notes sur les épicarides et les rhizocéphales des côtes de France. V. Non-spécificité du parasitisme du Liriopsis pygmaea. Bull. Soc. Zool. France 54, 607–609.

Pérez, C. (1931a). Notes sur les épicarides et les rhizocéphales des côtes de France. VII. *Peltogaster* et *Liriopsis*. *Bull. Soc. Zool. France* **56**, 509–512.

Pérez, C. (1931b). Statistique d'infestation des pagures par les *Chlorogaster*. *Compt. Rend.* **192**, 1274–1276.

Pérez, C. (1931c). Les rhizocéphales parasites des pagures. *Verhandl. Schweiz. Naturforsch. Ges.* **112**, 261–276.

Poisson, R. (1930). Observations sur *Anophrys sarcophaga* Cohn (=*A. maggii* Cattaneo) infusoire holotriche marin et sur son parasitisme possible chez certains crustacés. *Bull. Biol. France Belg.* **64**, 288–331.

Potts, F. A. (1906). The modification of the sexual characters of the hermit crab caused by the parasite *Peltogaster* (castration parisitaire of Giard). *Quart. J. Microscop. Sci.* **50**, 599–621.

Potts, F. A. (1912). *Mycetomorpha*, a new rhizocephalan (with a note on the seuxal condition of *Sylon*). *Zool. Jahrb., Abt. 1. Syst.* **33**, 575–594.

Potts, F. A. (1915). On the rhizocephalan genus *Thompsonia* and its relation to the evolution of the group. *Carnegie Inst. Wash., Papers Dept. Marine Biol.* **8**, 1–32.

Prince, E. E. (1897). Special report on the natural history of the lobster. *Dept. Mar. Fish., Can., 29th Ann. Rept.* Suppl. 1, I–IV, 1–36.

Prytherch, H. F. (1940). The life history and morphology of *Nematopsis ostrearum*, sp. nov., a gregarine parasite of the mud crab and oyster. *J. Morphol.* **66**, 39–65.

Rabin, H. (1965). Studies on gaffkemia, a bacterial disease of the American lobster, *Homarus americanus* (Milne-Edwards). *J. Invertebrate Pathol.* **7**, 391–397.

Rathbun, M. J. (1930). The cancroid crabs of America of the families Euryalidae, Portunidae, Atelecyclidae, Cancridae and Xanthidae. *Bull. U. S. Natl. Museum* No. 152, 1–609.

Reinhard, E. G. (1942). Studies on the life history and host-parasite relationship of *Peltogaster paguri*. *Biol. Bull.* **83**, 401–415.

Reinhard, E. G. (1944). Rhizocephalan parasites of hermit crabs from the Northwest Pacific. *J. Wash. Acad. Sci.* **34**, No. 2, 49–58.

Reinhard, E. G. (1945). *Paguritherium alatum* n. g. n. sp., an entoniscian parasite of *Pagurus longicarpus*. *J. Parasiol.* **31**, 198–204.

Reinhard, E. G. (1950). An analysis of the effects of a sacculinid parasite on the external morphology of *Callinectes sapidus* Rathbun. *Biol. Bull.* **98**, 277–288.

Reinhard, E. G. (1956). Parasitic castration of Crustacea. *Exptl. Parasitol.* **5**, 79–107.

Reinhard, E. G., and Buckeridge, Sister F. W. (1950). The effect of parasitism by an entoniscid on the secondary sex characters of *Pagurus longicarpus*. *J. Parasitol.* **36**, 131–138.

Reverberi, G. (1943). Le castrazione parassitaria e la determinazione del sesso nei crostacei. *Attualita Zool.* (*1943*), 1.

Reverberi, G. (1952). Parasitismo, iperparassitismo e sesso nei crostacei. *Pubbl. Sta. Zool. Napoli.* **23**, 285–296.

Ricketts, E. F., and Calvin, J. (1962). "Between Pacific Tides" (J. W. Hedgpeth, ed.), 3rd rev. ed. Stanford Univ. Press, Stanford, California.

Rogers-Talbert, R. (1948). The fungus *Lagenidium callinectes* Couch (1942) on eggs of the blue crab in Chesapeake Bay. *Biol. Bull.* **95**, 214–228.

Rosen, B. (1967). Shell disease of the blue crab, *Callinectes sapidus*. *J. Invertebrate Pathol.* **9**, 348–353.

Roskam, R. T. (1957). Gaffkaemia, a contagious disease, in *Homarus vulgaris*. *Conseil Perm. Intern. Exploration Mer, Shellfish Comm. Rept.* 4 pp. (mimeo.).

Sandoz, M. D., and Rogers, M. R. (1944). The effect of environmental factors on hatching, moulting, and survival of zoea larvae of the blue crab, *Callinectes sapidus* Rathbun. *Ecology* **25**, 216–228.

Sandoz, M. D., Rogers, M. R., and Newcombe, C. L. (1944). Fungus infection of eggs of the blue crab, *Callinectes sapidus* Rathbun. *Science* **99**, 124–125.

Sawyer, W. H., Jr., and Taylor, C. C. (1949). The effect of shell disease on the gills and chitin of the lobster (*Homarus americanus*). *Maine Dept. Sea Shore Fisheries, Res. Bull.* **1**, 1–10.

Schaanning, H. T. L. (1929). Ein eiendommelig varietet av hummer (*Homarus vulgaris*). *Stavanger Museums Aarsh. 1925–28* No. 5, 1–3.

Schäfer, W. (1954). Form und Funktion der Brachyuren-Schere. *Abhandl. Senckenberg. Naturforsch. Ges.* **489**, 1–65.

Schäperclaus, W. (1935). Die Ursache der pestartigen Krebssterben. *Z. Fischerei* **33**, 343–366.

Scharrer, B., and Lochhead, M. S. (1950). Tumors in the invertebrates: a review. *Cancer Res.* **10**, 403–419.

Schereschewsky, H. (1925). Microsporidien als Erreger einer Muskelerkrankung der Flusskrebse. *Zool. Anz.* **65**, 69–74.

Schikora, F. (1906). Die Krebspest. *Fischereiztg., Neudamm* **9**, 529–532, 549–553, 561–566, and 581–583.

Schikora, F. (1926). 50 Jahre Krebspest. *Fischereiztg., Neudamm* **29**, 225–228 and 250–253.

Shiino, S. M. (1931). Studies in the modification of sexual characters in *Eupagurus samuelis* caused by a rhizocephalan parasite *Peltogaster* sp. *Mem. Coll. Sci., Kyoto Imp. Univ.* **7B**, 63–101.

Shiino, S. M. (1933). Bopyrids from Tanabe Bay. I. *Mem. Coll. Sci., Kyoto Imp. Univ.* **8B**, 249–300.

Shiino, S. M. (1934). Bopyrids from Tanabe Bay. II. *Mem. Coll. Sci., Kyoto Imp. Univ.* **9B**, 258–287.

Shiino, S. M. (1936). Bopyrids from Tanabe Bay. III. *Mem. Coll. Sci., Kyoto Imp. Univ.* **11B**, 157–174.

Shiino, S. M. (1937). Bopyrids from Tanabe Bay. IV. *Mem. Coll. Sci., Kyoto Imp. Univ.* **12B**, 479–493.

Shiino, S. M. (1939a). Bopyrids from Tanabe Bay. V. *Annotationes Zool. Japon.* **18**, 11–16.

Shiino, S. M. (1939b). Bopyrids from Kyûshyû and Ryûkyû. *Records Oceanog. Works Japan* **10**, 79–99.

Shiino, S. M. (1942a). Bopyrids from the South Sea Islands with description of a hyperparasitic cryptoniscid. *Palao Trop. Biol. Studies* **2**, 437–458.

Shiino, S. M. (1942b). On the parasitic isopods of the family Entoniscidae, especially those found in the vicinity of Seto. *Mem. Coll. Sci., Kyoto Imp. Univ.* **17B**, 37–76.

Shiino, S. M. (1943). Rhizocephala of Japan. *J. Sigenkagku Kenkyusyo* **1**, No. 1, 1–36.

Shiino, S. M. (1949). On two new species of the bopyrid genus *Bopyrella* found in Japan. *Bull. Biogeograph. Soc. Japan* **14**, 45–50.

Shiino, S. M. (1958). Note on the bopyrid fauna of Japan. *Rept. Fac. Fisheries, Prefect. Univ. Mie* **3**, 29–73.

Shiino, S. M. (1964a). On three bopyrid isopods from California. *Rept. Fac. Fisheries, Prefect. Univ. Mie* **5**, 19–25.

Shiino, S. M. (1964b). On two species of bopyrid isopods parasitic on *Callianassa uncinata* Milne-Edwards from Chile. *Rept. Fac. Fisheries, Prefect. Univ. Mie* **5**, 27–32.

Shiino, S. M. (1964c). Results of Amami Expedition. 5. Bopyridae. *Rept. Fac. Fisheries, Prefect. Univ. Mie* **5**, 237–242.

Shiino, S. M. (1965). Phylogeny of the genera within the family Bopyridae. *Bull. Museum Natl. Hist. Nat. (Paris)* [2] **37**, 462–465.

Shuster, C. N., Jr., Ulmer, D. H. B., Jr., and Van Engel, W. A. (1963). A commentary on claw deformities in the blue crab. *Estuarine Bull.* **7**, Nos. 2/3, 15–23.

Sims, H. W. (1966). An annotated bibliography of the spiny lobsters, families Palinuridae and Scyllaridae. *Florida State Board Conserv., Tech. Ser.* **48**, 1–84.

Sims, H. W. (1967). Personal communication.

Sims, H. W. and Joyce, E. A., Jr. (1965). Partial albinism in a blue crab. *Quart. J. Florida Acad. Sci.* **28**, 373–374.

Smith, G. W. (1906). Rhizocephala. *Fauna Flora Neapel* **29**, 1–123.

Snieszko, S. F., and Taylor, C. C. (1947). A bacterial disease of the lobster (*Homarus americanus*). *Science* **105**, 500.

Sogandares-Bernal, F. (1962). Presumable microsporidiosis in the dwarf crayfishes *Cambarellus puer* Hobbs and *C. shufeldti* (Faxon) in Louisiana. *J. Parasitol.* **48**, 493.

Sogandares-Bernal, F., and Hutton, R. F. (1959). The identity of metacercaria B reported from the pink shrimp, *Penaeus duorarum* Burkenroad, by Woodburn *et al.* in 1957. *J. Parasitol.* **45**, 362, 378.

Sordi, M. (1958). Micosi dei Crostacei decapodi marini. *Riv. Parassitol.* **19**, 131–137.

Sparks, A. K., and Mackin, J. G. (1957). A larval trypanorhynchid cestode from commercial shrimps. *Texas J. Sci.* **9**, 475–476.

Sprague, V. (1950a). Notes on three microsporidian parasites of decapod Crustacea of Louisiana coastal waters. *Occasional Papers Marine Lab., Louisiana State Univ.* **5**, 1–8.

Sprague, V. (1950b). *Thelohania cambari* n. sp., a microsporidian parasite of North American crayfish. *J. Parasitol* **36**, 46 (abstr.).

Sprague, V. (1954). Protozoa. *U.S. Bur. Fisheries, Bull.* **55**, 243–256.

Sprague, V. (1963). *Minchinia louisiana* n. sp. (Haplosporidia, Haplosporidiidae), a parasite of *Panopeus herbstii. J. Protozool.* **10**, 267–274.

Sprague, V. (1965). *Nosema* sp. (Microsporida, Nosematidae) in the musculature of the crab, *Callinectes sapidus. J. Protozool.* **12**, 66–70.

Sprague, V. (1966). Two new species of *Plistophora* (Microsporida, Nosematidae) in decapods, with particular reference to one in the blue crab. *J. Protozool.* **13**, 196–199.

Sprague, V., and Beckett, R. L. (1966). A disease of blue crabs (*Callinectes sapidus*) in Maryland and Virginia. *J. Invertebrate Pathol.* **8**, 287–289.

Sprague, V., and Beckett, R. L. (1968). The nature of the etiological agent of "Gray Crab" disease. *J. Invertebrate Pathol.* **11**, 503.

Sprague, V., and Orr, P. E. (1955). *Nematopsis ostrearum* and *N. prytherchi* (Eugregarinida. Porosporidae) with special reference to the host-parasite relations. *J. Parasitol.* **41**, 89–104.

Stewart, J. E., and Dingle, J. R. (1968). Characteristics of hemolymphs of *Cancer irroratus, C. borealis*, and *Hyas coaractatus. J. Fisheries Res. Board Can.* **25**, 607–610.

Stewart, J. E., and MacDonald, J. F. (1962). A report to the fishing industry regarding lobster disease (gaffkaemia). *Fisheries Res. Board Can., Halifax, Grand Rivière, Newfoundland Lab., Circ.* No. 9, 1–2.

Stewart, J. E., Cornick, J. W., Spears, D. I., and McLeese, D. W. (1966). Incidence of *Gaffya homari* in natural lobster (*Homarus americanus*) populations of the Atlantic region of Canada. *J. Fisheries Res. Board Can.* **23**, 1325–1330.

Stunkard, H. W. (1957). The morphology and life history of the digenetic trematode, *Microphallus similis* (Jägerskiöld, 1900) Baer, 1943. *Biol. Bull.* **112**, 254–266.

Sund, O. (1914). Beretning om anlaeg av statens hummeravlsstation og driften i 1913. *Aarsberetn. Norges Fisk.* **4**, 525–532.

Sund, O. (1915). Statens hummeravlsstation, Korshavn. *Aarsberetn. Norges Fisk.* **5**, 176–181.

Taylor, C. C. (1948). Shell disease as a mortality factor in the lobster (*Homarus americanus*). *Maine Dept. Sea Shore Fisheries Fish Circ.* **4**, 1–8 (mimeo.).

Templeman, W. (1948). Abnormalities in lobsters. *Bull. Newfoundland Govt. Lab.* No. 18, 3–8.

Théodoridès, J. (1961). Sur la distinction entre les grégarines des familles des Cephaloidophoridae et des Porosporidae, parasites de crustacés décapodes. *Compt. Rend.* **252**, 3640–3642.

Théodoridès, J. (1962). Grégarines d'invertébrés marins de la région de Banyuls. I. Eugrégarines parasites de crustacés décapodes. *Vie Milieu* **13**, 95–122.

Thomson, J. S. (1896). A copepod parasite of *Nephrops norvegicus. Proc. Roy. Soc. Edinburgh* **13**, 246–250.

Timon-David, J. (1949). Sur un trématode parasite des crabes en Méditerrannée. *Ann. Parasitol. Humaine Comparee* **24**, 25–28.

Tucker, B. W. (1930). On the effects of an epicaridan parasite, *Gyge branchialis* on *Upogebia littoralis. Quart. J. Microscop. Sci.* **74**, 1–118.

Tuzet, O., and Ormières, R. (1961). Sur quelques grégarines de crustacés décapodes. *Ann. Sci. Nat. Zool. Biol. Animale* [12] **3**, 773–783.

Unestam, T. (1965). Studies on the crayfish plague fungus *Aphanomyces astaci.* I. Some factors affecting growth *in vitro. Physiol. Plantarum* **18**, 483–505.

Uspenskaya, A. B. (1953). The life cycles of nematodes of the genus *Ascarophis* vanBeneden. (Nematodes-Spirurata). (In Russian.) *Zool. Zh.* **32**, 828–832. (Transl. by J. M. Moulton, Bowdoin College, Brunswick, Maine, 1966.)

Uzmann, J. R. (1967a). Juvenile *Ascarophis* (Nematoda: Spiruroidea) in the American lobster, *Homarus americanus. J. Parasitol.* **53**, 218.

Uzmann, J. R. (1967b). *Histriobdella homari* (Annelida: Polychaeta) in the American lobster, *Homarus americanus. J. Parasitol.* **53**, 210–211.

Uzmann, J. R. (1967c). Personal communication.

Uzmann, J. R., and Haynes, E. B. (1969). A mycotic gill disease of the pandalid shrimp, *Dicephalopandalus leptocerus* (Smith). *J. Invertebrate Pathol.* **12**, 275–277.

Vago, C. (1966). A virus disease in Crustacea. *Nature* **209**, 1290.

Van Engel, W. A., Dillon, W. A., Zwerner, D., and Eldridge, D. (1966). *Loxothylacus panopaei* (Cirripedia, Sacculinidae) an introduced parasite on a xanthid crab in Chesapeake Bay, U. S. A. *Crustaceana* **10**, 110–112.

Veillet, A. (1945). Recherches sur le parasitisme des crabes et des galathées par les rhizocéphales et les épicarides. *Ann. Inst. Oceanog. Monaco* **22**, 193–341.

Verrill, A. E. (1908). Decapod Crustacea of Bermuda, I. Brachyura and Anomura. *Trans. Conn. Acad. Arts Sci.* **13**, 299–474.

Viosca, P., Jr. (1945). A critical analysis of practices in the management of warm-water fish with a view to greater food production. *Trans. Am. Fisheries Soc.* **73**, 274–283.

Ward, J. W. (1962). Helminth parasites of some marine animals, with special reference to those from the yellow-fin tuna, *Thunnus albacares* (Bonnaterre). *J. Parasitol.* **48**, 155.

Waterman, T. H., ed. (1960, 1961). "The Physiology of Crustacea," Vols. 1 and 2. Academic Press, New York.

Watson, M. E. (1915). Some new gregarine parasites from Arthropoda. *J. Parasitol.* **2**, 27–36.

Watson, M. E. (1916a). Three new gregarines from marine Crustacea. *J. Parasitol.* **2**, 129–136.

Watson, M. E. (1916b). Observations on polycistid gregarines from Arthropoda. *J. Parasitol.* **3**, 65–75.

Watson-Kamm, M. E. (1922). Studies on gregarines. II. *Illinois Biol. Monographs* **7**, 1–104.

Williams, A. B. (1965). Marine decapod crustaceans of the Carolinas. *U. S. Fish Wildlife Serv. Fishery Bull.* **65**, 1–298.

Wood, P. C. (1965a). A preliminary note on Gaffkaemia investigations in England. *Rapp. Proces-Verbaux Reunions, Conseil Perm. Intern. Exploration Mer.* **156**, 30–34.

Wood, P. C. (1965b). Gaffkaemia, the blood disease of lobsters. *Proc. Soc. Gen. Microbiol.* P. 14 (abstr.).

Woodburn, K. D., Eldred, B., Clark, E., Hutton, R. F., and Ingle, R. M. (1957). The live bait shrimp industry of the west coast of Florida (Cedar Key to Naples). *Florida State Board Conserv., Tech. Ser.* **21**, 1–31.

Yamaguti, S. (1934). Studies on the helminth fauna of Japan. Part 4. Cestodes of fishes. *Japan. J. Zool.* **4**, 1–112.

Yoshida, M. (1952). On the breeding character of the shrimp, *Leander serrifer*, parasitized by bopyrids. *Annotationes Zool. Japon.* **25**, 362–365.

ZoBell, C. E., and Rittenberg, R. (1938). The occurrence and characteristics of chitinoclastic bacteria in the sea. *J. Bacteriol.* **35**, 275–287.

IV

Mortalities of Marine Animals, with Emphasis on the Role of Disease

A. INTRODUCTION

Scattered throughout the scientific literature and the popular press are reports of mortalities of marine organisms, sometimes of catastrophic proportions. Where examined, such mortalities have been attributed to severe changes in the physical or biotic environment, although it should be noted that the precise cause of death of individual organisms has often been undetermined. Mortalities of fishes and a few commercially important invertebrates have received most attention, probably because of the possible immediate economic impact of resultant decreases in numbers available to man, and, to a lesser extent, because of inconveniences and economic losses caused by the presence of large numbers of decaying carcasses on beaches and river banks, and in inshore waters. Some mortalities seem to have their origin in changes in the physical environment: sudden increase or decrease in temperature, oxygen depletion in restricted areas, drastic salinity decrease, or wave action upon larvae at the surface. Biotic factors are definitely implicated in other mortalities: specific disease organisms which increase to epizootic proportions; massive increase of other (usually phytoplankton) organisms such as *Gymnodinium;* and predator pressure, which may force smaller fish into favorable regions or may actually cause stranding on the shore. Such mortalities, if of sufficient proportions, have been called

"catastrophes" by Oppenheimer (1962). They are of interest to paleonto-
logists, who find evidence of comparable events in the fossil record.

Probably the best-documented summary of mass mortalities in the
sea and their causes is that of Brongersma-Sanders (1957). Listed are
categories of causes of recent mass mortalities: vulcanism, earthquakes
and seaquakes, sudden change in salinity, change in temperature, noxious
waterblooms, lack of oxygen, poisonous gases, death after spawning,
stranding, severe storms, and vertical currents. It is interesting that
Brongersma-Sanders did not list disease as a possible factor, but of
course the categorization of mortality factors and estimates of their
relative significance can depend to some extent on the viewpoint and
background of the categorizer. Brongersma-Sanders is an oceanographer
and marine geologist. Her list of references is extensive and constitutes
an important source of information about causes of mass mortalities in
the sea, exclusive of those caused by disease.

Then, too, it is important to distinguish "mass mortality," which is
catastrophic, relatively sudden, and of short duration, from "natural
mortality," which, although variable with time and place, is continuing.
Numerous attempts have been made to categorize causes of natural mortality in marine populations. Oppenheimer and Kesteven (1953) have
proposed a classification of causes of mortality in natural fish populations
which lists six principal categories of directly operating factors: predators,
parasites, pathogens, lethal genes, food deficiency, and physical-chemical
factors (which may be of biotic or abiotic origin) at lethal values. Of
these categories—both density-dependent and density-independent—the
authors believed that the "principal control responsibility [for population
density oscillations] must rest with parasites and pathogens, and mostly
with the latter in view of their more rapid reproduction and presumably
easier dispersion." The authors also pointed out that any one of these
factors could, alone or in combination with others, render fish vulnerable
to other factors, particularly to increased predation.

The discussion that follows considers specific and limited examples
of mortalities in marine populations, without attempting to separate
what might be termed "mass mortalities" from "natural mortalities," since
deaths of individuals constitute a normal part of the life history of a
population, regardless of their intensity in a given area at a given time.
Since most interest and observations have been directed toward mass
deaths of commercial species, this kind of mortality will occupy most of
our attention; but we must never lose sight of the less spectacular but
no less significant continuing natural mortalities in the same populations.
Also, since the orientation of this book is toward diseases, there may be
some slight bias in that direction in the ensuing discussion.

B. MASS MORTALITIES OF NORTH AMERICAN
CLUPEOID FISHES

The clupeoid fishes (families Clupeidae and Dussumeriidae) are especially prominent in the widely scattered literature on mortalities of fishes, probably primarily because of their worldwide occurrence and abundance (they are numerically among the most abundant of fishes), and their great population density in localized areas. If mortalities occur in such densely schooling fish, they will be observed, examined, and reported; whereas widely scattered or occasional dead fish resulting from mortalities of a species relatively sparsely distributed in a comparable area might escape notice. Because of the dense schooling characteristic of clupeoids, even localized environmental changes exceeding tolerance limits could kill large numbers of individuals. Dense schooling could also act to promote the rapid transmission of disease and its dramatic rise to epizootic proportions. Another possibility is that the clupeoids as a group are relatively more susceptible to changes in the physical or biological environment; such changes are most pronounced in rivers and inshore waters where many species of this group occur. Many clupeoids are anadromous; others spend part of their early lives in estuaries.

Fig. 50. Eggs of Atlantic herring washed up on the shore after a spring storm.

Mortalities of clupeoids may occur at any stage of development. Storms or winds may cast pelagic eggs upon the shore, where dessication or freezing can occur (Fig. 50). Demersal eggs may be exposed to predation and to extremes of weather in intertidal areas, or to smothering in areas of heavy egg deposition. Immature fish may aggregate in coves (or be driven into them by predators), where the ebbing tide, oxygen depletion, and high temperature may combine to kill the entire school. Epizootic disease may occur at any stage in the life history of the fish, but particularly during the two most critical periods of what is for individual fish a precarious existence at best—the first year of life and the spawning period.

Observation by the author of mortalities of herring, *Clupea harengus*, along the Atlantic coast of North America during recent years—particularly mortalities resulting from epizootic fungus disease in the Gulf of Saint Lawrence in the mid-1950's—has led to this attempt to summarize and evaluate reports from diverse sources (scientific and otherwise) of mortalities of clupeoids, as an example of what might be done for many groups of marine fishes. Undoubtedly many reports, especially newspaper accounts of mortalities, have not come to the attention of the author, but the literature here encompassed seems to constitute a nucleus about which generalizations may be made. Although the scope has been restricted to the waters of North America, it should be recognized that mortalities of clupeoids have been reported from elsewhere (Eberle, 1929), and undoubtedly are cosmopolitan in nature.

1. Atlantic Herring (*Clupea harengus harengus*)

Mortalities of Atlantic herring have been observed and reported for many years, and have been studied by the author for more than a decade (Sindermann and Rosenfield, 1954a,b; Sindermann, 1956, 1958, 1963, 1966b). Generally there have been two causes for such mortalities: one a combination of predator pressure and lethal physical factors, and the other outbreaks of epizootic fungus disease.

Along the coast of the Gulf of Maine, it is not unusual for extremely localized mortalities of immature herring of age groups 0 and 1 to occur. Dead fish are usually found near and below the low tide line in coves or on open sloping shores (Fig. 51). As an example, in July, 1953, two successive mortalities of this nature occurred in Love's Cove, Southport, Maine, and were examined closely by the author and other personnel of the United States Fish and Wildlife Service and Maine Department of Sea and Shore Fisheries (Anonymous, 1953). At the time of the

FIG. 51. Mass mortality of juvenile Atlantic herring, caused by a combination of predator pressure and receding tide, Loves Cove, Southport, Maine.

mortalities, 20 to 30 seals were at the mouth of the cove, and a few silver hake and pollock were included in the kills. The generally accepted conclusion was that a large school of herring entered the cove on the ebbing tide, followed by predators, and that the combination of predator pressure, falling tide, and oxygen depletion produced the observed mortalities. Similar localized mass deaths among immature herring were observed and examined by the author on the Perry Shore of Passama-quoddy Bay in the late summer of 1953. A number of whales actively feeding and driving the small herring in the predawn hours probably contributed. Bigelow and Schroeder (1953) reported observation of a similar type of mortality due to stranding in Cohasset Bay, Massachusetts, in October, 1920, caused (according to fishermen) by activities of silver hake, which were also stranded on the beach. Allen (1916) reported an extensive mortality of young herring at Rye Beach, New Hampshire, in August, 1911. Similar mortalities were reported in the summers of 1925 and 1928 in Manchester Harbor, Massachusetts.

Entirely distinct from these extremely localized phenomena, and of much greater significance in terms of impact on the population, are wide-spread mortalities of herring caused by epizootic fungus disease. Such mortalities were observed and reported from the Gulf of St. Lawrence

in 1913–1914 (Cox, 1916) and in 1954–1956 (Leim, 1955, 1956; Sindermann, 1956, 1958). During both outbreaks, dead herring were first observed in late spring, and mortalities continued through early summer.
Dead fish were floating at the surface, washed up on the beaches, and
dredged up by trawlers. Dying fish were observed in inshore areas, where
they swam feebly and erratically, and eventually sank to the bottom.
The focus of 1954–1956 mortalities seemed to be Chaleur Bay, although
reports of mortalities came from such eastern points as Newfoundland
and Cape Breton Island. From sampling done throughout the epizootic,
it was estimated conservatively that at least one fourth of the herring
population was killed in both 1954 and 1955. Immediate and drastic
decline of the fishery, and its slow recovery since that time, supported
the original estimate. Although less completely documented, the 1914
epizootic caused a reduction of the St. Lawrence herring fishery to one
third its former volume for several years following (Cox, 1916). The
available evidence strongly suggests that significant population decimation
resulted from the disease outbreaks.

2. Pacific Herring (*Clupea harengus pallasi*)

During the late winter and early spring of 1942, mortalities of herring
were widespread along 50 miles of the southeast coast of Vancouver
Island, British Columbia (Tester, 1942a). After the peak of mortalities
had passed, many fish were seen close inshore, moving lethargically and
erratically. Examination of dead and dying fish did not disclose any
clear-cut pathological condition except a change in texture and color
of the liver, and abnormal red blood cells in some blood smears. It is
interesting that observations of these mortalities, reported for Pacific
herring by Tester, were remarkably similar to those reported from the
Gulf of St. Lawrence in 1954–1956, except that no association with any
known disease was made. Similarities were in the behavior of dying fish,
the later abnormal aggregation of fish close inshore, the fact that the
mortalities occurred near the spawning period, and the somewhat selective
mortality, in that certain other species were involved but the mortalities
did not include all species in the area. At the time of the Pacific mortalities, sardines in the same area died, and hake died in large numbers
shortly after the mortalities of herring ceased. In the recent St. Lawrence
study, alewives and mackerel were reported dying and were observed
dead in July, 1955. Examinations of mackerel disclosed a high incidence
of fungus infection (Ronald, 1960). It seems possible that a disease
similar to that described from the herring of the Atlantic was responsible

for Pacific herring mortalities, even though a pathogen was not identified in the Pacific studies.

Herring eggs on certain spawning grounds in the Strait of Georgia suffered a high mortality in the spring of 1942, during the same period when herring were dying (Tester, 1942b). Large patches of opaque, dead and putrefying eggs were observed near and just below the low tide zone. Similar high mortalities of herring eggs on the west coast of Vancouver Island were reported in 1928 and 1929. A possible relationship between death of herring and eggs was proposed by Tester, but proof was lacking, since the cause of mortality in each case was undetermined.

In March, 1949, a herring mortality occurred at Mud Bay, British Columbia, in quantity described as "in excess of one thousand tons" (Stevenson, 1949). These were mature fish, and the only abnormality noted was that livers were shrunken and darker than normal. Several possible explanations for the mortality were advanced, including the one the predators might have driven the school inshore on a falling tide. It seems significant that during the springs of 1948 and 1949, schools of "dopey" herring were observed swimming lethargically in the inshore waters of the east coast of Vancouver Island, long after the time when they would have normally migrated to deeper water. This observation is of interest because it agrees precisely with the 1942 report (Tester, 1942a) and with observations of the activity of fungus-infected Atlantic herring during the 1954–1956 epizootic.

3. Pacific Sardines (*Sardinops caerulea*)

During January, February, and March, 1941, sardines in the Strait of Georgia, British Columbia, were reported dying (Foerster, 1942). Dead fish were observed floating at the surface, washed up on the shore, and on the bottom, and schools of sluggish, abnormal fish were seen at the surface near shore. External symptoms included flexure of the spine of some fish and hemorrhagic areas beneath the scales of many of the fish. Internally, the liver was a greenish, jaundiced color. A generalized bacteremia was found in dying specimens, but was felt to be secondary— a consequence of general weakening of the fish from some other cause. No definite conclusion was drawn as to the cause of the mortality. Environmental factors were examined, but little correlation was found, except possibly lack of adequate food. There was no evidence of other fish species being involved in the 1941 mortalities, but sardines were again reported dying in January and February, 1942, on the southeast coast of

Vancouver Island (Tester, 1942a) in smaller numbers than in 1941. This time Pacific herring were found dying in the same area. The symptoms noted above are remarkably similar to those observed in experimental tanks of Atlantic herring, in which a gram-negative bacillus is responsible for generalized bacteremia. The same condition is occasionally seen in nature among immature Atlantic herring—many subcutaneous hemorrhages and fraying of the caudal fin being outstanding external symptoms. The spinal flexure seen on some of the dying Pacific sardines and the abnormal fish seen moving lethargically near shore are also reminiscent of the Pacific herring mortalities in the same area, and of observations of fungus-diseased Atlantic herring.

4. Menhaden (*Brevoortia tyrannus*)

Probably no other clupeid is as well known as the menhaden for mortalities about which so little is known. Unlike the sporadic mortalities of other species, mortalities of menhaden occur regularly and annually in some coastal areas, especially in the vicinity of New York and in Chesapeake Bay. According to Westman and Nigrelli (1955), mortalities occur in the New York area in late May and June, and dying fish (known as "spinners") exhibit erratic movement and exophthalmia. Gas emboli have been observed in capillaries, and these authors concluded that salinity variations and pollution may be associated with the mortalities.

Environmental factors, particularly oxygen deficiency produced by an influx of oxygen-deficient deeper waters or by reduced oxygen content due to high temperatures, are felt to be responsible for regular fish kills (which include large percentages of menhaden, in addition to other species such as striped bass, alewives, and shad) in the Chesapeake Bay area. It seems reasonable to expect that temperature changes could also constitute a source of severe environmental stress on menhaden. As in the New York area, mortalities occur from late spring to early autumn in shallow waters of the bay. Many of these kills in Chesapeake Bay have been examined carefully after their occurrence—for example, in Baltimore Harbor in September, 1954, where many menhaden were killed, possibly by oxygen-depleted water masses displaced by the hurricane of August 30–31. Many records of mortalities were gathered for the Maryland Department of Research and Education. Solomons, Maryland, by the late Romeo Mansueti (1954) in the expectation that some pattern might be found and subsequent prediction might be possible. Recent interest in the mortalities has focused on possible viral etiology (Anonymous, 1968).

5. Shad (*Alosa sapidissima*)

Reports of shad mortalities are relatively sparse when compared with those for other clupeids, and such reports usually concern deaths in freshwater, either associated with spawning or with abnormally high stream temperatures. Huntsman (1946) reported that "heat stroke" or suffocation killed several thousand shad in two rivers of New Brunswick and Nova Scotia after a warm humid period when stream temperatures rose to 88°F. Mortalities of shad after spawning have been reported (Cating, 1955) for rivers south of the Neuse in North Carolina, where the fish pile up in large numbers behind obstructions. Repeat spawners are rare in southern rivers, but spawning mortalities decline to the northward; there are some repeat spawners in the Chesapeake, and about 50% repeat spawners in the Connecticut River. This geographical difference in mortality may be due to temperature: the lower summer water temperatures of the more northern rivers favoring survival of the shad after spawning.

Summer mortalities of shad and threadfin shad, *Dorosoma petenense* (Gunter), have also been reported from California. Haley *et al.* (1967) associated the bacterium *Aeromonas liquefaciens*, combined with stress from low environmental oxygen resulting from organic pollution, with one such mortality in 1966.

6. Alewife (*Alosa pseudoharengus*)

Mortalities of alewives have been reported in freshwater studies (Pritchard, 1929; Dence, 1956). Mass deaths were annual occurrences in Lake Ontario according to Pritchard, and have been noted·more recently in Onondaga Lake, New York, by Dence. The species is of particular interest because evidence of mortality appears as "concretions," usually of the muscular portions of the fish, cast up on the shore (Graham, 1956). No obvious pathology was reported in the studies referred to, and it was suggested that freshwater did not provide the essential requirements for normal existence for members of the species.

A mortality of alewives in the marine environment was investigated by the author at Campbellton, New Brunswick, on the south shore of the Gulf of Saint Lawrence in July 1955. This occurred just after the mortalities of herring that were discussed in a previous section, and was probably caused by the same fungus disease that killed the herring. Dead alewives at the time of examination were too decomposed for positive diagnosis of disease, but previous work (Sindermann and Scattergood, 1954) had demonstrated that alewives were susceptible to the fungus and that the course of infection in this species was similar to that in herring. The epizootic peak in herring of the southern Gulf of Saint Lawrence undoubtedly provided great infection pressure on other susceptible species in the area.

Alewives, like shad, frequently encounter severe environmental conditions of high temperature and low oxygen during downstream migration after spawning. Often extensive areas of a river may be fouled with dead fish during early summer. The author examined such an extensive kill in sections of the lower Kennebec River in Maine in June, 1957. Alewives made up over 95% of the dead fish examined over a 5-mile section of river bank, after a period of very low runoff and extremely high temperatures. A similar and even more extensive kill occurred in the lower Charles River, Massachusetts, in June, 1959. Biologists who examined the occurrence attributed mortalities to low oxygen levels produced by heavy sewage concentrations.

7. Other Clupeoids

A mortality of round herring, *Etrumeus sadina,* was reported by Wells *et al.* (1961) from Pamlico Sound, North Carolina. Dead fish occurred in windrows on an extensive section of beach, after a period of high winds and precipitous temperature drop in mid-December—occurrences which led the authors to conclude that the mortalities were caused by sudden cold. An estimated 2 million individuals of this temperature-sensitive species were killed.

Mass deaths of threadfin shad, *Dorosoma petenense,* and gizzard shad, *Dorosoma cepedianum,* have been reported from Florida by Berry *et al.* (1956). Such mortalities seem associated with spawning, and do not seem related to changes in the physical environment, although Parsons and Kimsey (1954) found that threadfin shad died when exposed experimentally to a temperature drop of from 10° to 20°F. Cold temperature, particularly of sudden occurrence, has been implicated by several authors as a cause of fish mortalities. Gunter (1941, 1947a,b) has documented this relationship well for the Texas coast and Storey and Gudger (1936), Miller (1940), and Galloway (1941) for the Florida coast. Such cold mortalities often take place when fish are present in shallow water which chills quickly, or when fish occur beyond their normal range, or at the fringes of their normal range. As might be expected, fish with normal warm-water distributions seem more susceptible to cold mortality.

To summarize, mortalities of clupeoids have been associated with several environmental factors. Fungus disease has killed sea herring and alewives; stranding has resulted in localized mortalities of sea herring; storms have washed great quantities of eggs up on shore; and physical-chemical factors at lethal limits have been suggested as causes of deaths of Pacific sardines, alewives, shad, and menhaden.

A comparable summarization of reported mortalities could be attempted for several other groups of commercial marine fishes, such as the gadoids, but the generalization that would emerge—environmental causes, often with a strong suspicion of disease—would not be significantly different from the foregoing.

C. MASS MORTALITIES OF SHELLFISH

Many physical, chemical, and biological variables contribute directly or indirectly to mortalities of commercial marine shellfish (Fig. 52). Various environmental factors and some of their effects have been discussed by Dexter (1944), Brongersma-Sanders (1957), Coe (1957), Mackin (1951), Dickie and Medcof (1963), Medcof and Bourne (1964),

FIG. 52. Surf clams washed ashore on a New Jersey beach after a severe winter storm.

and Merrill and Posgay (1964). It seems clear that the actual cause of death in many mass mortalities is often undetermined, even after exhaustive studies such as those of Orton (1924a,b), who studied oyster mortalities in England in 1920–1921, and Roughley (1926), who examined oyster mortalities in Australia in 1924–1925.

Disease has been suspected as a cause of mortalities, but the actual disease agent has often proved to be elusive.

In the Japanese literature are numerous historical accounts of mass oyster mortalities of unknown causes dating back to 1915. Although disease was often suspected, specific pathogens were usually not identified. Takeuchi *et al.* (1960) mentioned large-scale deaths of oysters in Kanasawa Bay, beginning in 1915 and continuing for a number of years. Over 80% of the oysters in that bay died annually. Ogasawara *et al.* (1962) reported similar mass mortalities on the Miura peninsula, beginning in 1927 and continuing for 10 years. Oyster farms all along the coast of the peninsula lost from 50 to 80% of their crop annually. More recent mortalities of 2-year-old oysters have occurred in Hiroshima Bay and adjacent localities, beginning in 1945 (Fujita *et al.*, 1953). A 10-year study (Takeuchi, 1963; *et al.*, 1955, 1956, 1957, 1960) provided somewhat-inconclusive evidence that a bacterial pathogen was responsible for the mortalities, but further studies will be necessary. Takeuchi *et al.* (1960) implicated a gram-negative, motile, 1–3 μ bacillus, probably an *Achromobacter*, although the evidence presented was incomplete. Experimental infections were achieved with cultured bacteria, but the organisms could be isolated from healthy as well as sick oysters, and also from seawater. Moribund oysters were characterized by diffuse cell infiltration, massive increase in bacterial numbers, and tissue necrosis. No cultures of the isolates have been maintained.

A series of papers published in the Bulletin of the Tohoku Regional Fisheries Research Laboratory in 1965 described studies of mass mortalities of oysters in another area of Japan—Matsushima Bay, Miyagi Prefecture—that have occurred annually in late summer since 1961. Environmental, physiological, and pathological factors were examined. Pathological changes were observed, and the cause of mortalities was believed, inconclusively, to be related to metabolic disturbance associated with spawning. Mortalities exceeded 60% per year in certain areas of the Bay during the period 1960–1965, and were selective in that other bivalves did not die. A gram-positive bacterium was found in multiple abscesses in up to 20% of certain samples (Numachi *et al.*, 1965), but a causal relationship with mortalities was not felt to exist. Later studies by the Oxford (Maryland) Laboratory of the U. S. Bureau of Commercial Fisheries suggested that the disease condition is the same as that called "focal necrosis" in adult Pacific oysters from Washington, and in Japanese seed imported into Washington. The pathogen warrants further observation, because the abscesses may represent only the chronic stage of infection in more resistant hosts; the acute disease may be more significant in mortality. An amoeboid organism, often present in large numbers and accompanied by pronounced cellular host response, has also been found in oysters from the Matsushima Bay mortality area.

In August, 1966, I was able to observe evidence of significant levels of mortality in Matsushima Bay oysters of market size suspended from rafts. These were parent stocks of United States west coast imports. Mortalities, as indicated by fresh "boxes" and gapers, were as high as 35%, and the Japanese biologists accompanying me indicated that deaths would probably increase through August. Samples that we obtained had some evidence of "focal necrosis," but possibly of more significance were infections with an amoeboid organism that seemed to be concentrated in areas of highest mortalities. The organism was 5–8 μ, with a small (1–2 μ) nucleus having a discrete membrane and centrally located endosome. Extensive leukocytic infiltration was common, particularly in connective tissue adjacent to the gut. Infections also occurred in developing eggs. It appears then that at least two and possibly three pathogens are operative in native Japanese oyster populations at the present time: an amoeboid organism, a bacterium responsible for "multiple abscesses," and the Hiroshima Bay bacterium.

Pacific oysters, *Crassostrea gigas*, imported as seed from Japan and planted in waters of the state of Washington on the west coast of the United States, began dying in significant numbers in the late 1950's. Oysters in their second year after introduction were most commonly killed, and deaths were most often noted at the heads of bays, although occurrences were irregular. In the absence of other obvious environmental changes, and because of the selective nature of the mortalities, disease has been suspected. The pathological condition described as focal necrosis has also been found in seed from Japan. As many as 30% of individuals in a sample were affected. In addition, a haplosporidian parasite, morphologically similar to the pathogen *Minchinia nelsoni* associated with recent mortalities on the United States east coast, has been by staff members of the Bureau of Commercial Fisheries' Oxford (Maryland) laboratory in Pacific oysters from the state of Washington; a similar organism was recognized recently in a sample of seed oysters from Taiwan. Pereyra (1964) mentioned a "multinucleated MSX-like organism, possibly pathogenic" in a dying oyster from Oyster Bay, Washington. No clear association has yet been made, however, of specific pathogens with mortalities of *C. gigas* on the Pacific coast of the United States, and it is quite possible that other environmental factors are operative in the mortality areas.

Hirsch (1921), Dollfus (1923), and Korringa (1952) reported major mortalities of mussels, *Mytilus edulis*. probably due to a contagious disease, in the period 1900–1919. The disease reached a peak in 1914–1916. Sick mussels of all ages lost their byssal attachment, mantles were retracted, meats were thin, and adductor muscles were weak. Histological and bacteriological examinations were inconclusive. Soon thereafter (1919–1923) catastrophic mortalities of oysters, *Ostrea edulis*, occurred in western Europe. Deaths began in 1919 in Mar Piccolo, near Taranto, Italy (Cerruti, 1941), and quickly spread to England and other European countries, where they were examined by Orton (1924a,b), who suspected but was unable to demonstrate a bacterial pathogen. Although no infectious agent was directly associated with the mortalities, disease signs such as mantle retraction, pale digestive gland, muscle degeneration, gut inflammation, and shell and mantle pustules were seen. Ulcerations and pustules on the body and mantle, and shell pustules containing dead or moribund leukocytes were observed in oysters from England and Holland during periods of mortality (Orton, 1937). These signs are quite likely associated with a disease process. In addition to the exhaustive studies of Orton, Eyre (1923, 1924) isolated a fungus, *Cladothrix dichotoma* Cohn, and nine species of bacteria from sick and healthy oysters, but expressed doubt that any were true pathogens.

Korringa (1952) has given an excellent historical account of these mortalities. Cultured oyster beds in France, England, Denmark, Germany, and The Netherlands were affected almost simultaneously. Many natural beds were also destroyed. A few isolated populations (Helgoland and Brittany) were not affected until several years later. Mortalities did not occur in Portuguese oysters, *Crassostrea angulata*, during the time. Although environmental factors such as poor food supply and low temperatures were claimed to be causes of the catastrophic mortalities by a few authors (Gaarder and Alvsaker, 1941; Spärck, 1950), the available evidence strongly indicates an infectious disease (Cole, 1951; Fischer, 1951; Korringa, 1952).

A mortality with characteristics very similar to those seen in European *Ostrea edulis* was described by Roughley (1926) in populations of rock oysters, *Crassostrea commercialis*, from Australia. Oysters died in 1924 and 1925 in Georges River, New South Wales. Disease signs, such as abscesses and ulcerations, were observed and a bacterial pathogen was suspected, possibly combined with winter environmental stress.

Disease-associated mortalities with a history of long and frustrating scientific study were first observed in 1915 in oysters, *Crassostrea virginica,* of Prince Edward Island, Canada, in the Gulf of Saint Lawrence (Needler and Logie, 1947). In the period from 1915 to 1933, the disease spread around the Island, and destroyed most of the oyster stocks, some of which required 20 years to return to previous levels of abundance (Logie, 1956). During the outbreak period, oysters apparently developed resistance to the causative organism, whose identity remains undetermined. Beginning in 1955, mortalities (probably due to the same disease) began in waters of the adjacent mainland of New Brunswick across Northumberland Strait. Oyster populations along the entire northern coast of New Brunswick and Nova Scotia were decimated, but mass transfer of disease-resistant oysters from Prince Edward Island waters, beginning in 1957, has hastened the recovery of the fishery (Logie *et al.,* 1960; Drinnan and England, 1965).

Evidence for mass mortalities in deep-water mollusks has been published recently. Merrill and Posgay (1964), estimating natural mortality rates of sea scallops, *Placopecten magellanicus,* from Georges Bank by ratios of recently dead shells (clappers) to live animals, found ratios as high as 0.83, suggesting extensive mortalities. Medcof and Bourne (1964), also working with sea scallops of the western North Atlantic, identified a number of causes of natural mortality, including parasites and shell pests. They found no evidence of mortality from pathogenic microorganisms, although the flagellate *Hexamita* was isolated from scallops. Dickie and Medcof (1963) reported nine mass mortalities of scallops (up to 80% of existing populations) in the southern Gulf of Saint Lawrence since 1928, which have limited the abundance of fishable stocks. These authors concluded that sudden increases in water temperature were directly responsible. Other less spectacular mortalities (up to 25%) were believed to have been caused by unusual concentrations of predators. Evidence suggestive of mass mortality of Australian scallops has been supplied by Sanders (1966). Explorations for new beds off the coast of Victoria disclosed extensive concentrations of dead shells, but no living scallops in an area which had supported a fishery a decade earlier. Soft-shell clam, *Mya arenaria,* populations of the Northumberland Strait region of the Gulf of Saint Lawrence were found by Ingalls and Needler (1939, 1940) to have suffered mass mortalities in those years. Evidence of recent deaths, in the form of decomposing meats, was recorded for many beds, and quahaugs, *Mercenaria mercenaria,* were also found to have suffered heavy recent mortality. Not all bays were affected, and the authors gave no indication of possible causes of the mortalities observed.

Blue crab populations on the coasts of North and South Carolina have been affected by extensive mortalities beginning in 1965 (Lunz, 1967, 1968). Significant impact on population size was indicated by a marked drop in catch per unit effort in 1966 and 1967, as compared with the previous 5 years. Newspapers stated that great numbers of crabs were washed up on beaches or littered the bottoms of creeks, and that catches were drastically reduced. Disease has been suspected (Lunz, 1967), and two parasites have been identified from moribund crabs—one a vibrio with characteristics of *V. parahemolyticus* (Krantz *et al.*, 1969) the other an ameba, *Parameba* sp. (Sprague and Beckett, 1968). However, no clear association of either disease organism with mass mortalities has been made. These recent mortalities in wild crabs are apparently distinct from the long-recognized high levels of deaths in crab shedding floats (Beaven and Truitt, 1939) which may in part be associated with parasites or diseases (Couch, 1966; Sprague and Beckett, 1966).

A few mass mortalities of commercial shellfish have been definitely ascribed to epizootics caused by specific pathogens (Sindermann, 1963). Recurring mortalities of American oysters in the Gulf of Mexico were found to be caused by the fungus, *Dermocystidium marinum*. Exerting its effects in higher salinities and temperatures among dense aggregations of hosts, the pathogen can cause annual mortalities in excess of 50%. Development and use of a presumptive test, with thioglycollate medium (Ray, 1952), has established the presence of the organism in oysters throughout the Gulf of Mexico and northward along the Atlantic Coast as far as Connecticut. Although the fungus may at times reach epizootic levels in particular areas, its most significant effect is probably that of continuing attrition, year after year, during periods of high seawater temperatures. Effects of the disease on commercial beds are now controlled to some extent by planting and harvesting at prescribed times of the year and by spreading oysters thinly on the beds.

Major mortalities, with consequent severe depression of the oyster fishery, occurred in Delaware and Chesapeake bays on the United States east coast, beginning in the late 1950's. A haplosporidan parasite with distinctive characteristics, *Minchinia nelsoni*, has been associated with the mortalities. Epizootic areas have had oyster losses in excess of 90%, and some indications are appearing of increased resistance among survivors. The disease, like that caused by *Dermocystidium*, exists and exerts severe effects in salinities above 15‰. Seed beds and oyster stocks in low salinity areas have not been destroyed. Recently the organism has been found in oyster populations on the coasts of New York and North Carolina—well outside previous areas of high mortality.

Studies of these serious pathogens of oysters, *Dermocystidium marinum* and *Minchinia nelsoni*, have revealed the very important role of a "salinity barrier" to certain diseases. The fungus *D. marinum* exerts severe effects on oyster populations in high salinity waters of the bays along the Gulf of Mexico coast but does not flourish in low salinity areas. *Minchinia nelsoni*, which has seriously affected oyster stocks of the Middle Atlantic states, also occurs in higher salinities. Both pathogens seem confined to salinities above 15‰; this fact has made possible the continuation of production in parts of coastal areas affected by the epizootics.

Inhibitory effects of low temperatures have been well illustrated for these serious oyster pathogens. *Dermocystidium marinum* causes warm-weather mortalities in American oysters; in fact, the plantings of seed oysters are timed to take advantage of the relative quiescence of the disease in cooler seasons. Surveys of *Dermocystidium* have indicated marked decline in winter. *Minchinia nelsoni*, of Chesapeake and Delaware Bays, is similarly quiescent in winter. New infections are not apparent, prevalence of disease declines, existing infections seem less active, and mortalities are reduced.

Mackin (1961) attempted, from a review of the literature, to itemize characteristics of mortalities of oysters due to various causes. As one who has published extensively on the role of disease in oyster populations, he naturally turned his attention toward mortalities caused by infectious agents. Among many interesting comments in his paper, Mackin stated that "all oyster-producing bays are endemic areas for one or more diseases" and that "not only are bivalve molluscs frequent hosts for pathogens, but they are regularly parasitized by a unique group of low fungi." Mackin further stated his belief that "of all causes of mortality, disease ranks first." Disease, then, can cause significant, if temporary, reductions in population abundance of marine invertebrates. Such reductions may exceed 95% of existing stocks. Additionally, there is every indication that serious but undescribed diseases exist among marine invertebrates. Mackin (1962), for example, mentioned a number of pathological conditions in oysters that were not associated with known pathogens. Rust disease of Pacific king crabs, described in the present paper on the basis of an unpublished contract report, is a commonly recognized condition in the fishery, but has not been described in the published scientific literature.

Destruction of most of a population by epizootics and mass mortalities of course also reduces pathogen numbers, because the possibility of finding a new susceptible host at a critical point in the life cycle is reduced.

Less spectacular mortalities, which also have severe continuing depressive effects on host population size, are probably more common than large-scale or mass mortalities. Minor fluctuations in abundance may be attributable to such "background" mortalities. Also, the parasites and diseases that do not kill the host may act as indirect agents of mortality. Abnormal individuals are rendered more vulnerable to predation in many ways: Their body muscles may be partially destroyed; covering or erosion of their gills may interfere with respiration; or their normal protective coloration may be modified or obscured. For example, Hopkins (1957a) has observed that blue crabs prey more frequently on oysters which cannot close their shells as quickly or as tightly as normal oysters. Any increase in parasite burden must reduce the probability of survival in an environment where death, early and sudden, is the rule rather than the exception. For parasites with complex life cycles involving two or more hosts, consumption of an earlier host in the cycle—one weakened by the parasite—by the right predator may be critical to the completion of the cycle.

Another prominent effect of parasitization of marine mollusks and crustaceans is sterilization of the host. Larval trematodes are notable for destroying the gonads of gastropods and bivalves, and parasitic barnacles and certain isopods produce similar effects in crustaceans. In areas where levels of parasitization are high, the reproductive capacity of the host population may be seriously impaired. In a study of the ecological relation of the marine snail, *Littorina littorea*, and its trematode parasite, *Cryptocotyle lingua*, Sindermann and Farrin (1962), and Sindermann (1965, 1966a) found prevalences of the parasite of over 50% in certain coastal areas, indicating that the reproductive potential of snail populations was suppressed by that amount. An excellent review of parasitic castration of Crustacea has been provided by Reinhard (1956).

Effects of disease can be generally categorized as catastrophic, resulting in mass mortalities, or continuing, producing a constant drain on population numbers. Although disease is always with us, and mortalities have undoubtedly occurred in the past, new factors have been introduced by man to set the stage for the spread of epizootic disease. For example, oysters are transferred promiscuously from one geographical area to another; populations are often crowded in dense beds, sometimes in areas where natural populations did not exist previously; drastic physical and chemical changes have been made in oyster habitats; and new predators have been introduced. A dominant mortality factor—disease—has been aided by human activities; it must be controlled if we are to achieve maximum production of cultivated inshore mollusks and crustaceans.

It is, of course, true that many different environmental factors— physical, chemical, and biological—can kill oysters, crabs, or other animals of commercial value (Brongersma-Sanders, 1957). Any single factor may become overriding, however, at a particular time in the life of a species, and in this chapter I have described several examples of how the factor of disease can reduce the abundance of marine species. Furthermore, it is very likely that many mass mortalities are consequences of interaction of several environmental and population factors.

It is easy, of course, to overextend any point of view; there is no implication here that every decrease in abundance can be blamed on disease. An excellent case could also be made from the published literature for the significant role of predation, particularly during population peaks of particular predator species, as a major cause of fluctuations in abundance of commercially valuable species. Man-made changes in environment can also affect abundance. Because of industrial pollution, shellfish populations have been eliminated from certain localized areas within estuaries and along the coast. In addition, other types of pollution have made extensive areas in rivers and bays unavailable for the harvesting of shellfish. It is likely that mass mortalities are, and have always been, natural methods of population regulation—but, until recently, these mortalities would have been accepted with the same dazed bewilderment and inaction that must have characterized the behavior of our ancestors during the plagues of the Dark Ages. We can now look to methods of environmental control and stock manipulation, particularly for sedentary shallow water species such as oysters, clams, and even certain Crustacea, as part of the methodology of an increasingly complex system of cultivation of our inshore waters.

D. SUMMARY

The following summarizing statements can be made about mortalities of marine animals:

1. Distinction should be made between mass mortality and natural mortality, even though both are normal aspects of the life history of a marine species. Mass mortality implies an event that is catastrophic, relatively sudden, and of short duration, whereas natural mortality is continuing, although variable with time and place.

2. In the literature on mass mortalities in the sea there are comparatively few examples of a specific cause being proved beyond doubt, but many examples of a specific cause being strongly implicated by available evidence. Probably many mass mortalities represent interaction of several environmental and population factors.

3. Documentation (some better than others) exists for mass mortalities caused by vulcanism, earthquakes and seaquakes, sudden salinity change; temperature change; toxic phytoplankton blooms; lack of oxygen; poisonous gases; death after spawning; stranding; severe storms; vertical currents; and disease.

4. Natural mortality may be a result of factors which are density-dependent or independent, but the principal controls for population

density oscillations are probably disease and predation, both of which are density-dependent.

5. The mortalities attributed to effects of disease may in many instances involve contributions of environmental factors such as temperature extremes and inadequate food supply, or such population factors as density and migrations.

REFERENCES

Allen, G. M. (1916). The whalebone whales of New England. *Mem. Boston Soc. Nat. Hist.* **8**, 107–322.

Anonymous (Glude, J.) (1953). Dead herring off coast. *Comm. Fisheries Rev.* **15**, No. 10, 36.

Anonymous. (1968). Menhaden kill in Chesapeake Bay under study. *Comm. Fisheries Rev.* **30**, Nos. 8–9, 25.

Beaven, G. F., and Truitt, R. V. (1939). Crab mortality on Chesapeake Bay shedding floats 1938–1939. *Contrib. Chesapeake Biol. Lab.* **33**, 1–14.

Berry, F. H., Huish, M. T., and Moody, H. (1956). Spawning mortality of the threadfin shad, *Dorosoma petenense* (Günther), in Florida. *Copeia* p. 192.

Bigelow, H. B., and Schroeder, W. C. (1953). Fishes of the Gulf of Maine. *U. S. Fish Wildlife Serv., Fishery Bull.* **53**, 1–577.

Brongersma-Sanders, M. (1957). Mass mortality in the sea. *In* "Treatise on Marine Ecology and Paleoecology" (J. W. Hedgpeth, ed.) Mem. 67, Vol. 1, Chap. 29, pp. 941–1010, Geol. Soc. Am., New York.

Cating, J. (1955). Personal communication.

Cerruti, A. (1941). Osservazioni ed esperimenti sulle cause di distruzione delle larve d'ostrica a nel Mar Piccolo e nel Mar Grande di Taranto. *Arch. Oceanog. Limnol.* **1**, 165–201.

Coe, W. R. (1957). Fluctuations in littoral populations. *In* "Treatise on Marine Ecology and Paleoecology" (J. W. Hedgpeth, ed.), Mem. 67, Vol. 1, Chapter 28, pp. 935–939. Geol. Soc. Am., New York.

Cole, H. A. (1951). The British oyster industry and its problems. *Rappt. Proces-Verbaux Reunions, Conseil Perm. Intern. Exploration Mer* **128**, No. 2, 7–17.

Couch, J. A. (1966). Two peritrichous ciliates from the gills of the blue crab. *Chesapeake Sci.* **7**, 171–176.

Cox, P. (1916). Investigation of a disease of the herring (*Clupea harengus*) in the Gulf of St. Lawrence, 1914. *Contrib. Can. Biol. Fisheries* pp. 81–85.

Dence, W. (1956). Concretions of the alewife at Onondaga Lake, N. Y. *Copeia* pp. 155–158.

Dexter, R. W. (1944). Annual fluctuation of abundance of some marine mollusks. *Nautilus* **58**, 18–24.

Dickie, L. M., and Medcof, J. C. (1963). Causes of mass mortalities of scallops (*Placopecten magellanicus*) in the southwestern Gulf of Saint Lawrence. *J. Fisheries Res. Board Can.* **20**, 451–482.

Dollfus, R. P. (1923). La maladie des moules et la mortalité des huîtres en Zélande au course de ces dernières années. *Bull. Soc. Cent. Aquicult. Peche* **30**, 38–44.

Drinnan, R. E., and England, L. A. (1965). Further progress in rehabilitating oyster stocks. *Fisheries Res. Board Can., Gen. Ser. Circ., Biol. Sta., St. Andrews. N. B.* **48**, 1–4.

Eberle, G. (1929). Ein Massensterben von Heringen. *Natur Museum* **59**, 64–70.

Eyre, J. W. H. (1923). Some notes on the bacteriology of the oyster (including description of two new species). *J. Roy. Microscop. Soc.* 1923, 385–394.

Eyre, J. W. H. (1924). An account of investigations into the cause or causes of the unusual mortality among oysters in English oyster beds during 1920 and 1921, Part II. Appendix D. Final bacteriological report. *Min. Agr. Fish, Fish. Invest., London* [2] **6**, No. 4, 29–39.

Fischer, P. H. (1951). Causes de déstruction des mollusques: Maladies et mort. *J. Conchyliol.* **91**, 29–59.

Foerster, R. (1942). The mortality of young pilchards, 1941. *Fisheries Res. Board Can., Progr. Rept. Pacific Biol. Sta.* **48**, 3–8.

Fujita, T., Takayuki, M., Hirokawa, Y., and Fumio, A. (1953). Pathological-histological studies of the inflammation in Hiroshima Bay oysters (*Ostrea gigas*). *J. Japan Fisheries Soc.* **19**, 766–770.

Gaarder, T., and Alvsaker, E. (1941). Biologie und Chemie der Auster in den norwegischen Pollen. *Bergens Museums Arbok, Naturv.* No. 6, 1–236.

Galloway, J. C. (1941). Lethal effect of the cold winter of 1939–40 on marine fishes at Key West, Florida. *Copeia* pp. 118–119.

Graham, J. J. (1956). Observations on the alewife (*Pomolobus pseudoharengus* Wilson) in fresh water. *Toronto Stud. Biol. Ser.* **62**; *Publ. Ontario Fisheries Res. Lab.* **74**, 1–43.

Gunter, G. (1941). Death of fishes due to cold on the Texas coast, January, 1940. *Ecology* **22**, 203–208.

Gunter, G. (1947a). Differential rate of death for large and small fishes caused by hard cold waves. *Science* **106**, 472.

Gunter, G. (1947b). Catastrophism in the sea and its paleontological significance, with special reference to the Gulf of Mexico. *Am. J. Sci.* **245**, 662–676.

Haley, R., Davis, S. P., and Hyde, J. M. (1967). Environmental stress and *Aeromonas liquefaciens* in American and threadfin shad mortalities. *Progressive Fish Culturist* **29**, 193.

Hirsch, C. A. E. (1921). Ueber eine Muschelkrankheit in Holland. *Fischerbote* **13**, 217–223.

Hopkins, S. H. (1957). Interrelations of organisms. B. Parasitism. *In* "Treatise on Marine Ecology and Paleoecology" (J. W. Hedgpeth, ed.) Mem. 67, Vol. 1, Chap. 15, pp. 413–428. Geol. Soc. Am., New York.

Huntsman, A. G. (1946). Heat stroke in Canadian maritime stream fishes. *J. Fisheries Res. Board Can.* **6**, 476–482.

Ingalls, R. A., and Needler, A. W. H. (1939). Preliminary report on shore mollusc resources of the Northumberland Strait coast of Nova Scotia. *Fisheries Res. Board Can., Ms. Rept. Biol. Sta.* No. 161, 1–26.

Ingalls, R. A., and Needler, A. W. H. (1940). A report on shore mollusc resources of the Northumberland Strait coast of Novia Scotia. *Fisheries Res. Board Can., Ms. Rept. Biol. Sta.* No. 333, 1–29.

Korringa, P. (1952). Recent advances in oyster biology. *Quart. Rev. Biol.* **27**, 266–308 and 339–365.

Krantz, G. E., Colwell, R. R., and Lovelace, E. (1969). *Vibrio parahemolyticus* from the blue crab *Callinectes sapidus* in Chesapeake Bay. *Science* **164**, 1286–1287.

Leim, A. H. (1955). Herring mortalities in the Bay of Chaleur in 1955. *Fisheries Res. Board Can., Progr. Rept. Atlantic Biol. Sta.* **62**, 30–32.

Leim, A. H. (1956). Herring mortalities in the Gulf of Saint Lawrence, 1955. *Fisheries Res. Board Can. Ms. Rept. Biol. Sta.* No. 607, 1–9.

Logie, R. R. (1956). Oyster mortalities, old and new, in the Maritimes. *Fisheries Res. Board Can., Progr. Rept. Atlantic Coast Sta.* 65, 3–11.

Logie, R. R., Drinnan, R. E., and Henderson, E. B. (1960). Rehabilitation of disease-depleted oyster populations in eastern Canada. *Proc. Gulf Caribbean Fish. Inst. 13th Ann. Sess.* pp. 109–113.

Lunz, G. R. (1967). Annual Report 1965–1966. *Bears Bluff Lab., S. C., Contrib.* 44, 1–11.

Lunz, G. R. (1968). Annual Report 1966–1967, Bears Bluff Laboratories. *Rept. S. Carolina Wildlife Resources Dept. Fiscal Year 1966–1967,* 11 pp.

Mackin, J. G. (1951). Histopathology of infection of *Crassostrea virginica* (Gmelin) by *Dermocystidium marinum* Mackin, Owen, and Collier. *Bull. Marine Sci. Gulf Caribbean* 1, 72–87.

Mackin, J. G. (1961). Mortalities of oysters. *Proc. Natl. Shellfisheries Assoc.* 51, 21–40.

Mackin, J. G. (1962). Oyster disease caused by *Dermocystidium marinum* and other microorganisms in Louisiana. *Publ. Inst. Marine Sci.* 7, 132–229.

Mansueti, R. (1954). Personal communication.

Medcof, J. C., and Bourne, N. (1964). Causes of mortality of the sea scallop, *Placopecten magellanicus. Proc. Natl. Shellfisheries Assoc.* 53, 33–50.

Merrill, A. S., and Posgay, J. A. (1964). Estimating the natural mortality rate of the sea scallop (*Placopecten magellanicus*). *Intern. Comm. N. W. Atlantic Fisheries Res. Bull.* 1, 88–106.

Miller, E. M. (1940). Mortality of fishes due to cold on the southeast Florida coast, 1940. *Ecology* 21, 420–421.

Needler, A. W. H., and Logie, R. R. (1947). Serious mortalities in Prince Edward Island oysters caused by a contagious disease, *Trans. Roy. Soc. Can., Sect.* V [3] 41, 73–89.

Numachi, K., Oizumi, J., Sato, S., and Imai, T. (1965). Studies on the mass mortality of the oysters of Matsushima Bay. III. The pathological degenerations of oysters by Gram-positive bacteria and their frequency. *Tohoku Reg. Fisheries Res. Lab. Rept.* 25, 39–47.

Ogasawara, Y., Kobayashi, U., Okamoto, R., Furukawa, A., Hisaoka, M., and Nogami, K. (1962). The use of suppressed oyster seed spats in the oyster culture and its productive significance. *Naikai Reg. Fisheries Res. Lab. Res. Rept.* 19, 1–153.

Oppenheimer, C. H. (1962). On marine fish diseases. *In* "Fish as Food" (G. Borgstrom, ed.), Vol. 2, p. 541. Academic Press, New York.

Oppenheimer, C. H., and Kesteven, G. L. (1953). Disease as a factor in natural mortality of marine fishes. *Food Agr. Organ. U. N., FAO Fisheries Bull.* 6, 215–222.

Orton, J. H. (1942a). An account of the investigations into the cause or causes of the unusual mortality among oysters in English oyster beds during 1920 and 1921, Part I. *Min. Agr. Fish, Fish. Invest., London* [2] 6, No. 3, 1–199.

Orton, J. H. (1924b). An account of the investigations into the cause or causes of the unusual mortality among oysters in English oyster beds during 1920 and 1921, Part II. Appendix A. Interim report on oyster mortality investigations, 1920. *Min. Agr. Fish, Fish. Invest. London* [2] 6, No. 4, 3–14.

Orton, J. H. (1937). "Oyster Biology and Oyster Culture," Buckland Lectures for 1935. Arnold, London.

Parsons, J. W., and Kimsey, J. B. (1954). A report on the Mississippi threadfin shad. *Progressive Fish Culturist* 16, 179–181.

Pereyra, W. T. (1964). Mortality of Pacific oysters, *Crassostrea gigas* (Thunberg), in various exposure situations in Washington. *Proc. Natl. Shellfisheries Assoc.* **53**, 51–63.

Pritchard, A. (1929). The alewife (*Pomolobus pseudoharengus*) in Lake Ontario. *Publ. Ontario Fisheries Res. Lab.* **38**, 39–54.

Ray, S. M. (1952). A culture technique for diagnosis of infections with *Dermocystidium marinum* Mackin, Owen, and Collier in oysters. *Science* **116**, 360–361.

Reinhard, E. G. (1956). Parasitic castration of Crustacea. *Exptl. Parasitol.* **5**, 79–107.

Ronald, K. (1960). Herring mortalities in the coastal waters of the Gaspe Peninsula. *Rept. to the Min. Fisheries Province Quebec, 1954,* 5 pp.

Roughley, T. C. (1926). An investigation of the cause of an oyster mortality on the George's River, New South Wales, 1924–5. *Proc. Linnean Soc. N. S. Wales* **51**, 446–491.

Sanders, M. J. (1966). Victorian offshore scallop explorations. *Australian Fishery Newsletter* **25**, 11 and 13.

Sindermann, C. J. (1956). Diseases of fishes of the western North Atlantic. IV. Fungus disease and resultant mortalities of herring in the Gulf of St. Lawrence in 1955. *Maine Dept. Sea Shore Fish., Res. Bull.* **25**, 1–23.

Sindermann, C. J. (1958). An epizootic in Gulf of Saint Lawrence fishes. *Trans. N. Am. Wildlife Conf.* **23**, 349–360.

Sindermann, C. J. (1963). Disease in marine populations. *Trans. N. Am. Wildlife Conf.* **28**, 336–356.

Sindermann, C. J. (1965). Effects of environment on several diseases of herring from the western North Atlantic. *Spec. Publ. Intern. Comm. N. W. Atlantic Fish.* **6**, 603–610.

Sindermann, C. J. (1966a). Larval ecology of the trematode *Cryptocotyle lingua*. *Proc. 1st Intern. Congr. Parasitol. Rome, 1964* Vol. 1, pp. 12–13. Pergamon Press, Oxford.

Sindermann, C. J. (1966b). Diseases of marine fishes. *Advan. Marine Biol.* **4**, 1–89.

Sindermann, C. J., and Farrin, A. E. (1962). Ecological studies of *Cryptocotyle lingua* (Trematoda: Heterophyidae) whose larvae cause "pigment spots" of marine fish. *Ecology* **43**, 69–75.

Sindermann, C. J., and Rosenfield, A. (1954a). Diseases of fishes of the western North Atlantic. I. Diseases of the sea herring (*Clupea harengus*). *Maine Dept. Sea Shore Fish., Res. Bull.* **18**, 1–23.

Sindermann, C. J., and Rosenfield, A. (1954b). Diseases of fishes of the western North Atlantic. III. Mortalities of sea herring (*Clupea harengus*) caused by larval trematode invasion. *Maine Dept. Sea Shore Fish., Res. Bull.* **21**, 1–16.

Sindermann, C. J., and Scattergood, L. W. (1954). Diseases of fishes of western North Atlantic. II. *Ichthyosporidium* disease of the sea herring (*Clupea harengus*). *Maine Dept. Sea Shore Fish., Res. Bull.* **19**, 1–40.

Spärck, R. (1950). Investigation on the biology of the oyster. XII. On the fluctuations in the oyster stock of northwestern Europe. *Rept. Danish Biol. Sta.* **52**, 41–50.

Sprague, V., and Beckett, R. L. (1966). A disease of blue crabs (*Callinectes sapidus*) in Maryland and Virginia. *J. Invertebrate Pathol.* **8**, 287–289.

Stevenson, J. C. (1949). The mortality of herring at Mud Bay, March, 1949. *Fisheries Res. Board Can., Pacific Biol. Sta., Circ.* **18**, 1–3.

Storey, M., and Gudger, E. W. (1936). Mortality of fishes due to cold at Sanibel Island, Florida, 1886–1936. *Ecology* **17**, 640–648.

Takeuchi, T. (1963). Study of measures to control oyster mortalities. (In Japanese.) *Hiroshima-ken Suisan Shikenio Hokoku* **24**, 29–46.

Takeuchi, T., Matsubara, T., Hirokawa, Y., and Tsukiyama, A. (1955). Bacteriological study on the abnormal mortality of Hiroshima oysters (*Ostrea gigas*). I. *J. Japan. Fisheries Soc.* **20**, 1066–1070.

Takeuchi, T., Matsubara, T., Hirokawa, Y., and Tsukiyama, A. (1956). Bacteriological studies on the abnormal mortality of Hiroshima oysters (*Ostrea gigas*). II. *J. Japan. Fisheries Soc.* **21**, 1199–1203.

Takeuchi, T., Matsubara, T., Hirokawa, Y., and Matsuo, Y. (1957). Bacteriological studies on the abnormal mortality of Hiroshima oysters (*Ostrea gigas*). III. *J. Japan. Fisheries Soc.* **23**, 19–23.

Takeuchi, T., Takemoto, Y., and Matsubara, T. (1960). Haematological study of bacteria affected oysters. *Rept. Hiroshima Prefect. Fish. Expt. Sta.* **22**, No. 1, 1–7. (Transl. U. S. Joint Publ. Res. Serv. for Transl. Program, Bur. Comm. Fish., Milford, Conn. 1965.)

Tester, A. L. (1942a). A high mortality of herring eggs. *Fisheries Res. Board Can., Progr. Rept. Pacific Coast Sta.* **53**, 16–19.

Tester, A. L. (1942b). Herring mortality along the south-east coast of Vancouver Island. *Fisheries Res. Board Can., Progr. Rept. Pacific Coast Sta.* **52**, 11–15.

Wells, H. W., Wells, M. J., and Gray, I. E. (1961). Winter fish mortality in Pamlico Sound, North Carolina. *Ecology* **42**, 217–219.

Westman, J. R., and Nigrelli, R. F. (1955). Preliminary studies of menhaden and their mass mortalities in Long Island and New Jersey waters. *N. Y. Fish Game J.* **2**, 142–153.

V

Disease and Parasite Problems in Marine
Aquaria and in Cultivated Marine Populations

A. INTRODUCTION

Diseases and parasites can play very significant roles in marine aquaculture; in fact, even the limited scale of culture we now have has given us examples of devastating effects of disease outbreaks upon fish and shellfish populations. Most of the available information about diseases of captive marine fishes has been acquired through studies in marine aquaria, but similar diseases have emerged and are emerging as problems among the few species of marine fish now cultured. Shellfish have been cultivated by primitive methods for centuries, but the significance of disease has only recently been appreciated, and methods of disease control are still very inadequate.

A logical sequence for this chapter seems to be to consider first the diseases of fish in marine aquaria, as background for a summary of the limited knowledge of diseases in cultured marine fish populations. The fish diseases can then be followed by a consideration of disease in cultured shellfish populations, about which more is known.

B. FISH IN MARINE AQUARIA

The importance of disease control has become increasingly apparent with the establishment of new marine aquaria and hatcheries, where marine fishes are held in captivity or are reared under hatchery conditions. Studies in such artificial environments should prove to be fruitful sources of information about diseases and epizootics in marine species. A new technology for treatment of marine fish diseases, which includes modifications of techniques used in freshwater hatcheries and aquaria, is slowly developing (Nigrelli, 1943; Laird, 1956; Oppenheimer, 1962) and should undergo marked expansion in the next decade.

The first international congress of aquariology, dealing largely with marine aquaria, was held at Monaco in 1960; and the proceedings were published in four volumes in 1962. A number of papers on the treatment and control of marine fish diseases were presented at the congress. The extent of disease control possible in marine aquaria was effectively illustrated by Paccaud's paper (1962) on diseases of coral fish. These animals are extremely susceptible to a number of microbial infections, and seem incapable of any internal defense against such invasions. Preventive and curative measures included sterilization of water by germicidal lamps, addition of low-level antibiotics in food, and disinfectant dips. In the same volume, Højgaard (1962) described control measures against a dinoflagellate, *Oodinium ocellatum* (Brown), used in the Denmark Aquarium at Charlottenlund. The parasite occurred on the skin and gills of many fishes, especially coral fish. Control was effected with copper sulfate and lowered salinities. Chlupaty (1962) also reviewed the several diseases to which coral fish are susceptible and included published information on treatments. He found, as did Højgaard, that *Oodinium* was one of the most widespread parasites. Another skin disease of coral fish apparently caused by a ciliate protozoan similar or identical to *Cryptocaryon irritans* Brown, was reported by de Graaf (1962) from the Amsterdam Aquarium. The disease progressed rapidly and fish were killed, until a successful treatment with trypaflavine was devised.

As has been true with research on freshwater fish diseases, many of the real advances in understanding the role of diseases in the sea can be expected from studies of fish in captivity. This has been and will continue to be true, especially of the infectious diseases which, in epizootic form, may sweep through aquarium populations, or in enzootic form may cause continued attrition of valuable specimens. Infectious diseases, easily introduced with fish from natural habitats, may flourish in an artificial environment because of increased effectiveness of transmission from fish to fish in a restricted body of water, because of somewhat higher environmental temperatures, or because of inadequate diet and space, and consequent reduction in resistance of the fish. Undoubtedly the total stress of an unnatural environment is involved in disease outbreaks. Furthermore, abnormalities are more likely to be observed in marine aquaria because the fish are subject to much closer scrutiny than is ever possible in the sea. Also, the absence of predators in most aquarium situations permits abnormal individuals (for example, fish with advanced tumors) to live far beyond their expected survival time in nature. As was pointed out by Oppenheimer and Kesteven (1953), external signs of bacterial infections are often visible only when the fish is under water. These signs can best be seen in captive fish; in fact most of the bacterial diseases of marine fishes, such as dermatitis and tuberculosis, have been observed in captive populations (Aronson, 1926; ZoBell, 1946; Nigrelli and Vogel, 1963). Bacterial pathogens, because of high infectivity and short generation time, produce severe effects on fish held in marine aquaria. Oppenheimer and Kesteven (1953) reported that of all external lesions on fish in saltwater aquaria, bacterial tail rot or fin rot was most common. I have reached the same conclusion from 10 years' observations of Atlantic herring, *Clupea harengus harengus,* held in captivity for varying periods up to 2 years. The disease syndrome included progressive erosion of fins and tail, minute hemorrhages beneath scales, disorientation, and roughening, raising, and sloughing of the integument. *Vibrio ichthyodermis* (*Pseudomonas ichthyodermis*), the pathogen involved in Oppenheimer and Kesteven's study, reached epizootic proportions during summer, and many species of fishes were infected. Injections of various antibiotics were effective in reducing mortalities (Oppenheimer, 1962), as was terramycin added to the food (Farrin *et al.,* 1957).

Other examples of skin ulcerations and fin rot of bacterial origin in captive fishes were reported by A. G. Anderson (1911), Riddell and Alexander (1911), Wells and ZoBell (1934), Sindermann and Rosenfield (1954), and Conroy (1963). Oppenheimer (1958) described a progressive tail rot disease of Atlantic cod, *Gadus morhua* L., held in live boxes, accompanied by bacteremia and death, usually within 48 hours from onset of disease signs. Reinfections were obtained from cultured bacterial isolates, and the causative organism was characterized as a species of *Pseudomonas.* The disease developed in water temperatures of 5° to 9°C. Disease signs were remarkably similar to those seen by us in Atlantic herring. A paper by Ford (1928) discussed tail abnormalities in young herring that are highly reminiscent of the effects of bacterial disease, but which were attributed by Ford to "nibbling" of the tail by other members of the school. A bacterial dermatitis was reported by Pérès (1944) from many species of fishes held in the Aquarium of Monaco. The disease produced scale abnormalities, fraying of fins, sloughing of skin, and muscle ulceration, terminating within 48 hours in death of the affected fish. Disease signs were similar to the various types of dermatitis described above.

Lymphocystis, probably the best known virus disease of marine and fresh water fishes, occasionally appears in marine aquaria (Fig. 53). Manifestations of lymphocystis include whitish nodules on body and fins caused by hypertrophy of fibroblasts and osteoblasts. The connective tissue cells grow to enormous size (as great as 5 mm) and become sur-

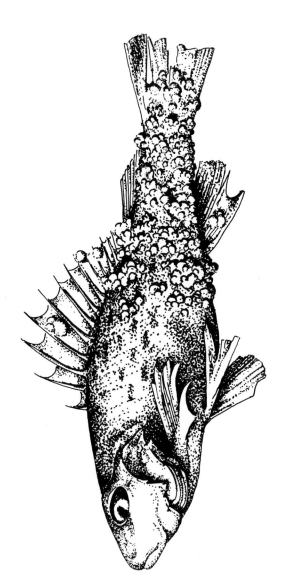

FIG. 53. Lymphocystis disease. (Redrawn from Weissenberg, 1920.)

rounded by a thick hyaline capsule. In severe cases much of the body surface may be involved. A great body of literature has accumulated on lymphocystis; much of the early work was well summarized by Nigrelli and Smith (1939); recent research on the disease has been reviewed by Weissenberg (1965) and Nigrelli and Ruggieri (1965). Observation of the disease among marine aquarium fishes (Nigrelli and Smith, 1939) indicated that it appeared in midsummer and disappeared in late autumn and winter. Infected fish recovered completely, and the disease was seldom fatal.

"Velvet disease" of marine fishes, caused by the dinoflagellate, *Oodinium ocellatum,* has assumed epizootic proportions in aquaria (Brown, 1931, 1934; Brown and Hovasse, 1946). One study in the aquarium of the Zoological Society of London disclosed heavy mortality from the disease over several years. Coldwater and subtropical fishes were affected and mortalities began soon after arrival of specimens from Bermuda. Deaths were attributed to massive numbers of the parasitic dinoflagellate on the gills and occasionally on the external surfaces of 28 species of fishes (Fig. 54). The parasite thus appeared to be non-specific in host selection. Laird (1956) reported it as a cause of major mortalities in a Singapore aquarium. Primarily a gill parasite, it caused hemorrhages and adhesions of gill filaments and apparently interfered with respiration of the host. In heavy infections it spread over skin and fins, giving the appearance of powdery or velvety patches. Nigrelli (1936) also reported this parasite dinoflagellate as common on skin and gills of many species in the New York Aquarium.

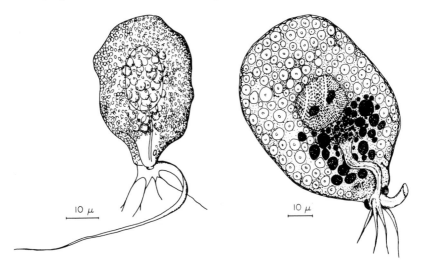

Fig. 54. Trophozoites of the parasitic dinoflagellate, *Oodinium ocellatum.* (Redrawn from Brown and Hovasse, 1946.)

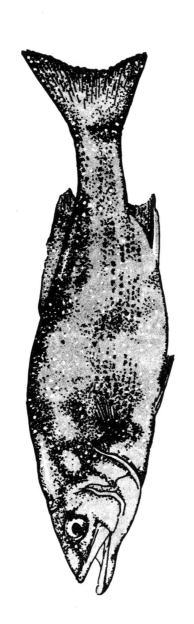

FIG. 55. White spot disease of sea trout, caused by the ciliate, *Cryptocaryon irritans*. (Redrawn from Sikama, 1938.)

A ciliate parasite, *Cryptocaryon irritans* Brown, is the marine counterpart of the ubiquitous freshwater *Ichthyophthirius multifiliis* Fouquet. The parasite, named and briefly described by Brown (1951, 1963), causes white spot disease, characterized by whitish pustules on gills and skin (Fig. 55). The parasite was probably first seen on marine hosts by Kerbert (1886). Epizootics caused by *Cryptocaryon* have been described in marine aquarium fishes in Japan, London, and Singapore (Brown, 1951; Laird, 1956). Infections rarely have been heavy in natural populations. In Fiji, only one species, the rock cod, *Epinephelus merra* Bloch, was infected of 36 species examined from the same coral reef, and all infections were very light (Laird, 1956), but in aquaria few species were resistant to infection. In Japan, 44 of 53 aquarium species were attacked (Sikama, 1938). Parasite numbers increased rapidly when the mature trophozoite dropped off the host and encysted on the bottom of the aquarium. Multiple divisions that followed produced large numbers of motile infective stages.

Nigrelli and Ruggieri (1966) reported *Cryptocaryon* from 27 species of fish of Indo-Pacific and Atlantic origin in the New York Aquarium. They described and illustrated stages in the life cycle, and gave cytological details. Pathology included excessive production of mucus by the host, petechial lesions on body and gills, erosion of gill tissue, and blindness. Heavy infections were fatal. An effective treatment was developed by use of formalin, cupric acetate, and tris(hydroxymethyl)aminomethane in seawater. The authors considered their parasite to be the same as that reported by Sikama (1937, 1938, 1960, 1961, 1962) as a species of *Ichthyophthirius,* and by Brown (1951, 1963), Laird (1956), and de Graff (1962), as *Cryptocaryon irritans.*

The emergence in the aquarium environment of other pathogens virtually unknown in fish from natural habitats was illustrated in a series of studies carried out in the aquarium of the Oceanographic Institute of Monaco. Two algae, *Leucosphaera oxneri* and *Thallamoebella parasitica,* were considered by Raabe (1937, 1940a,b) to be responsible for epizootics and mortalities in a number of marine fish species. Other parasites, including Myxosporida, Microsporida, and larval nematodes, were also implicated in aquarium mortalities (Raabe, 1936; Guiart, 1938). Mullet, *Mullus barbatus* L., from the Mediterranean frequently became emaciated and died from kidney destruction due to a myxosporidan of the genus *Myxidium.* Other fish apparently were killed by liver degeneration produced by the microsporidan *Nosema ovoïdeum* Raabe.

Monogenetic trematodes can reach epizootic proportions in marine aquaria. Jahn and Kuhn (1932) reported heavy infestation of the eyes of fishes of the families Serranidae and Lutjanidae by the monogenetic trematode, *Benedenia melleni* (MacCallum). Aquarium fish carried up to 2000 worms attached to eyes, gills, and nasal cavities, and frequently died. Survivors usually harbored progressively fewer parasites; this decrease was attributed to development of local immunity and to immune mechanisms of the host mucus (Nigrelli and Breder, 1934; Nigrelli, 1935a,b,c, 1937, 1947).

F. S. Russell (1923) reported lesions and emaciation of gray mullet, *Mugil capito*, kept in experimental ponds in Egypt, from heavy infestations of the copepod, *Caligus pageti*. The parasite had not been seen in wild populations.

A number of important prophylactic steps should be considered in marine aquaria; most of them are applicable to freshwater aquaria as well: (1) Prevent the spread of disease by controlling the water which has passed through tanks containing diseased fish; (2) sterilize aquaria periodically with chlorine; (3) keep uneaten foods from decaying in tanks; (4) prevent abnormal temperature, pH, and water flow, which lower resistance to disease; (5) provide food free of pathogens; (6) quarantine all new introductions for 2 to 3 weeks; and (7) isolate any abnormal fish immediately.

A recent popular article (J. Russell, 1966) described research oriented toward disease control at the Toba Aquarium, Mie Prefecture, Japan. A fish hospital with nine staff members carries on studies of diseases and tests drugs and other forms of treatment. Bacterial pathogens have been given major attention—particularly those thought to be responsible for dermatitis and exophthalmia. White spot disease caused by the ciliate *Cryptocaryon* was found to be the most deadly pathogen, and a treatment was devised—a dip of copper sulfate and Neguvon (a Japanese insecticide).

Probably the longest continuing efforts to understand, prevent, and treat diseases in marine aquaria are those of Ross Nigrelli and his associates at the New York Aquarium. Beginning in the 1930's and continuing to the present, Dr. Nigrelli has made significant contributions to knowledge of most of the important pathogens and diseased conditions of aquarium fish, particularly lymphocystis, myxobacteria, mycobacteria, tumors, dinoflagellates, and monogenetic trematodes.

C. FISH IN MARINE AQUACULTURE

Surprisingly few marine fishes are cultured successfully on a commerical scale at present. Some euryhaline species such as milkfish and mullets have been grown in captivity in the Far East for centuries, but culture of truly marine species is a recent development. There is no significant commercial production of marine fish by aquaculture methods

in the United States, but interest has been expressed recently in development of techniques for culture of pompano, mullets, flounders, and certain
other species. Berry and Iversen (1966) have summarized information
about pompano culture, listing recommendations and problem areas,
one of which was disease.

The Japanese have probably made the greatest advances in marine
aquaculture. Shellfish and more recently finfish have been cultivated—
the latter particularly in the Seto Inland Sea Region and in Mie Prefecture. One of the greatest obstacles to further development of marine
fish culture in Japan is disease, and efforts are being made to understand
and control the diseases of cultured marine fishes. In fact, a new scientific journal, Fish Pathology, has just been started there (1965) to publish
results of research on diseases of fish and shellfish. A number of diseases
have been described in this and other publications.

An ulcer disease, caused by a vibrio, was described by Kusuda (1966)
from cultivated fish of nine species in various parts of Japan. Included
were the most important cultured species: the yellowtail, Seriola quinqueradiata; ayu, Plecoglossus altivelis; and horse mackerel, Trachurus
japonicus. The ulcer disease was also seen in wrasses and mackerel taken
from natural waters. Diseased fish usually died within a few days after
infection, and mortalities on rearing grounds reached 98% for certain
species. The pathogen was isolated from diseased individuals, injected,
and reisolated from experimentally infected hosts. The same bacterium
was isolated from seawater samples taken in the Japan Sea and along
the coast. The pathogen was sensitive to a number of antibiotics and to
sulfonamides; diseased fish were cured by adding sulfisoxazole to food,
or by injecting streptomycin, chloramphenicol, or tetracycline. Kubota
and Hagita (1963) found that nitrofurazone (a phosphate-based chemical
developed specifically for treatment of fish) was effective against vibrio
infections of yellowtail.

Mie Prefecture, Japan, is one of the centers of marine fish culture,
especially yellowtail and ayu. Studies of diseases of these and other
species, carried on since 1955, were recently summarized by Kubota and
Takakuwa (1963). Among the bacterial diseases described were (1) a
vibrio disease of ayu; (2) a systemic vibrio disease of yellowtail, and
other carangids (Seriola purpurescens and Caranx delicatessimus); (3)
bacterial dermatitis of a number of fish caused by Pseudomonas sp.; and
(4) ulcer disease of puffers, also caused by a vibrio. The authors were
quick to say, however, that the diseases may not consitute clear entities—
that the same vibrio may be involved in several, and that infections may
be mixed. These possibilities were certainly evident from the descriptions
given.

The vibrio disease of Plecoglossus altivelis occurred in 1963 in kowari

—floating net enclosures used in fish culture in Mie Prefecture. White patches appeared on the skin, followed by sloughing and ulceration. Visceral inflammation and ulceration characterized advanced stages of the infection. Fish transferred to freshwater recovered. The disease was similar to one described by Kusuda and Akazawa (1963) from cultured *P. altivelis* in Kurita Bay on the Japan Sea, and also resembled a vibrio disease, described by Muroga and Egusa (1967), affecting *P. altivelis* being held in net cages in Lake Hamana, a salt lake on the south coast of Japan. Experimental infections were achieved by injection of bacterial isolates, and the organism was recovered from these infections. The pathogen was identified as *Vibrio anguillarum* on the basis of culture characteristics, and the ability to produce experimentally the signs of red disease in eels, including surface hemorrhages, congestion in fins, and areas of necrosis. Inoculated ayu displayed distinct pathological signs; the inoculation site became hemorrhagic, edematous, then necrotic. Intestine, kidney, and spleen also underwent marked pathological changes.

The vibrio disease of *Seriola quinqueradiata, S. purpurescens,* and *Caranx delicatessimus* in Mie Prefecture was apparently similar to that infecting *Plecoglossus altivelis*. Disease signs included skin ulceration, extensive muscular necrosis, and internal hemorrhages. There was some suggestion that other bacteria may have been involved, since successful treatment was reported after intramuscular injection of Sulxin, which was not usually effective against gram-negative bacteria.

The available literature indicates that halophilic vibrios are significant pathogens of cultured marine fishes in Japan, but much confusion exists at present as to the number of disease entities involved. Three vibrios, similar or identical to *V. anguillarum, V. parahemolyticus,* and *V. alginolyticus,* have been reported—usually though, with some qualifications about precise identification.

Bacterial dermatitis is a common and widespread disease of aquarium and cultured fish in Mie Prefecture. Externally visible hemorrhages and ulceration occur, with or without visceral pathology. The disease is thought to be enhanced by surface abrasions, drastic changes in water temperature, or inadequate diet. Kubota and Takakuwa (1963) stated that the causative organism was a pseudomonad, although other studies suggested a vibrio as the pathogen.

Recently a systemic fungus disease, probably due to *Ichthyophonus*, was recognized in cultured yellowtail (Egusa, 1967). This ubiquitous fungus has caused epizootics in freshwater salmonid hatcheries in the western United States in which raw marine clupeoid fishes, salmon viscera, infected trout viscera, and infected saltwater forage fishes were used as part of the hatchery diet. A similar situation may exist in Japanese marine fish culture.

Among the parasitic diseases of cultured marine fishes of Mie Prefecture discussed by Kubota and Takakuwa (1963), monogenetic trematodes caused greatest damage to yellowtails. Two species were significant: *Benedenia seriolae* Yamaguti and *Axine heterocerca* Goto. *Benedenia* occurred on the body surfaces; as many as 570 were counted on individual hosts. Numbers varied seasonally, being lowest during winter and spring. Heavy infestations caused reduction in growth rate, emaciation, and abrasions which rendered the fish vulnerable to bacterial dermatitis. The parasites developed in great numbers in regions where concentrations of small *kowari* existed. Kusuda (1960) proposed a successful freshwater treatment. *Benedenia seriolae* is also a serious problem among yellowtail fish-culture farms in Shizuoka Prefecture. Kasahara (1967a,b), who reported on biological studies oriented toward control measures, found that *B. seriolae* produced eggs repeatedly, and that the worm tolerated temperatures up to 28°C before it detached. Sodium pyrophosphate was an effective control. Hoshina (1968) extended the experimental studies on *Benedenia*. He found that larvae could survive free from the host for one day, and that the time from hatching to maturity was as little as 18 days at 22°–26°C.

Axine is a blood-sucking trematode which parasitizes the gills. Heavy infestations may cause severe anemia and may kill the host fish. Even light parasitization may cause emaciation. In 1963 most of the cultured yellowtail populations in Mie Prefecture were severely affected by this gill parasite. Some control was achieved by short-term brine dips.

Other parasites of cultured yellowtail, of relatively minor significance, include several unidentified species of monogenetic trematodes; the digenetic trematodes, *Echinostephanus hispidus* Yamaguti and *Tormopsolus orientalis* Yamaguti, from the intestines; several species of ectoparasitic copepods of the genera *Caligus* and *Lernaeopoda* on gills, buccal cavity, and fins; and a parasitic isopod in the gill cavity.

Significant advances in the use of brackish-water ponds for fish culture have been made in Israel in the past two decades. Commercial production concentrates on carp, mullet, and tilapia, and has reached a level of 10,000 tons annually. Serious disease problems were encountered early in the program (Tal and Shelubsky, 1952). Ectoparasites—monogenetic trematodes and parasitic crustacea—have been considered most harmful, particularly to young fry, and effective controls by insecticides have been developed (Shilo, 1953; Sarig and Lahav, 1959; Lahav and Sarig, 1964; Lahav et al., 1962, 1964, 1966; Paperna, 1963a,b, 1964; Sarig et al., 1965). Other serious problems in the brackish ponds of Israel include mortalities of fish due to low oxygen concentrations that follow algal blooms, and mortalities due to blooms of toxin-producing algae

(Shilo *et al.*, 1964; Shilo, 1965; Abeliovitch, 1967).

The role of disease in experimental marine fish-farming was the subject of a preliminary report by J. I. W. Anderson and Conroy (1968a). Flatfishes and salmonids maintained in seawater were affected by a number of diseases. An outbreak of lymphocystis occurred in a breeding population of Dover sole, *Solea vulgaris.* A vibrio disease, caused by an organism with characteristics of *Vibrio anguillarum,* affected most of the species being held in ponds and tanks. The most obvious external sign was ulceration of the belly and caudal peduncle. Hemorrhage and pathological changes occurred in the viscera. Antibiotic therapy was unsuccessful. Another bacterial disease, caused by a myxobacterium, affected rainbow trout held in cages in seawater. Progressive erosion of the upper jaw was the most prominent disease sign. Effective control was achieved by repeated dips in 1:2000 copper sulfate solution. An extensive infestation of Dover sole stocks by the monogenetic trematode, *Entobdella soleae,* was observed after the fish had been in captivity one year. Formalin baths (1:4000) were effective in controlling the problem. Leeches (*Piscicola* sp.) and parasitic copepods, *Lepeophtheirus nordmanni,* flourished on Dover sole and turbot, respectively. The only control measure proposed was washing with jets of freshwater. In addition to the diseases caused by microbial and other parasites, lipoid degeneration of the liver due to inadequate diet was observed in a population of juvenile turbot. Mortalities occurred until the diet was changed.

In summary, knowledge of disease control measures for captive marine fishes is still rudimentary. The extensive information about freshwater disease control—particularly that developed for hatcheries—often cannot be extended directly to the marine environment, as Oppenheimer (1962) has pointed out. The pH and salt content of seawater may alter the activity of antibiotics and other chemicals used in disease therapy. A growing interest exists, however, in therapeutic measures applicable to marine environments. Bacteria, Protozoa, and monogenetic trematodes constitute most serious menaces to captive and cultured marine species; severe mortalities have been caused by outbreaks of each. Other pathogens, particularly viruses, may play significant but as yet undetermined roles.

D. SHELLFISH CULTURE

Diseases can appear in shellfish populations held or grown under the following artificial conditions:

1. Short-term holding of market-size crustaceans such as lobsters and crabs in pounds, tanks, and live cars; and similar holding of market-size

clams and oysters in tanks and inshore beds.

2. Cultivation of shellfish such as oysters or mussels in natural waters, which involves catching seed in natural waters; spreading seed on growing beds, or transferring it to growing racks or rafts; and possibly transfer of partially grown stocks to other growing beds; or, in Crustacea, the cultivation of shrimp by trapping juveniles in tidal ponds, and possibly adding nutrient.

3. Production of molluscan shellfish larvae and spat in hatcheries, or the production of crustacean larvae and juveniles in hatcheries, in treated or recirculated seawater, followed in some cases by growth to market size under artificial conditions.

1. Short-Term Holding of Market-Size Shellfish

Numerous examples of disease-caused mortalities among captive shellfish have been recorded. The practice of holding crabs during molting in shedding tanks or floats aids the buildup of commensal ciliates on the gills, and contributes to mortalities. Molting blue crabs from Chesapeake Bay suffered serious mortalities in the summers of 1965 and 1966. Their gills had a massive infestation of peritrichous ciliates of the genera *Lagenophrys* and *Epistylus* (Couch, 1966, 1967). Mortalities were most severe among crabs in holding tanks just before or after molting, but crabs from natural waters were also heavily infested, and fishermen reported mortalities. Infestations of gills frequently seemed heavy enough to interfere with respiration.

Populations of American lobsters, *Homarus americanus*, held in live cars or pounds suffer major losses from two bacterial diseases: red tail or gaffkaemia caused by the coccus *Gaffkya homari*, and shell disease caused by chitin-destroying, gram-negative bacilli (considered in greater detail in Chapter III). Both diseases can be transmitted under crowded conditions that prevail in pounds. Gaffkaemia was first noted on the North American east coast in 1946. Disease signs include variable pink coloration of the ventral abdomen, pink hemolymph, prolonged clotting time, and drastic reduction in blood phagocytes. Diseased lobsters become progressively weaker, and mortalities may reach 50% after short periods of storage. Mortalities increase sharply if water temperature exceeds 15°C. Moribund lobsters often move to shoal water and die.

Two epizootics of gaffkaemia have occurred on the Maine coast, one in 1946–1947 and another in 1959–1960 (Goggins and Hurst, 1960). Losses reached as high as 58% of impounded populations. The pathogen was able to live and multiply outside the lobster, in the slime on lobster cars, crates, tanks, and live wells. *Gaffkya* was also isolated from mud of tidal pounds and from seawater several miles from infected pounds. The disease was transmitted experimentally by allowing presumably healthy lobsters to feed on infected individuals or by holding healthy lobsters in seawater containing the pathogen. Deaths followed in 14 to 21 days. Treatment of tidal pounds with calcium hypochlorite reduced populations of the pathogen in bottom mud, and reduced subsequent losses of impounded lobsters.

Gaffkya-like organisms have also been isolated from European lobsters, *Homarus vulgaris* Edwards, by Wood (1965a,b). He observed mortalities in storage tanks in southern England in 1962, and recovered *Gaffkya* with cultural and biochemical characteristics similar to Canadian and United States isolates.

The second bacterial disease of lobsters, known as shell disease, is caused by chitin-destroying, gram-negative bacilli. Hess (1937) isolated chitin-degrading bacteria from live American lobsters impounded at Yarmouth, Nova Scotia. The disease was characterized by a pitting and sculpturing of the exoskeleton. Initial lesions occurred on the walking legs and were distinguished by white outer margins, from which the bacteria were most readily isolated. Although disease signs were first seen in impounded lobsters, similar conditions were later observed in newly caught lobsters from several widely separated Canadian fishing grounds. Hess found the disease relatively rare in natural populations but noted severe shell erosion and weakening of lobsters stored in pounds over the winter.

Significant mortalities of captive lobsters accompanied the shell disease. Taylor (1948) stated that 71% of infected captive lobsters died from the disease, but observed no correlation between mortality and intensity of external shell erosion. Contraction of the disease by healthy lobsters placed in seawater tanks with infected individuals indicated direct transmission. The disease developed slowly, requiring at least 3 months before the advanced stages were reached. Progress of chitin destruction was directly temperature-dependent and new shell laid down after molting was not affected, except by reinfection.

2. Shellfish Culture in Natural Waters

Evidence is good for significant effects of disease on shellfish cultured in natural waters. Planted oyster beds in Delaware and Chesapeake bays on the United States east coast have been severely affected in the last decade by Delaware Bay disease, caused by the haplosporidan protozoan, *Minchinia nelsoni*. According to Andrews (1966), nearly half the planted beds in Virginia waters of Chesapeake Bay were forced out of production from 1959 to 1961 because of this disease, and planted beds in Delaware Bay were even more seriously affected. Andrews found that oysters became infected from May through October, and that mortality was highest in early summer and early autumn. Deaths could occur within 2 months following introduction, and mortalities in each of the first 2 years after introduction were usually 50–60%. Andrews and Wood (1967) surveyed Virginia oyster grounds for several years to determine disease intensity. The beds were classified according to prevalence of *M. nelsoni* and risk of loss due to the pathogen, as a guide to oystermen in planning their planting and harvesting.

Four states whose oyster industries have been seriously affected by Delaware Bay disease (Virginia, Maryland, Delaware, and New Jersey) have for several years been carrying on programs, partly financed by federal funds, to develop stocks of oysters resistant to the disease. Judging from the apparent development of resistance to a disease (Malpeque Bay disease) of similar severity but unknown etiology in oyster stocks of Prince Edward Island, Canada, a number of years ago (Logie, 1956), this approach to the problem of returning oyster beds to full production seems reasonable. Whether human efforts can hasten the process of selection now presumably in progress among natural populations exposed to epizootic Delaware Bay disease remains to be seen. Little published information on the results of these state programs is yet available, with the exception of an abstract and a recent paper from the Virginia group (Powell and Andrews, 1967; Andrews, 1968). The abstract (Powell and Andrews, 1967) stated that "early exposure of spat to the disease is important" (in reducing mortalities) and that "the work . . . has demonstrated that resistance can be both hereditary and acquired." Additional details of Virginia's resistant stock program have been published (Andrews, 1968). Findings indicated that "history and source of parental oysters was less important for survival than early exposure to an environment where the disease was active," and "survival of progeny and native oysters to market size in areas of intensive MSX activity where imported susceptibles had high death rates suggests that acquired resistance is involved." As Andrews has pointed out, if survival of oysters in epizootic areas is increased more by early exposure to disease and by acquired rather than innate resistance, the immediate need for producing seed from genetically resistant parents in controlled environments would be reduced.

Another disease of planted oysters, caused by the fungus *Dermocystidium marinum*, is greatly influenced by proximity of susceptible hosts. Mackin (1962) has speculated that epizootics may follow initiation of the practice of concentrating oyster plantings in small areas. It was his opinion that "this one factor has made those areas where crowded planting is the rule the areas of most intense development of oyster disease [Louisiana and Virginia]." He asked the question, "Has modern planting method itself precipitated the most acute crisis in oyster production ever observed?" His summary suggested the answer: "Part of the increasing toll of disease may be due to heavily crowded plantings, constant re-introduction of large numbers of susceptible oysters to areas of endemic disease, and repeated re-introduction of disease by exotic oyster populations."

The reduced effects of *Dermocystidium* disease during periods of lower water temperatures and in lower salinities have important implications for oyster culture in enzootic areas. The disease is active for most of the year in the Gulf of Mexico, but is quiescent for almost half the year in Chesapeake Bay. Ray and Chandler (1955) found that in Louisiana the entire crop of oysters could be lost in one summer because of *Dermocystidium*. Andrews and Hewatt (1957) reported that oysters could be held for two or three summers in Virginia before yield was reduced by the disease to a level which returned no profit. Losses could be minimized by limiting the number of summers that oysters were held in enzootic areas, and by maximum use of low salinity areas.

Age and size of oysters influence the prevalence of fungus infections and the mortality rate. Spat are thought to be refractory to infection until they are 3 to 4 months old, and death rates are low during the first year of life. Prevalence and mortality rate both increase with age and size. Thus it is important to plant the largest seed possible, and to harvest oysters as soon as they reach market size. To minimize losses due to *Dermocystidium*, Andrews and Hewatt (1957) recommended planting in early autumn, to take advantage of autumn and spring growth before infections occur. Harvesting in late spring was also advised.

Variations in susceptibility to the fungus pathogen, pointed out by Andrews and Hewatt (1957), have important implications for oyster planters. As an example, oyster seed from seaside bays of Virginia was so susceptible that its use in enzootic areas was precluded, if more than a single summer's exposure to the fungus was required. Comparison of seed from several states disclosed that the South Carolina stocks were least susceptible of those tested.

Other evidence for effects of disease has been derived from studies of populations of oysters grown on the bottom and by suspended culture in Japan. The Japanese literature contains numerous historical accounts of mass mortalities of oysters dating back to 1915. Although disease was often suspected, specific pathogens were usually not identified in the earlier work. Takeuchi *et al.* (1960) mentioned large-scale mortalities of oysters in Kanasawa Bay, beginning in 1915 and continuing for several years. Over 80% of the oysters in that bay died annually during the period. Ogasawara *et al.* (1962) reported similar mass mortalities on the Miura Peninsula, beginning in 1927 and continuing for 10 years. Oyster farms along the coast of the peninsula lost 50–80% of their crop annually. More recent mortalities of 2-year-old oysters have occurred in Hiroshima Bay and adjacent localities, beginning in 1945 (Fujita *et al.*, 1953). A 10-year study (Takeuchi *et al.*, 1960) provided somewhat inconcusive evidence that a bacterial pathogen caused the mortalities.

A series of papers published in the *Bulletin of the Tohoku Regional Fisheries Research Laboratory* (Imai *et al.*, 1965; Kan-no *et al.*, 1965; Mori *et al.*, 1965a,b; Numachi *et al.*, 1965; Tamate *et al.*, 1965) described mass mortalities of raft-cultured oysters in Matsushima Bay, Miyagi Prefecture, Japan, that have occurred annually in late summer since 1961. Environmental, physiological, and pathological factors were examined. Pathological changes were observed, and mortalities were considered to be related to metabolic changes during fattening and spawning. Mortalities exceeded 60% per year in certain areas of the Bay during 1961–1964. A gram-positive bacterium was found in multiple abscesses in as many as 20% of oysters in certain samples (Numachi *et al.*, 1965), but a causal relation with mortalities was not established. Later studies suggested that the disease condition is the same as that called focal necrosis, recognized in adult Pacific oysters from Washington examined at the Oxford Laboratory of the Bureau of Commercial Fisheries. The pathogen warrants further observation, since the abscesses may represent only the chronic stage of infection in resistant hosts, whereas the acute disease may have a significant effect on mortality (Sindermann and Rosenfield, 1967). Additionally, an amoeboid organism, often present in large numbers and accompanied by pronounced host response, was found in samples of oysters from the Matsushima Bay mortality area examined at the Oxford Laboratory.

A well documented example of the effects of a parasite on cultivated mussel populations is the invasion of the north European sea mussel stocks by the copepod, *Mytilicola intestinalis*. A voluminous body of literature (considered in greater detail in Chapter III) has accumulated about this parasite and its effects on mussels. Steuer (1902) first described the parasite from the intestines of Mediterranean edible mussels, *Mytilus galloprovincialis* L., and Pesta (1907) outlined the life history. Korringa (1950, 1959) described the relatively sudden appearance of *Mytilicola* in sea mussel stocks of the Netherlands in 1949, and its subsequent spread to many mussel beds during the following decade. The organism had been known in Mediterranean mussels since the beginning of the twentieth century (Monod and Dollfus, 1932). In 1938 it was found near Cuxhaven, Germany; from there it was assumed to have spread westward to the Netherlands. Dissemination was thought by Korringa and others to be aided by mussel-encrusted ships, by movement of planktonic larvae, and by transfer of seed mussels from infested areas. *Mytilicola* was also very abundant in localized areas of the English coast in 1946. Korringa stated that the condition of mussels was generally correlated with intensity of parasitization; mussels with fewer than 5 copepods were still healthy, those with 5 to 10 were visibly thinner, and more heavily infested lots suffered serious mortalities. According to Meyer-Waarden and Mann (1954) and Mann (1956), gonads of infested individuals weighed 10–30% less than those of nonparasitized mussels.

Infestation of sea mussels led to poor growth, thin meats (Cole and Savage, 1951; Mann, 1951), cream-colored rather than dark brown digestive diverticulum, failure of byssal development, and a dirty red-brown color of the meats. Reproduction of the parasite was accelerated by warm water, and the many young parasites present in the summer invaded and killed mussels. Mussels of all sizes died, including seed. Mussels fell from culture racks and died during transport to markets (Brienne, 1964). Density of mussel beds was believed to influence survival and multiplication of the parasite. Infections were light in areas where the mussels were thinly scattered and near the surface of the water. Because of the continued spread of *Mytilicola* in the Netherlands, an extensive scheme of repeated dredging of natural beds, transfer of lightly infested stocks, and destruction of heavily infested stocks was outlined by Korringa (1959) to create a barrier to further invasion.

Mytilicola in mussel populations grown on floats in Spain was studied by Andreu (1963). Infestation was greater near shore where tidal currents were weak. Vertical distribution of the parasite in cultured mussels grown on 6-meter ropes was uniform in areas of strong currents, but increased with depth where currents were weak. Andreu's findings agree well with those of Hepper (1955), who concluded from field observations that mussels raised from the bottom, or in fast-moving water at either end of an estuary, were less heavily infested with *Mytilicola* than those on the bottom, in slow-moving water, or in the mid-regions of estuaries. Hepper believed that control of the copepod was possible by using off-bottom culture or by locating culture beds in fast-moving water or at the brackish-water ends of estuaries.

3. Production of Shellfish in Artificial Environments

It is obvious that culture methods for marine animals will become increasingly complex, and may depend more and more on artificial environments. Among the invertebrates, a pressing need for disease control is already developing in shellfish hatcheries. Tubiash *et al.* (1965) described mass mortalities of bivalve mollusk larvae in hatchery tanks due to gram-negative, motile bacilli believed to be *Vibrio* sp. or *Aeromonas* sp. (Fig. 56) and found that all the pathogenic serotypes were sensitive to certain antibiotics. Combistrep and chloramphenicol were effective as therapeutic agents. Other epizootics in hatchery-reared oyster and clam larvae were found by Davis *et al.* (1954) to be caused by a fungus, later described as *Sirolpidium zoophthorum* by Vishniac (1955). Juvenile as well as larval bivalves were killed and epizootics in particular cultures destroyed most of the population in 2 to 4 days. Some control of epizootics, or reduction of their effects, can be expected by such measures as

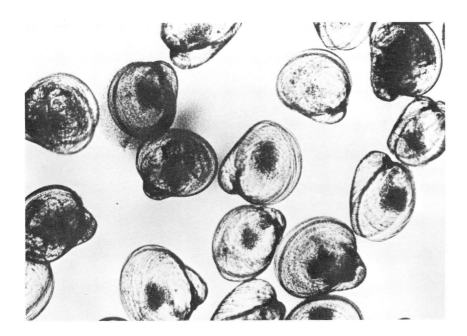

FIG. 56. Effects of bacterial disease in hatchery-reared bivalve larvae. Note dead individuals and bacterial "swarming" in center of photograph. (From Tubiash *et al.*, 1965.)

filtration and ultraviolet treatment of seawater, and use of bacteria-free algal cultures or sterilized artificial diets.

Hatcheries for the production of lobster larvae have been in existence in the United States and elsewhere for over half a century. Techniques were developed to hold "berried" (egg-bearing) females until larvae hatched, and to carry larvae through several molts. Larvae were then returned to the sea, but produced no demonstrable effect on the abundance of natural populations. Because of the high individual value of species such as lobsters, it might be possible to devise complete artificial culture systems to produce market-size individuals, but such a system is not available now. Even in the practice of short-term hatching and early larval rearing of lobsters, however, parasites and diseases have been problems. Egg-bearing female lobsters held in hatching troughs may die from the effects of *Gaffkya* infections before eggs are hatched. Similarly, female lobsters, as well as their eggs and larvae, may be infested with the annelid *Histriobdella*. Lobster eggs may also be destroyed by the suctorian *Ephelota*. These examples make it seem reasonable to expect that longer-term cultivation of lobsters or other crustacean species would encounter severe difficulties with parasites and diseases. Some evidence for this prediction can be found in a recent paper on the significance of disease in attempts at English prawn culture in seawater tanks (Anderson and Conroy, 1968b). Prawns, *Palaemon serratus*, were severely affected by a progressive systemic fungus disease which was first seen in egg-bearing females which had been captured at sea. Infection quickly spread to most groups of prawns being cultured. The etiological agent was tentatively assigned to the Phycomycete genus *Pythium*, and the authors noted the similarity between this disease and a mycosis caused by *Aphanomyces astaci* in European freshwater crayfish. Another important pathological condition seen in the prawns was brown spot disease, characterized by erosion of the exoskeleton and inflammation of underlying tissues. The disease was widespread among the cultured prawns. Anderson and Conroy alluded to other published examples of crustacean diseases caused by chitinivorous bacteria, but did not identify the organism responsible for brown spot disease. The concluding statement by Anderson and Conroy is of interest: "In any large-scale crustacean hatchery, diseases will undoubtedly occur and practical remedies will have to be sought. Mycoses would appear to be particularly hazardous and as far as we are aware no effective therapy is currently available."

The number of shellfish hatcheries in the United States and elsewhere is increasing gradually each year and plans now exist for growing various shellfish to market size under completely artificial conditions. If we can draw on experience with freshwater fish hatcheries, disease research must accompany any expansion of shellfish culture. Regardless of the degree of sophistication in other methodology, adequate disease control must be available, if catastrophic losses are to be avoided.

4. Effects of Transfers and Introductions of Shellfish

One final aspect of disease in cultured shellfish populations concerns results of transfers and introductions. Probably no marine animals have been moved from place to place more promiscuously than oysters. In most present-day oyster cultivation, seed stock is transferred to growing areas, often over great distances. Seed oysters may be introduced in areas where the species does not occur normally, under the mistaken impression that this strategy will prevent introduction of diseases that may be present in parent stocks.

Documentation now exists for the introduction of several oyster parasites and diseases from Japan to the west coast of United States. Pacific oysters, *Crassostrea gigas*, have been imported as seed stock into waters of the Pacific coast states since the 1930's, coincident with the decline in abundance of the native Olympia oyster, *Ostrea lurida*. The parasitic copepod, *Mytilicola orientalis*, was described from the digestive tract of the Japanese oyster in 1935. The parasite was transferred to the United States west coast with early imports of seed oysters from Japan, and was described as a new species in the United States in 1938. It is now common on the west coast. In 1946 the native west coast Olympia oyster was found to be infected; even small numbers of copepods caused poor condition of these oysters.

In addition to the copepod parasite, two disease entities were found recently in Japanese parent stocks. One, a bacterium that causes what has been called multiple abscesses or focal necrosis, has been found in up to 20% of samples of adult oysters from Japan. Seed oysters imported from Japan were found to be affected by this same disease, and the condition was also detected in adult oysters grown on the Washington coast. A second disease, caused by an amoeboid organism of yet undetermined taxonomic position, was found in 1966 in over 30% of oysters from an area of Matsushima Bay, Japan, examined at the Oxford Laboratory of the Bureau of Commercial Fisheries. Oyster mortalities in this area had been high since 1960. What may be a similar amoeboid organism has also been recognized in oysters grown in Humboldt Bay, California, from Japanese seed exported from Matsushima Bay (Sparks *et al.*, 1967). Annual mortalities in Humboldt Bay have apparently been increasing since 1960, and a dredged sample in which 50% of the oysters were recently dead (as indicated by persistence of two shell valves joined by the hinge ligament, and by unfouled inner shell surfaces) was observed by the author in the summer of 1966. Lesser mortalities of undetermined origin have occurred in other west coast growing areas.

We know, then, of three disease agents that are present in United States west coast oyster stocks: (1) parasitic copepod, (2) multiple abscess bacterium, and (3) amoeboid organism. All can cause pathological changes in oysters, and all apparently have been introduced from Japan. They, like a number of important shellfish predators, such as Japanese oyster drills and carnivorous flatworms, are now in United States waters and may affect native as well as introduced populations. It should be reemphasized, however, that as yet no clear association of specific pathogens with mortalities of *Crassostrea gigas* has been established on the Pacific coast of United States.

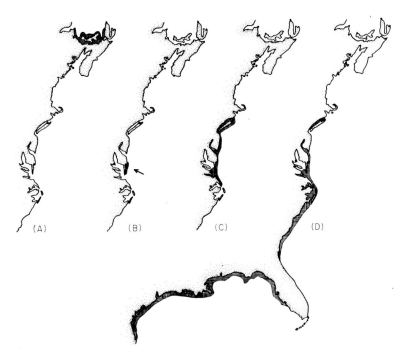

Fig. 57. Areas of the Atlantic coast of North America where disease-caused oyster mortalities have occurred: (A) Malpeque disease in the Gulf of Saint Lawrence, caused by an unknown pathogen; (B) seaside disease on the coasts of Virginia and Maryland, caused by the haplosporidan, *Minchinia costalis;* (C) Delaware Bay disease on the coasts of the Middle Atlantic states caused by the haplosporidan *Minchinia nelsoni;* and (D) *Dermocystidium* disease of the South Atlantic and Gulf coasts caused by the fungus, *Dermocystidium marinum.*

The oyster stocks of the North American east coast have also been severely affected by disease-associated mass mortalities during the past several decades (Sindermann, 1968). Four disease entities exist: Delaware Bay disease, *Dermocystidium* disease, Malpeque Bay disease, and seaside disease (caused by the haplosporidan *Minchinia costalis*). All are apparently distinct from diseases seen in Pacific oysters (Fig. 57). No significant quantities of Pacific oysters have been introduced commercially on the east coast nor has there been mass importation of foreign seed comparable to introductions made on the west coast. Different diseases seem to dominate in particular geographical areas on the east coast. There is and has been appreciable transfer of oysters from one geographical area of the coast to another, which may well have enhanced the spread of certain of these diseases.

Faced as we are with transfers and introductions—at present under very loose or no control, depending on state regulations—the proper course of action is difficult to prescribe. The obvious "hard-line" action would be strict quarantine and exclusion of imports. A more feasible approach would be strictly controlled introduction, but this method requires an extensive and expensive inspection and testing organization, probably on a federal level. Inspection could be combined with restriction of introduced exotic species to particular localities or, better still, to closed systems of culture, using only offspring for introductions in noncontaminated areas. In this way predators and most diseases could be excluded. It is difficult, however, to screen introductions for all possible pathogens, particularly the microbes. Cryptic life-cycle stages of known pathogens may exist, and organisms pathogenic to exotic species in their natural habitats may be poorly understood. Also, organisms which are not serious pathogens for the introduced species because of long association and natural immunity may have severe effects on native species in the area of introduction. On the other hand, pathogens with low infectivity may require large or repeated introductions to become established in a new area; or pathogens may, even after repeated introduction, remain at insignificant levels because of other limiting environmental factors. Often the course of events is very difficult to predict, although experimentation may help to define the level of risk involved.

E. SUMMARY

Considering fish and shellfish aquaculture as it now exists, several generalizations about disease seem reasonably justified:

1. Disease assumes greater significance in captive and cultured

marine populations than in natural populations, for many reasons, some of which are that (*a*) animals exist under more crowded conditions than in the natural habitat, thus facilitating transmission of pathogens and parasites; (*b*) shellfish are often cultivated in areas where natural populations did not exist, and their absence under natural conditions suggests some environmental limiting factor or factors; (*c*) fish and shrimp culture still depends largely on capture and impoundment of juveniles; many individuals may be slightly injured during capture, or may be already infected by certain pathogens; and (*d*) the nutrition of cultivated populations may be deficient because of abnormal or inadequate diets.

2. Diseases caused by vibrios have already assumed great importance among cultivated fish populations.

3. Pathogenic roles in cultivated populations of marine fish have been assumed by certain organisms that are often rare and innocuous parasites in natural populations. These organisms are often pathogens in marine aquaria also.

4. The larger animal parasites, especially those with complex life cycles, are usually of relatively minor importance in cultivated marine populations, but those with a single host—particularly the microbial parasites, with direct water-borne transmission and short generation times—are of great importance.

5. Molluscan shellfish culture, which at present is based on the most advanced marine aquacultural practices, has repeatedly experienced outbreaks of epizootic disease and resultant mass mortalities. Some control measures are available, but the limited knowledge about the diseases involved still prohibits really effective control.

6. Transfers and introductions of marine species, particularly shellfish, can increase disease problems in cultivated populations. Susceptible animals may be introduced in areas where particular diseases are enzootic or epizootic, or new diseases may be introduced when transfers are made from other geographic areas.

Disease is now and will continue to be a significant problem in marine aquaculture. At times it may determine the success or failure of a venture. It behooves us then to learn as much as we can about this severe limiting factor to the success of marine aquaculture.

REFERENCES

Abeliovitch, A. (1967). Oxygen regime in Beit-Shean fish ponds related to summer mass fish mortalities, preliminary observations. *Bamidgeh* **19**, 3–15.
Anderson, A. G. (1911). Bacteriological investigations as to the cause of an outbreak of disease amongst the fish at the Marine Laboratory, Bay of Nigg, Aberdeen. *Rept. Fishery Board Scot.* pp. 38–45.

Anderson, J. I. W., and Conroy, D. A. (1968a). The significance of disease in pre-liminary attempts to raise flatfish and salmonids in sea water. *Proc. 3rd Symp. Mond. Comm. Off. Intern. Epizoot. Etude Maladies Poissons (Stockholm, 1968) Unnumbered Separate* ·5 pp. (mimeo.).

Anderson, J. I. W., and Conroy, D. A. (1968b). The significance of disease in pre-liminary attempts to raise Crustacea in sea water. *Proc. 3rd Symp. Mond. Comm. Off. Intern. Epizoot. Etude Maladies Poissons, Separate* No. 3, 8 pp.

Andreu, B. (1963). Propagación del copépodo parásito *Mytilicola intestinalis* en el mejillon cultivado de las rías gallegas (N. W. de España). *Invest. Pesquera (Vigo)* **24**, 3–20.

Andrews, J. D. (1966). Oyster mortality studies in Virginia. V. Epizootiology of MSX, a protistan pathogen of oysters. *Ecology* **47**, 19–31.

Andrews, J. D. (1968). Oyster mortality studies in Virginia. VII. Review of epizootiology and origin of *Minchinia nelsoni. Proc. Natl. Shellfisheries Assoc.* **58**, 23–36.

Andrews, J. D., and Hewatt, W. G. (1957). Oyster mortality studies in Virginia. II. The fungus disease caused by *Dermocystidium marinum* in oysters of Chesapeake Bay. *Ecol. Monographs* **27**, 1–26.

Andrews, J. D., and Wood, J. L. (1967). Oyster mortality studies in Virginia. VI. History and distribution of *Minchinia nelsoni,* a pathogen of oysters, in Virginia. *Chesapeake Sci.* **8**, 1–13.

Aronson, J. D. (1926). Spontaneous tuberculosis in salt water fish. *J. Infect. Diseases* **39**, 315–320.

Berry, F. H., and Iversen, E. S. (1966). Pompano: Biology, fisheries and farming potential. *Proc. 19th Ann. Sess. Gulf Caribbean Fishery Inst.* pp. 116–128.

Brienne, H. (1964). Observations sur l'infestation des moules du pertuis Breton par *Mytilicola intestinalis* Steuer. *Rev. Trav. Office Peches Maritimes, Sci. Tech.* **28**, 205–230.

Brown, E. M. (1931). Note on a new species of dinoflagellate from the gills and epidermis of marine fishes. *Proc. Zool. Soc. London* 1931, Part I, pp. 345–346.

Brown, E. M. (1934). On *Oodinium ocellatum* Brown, a parasitic dinoflagellate causing epidemic disease in marine fish. *Proc. Zool. Soc. London* 1934, pp. 583–607.

Brown, E. M. (1951). *Cryptocaryon irritans* gen. et sp. n. *Proc. Zool. Soc. London* **120**, No. 11, 1–2 (agenda and abstr. of sci. meetings).

Brown, E. M. (1963). Studies on *Crytocaryon irritans* Brown. *Proc. 1st Intern. Congr. Protozool., Prague, 1961* pp. 284–287. Academic Press, New York.

Brown, E. M., and Hovasse, R. (1946). *Amyloodinium ocellatum* (Brown), a peridinian parasite on marine fishes. A complementary study. *Proc. Zool. Soc. London* **116**, 33–46.

Chlupaty, P. (1962). Krankheiten der Korallenfische und ihre Behandlung. *Bull. Inst. Oceanog. Monaco, Numero Special 1A, Premier Congr. Intern. Aquariol. A* pp. 81–92.

Cole, H. A., and Savage, R. E. (1951). The effect of the parasitic copepod, *Mytilicola intestinalis* (Steuer) upon the condition of mussels. *Parasitology* **41**, 156–161.

Conroy, D. A. (1963). Un caso de putrefaccion de la aleta caudal observado en la corvina. *Inst. Biol. Marina, Mar del Plata Cien. Invest.* **19**, 333.

Couch, J. A. (1966). Two peritrichous ciliates from the gills of the blue crab. *Chesapeake Sci.* **7**, 171–173.

Couch, J. A. (1967). A new species of *Lagenophrys* (Ciliatea: Peritrichida: Lagenophridae) from a marine crab, *Callinectes sapidus*. *Trans. Am. Microscop. Soc.* **86**, 205–211.

Davis, H. C., Loosanoff, V. L., Weston, W. H., and Martin, C. (1954). A fungus disease in clam and oyster larvae. *Science* **120**, 36–38.

De Graaf, F. (1962). A new parasite causing epidemic infection in captive coral fishes. *Bull. Inst. Oceanog. Monaco, Numero Special 1A, Premier Congr. Intern. Aquariol. A* pp. 93–96.

Egusa, S. (1967). Personal Communication.

Farrin, A. E., Scattergood, L. W., and Sindermann, C. J. (1957). Maintenance of immature sea herring in captivity. *Progressive Fish Culturist* **19**, 188–189.

Ford, E. (1928). Herring investigations at Plymouth. IV. The growth of young herrings in the neighbourhood of Plymouth. *J. Marine Biol. Assoc. U. K.* **15**, 305–319.

Fujita, T., Matsubara, T., Hirokawa, H., and Araki, F. (1953). On the inflammatorious changes of the *Ostrea gigas* in Hiroshima Bay. (In Japanese with English summary and title.) *Bull. Japan. Soc. Sci. Fisheries* **19**, 766–770.

Gibson, F. A. (1961). Gaffkaemia in stored lobsters. *Cons. Perm. Intern. Explor. Mer. Shellfish Comm., Rept. No.* **58**, 1 p. (mimeo.).

Guiart, J. (1938). Etude parasitologique et épidemiologique de quelques poissons de mer. *Bull. Inst. Oceanog.* **755**, 1–15.

Goggins, P. L., and Hurst, J. W., Jr. (1960). Progress report on lobster gaffkyaremia (Red Tail). Dept. of Sea and Shore Fisheries, Augusta, Maine. Unpublished mimeo.

Hepper, B. T. (1955). Environmental factors governing the infection of mussels, *Mytilus edulis*, by *Mytilicola intestinalis*. *Min. Agr. Fish. Food, Fish. Invest., London* [2] **20**, 1–21.

Hess, E. (1937). A shell disease in lobsters (*Homarus americanus*) caused by chitinovorous bacteria. *J. Biol. Board Can.* **3**, 358–362.

Højgaard, M. (1962). Experiences made in Danmarks Akvarium concerning the treatment of *Oodinium ocellatum*. *Bull. Inst. Oceanog. Monaco, Numero Special 1A, Premier Congr. Intern. Aquariol. A* pp. 77–79.

Hoshina, T. (1968). On the monogenetic trematode, *Benedenia seriolae*, parasitic on yellowtail, *Seriola quinqueradiata*. *Proc. 3rd Symp. Mond. Comm. Off. Intern. Epizoot. Etude Maladies Poissons* (*Stockholm, 1968*) Separate No. 25, 12 pp.

Imai, T., Numachi, K., Oizumi, J., and Sato, S. (1965). Studies on the mass mortality of the oyster in Matsushima Bay. II. Search for the cause of mass mortality and the possibility to prevent it by transplantation experiment. (In Japanese with English summary.) *Bull. Tohoku Regional Fisheries Res. Lab.* **25**, 27–38.

Jahn, T. L., and Kuhn, L. R. (1932). The life history of *Epibdella melleni* MacCallum 1927, a monogenetic trematode parasitic on marine fishes. *Biol. Bull.* **62**, 89–111.

Kan-no, H., Sasaki, M., Sakurai, Y., Watanabe, T., and Suzuki, K. (1965). Studies on the mass mortality of the oyster in Matsushima Bay. I. General aspects of the mass mortality of the oyster in Matsushima Bay and its environmental conditions. (In Japanese with English summary.) *Bull. Tohoku Regional Fisheries Res. Lab.* **25**, 1–26.

Kasahara, S. (1967a). Studies on the biology of *Benedenia seriolae*, an ectoparasitic trematode on the yellowtail. I. On the growth and spawning of the fluke in summer. (In Japanese with English summary.) *J. Fac. Fisheries Animal Husbandry Hiroshima Univ.* 7, 97–104.

Kasahara, S. (1967b). On the sodium pyrophosphate peroxyhydrate treatment for ectoparasitic trematodes on the yellowtail. (In Japanese.) *Fish Pathol.* 1, 48–53.

Kerbert, C. (1886). *Chromatophagus parasiticus*—a contribution to the natural history of parasites. *Rept. U. S. Comm. Fisheries* pp. 1127–1136, abstract of "Chromatophagus parasiticus, ein Beitrag zur Parasitenlehre." *Ned. Tijdschr. Dierk., Amsterdam* 5, 44–58 (1884).

Korringa, P. (1950). De annval van de parasiet *Mytilicola intestinalis* op de Zeeuwse mosselcultuur. *Visserijnieuws* 3, No. 7, Suppl., 1–7 (translation by S. H. Hopkins, Texas A. and M. Res. Found., 1951).

Korringa, P. (1959). Checking *Mytilicola*'s advance in the Dutch Waddensea. *Cons. Perm. Intern. Explor. Mer, 47th Meeting, 1959, Shellfish Comm. Rept. No.* 87, 1–3 (mimeo.).

Kubota, S. S., and Hagita, K. (1963). Studies on the diseases of marine-culture fishes. II. Pharmaco-dynamic effects of nitro-furazone for fish diseases. *J. Fac. Fisheries, Prefect. Univ. Mie* 6, No. 1, 125–144.

Kubota, S. S., and Takakuwa, M. (1963). Studies on the diseases of marine cultured fishes. I. General description and preliminary discussion of fish diseases in Mie Prefecture. *J. Fac. Fisheries, Perfect. Univ. Mie* 6, No. 1, 107–124; Transl. *Fisheries Res. Board Can. Biol. Sta., Nanaimo, B. C.* (1966).

Kusuda, R. (1960). On the fishery-biological studies of *Epibdella seriolae* Yamaguti infesting the surface skin of *Seriola quinqueradiata.* I. The timing of its appearance and its effects on the cultured *Seriola quinqueradiata.* (In Japanese; mimeo.) *Fishery Expt. Inst. Kyoto* (cited by Kubota and Takakuwa, 1963).

Kusuda, R. (1966). Studies on the ulcer disease of marine fishes. *Proc. 1st U. S.-Japan Joint Conf. Marine Microbiol., Tokyo, 1966* 13 pp. (mimeo. extr.).

Kusuda, R., and Akazawa, I. (1963). On the contagious diseases caused by bacteria in marine cultured fish. (In Japanese.) Discussions on the Promotion of Fisheries, Extra Issue, No. 3 (cited by Kubota and Takakuwa, 1963).

Lahav, M., and Sarig, S. (1964). Observations on the biology of *Lernaea cyprinacea* L., in fish ponds in Israel. *Bamidgeh* 16, 77–86.

Lahav, M., Shilo, M., and Sarig, S. (1962). Development of resistance to Lindane in *Argulus* populations of fish ponds. *Bamidgeh* 14, 67–75.

Lahav, M., Sarig, S., and Shilo, M. (1964). The eradication of *Lernaea* in storage ponds of carps through destruction of the copepodidal stage by Dipterex. *Bamidgeh* 16, 87–94.

Lahav, M., Sarig, S., and Shilo, M. (1966). Experiments in the use of Bromex-50 as a means of eradicating the ectoparasites of carp. *Bamidgeh* 18, 57–66.

Laird, M. (1956). Aspects of fish parasitology. *Proc. 2nd Joint Symp. Sci. Soc. Malaya Malayan Math. Soc., 1956* pp. 46–54.

Logie, R. R. (1956). Oyster mortalities, old and new, in the Maritimes. *Fisheries Res. Board Can., Progr. Rept. Atlantic Coast Sta.* 65, 3–11.

Mackin, J. G. (1962). Oyster disease caused by *Dermocystidium marinum* and other microorganisms in Louisiana. *Publ. Inst. Marine Sci.* 7, 132–229.

Mann, H. (1951). Qualitätsverminderung der Fleisches der Miesmuscheln durch den Befall mit *Mytilocola intestinalis. Fischereiwelt* 3, No. 8, 121–122.

Mann, H. (1956). The influence of *Mytilicola intestinalis* (Copepoda parasitica) on the development of the gonads of *Mytilus edulis*. *Cons. Perm. Intern. Explor. Mer, Rappt. Proces-Verbaux Reun.* **140**, No. 3, 57–58.

Meyer-Waarden, P. F., and Mann, H. (1954). Der Befall von *Mytilus edulis* durch *Mytilicola intestinalis* in den deutschen Wattengebieten 1950–1953. *Ber. Deut. Komm. Meeresforsch.* **13**, 347–362.

Monod, T., and Dollfus, R. P. (1932). Les copépodes parasites de mollusques. *Ann. Parasitol. Humaine Comparee* **10**, 129–204.

Mori, K., Imai, T., Toyoshima, K., and Usuki, I. (1965a). Studies on the mass mortality of the oyster in Matsushima Bay. IV. Changes in the physiological activity and the glycogen content of the oyster during the stages of sexual maturation and spawning. (In Japanese with English summary.) *Bull. Tohoku Regional Fisheries Res. Lab.* **25**, 49–63.

Mori, K., Tamate, H., Imai, T., and Itikawa O. (1965b). Studies on the mass mortality of the oyster in Matsushima Bay. V. Changes in the metabolism of lipids and glycogen of the oyster during the stages of sexual maturation and spawning. (In Japanese with English summary.) *Bull. Tohoku Regional Fisheries Res. Lab.* **25**, 65–88.

Muroga, K., and Egusa, S. (1967). *Vibrio anguillarum* from an endemic disease of ayu in Lake Hamana. *Bull. Japan. Soc. Sci. Fisheries* **33**, 636–640.

Nigrelli, R. F. (1935a). Studies on the acquired immunity of the pompano, *Trachinotus carolinus*, to *Epibdella melleni*. *J. Parasitol.* **21**, 438–439.

Nigrelli, R. F. (1935b). Experiments on the control of *Epibdella melleni* MacCallum, a monogenetic trematode of marine fishes. *J. Parasitol.* **21**, 438.

Nigrelli, R. F. (1935c). On the effect of fish mucus on *Epibdella melleni*, a monogenetic trematode of marine fishes. *J. Parasitol.* **21**, 438.

Nigrelli, R. F. (1936). The morphology, cytology, and life history of *Oodinium ocellatum* Brown, a dinoflagellate parasite on marine fishes. *Zoologica* **21**, 129–164.

Nigrelli, R. F. (1937). Further studies on the susceptibility and acquired immunity of marine fishes to *Epibdella melleni*, a monogenetic trematode. *Zoologica* **22**, 185–191.

Nigrelli, R. F. (1943). Causes of diseases and death of fishes in captivity. *Zoologica* **28**, 203–216.

Nigrelli, R. F. (1947). Susceptibility and immunity of marine fishes to *Benedenia* (=*Epibdella*) *melleni* (MacCallum), a monogenetic trematode. III. Natural hosts in the West Indies. *J. Parasitol.* **33**, Suppl., 25 (abstr.).

Nigrelli, R. F., and Breder, C. M. (1934). Susceptibility and immunity of certain marine fishes to *Epibdella melleni*. *J. Parasitol.* **20**, 259–269.

Nigrelli, R. F., and Ruggieri, G. D. (1965). Studies on virus diseases of fishes. Spontaneous and experimentally-induced cellular hypertrophy (Lymphocystis disease) in fishes of the New York Aquarium, with a report of new cases and an annotated bibliography (1874–1965). *Zoologica* **50**, 83–96.

Nigrelli, R. F., and Ruggieri, G. D. (1966). Enzootics in the New York Aquarium caused by *Cryptocaryon irritans* Brown, 1951 (=*Ichthyophthirius marinus* Sikama, 1961), a histophagous ciliate in the skin, eyes, and gills of marine fishes. *Zoologica* **51**, 97–102.

Nigrelli, R. F., and Smith, G. M. (1939). Studies on lymphocystis disease in the orange filefish, *Ceratocanthus schoepfi* (Walbaum), from Sandy Hook Bay, N. J. *Zoologica* **24**, 255–264.

Nigrelli, R. F., and Vogel, H. (1963). Spontaneous tuberculosis in fishes and in other cold-blooded vertebrates, with special reference to *Mycobacterium fortuitum* Cruz from fish and human lesions. *Zoologica* **48**, 131–144.

Numachi, K., Oizumi, J., Sato, S., and Imai, T. (1965). Studies on the mass mortality of the oyster in Matsushima Bay. III. The pathological changes of the oyster caused by gram-positive bacteria and the frequency of their infection. (In Japanese with English summary.) *Bull. Tohoku Regional Fisheries Res. Lab.* **25**, 39–47.

Ogasawara, Y., Kobayashi, U., Okamoto, R., Furukawa, A., Hisaoka, M., and Nogami, K. (1962). The use of the hardened seed oyster in the culture of the food oyster and its significance to the oyster culture industry. (In Japanese with English summary.) *Bull. Naikai Regional Fisheries Res. Lab.* **19**, 1–153.

Oppenheimer, C. H. (1958). A bacterium causing tail rot in Norwegian codfish. *Publ. Inst. Marine Sci., Univ. Texas* **5**, 160–162.

Oppenheimer, C. H. (1962). On marine fish diseases. *In* "Fish as Food" (G. Borgstrom, ed.), Vol. 2, p. 541. Academic Press, New York.

Oppenheimer, C. H., and Kesteven, G. L. (1953). Disease as a factor in natural mortality of marine fish. *FAO Fisheries Bull.* **6**, 215–222.

Paccaud, A. (1962). Essais divers pour enrayer los maladies des poissons dits "des coraux" en eau artificielle. *Bull. Inst. Oceanog. Monaco, Numero Special 1A, Premier Congr. Intern. Aquariol. A* pp. 57–75.

Paperna, I. (1963a). Some observations on the biology of *Dactylogyrus vastator* in Israel. *Bamidgeh* **15**, 8–28.

Paperna, I. (1963b). Dynamics of *Dactylogyrus vastator* Nybellin (Monogenea) populations on the gills of carp fry in fish ponds. *Bamidgeh* **15**, 31–50.

Paperna, I. (1964). Host reaction to infestation of carp with *Dactylogyrus vastator* Nybellin, 1924 (Monogenea). *Bamidgeh* **16**, 129–141.

Pérès, J. M. (1944). Note sur la maladie des écailles des téléostéens marins de l'Aquarium de Monaco. *Bull. Inst. Oceanog.* **859**, 1–7.

Pesta, O. (1907). Die Metamorphose von *Mytilicola intestinalis* Steuer. *Z. Wiss. Zool.* **88**, 78–98.

Powell, E. H., and Andrews, J. D. (1967). Production of MSX-resistant oysters. *Virginia J. Sci.* [N.S.] **18**, No. 4, 163 (abstr.).

Raabe, H. (1936). Études de microorganismes parasites des poissons de mer. 1. *Nosema ovoïdeum* Thél. dans le foie des rougets. *Bull. Inst. Océanog.* **696**, 1–12.

Raabe, H. (1937). Études de microorganismes parasites des poissons de mer. II. *Thallamoebella parasitica* n. g. n. sp. *Bull. Inst. Oceanog.* **737**, 1–16.

Raabe, H. (1940a). Études de microorganismes parasites des poissons de mer. III. *Leucosphaera oxneri* n. g. n. sp., algue provoquant les "points blancs" sur la peau des poissons. *Bull. Inst. Oceanog.* **785**, 1–11.

Raabe, H. (1940b). Épidémie des "petits nuages blancs" et des "taches blanches" sur la peau des poissons de mer. *Bull. Inst. Oceanog.* **786**, 1–12.

Ray, S. M., and Chandler, A. C. (1955). *Dermocystidium marinum*, a parasite of oysters. *Exptl. Parasitol.* **4**, 172–200.

Riddell, W., and Alexander, D. M. (1911). Note on an ulcerative disease of the plaice. *Proc. Trans. Liverpool Biol. Soc.* **26**, 155–161.

Roskam, R. T. (1957). Gaffkaemia, a contagious disease, in *Homarus vulgaris*. *Cons. Perm. Intern. Explor. Mer, Shellfish Comm. Rept.* 4 pp. (mimeo.).

Russell, F. S. (1923). A new species of *Caligus* from Egypt, *Caligus pageti* sp. n. *Ann. Mag. Nat. Hist.* **15**, 611–618.

Russell, J. (1966). Japan's fish hospital. *New Sci.* 31, 150–151.

Sarig, S., and Lahav, M. (1959). The treatment with Lindane of carp and fish ponds infected with the fish-louse, *Argulus*. *Proc. Gen. Fish. Council Medit.* 5, 151–156.

Sarig, S., Lahav, M., and Shilo, M. (1965). Control of *Dactylogyrus vastator* on carp fingerlings with Dipterex. *Bamidgeh* 17, 47–52.

Shilo, M. (1953). Prevention of mortality of fish fry caused by *Gyrodactylus* and *Dactylogyrus*. *Bamidgeh* 5, 26.

Shilo, M. (1965). Study of the isolation and control of blue-green algae from fish ponds. *Bamidgeh* 17, 83–93.

Shilo, M., Sarig, S., Shilo, M., and Zeev, H. (1964). Control of *Prymnesium parvum* in fish ponds with the aid of copper sulphate. *Bamidgeh* 16, 99–102.

Sikama, Y. (1937). Preliminary report on the white spot disease in marine fish. (In Japanese.) *Suisan-Gakukai* 7, No. 3, 149–160.

Sikama, Y. (1938). Über die Weisspünktchenkrankheit bei Seefischen. *J. Shanghai Sci. Inst., Sect. III* 4, 113–128.

Sikama, Y. (1960). Contribution to the biological study of the diseases and parasites of fish in Japan. No. 2. White spot disease in marine fish and some similar diseases. (In Japanese.) *Japan. Inst. Marine Sci., Nihon Univ., Sogo-Kaiyo-kagaku (Bull. Marine Sci.)* 2, 189–200.

Sikama, Y. (1961). On a new species of *Ichthyophthirius* found in marine fishes. *Sci. Rept. Yokosuka City Museum* 6, 66–70.

Sikama, Y. (1962). Study on white spot disease in marine fish. *Agriculture and Horticulture (Tokyo)* 10, No. 1, 29–90.

Sindermann, C. J. (1968). Oyster mortalities, with particular reference to Chesapeake Bay and the Atlantic Coast of North America. *U. S. Fish Wildlife Serv., Spec. Sci. Rept., Fisheries* 569, 1–10.

Sindermann, C. J., and Rosenfield, A. (1954). Diseases of fishes of the western North Atlantic. I. Diseases of the sea herring (*Clupea harengus*). *Maine Dept. Sea Shore Fish., Res. Bull.* 18, 1–22.

Sindermann, C. J., and Rosenfield, A. (1967). Principal diseases of commercially important bivalve Mollusca and Crustacea. *U. S. Fish Wildlife Serv., Fishery Bull.* 66, 335–385.

Sparks, A. K., Robbins, E. J., Des Voigne, D., Hsu, B. C. C., and Schwartz, L. (1967). Oyster pathology. Research in Fisheries . . . 1966. *Coll. Fish., Fish. Res. Inst., Univ. Washington, Seattle, Contrib.* 240, 37.

Steuer, A. (1902). *Mytilicola intestinalis* n. gen. n. sp. aus dem Darme von *Mytilus galloprovincialis* Lam. *Zool. Anz.* 25, 635–637.

Takeuchi, T., Takemoto, Y., and Matsubara, T. (1960). Hematological study of bacteria-infected oysters. (In Japanese.) *Rept. Hiroshima Prefect. Fish. Expt. Sta.* 22, 1–7.

Tal, S., and Shelubsky, M. (1952). Review of the fish farming industry in Israel. *Trans. Am. Fisheries Soc.* 81, 218–223.

Tamate, H., Numachi, K., Mori, K., Itikawa, O., and Imai, T. (1965). Studies on the mass mortality of the oyster in Matsushima Bay. VI. Pathological studies. (In Japanese with English summary.) *Bull. Tohoku Regional Fisheries Res. Lab.* 25, 89–104.

Taylor, C. C. (1948). Shell disease as a mortality factor in the lobster (*Homarus americanus*). *Maine Dept. Sea Shore Fish., Fish. Circ.* 4, 1–8 (mimeo.).

Tubiash, H. S., Chanley, P. E., and Leifson, E. (1965). Bacillary necrosis, a disease of larval and juvenile bivalve mollusks. I. Etiology and epizootiology. *J. Bacteriol.* **90,** 1036–1044.

Vishniac, H. S. (1955). The morphology and nutrition of a new species of *Sirolpidium.* *Mycologia* **47,** 633–645.

Weissenberg, R. (1920). Lymphocystisstudien. (Infektiöse Hypertrophie von Stütz-gewebszellen bei Fischen.) 1. Die reifen Geschwülste bei Kaulbarsch und Flunder. Lymphocystisgenese beim Kaulbarsch. *Arch. Mikroskop. Anat. Entwicklungs-mech.* **94,** 55–134.

Weissenberg, R. (1965). Fifty years of research on the lymphocystis virus disease of fishes (1914–1964). *Ann. N. Y. Acad. Sci.* **126,** 362–374.

Wells, N. A., and ZoBell, C. E. (1934). *Achromobacter ichthyodermis* n. sp., the etiological agent of an infectious dermatitis of certain marine fishes. *Proc. Natl. Acad. Sci. U. S.* **20,** 123–126.

Wood, P. C. (1965a). A preliminary note on Gaffkaemia investigations in England. *Cons. Perm. Intern. Explor. Mer, Rappt. Proces-Verbaux Reun.* **156,** 30–34.

Wood, P. C. (1965b). Gaffkaemia, the blood disease of lobsters. *Proc. Soc. Gen. Microbiol.* p. 14 (abstr.).

ZoBell, C. E. (1946). "Marine Microbiology," 240 pp. Chronica Botanica, Waltham, Massachusetts.

VI

Internal Defense Mechanisms in Marine Animals

A. INVERTEBRATES

1. Introduction

The scientific literature includes a large amount of information about the internal defense mechanisms of invertebrates. Cantacuzène (1923b, 1928), Huff (1940), Baer (1944), Bisset (1947a), and Cushing (1967) published general reviews of immunity in invertebrates, and Stauber (1961), Tripp (1963), and Feng (1967) have published excellent summarizations of this subject, with particular reference to the oyster. Feng's and Cushing's papers are part of a symposium on "Defense Reactions in Invertebrates" held in 1967 and chaired by Dr. Frederik B. Bang (Bang, 1967a). Stauber's general definitions and categories of response have been followed closely in the following paragraphs, and the papers mentioned above, as well as an excellent one by Hirsch (1959) reviewing the concepts of Metchnikoff, have been drawn on liberally for material in this chapter.

Some of the terms used in discussing the internal defenses of animals include: susceptibility, resistance, immunity, natural resistance, and acquired resistance. Often, the precise limits of such terms are not clearly defined. Schneider (1951), Read (1958), and Stauber (1961) have pointed out that susceptibility and resistance should be considered as separate biological entities. Susceptibility should be limited to the *degree of vulnerability* of an animal to penetration by a pathogen and to the

258

successful establishment of the pathogen. Susceptibility has been further defined by Read (1958) as "a physiological state of the host in which the parasite (pathogen) is supplied with its life needs, and in susceptibility is the state in which these life needs are not satisfied—neither state involving a host response." Resistance, on the other hand, should be restricted to the *responses* of an animal to invasion by parasites or pathogens. Read (1958) has effectively defined resistance as "those alterations of the physiological state of the host which represent a response to previous or present experience with the parasite (pathogen) or a chemically related entity." Included would be previous experience of the species with resulting natural selection.

Resistance, when properly restricted to responses of the host to parasite invasion, is usually divided into two categories; innate (natural) and acquired. Innate resistance depends on those responses of the host that appear upon first contact with a pathogen. It is usually a species or racial characteristic, but it may vary individually (Huff, 1940). Acquired resistance, as succinctly described by Stauber (1961), is host response which develops after initial exposure to an invading organism or its metabolites; if the host survives this contact, acquired resistance (immunity) may persist for varying periods once it has developed. It is usually characterized by enhanced response to the invasive organism upon subsequent contact with it, and—in the vertebrates only—it is usually associated with the presence of specific antibodies (Stauber, 1961).

The mechanisms of resistance of the animal, whether innate or acquired, may be cellular or humoral. Cellular responses of invertebrates include the following: (1) phagocytosis and digestion of foreign particles, or transport of the particles across an epithelial surface if they are indigestible; (2) leukocytosis and leukocytic infiltration—the mobilization of phagocytic cells in the blood-stream and their migration toward sources of irritation; (3) thrombosis—the formation of cellular or acellular clots to close gaps in the vascular system and immobilize invading microorganisms; (4) encapsulation—response to the presence of a large amount of foreign material or to certain types of indigestible material—characterized by envelopment by concentric layers of fibroblast-like cells. Humoral responses of invertebrates are actually special cases of cellular responses, in which "Cellular secretion, fragmentation, or biochemical alteration confers bacteriostatic, lytic, or other properties on body fluid" (Stauber, 1961). If these properties are present before introduction of microorganisms then they should properly be considered insusceptibility factors rather than factors of resistance, as was pointed out by Stauber. Some invertebrate body fluids do have striking bacteriolytic properties, as well as agglutinating activity which may facilitate phagocytosis and encapsulation. It is usually very difficult, however, to determine whether or not such properties result from previous experience with a pathogen. Recent but incomplete evidence for augmentation of bacteriocidal activity in the body fluids of at least one invertebrate (to be considered later in the chapter) suggests that mechanisms of resistance are operative—possibly in addition to insusceptibility factors.

In this section we shall attempt to review briefly some of the pertinent studies of internal defense mechanisms of marine invertebrates, recognizing the very important fact pointed out by Bang (1967a) that the "nonvertebrates" constitute an assemblage of evolutionarily very diverse animals with possibly very different ways of responding to the invasion of pathogens.

2. Cellular Mechanisms of Internal Defense

Beginning with Metchnikoff (1884, 1893), the greatest attention in invertebrate defense mechanisms has been paid to the amoebocytes, often of diverse nature, found in body fluids. In an organism such as the oyster and in many other invertebrates this cell is involved in at least five phenomena: (1) phagocytosis of invading microorganisms; (2) leukocytosis—the mobilization of phagocytic cells; (3) leukocytic infiltration (inflammation)—migration from blood vessels and concentration of leukocytes in the injured area; (4) thrombosis—the formation of cellular clots to close gaps in the vascular system; (5) encapsulation—the surrounding of an invading substance by modified amoebocytes.

The classic studies of Metchnikoff (1893, 1905), as recently reviewed by Hirsch (1959), stressed the importance of phagocytosis in invertebrate defense processes. Phagocytosis had been described as early as 1862 by Haeckel, but before Metchnikoff it was generally held that phagocytes were simple scavengers of foreign material; in fact, it was suspected that disease might actually be spread by transport of pathogens in phagocytes. Metchnikoff's basic contribution, using invertebrate animals, was the discovery of the critical role of phagocytes as host mechanisms of defense against invading microorganisms (Hirsch, 1959).

Stauber and his associates have done much to elucidate the process of phagocytosis in oysters (Stauber, 1950; Tripp, 1958a,b,c, 1960; Feng, 1962). Using a variety of injected substances, from serum albumin to India ink, they found that injected particles were phagocytized rapidly and that phagocytes containing particles were quickly distributed throughout the oyster. Particles were digested, or lysed, or, if indigestible, were carried by phagocytes across epithelia of the oyster and thus eliminated. Tripp determined that some digestible particles were also eliminated by diapedesis—migration of phagocytes through epithelial barriers—and Feng found that certain nonparticulate substances could be absorbed (pinocytized) by phagocytes. Similar studies and observations were made for the European oyster, *Ostrea edulis,* by Takatsuki (1934).

Several parasites and pathogens of mollusks have been reported as being phagocytized: the fungus *Dermocystidium marinum* by Mackin (1951), the haplosporidan *Minchinia nelsoni* by Farley (1968), the flagellate *Hexamita nelsoni* by Mackin *et al.* (1952). One of the most enlightening studies of phagocytosis in mollusks is that of Bang (1961), who used *in vitro* methods with oyster leukocytes and bacteria. He found that bacteria adhered to the leukocyte before phagocytosis, presumably by entanglement of bacterial flagella by pseudopodia. He also found that certain bacteria were not phagocytized.

Leukocytosis, the mobilization of phagocytes in the bloodstream, has been examined in the oyster by Stauber and his associates. Feng (1965), for example, determined that the number of circulating hemocytes increased with temperature, and that injection of sterile seawater or spinach chloroplasts caused reduction of hemocyte numbers. This decrease was probably the consequence of cellular clot formation.

The terms leukocyte, phagocyte, and amoebocyte have been used variably in the invertebrate literature—sometimes almost interchangeably. All terms refer to free cells in the circulating blood, usually amoeboid and often phagocytic. The leukocytes of bivalve mollusks have been divided by George (1941) into three types: (1) small cells with large nuclei and scant hyaline cytoplasm, often called small amoebocytes; (2) phagocytes, with much more cytoplasm; and (3) granular cells. The suggestion of Farley (1968) that the proper general term might be "hemocyte" seems to be a good one. He has pointed out that oysters have two basic types of blood cells: small agranular nonphagocytic cells with proportionally large nuclei, which he has labeled "hyaline hemocytes," and larger granular "phagocytes." The origin of leukocytes in mollusks is still uncertain, as was pointed out by Cheng (1967).

Knowledge about the value of leukocytic infiltration (inflammation) as an internal defense against infection is still very incomplete, even for higher vertebrates. In the vertebrates inflammation involves a sequence of phenomena including changes in permeability of blood vessels, leakage of blood fluids into tissues, adherence of leukocytes to blood vessel walls, and migration of leukocytes into tissues around the area of foreign invasion or injury. Counterparts of these phenomena exist in invertebrates, particularly for the adherence of amoebocytes to blood vessel walls and migration into invaded or injured tissues. This behavior of leukocytes was effectively demonstrated in the American oyster by Bang (1961) as part of a very lucid explanation of internal defense processes in this species.

The various phases of leukocyte infiltration of tissues (the counterpart of inflammation) can be effectively demonstrated in oysters infected by the haplosporidan *Minchinia nelsoni*. Infected oysters exhibit edema and cell infiltration with small lymphocyte-like amoebocytes. Proportions of cell types shift toward greater relative numbers of these lymphocyte-like cells—small, with large nuclei—which may or may not differentiate into phagocytes. Large amoebocytes frequently ingest the parasites, but do not seem to kill them, and may only spread them systemically in the host.

In addition to phagocytosis and leukocytic infiltration, encapsulation is a common form of internal defense among invertebrates. Encapsulation involves the surrounding of an invading substance by modified amoebocytes or connective tissue fibrocytes. Among mollusks it seems to be a response to infections by such pathogens as the fungus *Dermocystidium* and haplosporidan Protozoa and to invasions by larval cestodes and certain larval trematodes. Abscesses that are formed, particularly in the mantle, have outer margins of amoebocytes and fibrous connective tissue. Eventually the entire lesion may be walled off by an epithelial layer. Encapsulation has been demonstrated in snails penetrated by miracidia of trematodes abnormal to the species; the reaction occurred within 24 hours.

Tripp (1961), working with bacteria and other foreign particles injected into oysters and snails, found that bacteria were removed from blood and tissues in 48 hours, but that some bacteria could not be degraded by phagocytes. *Mycobacterium,* for example, multiplied within the phagocytes, but infected cells accumulated to form nodules surrounded by fibrous-like cells. It appears that since the amoebocytes were unable to eliminate the tubercle bacilli by migration or digestion, the mechanism of nodule formation—a special case of encapsulation—came into play.

Another special form of encapsulation—actually an extension of the process of "pearl" formation known for several centuries—has been labeled "nacrezation" by Cheng (1967). The presence of dead helminth larvae or of other irritants in the tissues, or between the shell and mantle, will stimulate secretion and deposition of nacreous layers about the foreign material, often incorporating the material in blisters on the inner surface of the shell. A similar process occurs when shell-invading annelids, *Polydora,* penetrate through the inner shell surface. Farley (1968) has described the process of recovery of oysters from *Minchinia nelsoni* infections which includes the walling off in shell pustules of phagocytized pathogens. This process, considered the terminal stage in removal of moribund pathogens, followed localization of phagocytized organisms in lesions or pustules in the mantle epithelium.

Farley's paper is probably the most comprehensive histopathological study of an oyster disease yet published. In addition to descriptions of phases of the disease caused by *M. nelsoni,* he summarized other references to oyster pathology and made valuable suggestions about terminology, such as substitution of "hemocyte" for the array of terms now used to describe blood cells.

The involvement of amoebocytes in clot formation or thrombosis is complex, and deserves particular attention, since either cellular or extracellular clots may be formed. Bang (1961) was able to demonstrate extensive intravascular cellular clots in oysters, caused by injecting an extract of ground gill tissue—an injury response. The clots adhered to the blood vessel wall, producing stasis of blood, and were resolved only very slowly. Extracellular clot formation, however, is well developed in several invertebrates such as horseshoe crabs and oysters, in each of which the predominant circulating cells are also directly involved in cellular clot formation. The presence of this extracellular gel or clot in oysters seems to inhibit bacterial motion and may thus render microorganisms more susceptible to phagocytosis. The origin of components or activators of the clotting process from amoebocytes, many of which are granular, is obviously possible.

The formation of a cellular clot at the site of injury or in response to injection of tissue extracts, as has been demonstrated by Bang, has great survival value. Amoebocytes accumulate in great numbers at injured surfaces; some clump within the blood vessels and adhere tightly to the vessel wall, so that circulation is greatly slowed or stopped in the area of injury. Probably the best demonstration of the part that phagocytes or amoebocytes play in formation of intravascular clots which immobilize foreign particles is in the work of Bang (1956), Shirodkar *et al.* (1960), and Levin and Bang (1964). A vibrio pathogenic to *Limulus* was found to cause fatal intravascular clotting, which could be induced by the injected endotoxin of the vibrio as well. The endotoxin caused the serum expressed from clots to form a solid gel *in vitro.*

Work with plasma of *Limulus* demonstrated that cellular material from amoebocytes was necessary to effect coagulation. Plasma free of all cellular elements did not clot either spontaneously or after addition of endotoxin, but did form a gel 10 minutes after addition of washed amoebocytes. In this respect *Limulus* amoebocytes are comparable to mammalian systems. The finding that cell-free *Limulus* plasma does not coagulate except in the presence of amoebocyte extracts is in keeping with other observations.

It seems probable that the disruption of amoebocytes by bacterial toxin, and the resulting immobilization of bacteria by an extracellular clot which may be demonstrated *in vivo* and *in vitro*, may be an important mechanism whereby invertebrates protect themselves against the gram-negative bacteria so abundant in the sea (Levin and Bang, 1964). Since minute quantities of endotoxin can initiate clotting, this antibacterial mechanism is very sensitive and possibly very primitive, as was suggested by Levin and Bang.

A similar mechanism for immobilization of bacteria has recently been demonstrated by Barker and Bang (1966) for the parasitic barnacle, *Sacculina carcini*. Cantacuzène (1925) had previously observed that infection of the parasite with gram-negative bacteria caused loss of coagulability of the hemolymph. Barker and Bang found that injection of *Vibrio* cultures caused the plasma to become incoagulable within 24 hours and brought death shortly thereafter. Gross masses of gelled material containing bacteria were found within the plasma spaces. It was further noted that exhaustion of the coagulation system led to bacteremia and death of the barnacle and frequently its crab host. The role of endo-toxin in extracellular clot formation in several animals has been recently reviewed by Levin (1967).

Interesting work on cellular mechanisms of immunity in sea stars has been done by Chaet and Albert (1958), Bang and Chaet (1959), and Bang and Lemma (1962). Experimental bacterial infections resulted in phagocytosis, followed by migration of phagocytes from the coelom and the animal via the dermal papulae. This phenomenon had been known since 1888 (Durham, 1888), but the new observation was the clumping of amoebocytes and their adherence to walls of the papulae, a basic concomitant of inflammation in vertebrates, where it is called "capillary stickiness." Some agglutination was produced by injection of live and killed bacteria, and even by sterile seawater, but the strongest clumping was caused by injection of extracts of amoebocytes themselves. This observation was similar to Bang's findings (1961) when oysters were injected with tissue extracts, and suggests release of an injury substance which initiates the clumping and sticking.

In summary, the phagocytes or amoebocytes play many roles in ad-dition to that of phagocytosis, which must of course remain as the pre-dominant internal defense mechanism of invertebrates: (1) They are important in inflammation, the infiltration of injured or diseased tissue; and (2) they are important in clotting, either by participating themselves in cellular clots, or by secretions or injury products that act with plasma components to produce extracellular clots.

3. Humoral Mechanisms of Internal Defense

The obvious role played by phagocytosis in the internal defense processes of invertebrates, combined with early failures to demonstrate specific humoral antibodies, led to the idea that invertebrates were unable to form antibodies (Huff, 1940). A number of examples of antibody production have been reported in the literature, but almost invariably qualifications must be made as to the results reported, and as to the degree of similarity of the substances involved to vertebrate antibodies (immunoglobulins). Much of the earlier literature fails to provide experimental data upon which conclusions were reached; the work must be repeated systematically, with modern methods. Bang (1967b) has already addressed himself to such a study.

Beyond these severely qualified generalizations, it seems expedient to discuss humoral protective mechanisms in two categories: those that are innate, and those that are acquired.

a. *Natural or Innate Protective Mechanisms*

Natural antibody-like substances—agglutinins, lysins, and various antimicrobial factors—have been demonstrated in the body fluids of many invertebrates. Tyler and Metz (1945) and Tyler and Scheer (1945), working with the Pacific Coast spiny lobster, *Panulirus interruptus*, detected a wide array of natural agglutinins in the blood against cells (blood and sperm) of many groups of animals. They further found by absorptions that these agglutinins were at least group or class specific. Absorption with cells of any one species rendered the lobster serum inactive for all other species within the same group, but did not remove activity for species belonging to other groups. By cross-absorption tests, the separate agglutinins were found. Some nonreciprocal results implied the presence of similar reactants on cells of species belonging to certain groups. These agglutinins were shown to be proteins of large molecular size, located electrophoretically in the nonhemocyanin peak. In a later study (Tyler, 1946) the body fluid of the starfish was found to possess a number of distinct agglutinins, each with broad group specificity. Feng (1967) has summarized the evidence for a wide range of natural agglutinins in mollusks. Hemagglutinins specific for human A antigen were reported for the butter clam, *Saxidomus gigantus*, by Johnson (1964). Oyster blood contains agglutinins for bird and mammal erythrocytes. Tripp (1966) reported oyster hemagglutinin to be heat labile, with an opsonic effect on phagocytosis of rabbit erythrocytes by oyster leukocytes *in vitro*. The origin of these or any natural agglutinins is still in some question (Wiener, 1951). The two possibilities are: (1) They may have been induced in response to naturally occurring antigens such as those involved in disease, or (2) they may be genetically determined. Without doubt, many natural antibodies in the vertebrates, and antibody-like substances in the invertebrates, are stimulated by infection or by intrusion of foreign antigens. Also, cross-reactions between antibodies produced by one kind of antigen and other unrelated but chemically similar antigens are known, and it is possible that these reactions account for many of the so-called natural antibodies. However, natural antibodies such as anti-A and anti-B in man suggest genetic origin, although Wiener (1951) even here has insisted that these too can be explained as response to antigenic stimuli of parasitic origin.

The array of demonstrable mechanisms of internal defense against bacteria possessed by crustaceans has recently been illustrated in a series of papers from the Halifax (Nova Scotia) Laboratory of the Fisheries Research Board of Canada (Cornick and Stewart, 1966; 1968a,b; Stewart 1966; 1968a,b; Stewart *et al.*, 1966a,b; 1967; Stewart and Dingle, 1968). Using the American lobster, *Homarus americanus*, and its bacterial pathogen, *Gaffkya homari*, as a test system, these investigators examined the phagocytic, agglutinative, and bactericidal activities of lobster serum. Active phagocytosis was demonstrated, but the pathogens were not destroyed within the phagocyte, as indicated by the fact that most experimental infections proved fatal. Longer term infections were characterized by pigmented nodules of tightly clumped tissue cells containing the pathogens—a possible example of encapsulation. Bactericidal activity of serum *in vivo* and *in vitro* was demonstrated against a variety of bacteria, but not *Gaffkya homari*. Growth of the pathogen was actually promoted by lobster serum *in vitro*. Natural agglutinins against representatives of several genera of bacteria were present in lobster serum, but none was active against *G. homari*. A study of the rock crab, *Cancer irroratus*, disclosed agglutinins for *Gaffkya* that were considered to be responsible, in part, for reduced pathogenicity of *G. homari* in the crab.

The discussion of the relative importance of cellular and humoral factors in resistance to infection began with Metchnikoff (1893) and continues to the present. Work since Metchnikoff has consisted largely of further description of serum components, such as properdin and complement of vertebrates, which have antibacterial properties (Skarnes and Watson, 1957). It has been clearly established in vertebrates that certain serum factors influence the phagocytic process. Cellular and humoral factors act together to produce maximum natural resistance to disease. In support of Metchnikoff, however, as was pointed out by Hirsch (1959), almost all studies on activities of blood fluids in recent decades have used serum as the test material. Metchnikoff's concept that serum contains cellular products released during clotting has been underemphasized by many modern workers; it is possible that many of the lysins and bactericidins present in serum may be of cellular origin.

b. Acquired Protective Mechanisms

As a single generalization, it seems that phagocytosis is the major mechanism of internal defense in invertebrates, whereas in the vertebrates specific serum antibodies come to assume a significant role. The picture is neither black nor white, however, and a number of fascinating studies bear on the matter of antibody-like defense mechanisms in invertebrates.

One series of studies of acquired humoral defense mechanisms in invertebrates concerns responses to parasite invasion. Recent work that strongly suggests the development of a humoral response, possibly an antibody, to invasion of snails by larval trematodes has been reported by Michelson (1964). He found that extracts from a high percentage of snails, *Biomphalaria glabrata*, infected with larval *Schistosoma mansoni* possessed a factor which immobilized miracidia, but that the percentages were low for uninfected snails or those with new infections. Absorption of extracts with cercariae of *S. mansoni* sharply reduced the immobilizing ability. The same extracts immobilized miracidia of *Fasciola hepatica* —an unrelated trematode—suggesting lack of species specificity of the immune response. Extracts of six other snail species, all refractory to *S. mansoni* infection, were tested; two had immobilizing activity and four lacked it. Thus it cannot be held that resistance of many snails to *S. mansoni* infection may be due to a universally distributed immobilizing substance.

Michelson (1963) determined that no miracidial-immobilizing activity for *S. mansoni* was developed as a result of experimental injections of *B. glabrata* with acid-fast bacilli, echinostome metacercariae, bovine albumin, or polystyrene spheres. Low levels of immobilizing activity developed, however, as a result of infection with nematodes of the genus *Daubaylia* and inoculation with *S. mansoni* eggs. Very high levels of immobilizing activity developed only with extracts of snails infected with *S. mansoni*. Thus some degree of specificity of response is suggested, and miracidial immobilization is clearly not a generalized nonspecific response to parasitemia. What seems to have been demonstrated is an acquired humoral protection against parasite invasion, with some degree of specificity.

The work reported by Michelson is related to work done 30 years earlier by Winfield, Nolf, and Cort. Using the freshwater snail, *Lymnaea stagnalis*, which may serve as the first and second intermediate host for the strigeid trematode, *Cotylurus flabelliformis*, Winfield (1932) demonstrated that snails infected with sporocysts were highly resistant to penetration of *Cotylurus* cercariae. He suggested that this immune mechanism is very necessary in the survival of snails infected with sporocysts, since it prevents them from being overwhelmed by repenetration of cercariae which escape. It may well be, however, that the failure of cercariae to penetrate snails already parasitized by sporocysts could result from some form of chemical exclusion rather than immunity. Nolf and Cort (1933) found the same response, although it was not absolute. They also observed that although cercariae actively penetrate uninfected snails, most fail to show any penetration reaction when they contact a snail infected with sporocysts.

Other species of snails were tested to see if there was a nonspecific immunity to penetration of cercariae of *Cotylurus flabelliformis* in normal second intermediate hosts infected with larval trematodes of different species. Several snails showed no difference in cercarial penetration, but in one case, when *Lymnaea* was infected with larvae of a bird schistosome (*Schistomatium*), more cercariae penetrated uninfected snails than infected. Other evidence from studies of multiple infections of snails (Ewers, 1960; Bourus, 1963) suggested the opposite; that infections with one species of trematode may actually render the host more susceptible to infection by another. So, although the evidence is by no means definitive enough, there is reasonable indication of acquired immunity in mollusks after infection with larval trematodes, and of a degree of specificity of the response.

A report by Ewers and Rose (1965) suggests genetic differences in susceptibility of marine snails, *Velacumantus australis*, to invasion by larval trematodes. An association of variant shell-banding patterns with lower incidences of larval trematode parasitization was made. Marked variations in susceptibility of strains or geographical races of freshwater snails have been described repeatedly in studies of human schistosomiasis (Wright, 1960, 1966). Miracidial penetration of nonsusceptible strains provokes an immediate and pronounced tissue reaction in the form of cellular infiltration followed by walling-off by fibroblasts, whereas miracidial penetration of susceptible strains produces no host response. Newton (1952) crossed susceptible and insusceptible strains. Results of infection experiments suggested that the cellular response to miracidial penetration was genetically determined.

Bang and his associates in the Department of Pathobiology, School of Hygiene, Johns Hopkins University, have for years explored the nature of humoral resistance of invertebrates to disease. Rabin and Bang (1964) found that the coelomic fluids of sipunculids, *Golfingia gouldi,* possessed antibacterial activity against a marine vibrio. Bacterial multiplication was inhibited, but prior inoculation of the worms with killed vibrio had no effect on the antibacterial activity. The coelomic fluid is normally sterile, and inoculated live bacteria were cleared in 24 hours. The vibrio used was a species pathogenic for the horseshoe crab, *Limulus.*

Other studies with sipunculids disclosed natural heteroagglutinins to human red-blood cells, but no increased activity as a result of inoculation (Triplett *et al.,* 1958). Sipunculids, however, produced a highly effective lysin against a parasitic ciliate of crabs, *Anophrys sarcophaga* (Bang and Bang, 1962). The lysin so produced seemed nonspecific since it could be invoked by injection of normal crab blood or marine bacteria; it first immobilized the ciliates and then lysed them. The activity declined after about a week, but could be reinvoked repeatedly. It is interesting and pertinent that the ciliate does not elicit antibody formation in its normal host, the crab *Carcinus;* if *Anophrys* is injected into certain other crabs, however, it may be immobilized and lysed, or it may multiply as it does in *Carcinus,* to kill the host (Poisson, 1930).

Rabin (1965), studying a disease of American lobsters, *Homarus americanus,* caused by the bacterium, *Gaffkya homari,* was unable to demonstrate increased resistance after inoculation of heat-killed organisms. Serum from uninfected and inoculated animals actually stimulated *in vitro* growth of *G. homari.*

An induced bactericidin in the spiny lobster, *Panulirus argus,* was demonstrated by Evans *et al.* (1968). Inoculation with formalin-killed bacteria isolated from the normal gut flora resulted in detectable bactericidal activity of hemolymph within 12 hours with a peak between 24 and 48 hours. Attempts with the same methods to induce a similar response in oysters were unsuccessful (Weinheimer *et al.,* 1969).

A recent study of bacteriophage (T2 coliphage) clearance in oysters by Acton and Evans (1968) did not disclose induction of phage-neutralizing antibodies, but secondary phage injections were cleared much more rapidly than primary injections. That the more rapid clearance was not specific was suggested by the fact that primary stimulation by an antigenically unrelated phage still produced accelerated clearance when oysters were later challenged with the T2 coliphage. Accelerated secondary clearance in oysters was always much less than that found in lemon sharks studied simultaneously. The sharks, like most other verte-brates, produce high levels of phage- neutralizing antibody.

Phage clearance as an indicator of immunological response in inverte-brates has been used by others. Teague and Friou (1964) failed to find evidence for phage clearance in crayfish (*Cambarus virulis*) but Taylor *et al.* (1964) reported increased secondary clearance rates in the shore crab, *Carcinus maenas*. As was true with oysters, no phage-neutralizing antibodies were demonstrated.

Clearance of injected foreign protein was used as a test system for assessment of humoral responses of sea urchins, *Strongylocentrotus purpuratus*, by Hilgard and Phillips (1968). Acceleration of uptake of labeled bovine serum albumin by coelomocytes did not occur following immunization attempts, but the foreign protein disappeared from the coelomic fluid sooner than labelled injected native proteins, indicating a selective response. Earlier, Phillips (1960) found, using a blocking antibody system, that specific antibody-like material could be produced by an anemone, *Anthopleura elegantissima*, a mollusk, *Tegula funebralis*, and a sipunculid, *Phascolosoma agassizi*.

Summarizing the matter of humoral protective mechanisms in in-vertebrates; (1) we can see clear evidence of natural nonspecific ag-glutinins, lysins, and antibacterial agents in some species; and (2) we have occasional evidence of partially nonspecific response to invading substances. Infection of snails with trematodes makes the host refractory to further invasion, by immobilization of miracidia. In sipunculid worms, lysins are produced against ciliate parasites.

4. Antimicrobial and Antitumor Substances

Very recently several papers have appeared that suggest antimicro-bial and even antitumor activity of shellfish extracts. This finding is not new or startling, since extracts of many plants and animals have been found to have such properties—but invertebrates may contain factors that could be useful as antimicrobial or antitumor agents.

Li *et al.* (1962, 1965) isolated a high-molecular-weight substance from abalones and oysters that he called "paolin" (Chinese for abalone extract) which provided some protection of mice against poliovirus (19% deaths vs 48%) and against influenza virus (40% vs 70%) when given in food in large doses. He also found 50% inhibition of tumors induced by adenovirus in mice. He noted that the activity was much greater (80 times) in summer than in winter, but was uncertain as to whether the substance was accumulated from some environmental source or was synthesized by shellfish. The substance in oysters appeared to be a muco-protein or attached to a mucoprotein, with three active fractions. It was heat stable, however, and could be autoclaved. Li *et al.* separated the fractions from abalones by cellulose ion-exchange chromatography, and found that one fraction had no antiviral activity but inhibited growth of a number of bacteria—both gram-negative and gram-positive—includ-ing *Streptococcus pyogenes* and a penicillin-resistant strain of *Staphylo-coccus aureus*. The other fractions contained no antibacterial activity but inhibited virus growth. As the authors were careful to point out, however, antiviral substances are known from widely divergent sources. For ex-ample, sodium chloride extracts of snow peas provide mouse protection against influenza virus, and calf thymus extract reduces mouse mortalities by inhibiting type 1 polio virus and herpes virus. Li has found comparable antiviral activity in snail mucus, jelly of fish eggs, jelly of jellyfish, and a mucoprotein from mushrooms (which also exerted mouse antitumor effects).

At about the time of Li's work, Schmeer (1964, 1966) and Schmeer and Beery (1965) found that extracts of clams, which were called "mer-cenene," inhibited the growth of tumors in mice. In a series of brief reports, Schmeer and colleagues found growth-inhibiting activity of clam (*Mercenaria mercenaria*) extracts against a variety of tumors, and at-tempted biological and chemical characterization of the active component of the extract.

Skarnes and Watson (1957) have provided a very detailed summary of the many kinds of antimicrobial factors reported from vertebrates. These authors discussed 14 antimicrobial substances; undoubtedly, as research on invertebrates continues, more antimicrobial factors will be described from various phyla. As an example, lysozyme was recently recognized by McDade and Tripp (1967) in oyster blood.

5. *Tissue Transplantation*

Tissue transplantation phenomena have provided an exciting chapter in research on mammalian, and especially human, immune responses. Recent work with lower vertebrates has disclosed a sequence of events comparable to that seen in mammals. With fish, for example, Hildemann (1962) has carried out a long series of studies that illustrate the principles involved. He transferred scales as autotransplants, homotransplants, and heterotransplants. Depending on the nature of the transplant, he found acceptance or rejection; he determined that rate of rejection varied directly with temperature; and he found accelerated rate of rejection in second-series grafts. Homografts and heterografts elicited antibody response and ultimate graft rejections. Comparable studies have been carried on recently with invertebrates, with ambiguous but interesting results.

Cushing (1957) transplanted mantle tissue of scallops, *Aequipecten irradians,* into the body wall, and found that autografts persisted for over a month. A series comparing survival of autografts and homografts indicated slightly better survival of autografts, but no second-series grafts were done.

Cushing and his associates (Triplett *et al.,* 1958) also did an extensive series of skin and tentacle transplants in the sipunculid worm, *Dendrostomum.* No reactivity of recipients was noted other than universal encapsulation of foreign or autologous tissue by amoebocytes and fibrocytes. Simultaneous attempts to demonstrate the appearance of specific agglutinins, lysins, and precipitins in *Dendrostomum* were also unsuccessful even though natural agglutunins for various red cells were observed. Recently, Cushing *et al.* (1965) reexamined the sipunculids with a new approach, after having found no differential response in tentacle implantation. They injected eggs of *Dendrostomum* and other worms into the coelom of *Dendrostomum,* as had been done earlier with tentacles. Homologous eggs were either not encapsulated by amoebocytes or were encapsulated only slightly, but eggs of other species, or stained or damaged homologous eggs, were completely encapsulated. This finding suggested that some degree of self-recognition exists in the internal defense armament of at least some invertebrates.

Tripp (1961), working with freshwater snails, *Biomphalaria glabrata* and *Planorbarius corneus,* found differential response to homologous and heterologous tissue. With homotransplant tissues of *B. glabrata,* only minimal inflammation (leukocyte infiltration) occurred and the implant was quickly integrated with host tissue. On the other hand, heterologous tissue from *P. corneus* implanted into *B. glabrata* caused greater inflammation, subsequent encapsulation, and deterioration; the graft became infiltrated by host fibroblasts. Here then is rather clear indication of response to foreign antigenic stimulation in snails.

Cushing (1962) also examined tissue transplantation phenomena in cephalopod mollusks. In an elaborate series of experiments with the octopus, he found no difference in response to autografts and homografts —all being integrated and surviving as long as the hosts survived (a maximum of 39 days). He made no heterotransplants or second-set grafts. Results thus far indicate only the lack of self-recognition within the species for the short duration of the experiment.

Coelomic implants of pyloric caecum material of starfish were used by

Ghiradella (1965) to examine responses to homologous and heterologous tissue. Two species, *Patira miniata* and *Asterias forbesi,* were able to discriminate between homologous and heterologous transplants. Homologous tissue remained essentially normal for five weeks, while heterologous tissue was eliminated within a week. Several methods of elimination were observed: phagocytic activity, and autotomy or rupturing of dermal branchiae; only one instance of encapsulation was seen.

The evidence for specific immune responses from transplants in invertebrates is incomplete and inconclusive. Some studies suggest a degree of species self-recognition, but others do not indicate even this level of response. Further studies with many other species are needed.

6. Summary

The information about internal defense mechanisms in invertebrates other than insects may be summarized as follows: (1) The search for specific acquired antibodies in invertebrates has not been successful, but antibody-like activity has been demonstrated in a number of species; (2) the weight of the somewhat sketchy evidence favors a major role for phagocytosis, augmented at times by relatively nonspecific innate or acquired humoral factors; (3) many invertebrates seem endowed with antibacterial activity of body fluids, and to some extent with natural agglutinins and lysins.

Thus most of the conclusions reached by Huff (1940) about immune mechanisms in invertebrates are still pertinent:

"In the invertebrates a natural immunity to the attacks of many infective organisms and their noxious products is the first line of defense. This natural immunity is poorly understood, but it is the result of complex processes, including phagocytosis and natural antibodies, many of which are probably inherent. Phagocytosis plays a spectacular part in immunity and, as in vertebrates, is effected both by free and fixed phagocytic cells. It is ineffective in some cases. There are examples of acquired immunity—both active and passive—in invertebrates, but the specificity of such immunity is open to some question. Antibodies may be produced following inoculation or infection, but these result most successfully when natural antibodies already exist. These antibodies differ widely from the corresponding ones in vertebrates, as exemplified by the bacteriolysins which are highly thermostable. No complement has been found, but complementary actions occur. It is too early yet to attempt to evaluate the relative parts played by the various immune mechanisms in protecting the invertebrates."

It is still too early a quarter of a century later for such an evaluation, but additional evidence has accumulated.

Active antibody production by invertebrates has been claimed repeatedly. The best evidence lies in studies of the stimulation of agglutinins in insects. Even here, however, "the unstable nature of the agglutinins, their low titers, and non-specific stimulation all point to lack of analogy with vertebrate antibodies" (Cushing and Campbell, 1957). Claims for the demonstration of antibody production in invertebrates should be viewed with considerable caution, according to these authors. In earlier work, failure to use proper controls, failure to determine natural antibody content, and failure to determine the specificity of observed responses could account for some of the conflicting results. Cushing and Campbell feel that the safest conclusion to be drawn at present is that the question of specific antibody production in invertebrates needs to be investigated systematically before definite answers can be reached.

One final thought has been proposed by Stauber (1961):

"That so few examples of acquired resistance are known among invertebrates may be quite logical. Because of the short generation time, small size, and often enormous reproductive potential of invertebrates, subsequent disease outbreaks would be much more likely to be circumvented by appearance of resistant stocks . . . . so that even with very high mortality rates, a residual stock of survivors under favorable conditions could quickly repopulate an area. . . . If this reasoning is adequate to explain the lack of evidence for acquired resistance in most invertebrates, then those with long life spans, such as *Limulus,* should be studied more fully in an attempt to demonstrate acquired resistance."

B. VERTEBRATES

Serum antibodies are now considered by many to be the most important element of vertebrate host resistance to infection. Examination of the older literature and the broad picture of internal defense mechanisms helps put the antibodies in their rightfully important, but not all-important, place (Hirsch, 1959). Phagocytosis, probably the primary internal defense mechanism in invertebrates, is of importance to the vertebrate as well. A number of studies of the phagocytic process in vertebrates have helped to clarify its role, and its relationship to specific humoral immunity. The critical aspect of the phagocytic process as related to immunity is the intracellular fate of engulfed microorganisms. Those taken in by phagocytes may be retained or ejected. Three fates are possible for those ingested and retained by phagocytes: (1) death (bactericidal effect), (2) survival without multiplication for varying periods (bacteriostatic effect), or (3) multiplication.

The bacteriostatic effect is illustrated by certain bacterial spores, which do not germinate within the phagocyte but which remain viable for considerable lengths of time. If the resistance of the host or of the cells is lowered, however, the spores may germinate within the dead or moribund phagocyte: This is an example of attenuated or latent infection, originally elucidated by Metchnikoff (1893).

Biochemical substances that exert antibacterial action are important to an understanding of the resistance of microorganisms to being killed by phagocytes. The acidity of vacuoles plays a major role. Phagocytes have been shown to utilize glycolysis rather than respiration as their main energy source (Suter, 1956); the lactic acid produced is responsible for low intracellular pH. That antimicrobial action results from lactate production and acid reaction is supported by studies of Dubos (1954) demonstrating that many bacteria, particularly gram-positives, are suppressed or killed by low concentrations of lactate, especially when the pH of the medium is low (Hirsch, 1959).

Phagocytes contain other antibacterial substances; the most clearly defined bactericidal factor of vertebrate phagocytes is lysozyme (Skarnes and Watson, 1957). This enzyme lyses the bacterial species whose cell walls are composed of a susceptible substrate, and in addition may have inhibitory or lethal effects on a wide range of bacteria in combination with other substances which might be present within phagocytes.

Specific acquired humoral immunity to infection has been well demonstrated in the vertebrates. The protective capacities of body fluids are strongly developed in a vertebrate with aquired immunity. These properties of the fluids are of cellular origin. The general chemical composition of antibodies, the site of their formation, and the nature of the interaction between antigens and antibodies have been described for the vertebrates. The important concept of specific interaction between antibody and the bacterial surface with resulting increase in vulnerability to phagocytosis has explained one important function of antibodies in host resistance (Hirsch, 1959). Acquired immunity may affect the intracellular fate of bacteria in additional ways, as was pointed out by Hirsch: (1) Bacteria usually resistant to being killed within phagocytes might be made susceptible because of interaction with immune serum before phagocytosis; or (2) the phagocytes might develop more effective antibacterial properties in their cytoplasm in the acquired immune state.

Resistance to fish diseases involves a complex of interacting factors, including individual variability, species characteristics, seasonal influences, and nutritional effects. Immunity has both cellular and humoral aspects and extends from obvious phagocytic, lytic, and agglutinating activity to include such insusceptibility factors as the skin and mucus barriers and gastric secretions. Some of the mechanisms of natural and acquired resistance to disease in fish have been summarized by Bissett (1947a,b), Dreyer and King (1948), and Snieszko (1958). McDermott (1956) and Hirsch (1959) have reviewed the cellular and humoral mechanisms of immunity. Internal defense mechanisms of fishes are similar to those of higher vertebrates—including phagocytosis, antibody production, inflammation, hypertrophy, and metaplasia. The process of inflammation in fishes, as in other vertebrates, includes increased blood supply, migration of leukocytes into affected tissues, and loss of fluid through blood vessel walls. Inflammation may be localized or extensive, involving entire organs or body areas. Cell hypertrophy is common in a number of parasitic diseases of fishes. Monogenetic trematodes such as *Nitzschia sturionis* cause hypertrophy of epithelial cells of the gills (Lutta, 1941). Connective tissue hypertrophy is particularly apparent in encapsulation of tissue-invading Protozoa and helminths. Later phases of this process can involve pigment and calcium deposition that leads to destruction of the parasite. Metaplasia also occurs in parasitic diseases. Mucoid transformation of epithelia, with increase in numbers of mucus-secreting cells is common in fishes. Abundant mucus secretion is a defense mechanism characteristic of protozoan, trematode, or copepod parasitization of gills, and worm invasion of the digestive tract.

Tissue transplantation studies with fish have indicated incompatibilities which parallel those of higher vertebrates. A simple technique of scale transfers, first used by Goodrich and Nichols (1933), and elaborated by Hildemann (1956, 1957, 1958, 1962) and Hildemann and Cooper (1963), makes the fishes animals of choice for transplantation studies. Autotransplants reestablish blood supply within 48 hours, but homo- and heterotransplants establish blood supply more slowly and rejection responses follow; the severity of rejection depends on the relationship of donor and recipient. Second-series homografts are rejected more rapidly.

A number of papers have appeared recently which clearly substantiate earlier findings (Blake and Anderson, 1930; Toth, 1932; Nybelin, 1935; Schäperclaus, 1938; Snieszko *et al.*, 1938; Smith, 1940) of specific immunological competence in fish. Clem and Sigel (1963), Sigel *et al.* (1963), and Sigel and Clem (1965) studied immune responses in marine teleosts and elasmobranchs to injected viral and bacterial antigens. Lemon shark, *Negaprion brevirostris* (Poey), produced significant titers of hemagglutination-inhibition antibodies with a high degree of specificity in response to injected influenza virus. Titers were lower and specificity was less in similar studies of the margate, *Haemulon album* Cuvier. A very low degree of immunological reactivity was evident in the sea lamprey, *Petromyzon marinus* L. Goncharov (1962) hyperimmunized several cyprinid species at 15°–25°C with killed *Pseudomonas fluorescens* and other bacteria, and produced agglutinin titers as high as 10,240. The agglutinins were specific, and the reaction was temperature-dependent, since antibodies were not formed at 6°–7°C. Krantz *et al.* (1963, 1964), in research oriented toward control of freshwater hatchery diseases through immunization, reported significant antibody response in trout to killed bacteria injected with adjuvant. Maximum agglutinin titers were reached 3 to 4 months after injection. Fish immunized with formalin-killed *Aeromonas salmonicida*, the etiological agent of furunculosis, were protected during challenge with viable pathogens, but untreated controls were not. The authors pointed out, however, that augmented natural defense mechanisms often cannot prevent infection when the fish is confronted by severe physiological or environmental stresses. Post (1963) had used a similar immunization method to achieve moderate protection of rainbow trout, *Salmo gairdneri*, against *Aeromonas hydrophila*.

Spence *et al.* (1965) were able to produce appreciable antibody titers in rainbow trout immunized against *Aeromonas salmonicida;* the antiserum so produced provided passive protection of juvenile Pacific salmon when injected intraperitoneally. Several authors, including Post (1962), have suggested oral immunization as a practical mass prophylactic method, but evidence as to its efficacy is conflicting. Duff (1942) reported resistance of trout to furunculosis after they were fed killed *Aeromonas salmonicida*, and Ross and Klontz (1965) found increased survival of rainbow trout after oral immunization against "redmouth disease." Snieszko and Friddle (1949), however, were unable to demonstrate protection of young brook trout, *Salvelinus fontinalis*, against furunculosis by oral immunization, and Spence *et al.* (1965) found that oral immunization did not protect Pacific salmon exposed to *Aeromonas salmonicida*.

Poikilothermic vertebrates such as fish are excellent subjects for basic studies of immune responses. Allen and McDaniel (1937), Pliszka (1939), Cushing (1942), and Bisset (1946, 1948a,b) have summarized effects of temperature on antibody production, and have demonstrated that production was limited below 10°C. Sindermann and Honey (1964) found that certain natural heteroagglutinins of winter skates, *Raja ocellata* Mitchill, varied seasonally, and that titers were lowest at times of minimum environmental temperatures. Vladimirov (1968) reported that lysozyme activity in fish varied with season and with intensity of antibody formation, increasing threefold in summer. Nybelin (1943, 1968) found that agglutinin production occurred in cold-water fish but not in warm-water fish at 5°C, and concluded that antibody production was not a direct function of temperature, but rather that reactivity paralleled the other metabolic processes of the body. Hildemann (1957) noted acceleration of rates of homograft rejection in fish coincident with increasing environmental temperature. The immune response was measured by survival

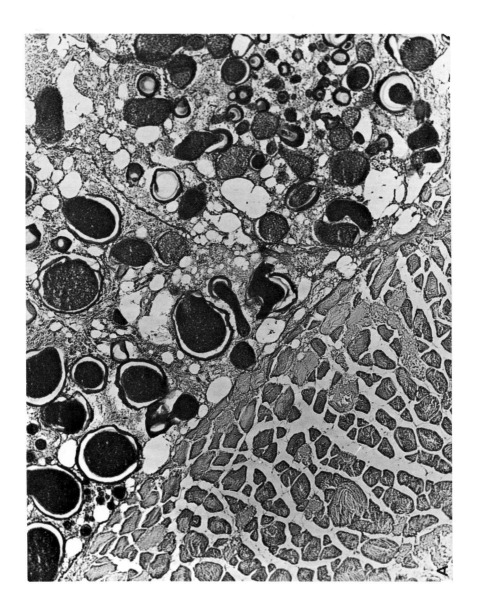

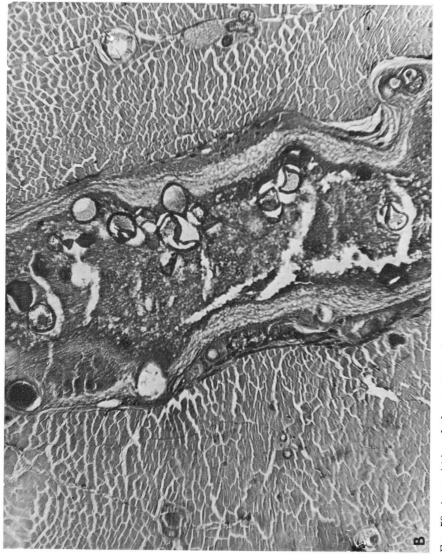

Fig. 58. Acute (A) and chronic (B) infections of Atlantic herring body muscles with the fungus *Ichthyophonus*. Note extensive necrosis in acute infection and extensive encapsulation in chronic infection.

time and inflammatory reactions. Duration and intensity of inflammation were closely correlated with rapidity of donor-tissue destruction. Fine and Drilhon (1961) demonstrated the formation of precipitins in eels in response to injections of human serum. Wolf (1941, 1954), Snieszko (1957), and Ehlinger (1964) found differences among strains of brook trout in resistance to ulcer disease and furunculosis. Papermaster *et al.* (1964), in studies of the evolution of immune responses, found a rising level of reactivity and complexity as the phylogenetic scale from hagfish to teleost was ascended.

Goncharov (1959a) reported high antibody titers in freshwater fish immunized against *Achromobacter punctatum* (*Pseudomonas punctata*), and also pointed out the prevalence of cross-agglutinations in work with such immune sera. Earlier, Mann (1939) had shown that carp affected by ascites (Bauchwassersucht) developed high agglutination titers against *Pseudomonas punctata,* but Roegner-Aust *et al.* (1950) and Goncharov (1959b) presented arguments that a virus was the primary etiological agent. Sorvachev *et al.* (1962) described prophylactic immunization of carp with an attenuated virus vaccine. According to their report, the 1- and 2-year-old progeny of hyperimmunized carp suffered little mortality during a severe outbreak of ascites, whereas young of unvaccinated fish died in great numbers. Such findings are unique, and are more suggestive of maintenance of immunity by natural infections. Despite some continuing disagreement about the causative organism, summarized by Schäperclaus (1965) and others in a recent symposium (Snieszko *et al.,* 1965), a body of literature on the epizootiology of this very important disease (ascites) of carp has accumulated. Included are indications of acquired immunity after infection, a possible role of bacteriophage, changes in virulence, and adaptation to new hosts—all problems that may be pertinent to certain marine fish diseases.

Fungus or myxosporidan invasion of fish often produces only tissue destruction with little indication of inflammatory response. Intramuscular parasites may cause hyalinization and lysis of muscle tissue until only granular debris and spores remain. In some individuals, however, fungus invasion elicits extensive formation of fibrous connective tissue by the host (Fig. 58).

The clearest evidence of acquired humoral immunity in fish, as in higher vertebrates, has been demonstrated with viral and bacterial diseases, but there are also some examples of immunity to animal parasite invasion. Acquired immunity is the development, on contact with a pathogen, of resistance to reinfection. In parasitic diseases, such immunity takes the form of heightened resistance to superinvasion. McCoy (1930), using the marine fish *Lutjanus griseus* and two species of the trematode genus *Haemocreadium*, found that in heavy infestations the duration of gut parasitization was short and some worms did not mature. Infestations with only a few worms, on the other hand, persisted for a long period.

Probably the best example of local immunity to superinfection concerns parasitization of the eyes of captive marine fishes (Serranidae and Lutjanidae) by the monogenetic trematode, *Benedenia melleni*. Jahn and Kuhn (1932) found infestations in aquarium fish of the two families that reached 2000 worms per host, attached to eyes, gills, and nasal cavities. Many fish so parasitized were killed, but the infestation level among survivors gradually decreased, apparently due to acquired immunity of the fish. These interesting observations were extended by Nigrelli and Breder (1934) and Nigrelli (1935a,b,c, 1937, 1947). Survivors of epizootics gradually lost their ectoparasitic *Benedenia,* and were not reinfested. Development of local immunity was proposed to explain the fact that worms did not attach at sites previously occupied by other individuals. Mucus of resistant fish had a strong adverse effect on the trematodes, whereas that of unexposed fish had only a slight effect.

Sigel *et al.* (1968), summarizing a number of continuing studies, suggested that the immune mechanism of fishes is not as fully developed as that of higher vertebrates, and that fishes must have compensatory mechanisms which insure their survival. The authors then went on to point out the naturally occurring substances in fishes, principally elasmobranchs, which may be involved in resistance to infection. Serum from sharks killed influenza virus and neutralized Rous sarcoma virus when mixtures of serum and virus were injected into chickens. Shark serum inoculations in hamsters prior to injections of adenovirus caused partial suppression of tumor development and growth. Bacteria were also destroyed by shark serum. All of the effects were reported to take place only when shark antibodies were accompanied by at least one component of shark complement. In other studies, grunts, *Haemulon sciurus*, were found to be capable of producing interferon after inoculation of virus or endotoxin.

Recent Russian studies of immunity in fish, summarized by Vladimirov (1968), indicate that the specificity of phagocytosis increases sharply with age; that complement of fish has a lower level of activity than other vertebrates; that lysozyme occur more frequently and with greater activity in predatory fish; that lysozyme titers increase simultaneously with antibody titers in immunized fish; and that fish antibodies are similar to warm-blooded animals in specificity, but that the level of antibody formation in fishes is lower than in mammals.

REFERENCES

Acton, R. T., and Evans, E. E. (1968). Bacteriophage clearance in the oyster (*Crassostrea virginica*). *J. Bacteriol.* **95,** 1260–1266.

Allen, F. W., and McDaniel, E. C. (1937). A study of the relation of temperature to antibody formation in cold-blooded animals *J. Immunol.* **32,** 143–152.

Avery, O. T. (1932). The role of specific carbohydrates in pneumococcus infection and immunity. *Ann. Internal Med.* [N.S.] **6,** 1–9.

Baer, J. G. (1944). Immunité et réactions immunitaires chez les invertébrés. *Schweiz. Z. Allgem. Pathol. Bakteriol.* **7,** 442–462.

Bang, F. B. (1956). A bacterial disease of *Limulus polyphemus. Bull. Johns Hopkins Hosp.* **98,** 325–351.

Bang, F. B. (1961). Reaction to injury in the oyster (*Crassostrea virginica*). *Biol. Bull.* **121,** 57–68.

Bang, F. B. (1967a). Introduction. Symposium on "Defense Reactions in Invertebrates." *Federation Proc.* **26,** 1664–1665.

Bang, F. B. (1967b). Serological responses among invertebrates other than insects. *Federation Proc.* **26,** 1680–1684.

Bang, F. B., and Bang, B. G. (1962). Studies on sipunculid blood: Immunologic properties of coelomic fluid and morphology of "urn cells." *Cahiers Biol. Marine* **3,** 363–374.

Bang, F. B., and Chaet, A. B. (1959). The effect of starfish toxin on amebocytes. *Biol. Bull.* **117,** 403–404 (abstr.).

Bang, F. B., and Lemma, A. (1962). Bacterial infection and reaction to injury in some echinoderms. *J. Insect Pathol.* **4,** 401–414.

Barker, W. H., Jr., and Bang, F. B. (1966). The effect of infection by gram-negative bacteria, and their endotoxins, on the blood-clotting mechanism of the crustacean *Sacculina carcini,* a parasite of the crab *Carcinus maenas. J. Invertebrate Pathol.* **8,** 88–97.

Bengston, I. A. (1924). Studies on organisms concerned as causative factors in botulism. *Hyg. Lab. Bull.* **132,** 1–96.

Bisset, K. A. (1946). The effect of temperature on non-specific infections of fish. *J. Pathol. Bacteriol.* **58,** 251–258.

Bissett, K. A. (1947a). Bacterial infection and immunity in lower vertebrates and invertebrates. *J. Hyg.* **45,** 128–135.

Bisset, K. A. (1947b). Natural and acquired immunity in frogs and fish. *J. Pathol. Bacteriol.* **59,** 679–682.

Bisset, K. A. (1948a). Natural antibodies in the blood serum of freshwater fish. *J. Hyg.* **46,** 267–268.

Bisset, K. A. (1948b). The effect of temperature upon antibody production in cold-blooded vertebrates. *J. Pathol. Bacteriol.* **60,** 87–92.

Blake, I., and Anderson, E. J. M. (1930). The identification of *Bacillus salmonicida* by the complement fixation test—a further contribution to the study of furunculosis of the Salmonidae. *Salmon Fishery (Edinburgh)* **1.**

Bourus, T. K. R. (1963). Larval trematodes parasitizing *Lymnaea stagnalis appressa* Say in Ontario with emphasis on multiple infections. *Can. J. Zool.* **41,** 937–941.

Cantacuzène, J. (1912). Sur certains anticorps naturels observés chez *Eupagurus prideauxii. Compt. Rend. Soc. Biol.* (Paris) **73,** 663–664.

Cantacuzène, J. (1913a). Observations relatives a certaines propriétés du sang de *Carcinus maenas* parasité par la sacculine. *Compt. Rend. Soc. Biol.* (Paris) **74,** 109–111.

Cantacuzène, J. (1913b). Recherches sur la production expérimentale de l'anticorps chez quelques invertébrés marins. *Compt. Rend. Soc. Biol.* (*Paris*) **74**, 111–113.

Cantacuzène, J. (1913c). Sur la production d'anticorps artificiels chez *Eupagurus prideauxii*. *Compt. Rend. Soc. Biol.* (*Paris*) **74**, 293–295.

Cantacuzène, J. (1916). Production expérimentale d'hémo-agglutinines et de précipitines chez *Helix pomatia*. *Compt. Rend. Soc. Biol.* (*Paris*) **79**, 528–530.

Cantacuzène, J. (1919). Anticorps normaux et expérimentaux chez quelques invertébrés marins. *Compt. Rend. Soc. Biol.* (*Paris*) **82**, 1087–1089.

Cantacuzène, J. (1922a). Sur le sort ulterieur des urnes chez *Sipunculus nudus* au cours de l'infection et de l'immunisation. I. *Compt. Rend. Soc. Biol.* (*Paris*) **87**, 264–267.

Cantacuzène, J. (1922b). Sur le sort ulterieur des urnes chez *Sipunculus nudus* au cours de l'infection et de l'immunisation. II. *Compt. Rend. Soc. Biol.* (*Paris*) **87**, 283–285.

Cantacuzène, J. (1923a). Cytolysine et cytoagglutinine provoquées par l'inoculation de liquide cavitaire de *Sipunculus nudus* chez *Maia squinado*. *Compt. Rend. Soc. Biol.* (*Paris*) **89**, 266–268.

Cantacuzène, J. (1923b). Le problème de l'immunitè chez les invertébrés. *Compt. Rend. Soc. Biol.* (*75th Ann.*) pp. 48–119.

Cantacuzène, J. (1925). Réactions de crabe sacculine vis à vis d'une infection expérimentale de la sacculine. *Compt. Rend. Soc. Biol.* (*Paris*) **93**, 1417–1419.

Cantacuzène, J. (1928). Recherches sur les réactions d'immunité chez les invertébrés. I. Réactions d'immunité chez *Sipunculus nudus*. *Arch. Roumaines Pathol. Exptl. Microbiol.* **1**, 7–80.

Cantacuzène, J., and Damboviceanu, A. (1934a). Caractères biologiques de l'extrait des acconties d'*Adamsia palliata* après déprotéinisation. *Compt. Rend. Soc. Biol.* (*Paris*) **117**, 136–138.

Cantacuzène, J., and Damboviceanu, A. (1934b). Caractères physico-chimiques du poison des acconties d'*Adamsia palliata*. *Compt. Rend. Soc. Biol.* (*Paris*) **117**, 138–140.

Chaet, A. B., and Albert, M. (1958). Evidence for the toxic theory. *Federation Proc.* **17**, 24.

Cheng, T. C. (1967). Marine molluscs as hosts for symbioses with a review of known parasites of commercially important species. *Advan. Marine Biol.* **5**, 1–424.

Clem, L. W., and Sigel, M. M. (1963). Comparative immunochemical and immunological reactions in marine fishes with soluble viral and bacterial antigens. *Federation Proc.* **22**, 1138–1144.

Cornick, J. W., and Stewart, J. E. (1966). Microorganisms isolated from the hemolymph of the lobster, *Homarus americanus*. *J. Fisheries Res. Board Can.* **23**, 1451–1454.

Cornick, J. W., and Stewart, J. E. (1968a). Interaction of the pathogen *Gaffkya homari* with natural defense mechanisms of *Homarus americanus*. *J. Fisheries Res. Board Can.* **25**, 695–709.

Cornick, J. W., and Stewart, J. E. (1968b). Pathogenicity of *Gaffkya homari* for the crab *Cancer irroratus*. *J. Fisheries Res. Board Can.* **25**, 795–799.

Cushing, J. E. (1942). An effect of temperature upon antibody production in fish. *J. Immunol.* **45**, 123–126.

Cushing, J. E. (1957). Tissue transplantation in *Pecten irradians*. *Biol. Bull.* **113**, 327 (abstr.).

Cushing, J. E. (1962). Blood groups in marine animals and immune mechanisms of lower vertebrates and invertebrates. (Comparative immunology.) *Proc. Conf.*

Immuno-Reprod., La Jolla, Calif., 1962 pp. 205–207 Population Council, New York.

Cushing, J. E. (1967). Invertebrates, immunology and evolution. *Federation Proc.* 26, 1666–1670.

Cushing, J. E., and Campbell, D. H. (1957). "Principles of Immunology," 344 pp. McGraw-Hill, New York.

Cushing, J. E., Boraker, D., and Keough, E. (1965). Reactions of sipunculid worms to intracoelomic injections of homologous eggs. *Federation Proc.* 24, 504.

Dreyer, N. B., and King, J. W. (1948). Anaphylaxis in the fish. *J. Immunol.* 60, 277–282.

Dubos, R. J. (1954). "Biochemical Determinants of Microbial Disease." Harvard Univ. Press, Cambridge, Massachusetts.

Duff, D. C. B. (1942). The oral immunization of trout against *Bacterium salmonicida*. *J. Immunol.* 44, 87–94.

Durham, H. E. (1888). On the emigration of ameboid corpuscles in starfish. *Proc. Roy. Soc.* B43, 327–330.

Ehlinger, N. E. (1964). Selective breeding of trout for resistance to furunculosis. *N. Y. Fish Game J.* 11, 78–90.

Evans, E. E., Painter, B., Evans, M. L., Weinheimer, P., and Acton, R. T. (1968). An induced bactericidin in the spiny lobster, *Panulirus argus*. *Proc. Soc. Exptl. Biol. Med.* 128, 394–398.

Ewers, W. H. (1960). Multiple infections of trematodes in a snail. *Nature* 186, 990.

Ewers, W. H., and Rose, C. R. (1965). Trematode parasitism and polymorphism in a marine snail. *Science* 148, 1747–1748.

Farley, C. A. (1968). *Minchinia nelsoni* (Haplosporida, Haplosporidiidae) disease syndrome in the American oyster, *Crassostrea virginica*. *J. Protozool.* 15, 585–599.

Feng, S. Y. (1962). The response of oysters to the introduction of soluble and particulate materials and the factors modifying the response. Ph.D. Thesis, Rutgers University, New Brunswick, N. J.

Feng, S. Y. (1965). Heart rate and leucocyte circulation in *Crassostrea virginica* (Gmelin). *Biol. Bull.* 128, 198–210.

Feng, S. Y. (1967). Responses of molluscs to foreign bodies, with special reference to the oyster. *Federation Proc.* 26, 1685–1692.

Fine, J., and Drilhon, A. (1961). Existence de globulines de faible mobilité électrophorétique dans le sérum de l'anguille soumise à des injections répétées de sérum humain. *Compt. Rend.* 252, 3891–3893.

George, W. C. (1941). Comparative hematology and the functions of the leucocytes. *Quart. Rev. Biol.* 16, 426–439.

Ghiradella, H. (1965). The reaction of two starfishes, *Patira miniata* and *Asterias forbesi*, to foreign tissue in the coelom. *Biol. Bull.* 128, 77–89.

Goncharov, G. D. (1959a). Results and aims of the study of infectious fish diseases. (In Russian.) *Tr. Soveshch. po Bolezn. Ryb, Ikhtiol Kom., Akad. Nauk SSSR* pp. 11–15.

Goncharov, G. D. (1959b). Viral rubella of fish in the USSR and abroad. (In Russian.) *Tr. Soveshch. po Bolezn. Ryb, Ikhtiol Kom., Akad. Nauk SSSR* pp. 32–37.

Goncharov, G. D. (1962). Immunological reactions of fish. (In Russian.) *Tr. Inst. Biol. Vodokhranilishch, Akad. Nauk SSSR* 12, 53–56.

Goodrich, H. B., and Nichols, R. (1933). Scale transplantation in the goldfish, *Carassius auratus*. *Biol. Bull.* **65**, 253.

Haeckel, E. (1862). Die Radiolarien. pp. 104–106, Geo. Reimer, Berlin.

Hildemann, W. H. (1956). Histocompatibility genetics of scale transplantation. *Transplant. Bull.* **4**, 132–134.

Hildemann, W. H. (1957). Scale homotransplantation in goldfish (*Carassius auratus*). *Ann. N. Y. Acad. Sci.* **64**, 775–790.

Hildemann, W. H. (1958). Tissue transplantation immunity in goldfish. *Immunology* **1**, 46–53.

Hildemann, W. H. (1962). Immunogenetic studies of poikilothermic animals. *Am. Naturalist* **96**, 195–204.

Hildemann, W. H., and Cooper, E. L. (1963). Immunogenesis of homograft reactions in fishes and amphibians. *Federation Proc.* **22**, 1145–1151.

Hilgard, H. R., and Phillips, J. H. (1968). Sea urchin response to foreign substances. *Science* **161**, 1243–1245.

Hirsch, J. G. (1959). Immunity to infectious diseases: Review of some concepts of Metchnikoff. *Bacteriol. Rev.* **23**, 48–60.

Huff, C. G. (1940). Immunity in invertebrates. *Physiol. Rev.* **20**, 68–88.

Jahn, T. L., and Kuhn, L. R. (1932). The life history of *Epibdella melleni* Mac-Cullum 1927, a monogenetic trematode parasitic on marine fishes. *Biol. Bull.* **62**, 89–109.

Johnson, H. M. (1964). Human blood group A_1 specific agglutinin of the butter clam, *Saxidomus giganteus*. *Science* **146**, 548–549.

Krafka, J., Jr. (1929). The production of anaphylaxis in the crawfish. *Am. J. Hyg.* **10**, 261–264.

Krantz, G. E., Reddecliff, J. M., and Heist, C. E. (1963). Development of antibodies against *Aeromonas salmonicida* in trout. *J. Immunol.* **91**, 757–760.

Krantz, G. E., Reddecliff, J. M., and Heist, C. E. (1964). Immune response of trout to *Aeromonas salmonicida*. Part I. Development of agglutinating antibodies and protective immunity. *Progressive Fish Culturist* **26**, 3–10.

Levin, J. A. (1967). Blood coagulation and endotoxin in invertebrates. *Federation Proc.* **26**, 1707–1712.

Levin, J. A., and Bang, F. B. (1964). A description of cellular coagulation in *Limulus*. *Bull. Johns Hopkins Hosp.* **115**, 337–345.

Li, C. P., Prescott, B., Jahnes, W. G., and Martino, E. C. (1962). Antimicrobial agents from mollusks. *Trans. N. Y. Acad. Sci.* [2] **24**, 504–509.

Li, C. P., Prescott, B., Eddy, B., Caldes, G., Green, W. R., Martino, E. C., and Young, A. M. (1965). Antiviral activity of paolins from clams. *Ann. N. Y. Acad. Sci.* **130**, 374–382.

Lutta, A. S. (1941). Infection of Aral Sea sturgeon (*Acipenser nudiventris*) with the gill trematode *Nitzschia sturionis*. (In Russian.) *Tr. Leningr. Obshch. Estetsvoispyt.* **68**, 40–60.

McCoy, O. R. (1930). Experimental studies on two fish trematodes of the genus *Haemocreadium* (Family Allocreadiidae). *J. Parasitol.* **17**, 1–13.

McDade, J. E., and Tripp, M. R. (1967). Lysozyme in the hemolymph of the oyster, *Crassostrea virginica*. *J. Invertebrate Pathol.* **9**, 531–535.

McDermott, W. (1956). Natural resistance to infections. *Ann. N. Y. Acad. Sci.* **66**, 233–414.

Mackin, J. G. (1951). Histopathology of infection of *Crassostrea virginica* (Gmelin) by *Dermocystidium marinum* Mackin, Owen, and Collier. *Bull. Marine Sci. Gulf Caribbean* **1,** 72–87.

Mackin, J. G., Korringa, P., and Hopkins, S. H. (1952). Hexamitiasis of *Ostrea edulis* L. and *Crassostrea virginica* (Gmelin). *Bull. Marine Sci. Gulf Caribbean* **1,** 266–277.

Mann, H. (1939). Serologische Untersuchungen an mit austeckender Bauchwassersucht befallenen Karpfen. *Z. Fischerei* **37,** 101–126.

Metchnikoff, E. (1884). Über eine Sprosspelzkrankheit der Daphnien. *Virchow's Archiv.* **96,** 177–195.

Metchnikoff, E. (1893). Lectures on the comparative pathology of inflammation. Delivered at Pasteur Inst., 1891 (Transl. by F. A. Starling and E. H. Starling). Kegan Paul, Trench, Trubner and Co., London.

Metchnikoff, E. (1905). "Immunity in Infective Diseases" (Transl. by F. G. Binnie). Cambridge Univ. Press, London and New York.

Michelson, E. H. (1963). Development and specificity of miracidial immobilizing substances in extracts of the snail, *Australorbis glabratus* exposed to various agents. *Ann. N. Y. Acad. Sci.* **113,** 486–491.

Michelson, E. H. (1964). Miracidia-immobilizing substances in extracts prepared from snails infected with *Schistosoma mansoni. Am. J. Trop. Med. Hyg.* **13,** 36–42.

Newton, W. L. (1952). The comparative tissue reaction of two strains of *Australorbis glabratus* to infection with *Schistosoma mansoni. J. Parasitol.* **38,** 362–366.

Nigrelli, R. F. (1935a). Studies on the acquired immunity of the pompano, *Trachinotus carolinus,* to *Epibdella melleni. J. Parasitol.* **21,** 438–439.

Nigrelli, R. F. (1935b). Experiments on the control of *Epibdella melleni* MacCallum, a monogenetic trematode of marine fishes. *J. Parasitol.* **21,** 438.

Nigrelli, R. F. (1935c). On the effect of fish mucus on *Epibdella melleni,* a monogenetic trematode of marine fishes. *J. Parasitol.* **21,** 438.

Nigrelli, R. F. (1937). Further studies on the susceptibility and acquired immunity of marine fishes to *Epibdella melleni,* a monogenetic trematode. *Zoologica* **22,** 185–191.

Nigrelli, R. F. (1947). Susceptibility and immunity of marine fishes to *Benedinia* (=*Epibdella*) *melleni* (MacCallum), a monogenetic trematode. III. Natural hosts in the West Indies. *J. Parasitol.* **33,** Suppl., 25 (abstr.).

Nigrelli, R. F., and Breder, C. M. (1934). Susceptibility and immunity of certain marine fishes to *Epibdella melleni. J. Parasitol.* **20,** 259–269.

Nolf, L. O., and Cort, W. W. (1933). On immunity reactions of snails to the penetration of the cercariae of the strigeid trematode *Cotylurus flabelliformis* (Faust). *J. Parasitol.* **20,** 38–48.

Nybelin O. (1935). Ueber Agglutininbildung bei Fischen. *Z. Immunitaetsforsch.* **84,** 74–79.

Nybelin, O. (1943). Influence of temperature on formation of agglutinins in fish. (In Swedish.) *J. Swedish Med. Assoc.* **19,** 1246–1255.

Nybelin, O. (1968). The influence of temperature on the formation of agglutinins in fish. *Proc. 3rd Symp. Mond. Comm. Off. Intern. Etude Maladies Poissons* (*Stockholm, 1968*) *Unnumbered Separate,* 3 pp. (mimeo.).

Papermaster, B. W., Condie, R. M., Finstad, J., and Good, R. A. (1964). Evolution of the immune response. I. The phylogenetic development of adaptive immunologic responsiveness in vertebrates. *J. Exptl. Med.* **119,** 105–130.

Phillips, J. H. (1960). Antibodylike materials of marine invertebrates. *Ann. N. Y. Acad. Sci.* **90**, 760–769.

Pliszka, F. V. (1939). Weitere Untersuchungen über Immunitätsreaktionen und über Phagozytose bei Karpfen. *Zentr. Bakteriol. Parasitenk. Abt. I. Orig.* **143**, 451–460.

Poisson, R. (1930). Observation sur *Anophrys sarcophaga* (Cohn) et *A. maggii* (Cattaneo), infusoire holotriche marin, et sur son parasitisme chez certain crustacés. *Bull. Biol. France Belg.* **64**, 288–331.

Post, G. (1962). Immunization as a method of disease control in fish. *U. S. Trout News* **7**(3), 14–17.

Post, G. (1963). The immune response of rainbow trout (*Salmo gairdnerii*) to *Aeromonas hydrophila. Utah Fish Game Bull.* **63**(7), 82 pp.

Rabin, H. (1965). Studies on gaffkemia, a bacterial disease of the American lobster, *Homarus americanus* (Milne-Edwards). *J. Invertebrate Pathol.* **7**, 391–397.

Rabin, H., and Bang, F. B. (1964). *In vitro* studies of the antibacterial activity of *Golfingia gouldii* (Pourtalés) coelomic fluid. *J. Insect Pathol.* **6**, 457–465.

Ramsdell, S. G. (1927). The smooth muscle reaction in the serum treated earthworm. *J. Immunol.* **13**, 385–387.

Read, C. P. (1958). Status of behavioral and physiological "resistance." *Rice Inst. Pam.* **45**, 36–54.

Roegner-Aust, S., Brunner, G., and Jaxtheimer, R. (1950). Elektronenmikroskopische Untersuchungen über den Erreger der Infektiösen Bauchwassersucht der Karpfen. Bakterium?-Virus? *Allgem. Fischereiztg.* **75**, 17–19.

Ross, A. J., and Klontz, G. W. (1965). Oral immunization of rainbow trout (*Salmo gairdneri*) against an etiologic agent of "Redmouth Disease." *J. Fisheries Res. Board Can.* **22**, 713–719.

Ruediger, G. F., and Davis, D. J. (1907). Phagocytosis and opsonins in the lower animals. *J. Infect. Diseases* **4**, 333–336.

Schäperclaus, W. (1938). Die Immunisierung von Karpfen gegen Bauchwassersucht auf natürlichem und künstlichem Wege. *Fischereiztg.* (*Neudamm*) **41**, 193–196.

Schäperclaus, W. (1965). Etiology of infectious carp dropsy. *Ann. N. Y. Acad. Sci.* **126**, 587–597.

Schmeer, M. R. (1964). Growth-inhibiting agents from *Mercenaria* extracts. Chemical and biological characteristics. *Science* **144**, 413–414.

Schmeer, M. R. (1966). Mercenene: Growth-inhibiting agent of *Mercenaria* extracts —further chemical and biological characterization. *Ann. N. Y. Acad. Sci.* **136**, 211–218.

Schmeer, M. R., and Beery, G. (1965). Mercenene: Growth-inhibitor extracted from clam *M. campechiensis*. Preliminary investigation of *in vivo* and *in vitro* activity. *Life Sci.* **4**, 2157–2165.

Schneider, T. A. (1951). Nutrition and resistance-susceptibility to infection. *Am. J. Trop. Med.* **31**, 174–182.

Shirodkar, M. V., Warwick, A., and Bang, F. B. (1960). The *in vitro* reaction of *Limulus* amebocytes to bacteria. *Biol. Bull.* **118**, 324–337.

Sigel, M. M., and Clem, L. W. (1965). Antibody response of fish to viral antigens. *Ann. N. Y. Acad. Sci.* **126**, 662–677.

Sigel, M. M., Moewus, L., and Clem, L. W. (1963). Virological and immunological studies on marine fish. *Bull. Office Intern. Epizooties* **59**, 143–145.

Sigel, M. M., Russell, W. J., Jensen, J. A., and Beasley, A. R. (1968). Natural immunity in marine fishes. *Proc. 3rd Symp. Mond. Comm. Off. Intern. Epizool. Etude Maladies Poissons,* (*Stockholm, 1968*) Separate No. 6, 3 pp.

Sindermann, C. J., and Honey, K. A. (1964). Serum hemagglutinins of the winter skate, *Raja ocellata* Mitchill, from the western North Atlantic Ocean. *Copeia* pp. 139–144.

Skarnes, R. C., and Watson, D. W. (1957). Antimicrobial factors of normal tissues and fluids. *Bacteriol. Rev.* **21**, 273–294.

Smith, W. W. (1940). Production of anti-bacterial agglutinins by carp and trout at 10°C. *Proc. Soc. Exptl. Biol. Med.* **45**, 726–729.

Snieszko, S. F. (1957). Disease resistant and susceptible populations of brook trout (*Salvelinus fontinalis*). *U. S. Fish Wildlife Serv., Spec. Sci. Rept., Fisheries* **208**, 126–128.

Snieszko, S. F. (1958). Natural resistance and susceptibility to infections. *Progressive Fish Culturist* **20**, 133–136.

Snieszko, S. F., and Friddle, S. B. (1949). Prophylaxis of furunculosis in brook trout (*Salvelinus fontinalis*) by oral immunization and sulfamerazine. *Progressive Fish Culturist* **11**, 161–168.

Snieszko, S. F., Piotrowska, W., Kocylowski, B., and Marek, K. (1938). Badania bakteriologiczne i serologiczne nad bakteriami posocznicy karpi. *Rozpravy Biol. Zak. Med. Wet.* **16**, 1–15.

Snieszko, S. F., Nigrelli, R. E., and Wolf, K. E. (1965). Viral diseases of poikilothermic vertebrates. *Ann. N. Y. Acad. Sci.* **126**, 1–680.

Sorvachev, K. F., Zadvorochnov, S. F., and Isayev, F. A. (1962). On the immunization of fish. (In Russian). *Biokhimiya* **27**, 202–207.

Spence, K. D., Fryer, J. L., and Pilcher, K. S. (1965). Active and passive immunization of certain salmonid fishes against *Aeromonas salmonicida. Can. J. Microbiol.* **43**, 397–405.

Stauber, L. A. (1950). The fate of India ink injected intracardially into the oyster, *Ostrea virginica* (*Gmelin*). *Biol. Bull.* **98**, 227–241.

Stauber, L. A. (1961). Immunity in invertebrates, with special reference to the oyster. *Proc. Natl. Shellfisheries Assoc.* **50**, 7–20.

Stewart, J. E., and Dingle, J. R. (1968). Characteristics of hemolymphs of *Cancer irroratus, C. borealis* and *Hyas coarctatus. J. Fisheries Res. Board Can.* **25**, 607–610.

Stewart, J. E., Dingle, J. R., and Odense, P. H. (1966a). Constituents of the hemolymph of the lobster, *Homarus americanus* Milne Edwards. *Can. J. Biochem.* **44**, 1447–1459.

Stewart, J. E., Cornick, J. W., Spears, D. I., and McLeese, D. W. (1966b). Incidence of *Gaffkya homari* in natural lobster *Homarus americanus* populations of the Atlantic region of Canada. *J. Fisheries Res. Board Can.* **23**, 1325–1330.

Stewart, J. E., Cornick, J. W., and Dingle, J. R. (1967). An electronic method for counting lobster (*Homarus americanus* Milne Edwards) hemocytes and the influence of diet on hemocyte numbers and hemolymph proteins. *Can. J. Zool.* **45**, 291–304.

Suter, E. (1956). Interactions between phagocytes and pathogenic microorganisms. *Bacteriol. Revs.* **20**, 94–132.

Takatsuki, S. (1934). Beiträge zur Physiologie des Austerherzens unter besonderer Berücksichtigung servier physiologischen Reaktionen. *Sci. Rept. Tokyo Bunrika Daigaku* **B2**, 55–62; also in *Rept. Hiroshima Prefect. Fish. Expt. Sta.* **20**, No. 1.

Taylor, A. E., Taylor, G., and Collard, P. (1964). Secondary immune response to bacteriophage T_1 in the shore crab *Carcinus maenas*. *Nature* **123**, 775.

Teague, P. O., and Friou, G. J. (1964). Lack of immunological responses by an invertebrate. *Comp. Biochem. Physiol.* **12**, 471–478.

Toth, L. (1932). Agglutination and Hämolyse bei Fischen. *Z. Immunitaetsforsch.* **75**, 277–283.

Triplett, E. L., Cushing, J. E., and Durall, G. L. (1958). Observations on some immune reactions of the sipunculid worm *Dendrostomum zostericolum*. *Am. Naturalist* **92**, 287–293.

Tripp, M. R. (1958a). Studies on the defense mechanism of the oyster, *Crassostrea virginica*. Ph.D. Thesis, Rutgers University, New Brunswick, N. J.

Tripp, M. R. (1958b). Disposal by the oyster of intracardially injected red blood cells of vertebrates. *Proc. Natl. Shellfisheries Assoc.* **48**, 142–147.

Tripp, M. R. (1958c). Studies on the defense mechanisms of the oyster, *Crassostrea virginica*. *J. Parasitol.* **44**, Suppl., 35–36 (abstr.).

Tripp, M. R. (1960). Mechanisms of removal of injected microorganisms from the American oyster, *Crassostrea virginica* (Gmelin). *Biol. Bull.* **119**, 273–282.

Tripp, M. R. (1961). The fate of foreign materials experimentally introduced into the snail *Australorbis glabratus*. *J. Parasitol.* **47**, 745–751.

Tripp, M. R. (1963). Cellular responses of mollusks. *Ann. N. Y. Acad. Sci.* **113**, 467–474.

Tripp, M. R. (1966). Hemagglutinin in the blood of the oyster *Crassostrea virginica*. *J. Invertebrate Pathol.* **8**, 478–484.

Tyler, A. (1946). Natural heteroagglutinins in the body fluids and seminal fluids of various invertebrates. *Biol. Bull.* **90**, 213–219.

Tyler, A., and Metz, C. B. (1945). Natural heteroagglutinins in the serum of the spiny lobster, *Panulirus interruptus*. I. Taxonomic range of activity, electrophoretic and immunizing properties. *J. Exptl. Zool.* **100**, 387–406.

Tyler, A., and Scheer, B. T. (1945). Natural heteroagglutinins in the serum of the spiny lobster, *Panulirus interruptus*. II. Chemical and antigenic relation to blood proteins. *Biol. Bull.* **89**, 193–200.

Vladimirov, V. L. (1968). Immunity in fish. *Proc. 3rd Symp. Mond. Comm. Off. Intern. Epizoot. Etude Maladies Poissons*, (Stockholm, 1968) Separate No. 21, 8 pp.

Weinheimer, P. F., Acton, R. T., and Evans, E. E. (1969). Attempt to induce a bactericidal response in the oyster. *J. Bacteriol.* **97**, 462–463.

Wiener, A. S. (1951). Origin of naturally occurring hemagglutinins and hemolysins. A review. *J. Immunol.* **66**, 287–295.

Winfield, G. F. (1932). On the immunity of snails infested with the sporocysts of the strigeid, *Cotylurus flabelliformis*, to the penetration of its cercariae. *J. Parasitol.* **19**, 130–133.

Wolf, L. E. (1941). Further observations on ulcer disease of trout. *Trans. Am. Fisheries Soc.* **70**, 369–381.

Wolf, L. E. (1954). Development of disease-resistant strains of fish. *Trans. Am. Fisheries Soc.* **83**, 342–349.

Wright, C. A. (1960). Relationships between trematodes and molluscs. *Ann. Trop. Med. Parasitol.* **54**, 1–7.

Wright, C. A. (1966). The pathogenesis of helminths in the Mollusca. *Helminthol. Abstr.* **35**, 207–224.

VII

Relation of Human Diseases to Diseases of Marine Animals

A. INTRODUCTION

Surprisingly few diseases of humans are related to the marine environment or to parasites and diseases of animals which inhabit the oceans. There are, however, isolated examples of disease interactions between man and marine organisms that can be harmful. Excluded from the following consideration are the biotoxins characteristic of certain fish, particularly in tropical waters (Halstead, 1958, 1965–67; Randall, 1958); biotoxins accumulated by shellfish, resulting in paralytic shellfish poisoning; ions, particularly those of heavy metals, accumulated by shellfish which cause human illnesses such as *Minamata* disease in Japan (Sato *et al.,* 1959); and toxins produced by microorganisms in processed seafood, causing botulism in humans (Pederson, 1955)—since none of these is of direct consequence as a disease of marine animals.

B. MICROBIAL DISEASES

One large category of human diseases that are not technically derived from parasites or diseases of marine animals, but which may result from passive transfer of human pathogens by marine species, concerns viral and bacterial infections. Pollution of estuarine and inshore waters, uptake

290

and retention of microorganisms by fish and shellfish, and ingestion of such passive carriers uncooked, can unite to produce human infection (Shewan and Liston, 1954; Mason and McLean, 1962). Examples of typhoid fever and infectious hepatitis outbreaks traceable to ingestion of raw shellfish can be found in the scientific literature, and are often over-emphasized in the newspapers. Almost invariably, when oysters or clams have been implicated, the outbreak has been traced to polluted growing areas, usually legally closed to the taking of shellfish. It seems likely that increasing conditions of estuarine and inshore pollution will lead to an increasing role of inshore fish and shellfish in transfer of human pathogens. As long as raw marine products from inshore waters are eaten by humans, the possibility of disease transmission, either mechanically or as a result of multiplication of a pathogen within the marine host, must be recognized. Glantz and Krantz (1965) have used serotyping of *Escherichia coli* to show a relationship between bacterial isolates from fish and pollution of water. Bacteria of human origin were retained in the digestive tract of fish for short periods, but experimental studies disclosed no illness in fish fed on *E. coli* serotypes pathogenic to man.

Janssen and Meyers (1968), in a very provocative recent paper, reported specific antibodies in white perch serum to several bacteria pathogenic to humans. Such antibodies were found only in fish netted in Chesapeake Bay waters adjacent to heavily populated areas; they were not found in fish from waters adjacent to sparsely populated areas. The authors suggested that fish may become actively infected with human pathogens in polluted waters, and may constitute a public health hazard. Further studies are certainly necessary before such a statement can be made with any degree of assurance. Molluscan shellfish, however, can be much more dangerous than fish in this respect. They are filter feeders, and thus can accumulate microorganisms from a polluted environment; most of them are harvested from estuaries and inshore waters, where pollution is more severe than in the open sea; and they are eaten raw much more frequently in western countries than are fish.

During the past decade, increasing numbers of summer bacterial enteritis outbreaks in Japan have been traced to human ingestion of raw marine fishes and invertebrates (Aiso and Matsuno, 1961; Sakazaki *et al.*, 1963). The largest outbreak, which affected 20,000 people, occurred in Niigata Prefecture in 1955; it was traced to eating cuttlefish from the Sea of Japan. Similar but less extensive outbreaks in 1959 were traced to eating saurel. Examples of the involvement of marine products in gastroenteritis outbreaks can be seen in the statistics of the Japanese Ministry of Health and Welfare. In 1963, of 524 outbreaks of food poisoning, 319 or 60% involved fish and shellfish. The causative organism in many cases was the halophilic bacterium, *Vibrio parahemolyticus* (Fujino), also called *Pseudomonas enteritis, Pasteurella parahemolytica,* and *Oceanomonas parahemolytica.* Numerous pathogenic and nonpathogenic strains have been isolated from coastal seawater, plankton organisms, bottom mud, and the body surfaces and intestines of marine animals. Thirty-two serotypes have been recognized. The oriental custom of eating fish raw has certainly contributed to the frequency of outbreaks, which are largely confined to the summer months. An extensive body of Japanese literature on *V. parahemolyticus* has accumulated[*] (Aiso and Fujiwara, 1963; Aiso and Matsuno, 1961; Fujiwara *et al.,* 1964; Iida *et al.,* 1957; Kawashima *et al.,* 1961; Sakazaki *et al.,* 1963; Takikawa, 1958; Zen-Yoji *et al.,* 1963).

Vibrio parahemolyticus has not been specifically identified as a pathogen of marine fish, although Kusuda (1965, 1966) reported vibrios causing ulcer disease of cultured marine fish to be "closely related to" or bearing "strong resemblance to *V. parahemolyticus* causing intestinal inflammation in man, and to *V. anguillarum* causing red fin disease in marine eels." There were enough differences, however, for him to state (1966) that "it is proper to believe that the bacteria (isolated from fish) are neither of the two types mentioned above." Akazawa (1968) in a brief published summary of ulcerative disease of marine fishes from the Japanese west coast, mentioned isolation of vibrios which he subdivided on the basis of undescribed biochemical and serological tests into *V. parahemolyticus, V. anguillarum,* and *V. alginolyticus.* More detailed evidence would be needed before isolates of *V. parahemolyticus* causing human digestive disturbances and isolates identified as *V. parahemolyticus* from diseased fish were considered to be identical.

Organisms with characteristics of *V. parahemolyticus* have been isolated from marine sources elsewhere in the world. Ward (1968) isolated serologically related forms from estuarine sediments in United States coastal areas, and mentioned two vibrio isolates from British waters which were similar to *V. parahemolyticus* in pathogenicity to mice. Baross and Liston (1968) reported *V. parahemolyticus* from sea water, sediments, and shellfish from the Puget Sound region on the North American west coast. Probably the most interesting recent report concerning the pathogen is that of Krantz *et al.* (1969). *V. parahemolyticus* was isolated from moribund tank-held blue crabs, *Callinectes sapidus,* from the Chesapeake Bay region of the middle Atlantic coast of the United States. The authors suggested that the vibrio is very likely a

[*] Most of the Japanese references cited, and some translations, were obtained through the courtesy of Dr. G. M. Dack, Director, Food Research Institute, University of Chicago.

pathogen of marine animals, and secondarily a potential human pathogen. It should be noted, however, that no human disorder has been related to V. *parahemolyticus* outside the Orient, that experimental infections of crabs were not reported, and that other pathogens have recently been described as causes of blue crab mortalities.

Among the human illnesses associated with microbial infectious agents of marine fish origin are severe inflammations of superficial wounds among fish handlers caused by the bacterium *Erysipelothrix insidiosa* (Trevisan) —also known as *E. rhusiopathiae* as described by Sheard and Dicks (1949), Wellman (1950, 1957), and Langford and Hansen (1954). Processing plant employees may be temporarily incapacitated by these infections, known as erysipeloid which are particularly common after injury by spines of such fish as sea robins or redfish. The causative organism has been isolated repeatedly from fish slime (Sneath *et al.*, 1951; Price and Bennett, 1951) but is not pathogenic to fish. Oppenheimer and Kesteven (1953) and Wellmann (1957) reported that known strains of the bacterium grew well in seawater medium.

C. HELMINTHIC DISEASES

A number of heterophyid trematodes, normally parasites of birds and mammals, with metacercariae in some marine and estuarine fishes, can infect humans who ingest raw fish. Larval trematodes, *Heterophyes heterophyes* (Siebold), infective to man, occur on the integument or in the flesh of mullets, *Mugil cephalus* and *Mugil japonicus*, found in brackish water in the Philippines, Egypt, Japan, and China (Belding, 1942). Species of *Microphallus* (*Spelotrema*) have been implicated as human parasites by Africa and Garcia (1935). They found *Heterophyes brevicaeca* (renamed *Spelotrema brevicaeca* by Tubangi and Africa, 1938) during autopsies in the Philippines. Two species of the heterophyid genus *Nanophyetus—N. salmincola* Chapin and *N. schikhobalowi* Skrjabin and Podjapolskaya—have been reported as rare parasites of human beings (Chapin, 1926; Skrjabin and Podjapolskaya, 1931). *Nanophyetus salmincola* is of particular interest because it harbors *Neorickettsia helminthoeca*, which causes "salmon poisoning" disease of dogs, and has been shown to persist for 3 years in sea-run salmon (Farrell *et al.*, 1964). Another heterophyid, *Cryptocotyle lingua*, a common parasite of sled dogs and gulls, with metacercariae in a number of marine fishes (especially herring) has been reported from inhabitants of northern Europe (Christensen and Roth, 1949). It is likely that still other heterophyid metacercariae from estuarine and inshore fish may occasionally infest man.

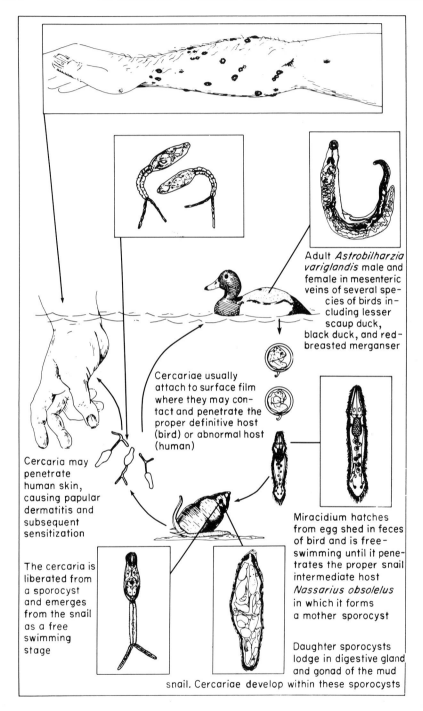

Adult *Astrobilharzia variglandis* male and female in mesenteric veins of several species of birds including lesser scaup duck, black duck, and red-breasted merganser

Cercariae usually attach to surface film where they may contact and penetrate the proper definitive host (bird) or abnormal host (human)

Cercaria may penetrate human skin, causing papular dermatitis and subsequent sensitization

The cercaria is liberated from a sporocyst and emerges from the snail as a free swimming stage

Miracidium hatches from egg shed in feces of bird and is free-swimming until it penetrates the proper snail intermediate host *Nassarius obsolelus* in which it forms a mother sporocyst

Daughter sporocysts lodge in digestive gland and gonad of the mud snail. Cercariae develop within these sporocysts

One human disease entity that has emerged in the past 20 years, and which is related to parasitization of mollusks, is marine schistosome dermatitis, often called "seabathers' eruption" or "clam diggers' itch." The larval trematodes of several genera in the family Schistosomatidae responsible for this condition normally mature in blood vessels of migratory birds. They may, however, invade human skin exposed to seawater near concentrations of the marine snails that act as intermediate hosts (Fig. 59). Penner (1942, 1950) first pointed out the existence of marine dermatitis-producing schistosomes; these have since been identified from many parts of the world (Chu, 1952; Hutton, 1952; Stunkard and Hinchliffe, 1952; Sindermann and Gibbs, 1953; Chu and Cutress, 1954; Bearup, 1956; Grodhaus and Keh, 1958; Sindermann, 1960; Ewers, 1961). Cercariae normally die after invading the skin, causing papular dermatitis which may in some individuals be severe. Secondary bacterial infections are common among clam diggers chronically exposed to the parasites. Studies by Sindermann (1960) of *Austrobilharzia variglandis,* an avian schistosome which parasitizes the mud snail, *Nassarius obsoletus,* in New England, indicated that external environmental conditions of salinity, temperature, and oxygen influenced cercarial emergence, and that infection levels varied geographically and with location of the host in the tide zone. Highest prevalence of infections, hence greatest risk of dermatitis, occurred in the high tide zone near bird sanctuaries in early autumn.

Certain species of the trematode genus *Philophthalmus,* which occur as larvae in marine snails (Penner and Fried, 1961, 1963) and as adults in the eye membranes of gulls, may be capable of infecting human beings. Two cases of such infection by freshwater members of the genus have been reported (Markovic, 1939; Dissanaike and Bilimoria, 1958) and experimental infections in mammals have been achieved (Alicata and Ching, 1960).

A human infection with the Echinostome trematode, *Himasthla muehlensi,* was reported by Vogel (1933). The infection was apparently obtained by eating raw hard clams, *Mercenaria mercenaria,* from the east coast of the United States. Only very minor morphological differences separate *H. muehlensi* from the common clam parasite, *H. quissetensis,* and it is probable that they are conspecific. Cheng (1965a, 1967) has offered an interesting hypothesis to account for occasional instances of severe gastrointestinal upsets after ingestion of raw hard clams from the

---

FIG. 59. Life cycle of *Austrobilharzia variglandis,* an avian schistosome, and human pathology resulting from accidental invasion of the skin by cercariae. (Based in part on Stunkard and Hinchliffe, 1952, and Sindermann, 1960.)

New England coast. Clams from this area harbored large numbers of *H. quissetensis* metacercariae, and toxic short-chain fatty acids were found to accumulate in the clam tissues adjacent to the worms. Cheng postulated that if enough raw clams containing the toxic fatty acids were eaten, transient digestive disturbances could result. In another study, Cheng (1965b) also reported that tissues of American oysters parasitized by the trematode *Bucephalus* contained appreciable amounts of short-chain fatty acids, particularly butyric acid, and again postulated that accumulations of such fatty acids in parasitized oysters could cause temporary gastroenteric disturbances in human beings.

Only a few cestodes from the marine environment constitute problems for people. Larval tapeworms, *Diplogonoporus grandis* (Blanchard), infective to man, occur in marine fishes of Japan. Larval *Diphyllobothrium latum* infect pike and turbot in brackish waters of the Baltic Sea (Schneider, 1902; Levander, 1909; Petrushevski, 1931; Wikgren and Muroma, 1956; Engelbrecht, 1958), and are dangerous parasites of man. Since *D. latum* is typically a parasite of freshwater fishes, it will not be considered in detail here, but pertinent information may be found in Cameron (1945), and Dogiel *et al.* (1958). Another species of *Diphyllobothrium, D. pacificum,* has been identified as a parasite of man along the coastal area of Peru, and infection was considered by Baer *et al.* (1967) and Baer (1969) to result from eating plerocercoid-infected raw sea fishes in a national dish called "cebiche." Experimental infections of mammals with plerocercoids from bonito (*Sarda chilensis*) and sierra (*Scomberomorus maculatus*) were unsuccessful, but Baer concluded that man is infected via the fish paratenic host.

Eosinophilic meningitis and meningoencephalitis has also become an important public health problem in the Indo-Pacific area, and has been the object of intensive epidemiological and other studies since 1960. Evidence has accumulated to indicate that the disease can sometimes be caused by larval *Angiostrongylus cantonensis* (Chen), a nematode parasite of rats that may invade the central nervous system of man. Infection of the mammalian definitive host—normal or abnormal—can result from ingestion of a molluscan intermediate host or a paratenic host, such as fish, harboring third-stage larvae. Cheng and Burton (1965) have demonstrated that oysters and clams can serve as experimental intermediate hosts and that first-stage larvae concentrated from the feces of infected rats could survive for 27 hours in salinities of 20%.

Ingestion of raw fish has been a suspected route of transmission in outbreaks of human eosinophilic meningitis in the Pacific area (Rosen *et al.*, 1961, 1962). Rosen (1966) reported two fatal causes of meningoencephalitis from Hawaii and Taiwan, and hypothesized that most of the numerous nonfatal cases of eosinophilic meningitis in the Pacific area were caused by *Angiostrongylus cantonensis*. The evidence (Rosen *et al.*, 1967) was (1) *A. cantonensis* has been recovered from the central nervous system of two patients with meningoencephalitis, and (2) the parasite has been found, when searched for, on every island in the Pacific area where eosinophilic meningitis has been observed. The authors stated, however, that if most cases of eosinophilic meningitis on Pacific islands are caused by *A. cantonensis*, more than one method of transmission is involved. Possible routes of infection include direct ingestion of raw molluscan intermediate hosts; accidental ingestion of mollusks or nematode larvae with raw vegetables; ingestion of raw transport hosts such as planarians, freshwater shrimps, crabs, and fish; contamination of drinking water; and skin penetration. Wallace and Rosen (1967) were able to infect tilapia, *Tilapia mossambica*, and a marine carangid fish, *Trachurops crumenophthalmus* (Bloch) (known as "bigeye scad" or "ature"), by experimental feeding with infected freshwater snail tissues. Third-stage larvae infective to rats were found in viscera and musculature of both fish species as long as 28 days after feeding. No data were presented to indicate that *T. crumenophthalmus* were naturally infected with *A. cantonensis* larvae. However, Wallace and Rosen (1966) were also able to experimentally infect the freshwater shrimp, *Macrobrachium lar*. Infective third-stage larvae were recovered from the cephalothorax and abdomen for as long as 29 days. Larvae resembling *A. cantonensis* were found in several species of field-caught freshwater shrimps, but in low prevalences.

Alicata (1966) recently postulated a role for the giant land snail, *Achatina fulica*, in distributing the parasite through the Indo-Pacific area. He also suggested that the nematode had been only recently introduced in the Pacific Islands. Punyagupta (1965) surveyed the occurrence of eosinophilic meningitis and *Angiostrongylus cantonensis* in Thailand, and described severe cases of myeloencephalitis. He considered *A. cantonensis* the etiological agent involved in meningitis cases, and believed that even a few larvae could produce clinical symptoms. Heyneman and Lim (1967) found that larvae of the parasite occurred in the mucous trails of terrestrial mollusks. They also found that lettuce in the market of Kuala-Lampur contained *A. cantonensis* larvae, suggesting that raw vegetables may be important in transmitting the parasite.

Thus, although a tenuous epidemiological association of *Angiostrongylus* with meningitis outbreaks in areas of the South Pacific has been made, the role of marine fish is not clear, as has been pointed out by Jacobs (1963). As research progresses, routes of infection other than those involving marine animals seem more important. An expanding, if at times confusing, body of epidemiological literature on the disease and its presumed etiological agent is available. In addition to work already cited, see Bailey (1948), Mackerras and Sandars (1955), Franco *et al.* (1960), Horio and Alicata (1961), Alicata (1962, 1963), Alicata and Brown (1962a,b), Beaver and Rosen (1964), Wallace and Rosen (1965), and Punyagupta (1966).

Recent reports from The Netherlands (Van Thiel *et al.*, 1960; Kuipers *et al.*, 1960a,b; Roskam, 1960; Van Thiel, 1962; Kuipers, 1964) described severe reactions to invasion of the wall of the human digestive tract by larval nematodes of the family Heterocheilidae (principally of the genus *Anisakis*), ingested alive with lightly salted "green" herring (Fig. 60). The disease, described as eosinophilic phlegmonous enteritis, is relatively rare, even in a population that consumes countless numbers of herring. It has become important only since 1955, when gutting and curing ashore of herring held on ice since capture superseded the earlier practice of gutting and curing at sea. This lapse of time allowed some worms to penetrate from the viscera of the herring into the abdominal wall, where they remained when the viscera were removed. This fact was considered by Van Thiel (1962) to explain why "anisakiasis" was not known before 1955, but Roskam (1966, 1967) also found a tenfold increase in infestation intensities in North Sea herring from 1959 to 1965 and a further increase in 1966, which must be considered in the epidemiology of the disease. Van Thiel (1966) found adult *Anisakis* in a number of marine mammals, particularly in the gray seal, *Halichoerus grypus*. The fact that these animals have been increasing in number around the Scottish coast—the feeding grounds of adult herring—may have acted to increase the abundance of larvae in herring and to increase the risk of human infestation.

The severe localized reaction of the intestinal wall tissue against larval penetration seems confined to the areas sensitized by previous penetration of another larva. The slight chance of two larvae penetrating at the same spot, according to Roskam (1963), explains the rarity of the disease in a population (the Dutch) exposed to millions of larval nematodes in uncooked herring. Measures have been taken in The Netherlands to increase the salt in the curing process, and to prolong the time in brine. Roskam (1967), however, reported that these measures have been ineffective, mainly because of control difficulties, and that consumer confidence in lightly salted herring continued to decline. Some deaths associated with suspected anisakiasis have occurred in recent years, but they were invariably due to complications from exploratory surgery, rather than from the effects of nematode invasion.

Following the experience in The Netherlands with "herring worm

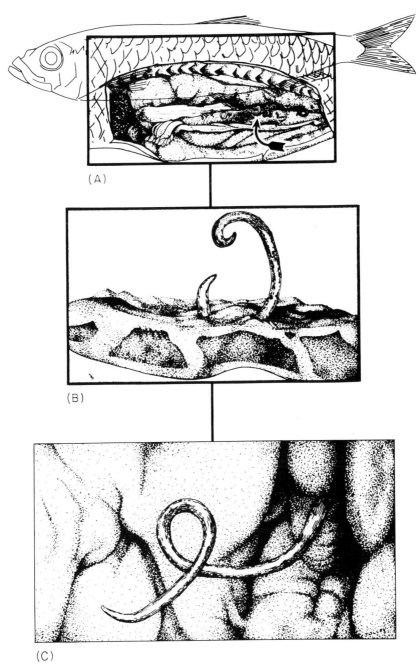

(A)

(B)

(C)

Fig. 60. Anisakiasis. (A) Larval nematodes encysted in viscera of the sea herring; (B) migrating larva which has invaded lateral body muscles of the herring after death of the host; (C) larval anisakid which has invaded the wall of the human digestive tract. (Based in part on Kuipers *et al.*, 1960a.)

disease," Vik (1966) examined a number of Scandinavian marine fishes for anisakid larvae. Mackerel and sea herring harbored an average of 10 or more larvae per fish; capelin and salmon harbored fewer. Larvae migrated from the viscera to body muscles after death of the fish host. Vik pointed out that only one Norwegian dish, *gravfisk*, in which fish is lightly salted and sugared for a few days, then eaten raw with a vinegar sauce, involved risk of *Anisakis* infection. Even here danger of infection could be almost eliminated by cleaning fish soon after capture, or by freezing them for 24 hours before use.

Ashby *et al.* (1964) reviewed the literature on eosinophilic granuloma of the human digestive tract, and added several cases from England. They indicated, however that while larval nematodes from fish may be of etiological significance in North Sea countries, the ova or larvae of a number of different parasites contaminating animal food products may be important in other geographical areas. The possible role of other parasites in eosinophilic granulomata has been reinforced by Williams (1965), who pointed out that larval nematodes belonging to the Ancylostomidae, Ascaridae, and Gnathostomidae (which often occur in large numbers in animals other than fish) may also be involved.

The identity of the worm or worms causing human anisakiasis in Europe is still very much in doubt. *Eustoma (Anacanthocheilus) rotundatum (Pseudanisakis rotundata)*, a common larval nematode of the subfamily Acanthocheilinae, occurs as a larva in the mesenteries and viscera of many North Atlantic fishes, including cod, haddock, redfish, flatfishes, and herring (Kahl, 1938). The larvae of this and other namatodes may occasionally invade the flesh, particularly after the host fish is killed. Several papers from The Netherlands (Kuipers *et al.*, 1960a,b; Roskam, 1960; Van Thiel *et al.*, 1960) identified *E. rotundatum* as the probable cause of the acute abdominal syndrome in humans, but Van Thiel later (1962) considered it a species of *Anisakis,* as did Berland (1961) and Roskam (1963). Van Thiel (1966) proposed the name *Anisakis marina* (L.) for all the anisakids from North Sea and North Atlantic marine mammals. The taxonomy of the parasite, like that of other Heterocheilidae (Punt, 1941, 1947), is still confused. Williams (1965) summarized the available information on the identity of larval nematodes involved in European "herring worm disease." He offered the opinion that a number of larval nematodes other than *Eustoma (Anacanthocheilus) rotundatum* (which had been originally designated specifically in The Netherlands) may be agents of the disease, and that care must be taken in attempts to identify larval nematodes from the human intestine.

Anisakiasis, has, however, emerged in recent years as a new and possibly serious public health problem in Japan, where raw fish are commonly eaten. About 100 cases have been identified, and many others may have been undiagnosed or misdiagnosed. In most of the recognized cases, *Anisakis*-like larvae were found in an eosinophilic phlegmon or abscess in the stomach or intestinal submucosa. Yokogawa and Yoshimura (1966, 1967) compared *Anisakis*-like larvae from a human infection with larvae from mackerel and found them morphologically similar. Oshima (1966) identified two species of adult anisakid nematodes from marine mammals taken near Japan, *Anisakis simplex* in the bluewhite dolphin and blackfish, and *A. phiseteris* in the sperm whale. Larvae thought to be *A. simplex* were common in muscles of Alaska pollock, cod, salmon, herring, bonito, mackerel, horse mackerel, and squid. The life cycle postulated by Oshima includes a crustacean intermediate and possible fish or squid paratenic hosts. Asami (1966), using anisakid larvae from the body cavity of mackerel, infected guinea pigs and studied infectivity and susceptibility. He found that starvation and suppression of gastric secretion facilitated infection. Encapsulated and free larvae were both equally infective.

The disease has been reported (Yokogawa and Yoshimura, 1966, 1967) from widely distributed localities in Japan. It is considered so serious there that a working group on anisakiasis was formed in 1965, with an initial membership of about 20. Since symptoms may be variable, diagnosis constitutes a difficult problem; one major effort of the working group has been development of an immunological (intradermal) test for infection. An appreciable body of Japanese literature on anisakiasis has accumulated in the past few years (Nishimura, 1963; Yamaguchi *et al.*, 1964; Yoshimura and Yokogawa, 1964; Asami *et al.*, 1964, 1965; Otsuru *et al.*, 1965; Yokogawa and Yoshimura, 1965; Kojima, 1966; Yoshimura, 1966a,b,c; Yamaguchi, 1966). In view of the importance of raw fish in the Japanese diet, it seems proper to ask why all Japanese are not infected. Some answers may be that many cases may exist without severe symptoms or may be misdiagnosed; or that in most instances of exposure the larvae do not penetrate; or if the worms do penetrate, they soon die without eliciting symptoms. Also, the findings of European workers—that severe symptoms are elicited only after penetration of an area of intestine already sensitized by previous invasion—may be pertinent. Man is an abnormal host for anisakids, and, as is true for other helminths such as *Angiostrongylus*, severe pathology may sometimes be produced in an abnormal host—much more severe than in the natural host, as was pointed out by Cheng (1965a).

The oriental custom of eating raw fish has exposed the human population of the Far East to parasitization by other larval nematodes—

particularly *Gnathostoma spinigerum* Owen, but this nematode has been reported thus far only from freshwater fishes (Miyazaki, 1960).

Most marine fish and shellfish parasites and pathogens are not adapted to develop in human beings. Even the parasites which normally develop in sea birds or mammals may not mature or may be otherwise imperfectly adapted to the human host. We are left therefore with only a few problem areas: the microbes causing erysipeloid, gastroenteritis, typhoid fever, and hepatitis, which are probably not pathogenic to marine animals at all (with the possible exception of *Vibrio parahemolyticus*), and the few larval helminths which may on rare occasions persist or develop in humans.

REFERENCES

Africa, C. M., and Garcia, E. Y. (1935). Heterophyid trematodes of man and dogs in the Phillipines with descriptions of three new species. *Philippine J. Sci.* **57**, 253–267.

Aiso, K., and Fujiwara, K. (1963). Feeding tests of "pathogenic halophilic bacteria." *Ann. Rept. Inst. Food Microbiol., Chiba Univ.* **15**, 34–38.

Aiso, K., and Matsuno, M. (1961). The outbreaks of enteritis-type food poisoning due to fish in Japan and its causative bacteria. *Japan. J. Microbiol.* **5**, 337–364.

Akazawa, H. (1968). Bacterial disease of marine fishes. *Bull. Japan Soc. Sci. Fish.* **34**, 271–272.

Alicata, J. E. (1962). *Angiostrongylus cantonensis* (Nematoda: Metastrongylidae) as a causative agent of eosinophilic meningoencephalitis of man in Hawaii and Tahiti. *Can. J. Zool.* **40**, 5–8.

Alicata, J. E. (1963). Incapability of vertebrates to serve as paratenic host for infective larvae of *Angiostrongylus cantonensis*. *J. Parasitol.* **49**, 48.

Alicata, J. E. (1966). Distribution of *Angiostrongylus cantonensis* in the Indian and Pacific Ocean areas, and the probable role of the giant African snail, *Achatina fulica*, in the dissemination of the parasite. *Proc. 11th Pacific Sci. Congr., Tokyo, 1966* Vol. 8, Symp. No. 43, p. 5 (abstr.). *Science Council of Japan*.

Alicata, J. E., and Brown, R. W. (1962a). Preliminary observations on the use of an intradermal test for the diagnosis of eosinophilic meningoencephalitis in man caused by *Angiostrongylus cantonensis*. *Can. J. Zool.* **40**, 119–124.

Alicata, J. E., and Brown, R. W. (1962b). Observations on the method of human infection with *Angiostrongylus cantonensis* in Tahiti. *Can. J. Zool.* **40**, 755–760.

Alicata, J. E., and Ching, H. L. (1960). On the infection of birds and mammals with the cercaria and metacercaria of the eye-fluke, *Philophthalmus*. *J. Parasitol.* **46**, Suppl., 16 (abstr.).

Asami, K. (1966). Larval anisakiasis in Japan. II. *Proc. 11th Pacific Sci. Congr., Tokyo, 1966* Vol. 8, Symp. No. 43, p. 3 (abstr.). *Science Council of Japan*.

Asami, K., Imano, H., Watanuki, T., and Sakai, H. (1964). Eosinophilic granuloma in the stomach probably caused by *Anisakis* infection. *Japan. J. Parasitol.* **13**, 325–326.

Asami, K., Watanuki, T., Sakai, H., Imano, H., and Okamoto, R. (1965). Two cases of stomach granuloma caused by *Anisakis*-like larval nematodes in Japan. *Am. J. Trop. Med. Hyg.* **14**, 119–123.

Ashby, B. S., Appleton, P. J., and Dawson, I. (1964). Eosinophilic granuloma of gastro-intestinal tract caused by herring parasite *Eustoma rotundatum*. *Brit. Med. J.* **I**, 1141–1145.

Baer, Jean G. (1969). *Diphyllobothrium pacificum*, a tapeworm from sea lions endemic in man along the coastal area of Peru. *J. Fisheries Res. Board Can.* **26**, 717–723.

Baer, Jean G., Miranda, H., Fernandez, W., and Medina, J. (1967). Human diphyllobothriasis in Peru. *Z. Parasitenk.* **28**, 277–289.

Bailey, C. A. (1948). An epidemic of eosinophilic meningitis, a previously undescribed disease, occurring on Ponape, Eastern Carolins. *Naval Med. Res. Inst. Proj.* NM 005 007, Rept. No. 7.

Baross, J., and Liston, J. (1968). Isolation of *Vibrio parahemolyticus* from the northwest Pacific. *Nature* **217**, 1263–1264.

Bearup, A. J. (1956). Life cycle of *Austrobilharzia terrigalensis* Johnston, 1917. *Parasitology* **46**, 470–479.

Beaver, P. C., and Rosen, L. (1964). Memorandum on the first report of *Angiostrongylus* in man, by Nomura and Lin, 1945. *Am. J. Trop. Med.* **13**, 589–590.

Belding, D. L. (1942). "Textbook of Clinical Parasitology," 888 pp. Appleton, New York.

Berland, B. (1961). Nematodes from some Norwegian marine fishes. *Sarsia* **2**, 1–50.

Cameron, T. W. M. (1945). Fish-carried parasites in Canada. *Can. J. Comp. Med. Vet. Sci.* **9**, 245–254, 283–286, and 302–311.

Chapin, A. (1926). A new genus and species of trematode, the probable cause of salmon-poisoning in dogs. *North Am. Veterinarian* **7**, 36–37.

Cheng, T. C. (1965a). Parasitological problems associated with food protection. *J. Environ. Health* **28**, 208–214.

Cheng, T. C. (1965b). Histochemical observations on changes in the lipid concentration of the American oyster, *Crassostrea virginica* (Gmelin), parasitized by the trematode *Bucephalus* sp. *J. Invertebrate Pathol.* **7**, 398–407.

Cheng, T. C. (1967). Marine molluscs as hosts for symbioses with a review of known parasites of commercially important species. *Advan. Marine Biol.* **5**, 1–424.

Cheng, T. C., and Burton, R. W. (1965). The American oyster and clam as experimental intermediate hosts of *Angiostrongylus cantonensis*. *J. Parasitol.* **51**, 296.

Christensen, N., and Roth, H. (1949). Investigations on internal parasites of dogs. *Kgl. Vet.-og Land-bohøjskole, Ars.* pp. 1–73.

Chu, G. W. T. C. (1952). First report of the presence of a dermatitis-producing marine larval schistosome in Hawaii. *Science* **115**, 151–153.

Chu, G. W. T. C., and Cutress, C. E. (1954). *Austrobilharzia variglandis* (Miller and Northup, 1926) Penner, 1953 (Trematoda: Schistosomatidae) in Hawaii with notes on its biology. *J. Parasitol.* **40**, 515–523.

Dissanaike, A. S., and Bilimoria, D. P. (1958). On an infection of a human eye with *Philophthalmus* sp. in Ceylon. *J. Helminthol.* **32**, 115–118.

Dogiel, V. A., Petrushevskii, G. K., and Polyanski, Y. I., eds. (1958). "Parasitology of Fishes." Leningrad Univ. Press, Leningrad (in Russian). (Transl. by Z. Kabata. Oliver & Boyd, Edinburgh and London, 1961.)

Engelbrecht, H. (1958). Untersuchungen über den Parasitenbefall der Nutzfische im Greifswalder Bodden und Kleinen Haff. *Z. Fischerei* [N. S.] **7**, 481–511.

Ewers, W. H. (1961). A new intermediate host of schistosome trematodes from New South Wales. *Nature* **190**, 283–284.

Farrell, R. K., Lloyd, M. A., and Earp, B. (1964). Persistence of *Neorickettsiae helminthoeca* in an endoparasite of the Pacific salmon. *Science* **145**, 162–163.

Franco, R., Bories, S., and Couzin, B. (1960). A propos de 142 cas de méningite a éosinophiles observés à Tahiti et en Nouvelle-Calédonie. *Med. Trop.* **20**, 41–55.

Fujiwara, K., Katoh, H., Tatsumi, K., Sawada, F., and Tsuchiya, Y. (1964). A selective medium for the isolation of *Vibrio parahaemolyticus*. (Tellulite medium-TTGA Agar). (In Japanese with English summary.) *J. Food Sanit.* **5**, 211–214.

Glantz, P. J., and Krantz, G. E. (1965). *Escherichia coli* sterotypes isolated from fish and their environment. *Health Lab. Sci.* **2**, 54–63.

Grodhaus, G., and Keh, B. (1958). The marine dermatitis-producing cercaria of *Austrobilharzia variglandis* in California (Trematoda: Schistosomatidae). *J. Parasitol.* **44**, 633–638.

Halstead, B. M. (1958). Poisonous fishes. *Public Health Rept.* (U. S.) **73**, 1–302.

Halstead, B. M. (1965–1967). "Poisonous and Venomous Marine Animals of the World," Vols. I and II. U. S. Govt. Printing Office, Washington, D. C.

Hart, J. C. (1945). Typhoid fever from clams. *Conn. Health Bull.* **59**, 289–292.

Heyneman, D., and Lim, B. (1967). *Angiostrongylus cantonensis:* Proof of direct transmission with its epidemiological implications. *Science* **158**, 1057–1058.

Horio, S. R., and Alicata, J. E. (1961). Parasitic meningo-encephalitis in Hawaii. A new parasitic disease of man. *Hawaii Med. J.* **21**, 139–140.

Hutton, R. F. (1952). Schistosome cercariae as the probable cause of seabather's eruption. *Bull. Marine Sci. Gulf Caribbean* **2**, 346–359.

Iida, H., Iwamoto, T., Karashimada, T., and Kumagai, M. (1957). Studies on the pathogenesis of fish-borne food-poisoning in summer. II. Studies on cholinesterase inhibition by culture filtrates of various bacteria. *Japan. J. Med. Sci. Biol.* **10**, 177–185.

Jacobs, L. (1963). Parasites in food. *In* "Chemical and Biological Hazards in Foods" (J. C. Ayres *et al.*, eds.), p. 521. Iowa State Univ. Press, Ames, Iowa.

Janssen, W. A., and Meyers, C. D. (1968). Fish: Serologic evidence of infection with human pathogens. *Science* **159**, 547–548.

Kahl, W. (1938). Nematoden in Seefischen. II. Erhebungen über den Befall von Seefischen mit Larven von *Anacanthocheilus rotundatus* (Rudolf) und die durch diese Larven hervorgerufenen Reaktionen des Wirtsgewebes. *Z. Parasitenk.* **10**, 513–525.

Kawashima, S., Hayashi, T., Watanabe, A., and Yamashita, N. (1961). Outbreaks of food poisoning caused by pathogenic halophiles and the methods for prevention. *Food Sanit. Res.* **125**, 1–71.

Kojima, K. (1966). Parasitic granuloma with special reference to histopathological findings of the *Anisakis*-like larva infection. (In Japanese.) *Japan J. Parasitol.* **15**, 30–31.

Krantz, G. E., Colwell, R. R., and Lovelace, E. (1969). *Vibrio parahemolyticus* from the blue crab *Callinectes sapidus* in Chesapeake Bay. *Science* **164**, 1286–1287.

Kuipers, F. C. (1964). Eosinophilic phlegmonous inflammation of the alimentary canal caused by a parasite from herring. *Pathol. Microbiol.* **27**, 925.

Kuipers, F. C., Van Thiel, P. H., and Roskam, R. T. (1960a). Eosinofiele flegmone van de dunne darm, veroorzaakt door een niet ann het lichaam van de mens aangepaste worm. *Ned. Tijdschr. Geneesk.* **104**, 422–427.

Kuipers, F. C., Van Thiel, P. H., Rodenburg, W., Wielinga, W. J., and Roskam, R.

T. (1960b). Eosinophilic phlegmon of the alimentary canal caused by a worm. *Lancet* **II**, 1171–1173.

Kusuda, R. (1965). Study of the ulcer disease of marine fish. *Bull. Kyoto Fish. Expt. Sta. No.* **25**, 116 pp.

Kusuda, R. (1966). Studies on the ulcer disease of marine fishes. *Proc. First U. S.-Japan Joint Conf. Microbiol.* **1966**, 13 pp.

Kusuda, R., and Akazawa, I. (1963). On a contagious disease of cultured marine fishes caused by a bacillus. (In Japanese) *Suisan Zoshoku, Extra No.* 3, pp. 31–67.

Langford, G. C., Jr., and Hansen, P. A. (1954). The species of *Erysipelothrix*. *Antonie van Leeuwenhoek, J. Microbiol. Serol.* **20**, 87–92.

Levander, K. M. (1909). Beobachtungen über die Nahrung und die Parasiten der Fische des finnischen Meerbusens. *Finnl. Hydrograph.-Biol. Untersuch.* **5**, 1–44.

Mackerras, M. J., and Sandars, D. F. (1955). Life history of rat lung worm, *Angiostrongylus cantonensis* (Chen) (Nematoda: Metastrongylidae). *Australian J. Zool.* **3**, 1–21.

Markovic, A. (1939). Der erste Fall von Philophthalmose beim Menschen. *Arch. Ophthalmol.* **140**, 515–526.

Mason, J. O., and McLean, W. R. (1962). Infectious hepatitis traced to the consumption of raw oysters. An epidemiologic study. *Am. J. Hyg.* **75**, 90.

Miyazaki, I. (1960). On the genus *Gnathostoma* and human gnathostomiasis, with special reference to Japan. *Exptl. Parasitol.* **9**, 338–370.

Nishimura, T. (1963). On a certain nematode larva found from the abscess of the mesentery of man. *Trans. 19th Branch-Meeting Parasitol., West. Div., Parasitol. Soc. Japan, 1963* p. 27.

Oppenheimer, C. H., and Kesteven, G. L. (1953). Disease as a factor in natural mortality of marine fish. *FAO Fisheries Bull.* **6**, 215–222.

Oshima, T. (1966). Parasitic granuloma with special reference to biological aspects on the anisakiasis. (In Japanese.) *Japan. J. Parasitol.* **15**, 32–33.

Otsuru, M., Hatsukano, T., Oyanagi, T., and Kenmochi, M. (1965). The visceral migrans of gastro-intestinal tract and its vicinity caused by some larval nematode. (In Japanese.) *Japan. J. Parasitol.* **14**, 542–555.

Pederson, H. D. (1955). On type E. botulism. *J. Appl. Bacteriol.* **18**, 619.

Penner, L. R. (1942). Studies on dermatitis-producing schistosomes in Eastern Massachusetts, with emphasis on the status of *Schistosomatium pathlocopticum* Tanabe, 1923. *J. Parasitol.* **28**, 103–116.

Penner, L. R. (1950). *Cercaria littorinalinae* sp. nov., a dermatitis-producing schistosome larva from the marine snail, *Littorina planaxis* Philippi. *J. Parasitol.* **36**, 466–472.

Penner, L. R., and Fried, B. (1961). Studies on ocular trematodiasis. I. Marine acquired philophthalmiasis. *J. Parasitol.* **47**, Suppl., 31 (abstr.).

Penner, L. R., and Fried, B. (1963). *Philophthalmus hegneri* sp. n., an ocular trematode from birds. *J. Parasitol.* **49**, 974–977.

Petrushevski, G. K. (1931). Über die Verbreitung der Plerocercoide von *Diphyllobothrium latum* in den Fischen der Newabucht. *Zool. Anz.* **94**, 139–147.

Price, J. E. L., and Bennett, W. E. J. (1951). The erysipeloid of Rosenbach. *Brit. Med. J.* **II**, 1060–1063.

Punt, A. (1941). Recherches sur quelques nématodes parasites de poissons de la Mer du Nord. *Mem. Musee Hist. Nat. Belg.* **98**, 1–109.

Punt, A. (1942). Recherches sur quelques nématodes parasites de poissons de la Mer du Nord. Thesis, Amsterdam.

Punt, A. (1947). Quelques nématodes parasites de poissons de la Mer du Nord. II. *Bull. Musee Hist. Nat. Belg.* **23**, No. 8, 1–13.

Punyagupta, S. (1965). Eosinophilic meningoencephalitis in Thailand: Summary of nine cases and observations on *Angiostrongylus cantonensis* as a causative agent and *Pila ampullacea* as a new intermediate host. *Am. J. Trop. Med. Hyg.* **14**, 370–374.

Punyagupta, S. (1966). Eosinophilic meningoencephalitis in Thailand with special reference to *Angiostrongylus cantonensis* infection. *Proc. 11th Pacific Sci. Congr., Tokyo, 1966* Vol. 8, Symp. No. 43, p. 7 (abstr.). *Science Council of Japan.*

Randall, J. E. (1958). A review of ciguatera, tropical fish poisoning, with tentative explanation of its cause. *Bull. Marine Sci. Gulf Caribbean* **8**, 236.

Rosen, L. (1966). Eosinophilic meningitis and *Angiostrongylus cantonensis* in the Pacific area. *Proc. 11th Pacific Sci. Congr., Tokyo, 1966* Vol. 8, Symp. No. 43, p. 6 (abstr.). *Science Council of Japan.*

Rosen, L., Laigret, J., and Bories, S. (1961). Observations on an outbreak of eosinophilic meningitis on Tahiti, French Polynesia. *Am. J. Hyg.* **74**, 26–42.

Rosen, L., Chappell, R., Laqueur, G. L., Wallace, G. D., and Weinstein, P. P. (1962). Eosinophilic meningoencephalitis caused by a metastrongylid lung-worm of rats. *J. Am. Med. Assoc.* **179**, 620–624.

Rosen, L., Loison, G., Laigret, J., and Wallace, G. D. (1967). Studies on eosinophilic meningitis. 3. Epidemiologic and clinical observations on Pacific islands and the possible etiologic role of *Angiostrongylus cantonensis. Am. J. Epidemiol.* **85**, 17–44.

Roskam, R. T. (1960). A human disease caused by a nematode from herring. *Cons. Intern. Explor. Mer, C. M., Herring Comm. Paper* No. 98, 3 pp. (mimeo.).

Roskam, R. T. (1963). Pathogenic aquatic organisms. *Bull. Office Intern. Epizooties* **59**, 135–142.

Roskam, R. T. (1966). *Anisakis* larvae in North Sea herring. *Cons. Intern. Explor. Mer, C. M., Herring Comm. Paper* No. 13, 2 pp. (mimeo.).

Roskam, R. T. (1967). *Anisakis* and *Contracaecum* larvae in North Sea herring. *Cons. Intern. Explor. Mer, C. M. Pelagic Fish (N) Comm., Paper* No. 19, 3 pp. (mimeo.).

Sakazaki, R., Iwanami, S., and Fukumi, H. (1963). Studies on the enteropathogenic, facultatively halophilic bacteria, *Vibrio parahaemolyticus.* I. Morphological, cultural, and biochemical properties and its taxonomical position. *Japan. J. Med. Sci. Biol.* **16**, 161–188.

Sato, T., Fukuyama, T., Yamada, M., and Takayagani, J. (1959). Minamata disease. Hg content in poisoned cats, fish and silt from Minamata Bay. *Bull. Inst. Public Health (Tokyo)* **8**, 183.

Schneider, G. (1902). Ichthyologische Beiträge. III. Über die in den Fischen des Finnischen Meerbusens vorkommenden Endoparasiten. *Acta Zool. Fenn. Soc. F. Fl. Fenn.* **22**, No. 2, 1–88.

Sheard, K., and Dicks, H. G. (1949). Skin lesions among fishermen at Houtman's Abrolhos, Western Australia, with an account of erysipeloid of Rosenbach. *Med. J. Australia* **2**, 352–354.

Shewan, J. M., and Liston, J. (1954). A review of food poisoning caused by fish and fishery products. *Appl. Bacteriol.* **17**, 522.

Sindermann, C. J. (1960). Ecological studies of marine dermatitis-producing schistosome larvae in northern New England. *Ecology* **41**, 678–684.

Sindermann, C. J., and Gibbs, R. F. (1953). A dermatitis-producing schistosome which causes "clam diggers itch" along the central Maine coast. *Maine Dept. Sea Shore Fish., Res. Bull.* 12, 20 pp.

Skrjabin, K. I., and Podjapolskaya, W. P. (1931). *Nanophyetus schikhobalowi* n. sp. ein neuer Trematode aus dem Darm de Menschen. *Zentr. Bakteriol. Parasitenk., Abt. I. Orig.* **119**, 294–297.

Sneath, P. H. A., Abbott, J. D., and Cunliffe, A. C. (1951). The bacteriology of erysipeloid. *Brit. Med. J.* **II**, 1063–1066.

Stunkard, H. W., and Hinchliffe, M. G. (1952). The morphology and life-history of *Microbilharzia variglandis* (Miller and Northup, 1926) Stunkard and Hinchliffe, 1951, avian blood-flukes whose larvae cause "swimmer's itch" of ocean beaches. *J. Parasitol.* **38**, 248–265.

Takikawa, I. (1958). Studies on pathogenic halophilic bacteria. *Yokohama Med. Bull.* **9**, 313–322.

Tubangi, M. A., and Africa, C. M. (1938). The systematic position of some trematodes reported from the Philippines. *Philippine J. Sci.* **67**, 117–127.

Van Thiel, P. H. (1962). Anisakiasis. *Parasitology* **52**, Suppl., 16–17 (abstr.).

Van Thiel, P. H. (1966). The final host of the herringworm *Anisakis marina*. *Trop. Geograph. Med.* **18**, 310–328.

Van Thiel, P. H., Kuipers, F. C., and Roskam, R. T. (1960). A nematode parasitic to herring, causing acute abdominal syndromes in man. *Trop. Geograph. Med.* **2**, 97–113.

Vik, R. (1966). *Anisakis* larvae in Norwegian food fishes. *Proc. 1st Intern. Congr. Parasitol., Rome, 1964* Vol. 1, pp. 568–569. Pergamon Press, Oxford.

Vogel, H. (1933). *Himasthla muehlensi* n. sp. ein neuer menschlicher Trematode de Familie Echinostomidae. *Zentr. Bakteriol., Parasitenk., Abt. I. Orig.* **127**, 385–391.

Wallace, G. D., and Rosen, L. (1965). Studies on eosinophilic meningitis. 1. Observations on the geographic distribution of *Angiostrongylus cantonensis* in the Pacific area and its prevalence in wild rats. *Am. J. Epidemiol.* **81**, 52–62.

Wallace, G. D., and Rosen, L. (1966). Studies on eosinophilic meningitis. 2. Experimental infection of shrimp and crabs with *Angiostrongylus cantonensis*. *Am. J. Epidemiol.* **84**, 120–131.

Wallace, G. D., and Rosen, L. (1967). Studies on eosinophilic meningitis. 4. Experimental infection of fresh-water and marine fish with *Angiostrongylus cantonensis*. *Am. J. Epidemiol.* **85**, 395–402.

Ward, B. Q. (1968). Isolations of organisms related to *Vibrio parahemolyticus* from American estuarine sediments. *Applied Microbiol.* **16**, 543–546.

Wellmann, G. (1950). Pathogenität und Wachstum der auf Fischen vorkommenden Rotlaufbacterien. *Abhandl. Fisch.* **3**, 489.

Wellmann, G. (1957). Über die Ubiquität des Rotlauferregers (*Erysipelothrix rhusiopathiae*). *Z. Fischerei* [N.S.] **6**, 191–193.

Wikgren, B., and Muroma, E. (1956). Studies on the genus *Diphyllobothrium*. A revision of the Finnish finds of diphyllobothrid plerocercoids. *Acta Zool. Fenn. Soc. F. Fl. Fenn.* **93**, 1–22.

Williams, H. H. (1965). Roundworms in fishes and so-called "herring-worm disease." *Brit. Med. J.* **I**, 964–967.

Yamaguchi, T. (1966). Parasitic granuloma with special reference to the infection and prevention of anisakiasis. (In Japanese.) *Japan. J. Parasitol.* **15**, 31–32.

Yamaguchi, T., Yanagawa, H., Kunishige, A., and Usuya, N. (1964). Studies on larva migrans. 12. Human cases of *Anisakis* infection. *Japan. J. Parasitol.* **13**, 589.

Yokogawa, M., and Yoshimura, H. (1965). *Anisakis*-like larvae causing eosinophilic granulomata in the stomach of man. *Am. J. Trop. Med. Hyg.* **14**, 770–773.

Yokogawa, M., and Yoshimura, H. (1966). Human larval anisakiasis in Japan. *Proc. 11th Pacific Sci. Congr., Tokyo, 1966* Vol. 3, Symp. No. 43, p. 4 (abstr.). *Science Council of Japan.*

Yokogawa, M., and Yoshimura, H. (1967). Clinicopathologic studies on larval anisakiasis in Japan. *Am. J. Trop. Med. Hyg.* **16**, 723–728.

Yoshimura, H. (1966a). Migrations of *Anisakis*-like larvae causing eosinophilic granuloma of human alimentary tract. (In Japanese.) *Minophagen Med. Rev.* **11**, 105–114.

Yoshimura, H. (1966b). Migrations of *Anisakis*-like larvae into the human alimentary tracts with special reference to clinical pathology. (In Japanese.) *Nihon Iji Shinpo* **2204**, 10–16.

Yoshimura, H. (1966c). Parasitic granuloma with special reference to clinical pathology of *Anisakis*-like larva infection in the digestive apparatus of man. (In Japanese.) *Japan. J. Parasitol.* **15**, 29–30.

Yoshimura, H., and Yokogawa, M. (1964). On the human cases of the infection with *Anisakis*-like larva, causing the eosinophilic granuloma of the stomach wall. *Japan. J. Parasitol.* **13**, 559–560.

Zen-Yoji, H., Sakai, S., Terama, T., Kudo, Y., and Hitogoto, H. (1963). Studies on the enteropathogenic halophilic bacteria. I. On the epidemiology of the food poisoning due to halophilic bacteria in Tokyo District during 1961 and bacteriological examination. (In Japanese with English summary.) *J. Japan. Infect. Diseases Assoc.* **37**, 195–204.

GIFT OF
A.V. FARMANFARMAIAN
PROFESSOR OF PHYSIOLOGY

VIII

Assessment of the Role of Disease in Marine Populations

A. INTRODUCTION

Many of the great fisheries of the world have experienced major fluctuations in supply. The causes of these fluctuations, although subjects of much discussion, have rarely been precisely determined. Reduction in abundance of commercially valuable marine species has been attributed to overfishing, failure of spawning, sudden and drastic changes in temperature and salinity, and many other factors. One biological factor that has received too little attention is disease. The fact that marine animals become ill and die, often in vast numbers, has been largely ignored. Events in commercial fish and shellfish populations in this century, however, have forced us to look closely at disease as a cause of mass mortalities of epic proportions, and of subsequent declines in abundance of commercial species.

The significance of marine diseases may be assessed from the viewpoint of the host population or from that of the human predator. Epizootics may reduce the numbers available to man, and in at least some marine species disease may be a primary mechanism for regulation of population size. Diseases that weaken or disorient individuals, or make them more conspicuous, can be of great importance in determining survival. Protozoan, helminth, and copepod parasites of the flesh, although not often direct causes of death, can act to weaken or slow the host and are also of great economic significance in the landed catch.

309

B. EPIZOOTICS AND MASS MORTALITIES
IN FISH POPULATIONS

Mass mortalities of marine, estuarine, and anadromous fishes are common, even though many such events may escape scientific attention. Newspaper articles and interviews with fishermen probably provide the best criteria for evaluating the extent of mortalities, except for the events that occur beyond the continental shelves.

Disease has often been suspected of being a cause of mass mortalities, but its role has seldom been proved without question. Too often scientific studies are not made, or are made too late, or the results of the studies are inconclusive. Interest in the event is usually directly proportional to the numbers of fish dying at any particular moment; long-term studies necessary to understand the role of suspected pathogens have rarely been carried on.

The often dramatic increase in disease prevalence that we term an epizootic is the result of interactions of variables such as susceptibility of the host population, virulence and infectivity of the pathogen, effectiveness of transmission, and physical factors in the environment. Basically, an epizootic of an infectious disease requires that one or more of the following conditions exist: (1) The pathogen must be newly introduced in a susceptible population; (2) infection pressure (dosage) or virulence of the pathogen must increase; or (3) resistance of the population must be lowered. The role of environmental influences and stresses such as state of nutrition, temperature, and salinity on disease prevalence must also be considered. Determination of the factors prevailing at the time of an outbreak requires broadly based and continuous studies in ecology, immunology, and pathology. Despite the fact that such ideal studies have not often been made in the past, an appreciable amount of documentation has been assembled for a few fish diseases with histories of epizootic prevalences and mortalities. Outstanding in this respect is the fungus disease of herring and other species, referred to in Chapter II, caused by *Ichthyophonus hoferi*. Outbreaks of this pathogen in herring of the western North Atlantic have been known since 1898 (Cox, 1916; Fish, 1934; Scattergood, 1948; Sindermann, 1956, 1958). The most recent epizootic occurred in the Gulf of Saint Lawrence in 1954–1955, when an estimated one half of the herring population was killed by the disease. The estimate was based on sampling and field observations during the outbreak, and was supported by the behavior of the fishery during the immediate postepizootic years. Landings declined rapidly to about half

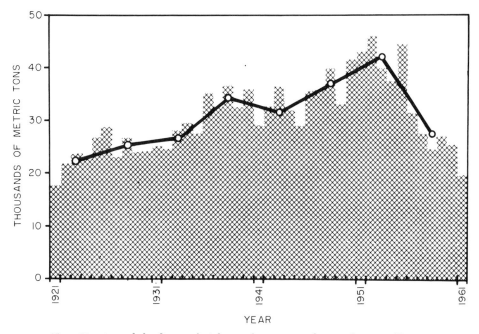

Fig. 61. Annual landings of Atlantic herring in the southern Gulf of Saint Lawrence, 1920–1961, showing effects of 1954–1955 fungus disease epizootic. (From Sindermann, 1963.)

their previous level, even though fishing effort and market demand remained unchanged (Fig. 61). Earlier work (Cox, 1916) indicated that comparable reductions in population abundance and in the catch followed the outbreaks of 1898 and 1914. Reports of outbreaks in the Gulf of Maine also suggested major dislocations in the fishery (Scattergood, 1948). It is interesting and perhaps pertinent that the two most recent outbreaks (the only ones for which we have adequate fishery data) occurred at times of herring abundance, as indicated by landing statistics and general observations.

One of the most remarkable aspects of the fungus disease of herring in the western North Atlantic has been its apparent periodicity—six recorded outbreaks, 14 to 25 years apart. The two principal areas involved, Gulf of Maine and Gulf of Saint Lawrence, each with discrete populations of herring, have been out of phase during the most recent outbreaks; an epizootic peak in one gulf coincided with very low disease prevalence in the other. The comparatively brief interval between outbreaks suggests at best only transient increase in resistance of herring populations to the disease. This hypothesis is supported by relatively low disease prevalence (average, 27%) at the epizootic peak, which

constitutes low selection pressure; by the fact that the most recent outbreak was at least as severe as the first recorded outbreak in 1898; and
by determination of mortality rates in experimental epizootics of comparable intensity (Sindermann, 1958).

Another disease with an even longer history of epizootic prevalences
is the red disease of eels caused by *Vibrio anguillarum*. Italian literature
dating back to Bonaveri in 1718 (cited by Hofer, 1904) records repeated
and severe outbreaks on the coast of Italy throughout the eighteenth and
nineteenth centuries, and gives some estimates of numbers of eels killed.
For example, Spallanzani in 1790 described an outbreak that killed almost 100,000 pounds of eels from the Comachio Lagoons on the east
coast of Italy near Ravenna in one 38-day observation period. The continuing presence of the disease in Italy was reported by Ghittino (1963).
Literature from northern Europe, particularly Scandinavia, provides other
evidence of widespread epizootics in which great numbers of eels were
killed (Bruun and Heiberg, 1932, 1935). An outbreak in eels of the Baltic
coast of Germany in 1959, reported by Mattheis (1960), followed a period
of several decades of low prevalence. Mattheis also observed that an
epizootic in eels preceded by 1 year an outbreak in pike.

The very recent epizootic of bacterial etiology in Chesapeake Bay
white perch seriously reduced the population, as indicated by field observations of shoals of dead fish, and numbers washed up on shore, as
well as by a sharp decline in production. The fishery in 1964, the first
postepizootic year, was markedly reduced in comparison with previous
years. Landings of white perch in 1964 were only 622,000 pounds, as
compared with an average of 1,500,000 pounds for the three preceding
years; no indication existed that other major variables had changed. Statements by sportsmen and local residents indicated that white perch were
extraordinarily abundant in 1962, the year immediately preceding the
outbreak.

One well-documented outbreak of parasitic disease with resultant
mass mortality of fish was reported by Dogiel and Lutta (1937). Infestation of sturgeon, *Acipenser nudiventris*, of the Aral Sea with the monogenetic trematode, *Nitzschi sturionis*, caused almost complete extermi-
nation of the fish population. The Aral Sea sturgeon had been free of the
trematode until 1936, when another sturgeon, *A. stellatus*, carrying *Nitzschia* as a relatively innocuous gill parasite, was introduced. The parasite
transferred to *A. nudiventris* and multiplied rapidly, causing mass mortalities which drastically reduced the population of sturgeon for several
years.

Mass mortalities appear to be, and often are, catastrophic events.
Their long-term effects may be severe, even resulting in extinctions in

part of the host range, or they may be slight, causing only minor depressions in population size. If reduction is severe enough and the ecological niche is vacated long enough, the species may be replaced by another with similar ecological requirements. The original species may then persist in low abundance for a long period. This is probably the extreme consequence of disease. The more probable course of events, in view of the high reproductive potential of most teleosts, is a gradual return to former population size and only temporary disturbances of many parts of the ecosystem in which the species is enmeshed. An extensive and still emerging documentation of the degree of this dislocation can be found in studies of the fisheries in the Gulf of Saint Lawrence during and after the recent epizootic of fungus disease (Kohler, 1961; Sindermann, 1963; Tibbo and Graham, 1963). Herring were most seriously involved. Landings during the postepizootic years were less than half their previous level; mean ages in landings decreased; growth rates increased; fewer age groups were represented in the fishery; and relative abundance of herring larvae decreased sharply. Alewives, which have been described as less susceptible to the pathogen (Sindermann and Scattergood, 1954), acquired infections and were killed in sufficient numbers to be observed. Mackerel were also heavily infected; mortalities occurred; and landings decreased during the postepizootic years. Cod did not become infected but fed on disabled herring to such an extent that their growth rate during the epizootic period exceeded anything previously recorded. Cod landings in the southern Gulf of Saint Lawrence almost doubled during the immediate postepizootic period, due almost entirely to increased weight of individual fish caught, rather than to increased numbers of fish taken. Lobsters, important bottom scavengers, showed a similar but less dramatic increase in growth rate. Here then were both negative and positive short-term effects of an epizootic in herring: the negative brought about by increased infection pressure and mortalities of other species, and the positive by a temporarily increased food supply for important predators and scavengers, resulting in accelerated growth of species which (in this example) had a higher unit value to man.

C. BACKGROUND EFFECTS

Epizootics provide the dramatic and obvious examples of disease as a factor of resistance to the biotic potential of marine fishes. The more pedestrian, less conspicuous, but probably more significant, effects of disease are those that have been variously described as low level or background effects. Disease may cause continuous subtraction of individuals by weakening and disorienting infected fish, reducing their ability to escape predators and to survive variations in the physical environment; by blinding fish; by making infected fish more conspicuous; or by altering behavior in ways that render fish more vulnerable to predation. A disoriented, erratic, circular swimming movement at or near the surface has been observed as a generalized sign of a number of diseases. It was first described by Plehn and Mulsow (1911) as a sign of *Ichthyophonus* infection in European salmonids, and has since been seen during mass mortalities of Pacific and Atlantic herring. Exophthalmia, with subsequent destruction of the eye, is another generalized sign of several diseases, including bacterial infection and larval trematode invasion. Cataracts, usually of both eyes, were noted by Raney (1952) in striped bass. Spinal curvatures, evidently of neuromuscular origin, have also been described as generalized signs of bacterial and fungal infections. In studies of herring diseases it has been noted that individuals with bacterial infections exhibited characteristic and easily visible whitish patches near the tail. Field observations of immature herring schools disclosed that individuals so affected were easily seen even in turbid water and during twilight. Other studies brought out the fact that diseased herring aggregated differentially in deeper water, and that samples of immature members of this pelagic species taken in bottom trawls contained higher frequencies of abnormal fish than did samples taken with conventional surface gear (purse seines and gill nets) in the same areas. Bruun and Heiberg (1932) and others have noted that eels with red disease were lethargic and often motionless on the bottom where they could be caught easily by hand. Locomotion became disoriented and swimming became a series of stiff, wriggling movements.

Examinations of fish with extensive intramuscular myxosporidan cysts and necrosis, with heavy larval nematode infestation of muscles, or with many copepods embedded in their flesh, lead inevitably to the conclusion that such a parasite burden, although it may not be the primary cause of death, must seriously reduce statistical chances for survival of the host in an environment in which early and sudden death is the rule.

Disease may also reduce the reproductive capacity of marine fish populations. Castration has been reported (Pinto, 1956) in European sardines as a result of invasion of the testes by *Eimeria sardinae*. Later studies disclosed that over 50% of the individuals sampled were parasitized. Mechanical interference with the discharge of sex products can result from massive visceral infections of American smelts by *Glugea hertwigi*. Cysts of the parasite occupy much of the body cavity, occlude the vent, and prevent normal spawning.

D. ECONOMIC EFFECTS

Economic effects of disease in marine fishes may be categorized as reduction in numbers of food fish available to the fishery; weight loss by diseased individuals; rejection of abnormal fish by consumers, and subsequent loss of interest in fishery products as food; and indirect effects, either favorable or unfavorable, on survival of other species in a food chain. Examples of economic effects in each of the categories have been mentioned in earlier chapters.

Second only to mortality induced directly or indirectly by disease is the often significant weight loss of diseased fish. Williams (1963) has drawn attention to possible losses of thousands of pounds of fishery products annually because of nutrient requirements of fish parasites or disruption of the host's metabolism by disease organisms. The copepod, *Lernaeocera branchialis,* for example, usually causes significant weight loss, so that parasitized fish are 20–30% below average weight. This loss can be an important economic factor if 50–80% of the fish landed are parasitized, as is often true. Williams referred to some very enlightening observations of Kabata (1958), who calculated the weight loss to the Scottish haddock fishery due to parasitization by *Lernaeocera.* About 15 of every 100 North Sea haddock carry this tissue-invading parasite. Assuming very conservatively that each infested fish would lose 1 ounce (almost certainly an underestimate), the loss to the total Scottish haddock catch would have been about 2 million pounds for the single reference year 1954. This loss is significant by itself, but is calculated for only one of the many parasites that affect any commercial fish species; the total effect of parasitism and disease is of course much greater.

Rejection of diseased fish by dealers or consumers can also be economically important. Mann (1954) has summarized some of the economic effects of parasites and diseased conditions of fish from the eastern North Atlantic. He was concerned particularly with fish as they appeared on the market, and indicated that protozoans, larval nematodes, and tissue-invading copepods created the most serious problems. Cited as an example was a microsporidan (*Glugea stephani*) infection of the intestine, gallbladder, liver, and mesenteries of plaice. The parasitized fish gradually became thinner, probably owing to destruction of digestive epithelium. Also considered was another microsporidan, *Plistophora ehrnebaumi* Reichenow, which caused destruction of body muscles of catfish, *Anarrhichas lupus,* and produced large, unsightly tumors. Mann mentioned a large catch of catfish landed at Hamburg in 1952, from West

Iceland waters, of which 10% had to be discarded as unsuitable for human consumption.

Ulcers and cysts caused by *Sphyrion* invasion of redfish and other species make it necessary to remove the diseased areas during processing. Some heavily infested fish cannot be processed at all (Priebe, 1963). Since up to 25% of the catch may be parasitized, the filleting operation is slowed and many pounds of fillets must be discarded. In the Gulf of Maine, the high frequency and intensity of parasitization of redfish results in such great increase in processing costs and decrease in processed yield that it may soon be necessary to downgrade the species in that area from a food fish to an industrial fish, utilized only as a source of fish meal and oil.

Hargis (1958) has cited data from fish processors, indicating that candling and trimming to detect and remove flesh parasites can increase costs of packaging as much as 80%. Of particular significance were *Sphyrion* "buttons" in redfish, *Porrocaecum* larvae in cod, and *Stephanostomum* metacercariae in flounders.

Larval nematodes are most likely to produce consumer complaints if found in marketed fish. Larval anisakids occur in mesenteries and gonads of European herring. Mann (1954) reported them as infrequent in small herring but common in adult herring of the Norwegian coast. Larval anisakids are also common in herring of the North American east and west coasts. Larval nematodes invade the liver of gadoids, disrupt normal function, and often cause extensive atrophy. This condition is prevalent in haddock, where larval worms may occur in the flesh as well. Presence of conspicuous larval cod worms (*Porrocaecum*) in the flesh can lead to rejection of infested fish. Certain inshore grounds off Canada have not been fished for cod because of a history of consistently high nematode parasitization.

Spaghetti worms (larval cestodes) in sciaenid fishes from the Gulf of Mexico should also be included here, since they are very conspicuous, and cause many food fishes to be discarded.

E. ROLE OF DISEASE IN THE EARLY LIFE
HISTORIES OF MARINE ANIMALS

It is generally accepted that much of the mortality of a given year class of marine animals occurs in the embryonic and larval stages, and that the strengths of year classes are determined by relative survival

of young. Variables such as oxygen, temperature, salinity, and food supply are undoubtedly important, as is the very obvious and extensive
predation on eggs and larvae. Effects of disease, which may also be very
significant, are less clearly understood, but are amenable to descriptive
and experimental studies.

Some beginnings have been made in elucidating the effects of parasitism and disease on survival of eggs, larvae, and postlarvae of marine
animals. Among the vertebrates, a microsporidan, *Plistophora gadi,*
pathogenic to fingerling cod from the Barents Sea, was described by
Polyanski (1955). The parasite produced intramuscular cysts and ulceration, and may be identical to the *Plistophora* sp. described earlier by
Drew (1909). Polyanski found it to be rare in Barents Sea cod, but
considered it highly pathogenic to fingerlings because of pronounced
changes in musculature and resultant ulceration. Massive infections were
assumed to be fatal.

A mass mortality of young-of-the-year smelts, *Osmerus mordax*
(Mitchill), was reported by Legault and Delisle (1967) from Quebec.
Extensive invasion by the microsporidan, *Glugea hertwigi*, was considered to be the cause. Visceral adhesions and distintegration of intestinal tissues were common. Although the mortalities occurred in freshwater, smelts and the same microsporidan are abundant in marine and
estuarine waters as well, and similar mortalities of juveniles could occur
there.

Mortalities of herring larvae in marine aquaria owing to parasite
invasion were reported by Rosenthal (1967). Four parasites were introduced with wild plankton used as food: a nematode, *Contracaecum* sp.;
a larval cestode, *Scolex pleuronectis;* the copepodite stage of *Lernaeocera;*
and the copepod, *Caligus rapax.* Larval herring were killed in about 11
days by the nematode and within a few hours by *Lernaeocera* copepo-
dites. The other two parasites did not seriously harm their larval hosts.
Contracaecum larvae were also considered by Roskam (1967) to be a possibly significant factor in mortality of juvenile herring. The larval nematodes were abundant in North Sea plankton (Van Banning, 1967), and
were abundant in juvenile herring from 11 to 14 cm long, but infestation
intensity fell off drastically with increasing length, suggesting that either
the larvae or the infested herring disappeared rapidly. Roskam hypothesized that the decline in intensity was due to mortality of the infested
fish.

Another parasite of larval and postlarval herring, a microsporidan of
the genus *Plistophora*, was reported by Sindermann (1961). The parasite
produced macroscopic intramuscular cysts in the body wall overlying
the viscera, and occurred in up to 3% of samples from the coastal waters

of the Gulf of Maine. A decade of parasite examinations (Sindermann, 1963) did not disclose the microsporidan in juvenile or adult herring.

Bacteria can also affect survival of herring and other larvae. Dannevig and Hansen (1952) found that herring and plaice larvae were killed by *Vibrio anguillarum* and possibly by the myxosporidan, *Myxosoma cerebralis*.

Some evidence is accumulating about the effects of diseases on the early life history stages of invertebrates. Bacterial pathogens, identified as *Aeromonas* sp. or *Vibrio* sp., were isolated by Guillard (1959) and Tubiash, Chanley, and Leifson (1965) from cultures of hatchery-reared bivalve larvae. The organisms killed larvae and juveniles of five commercial bivalve species: American oysters, *Crassostrea virginica;* European oysters, *Ostrea edulis;* hard-shell clams, *Mercenaria mercenaria;* bay scallops, *Aequipecten irradians;* and shipworms, *Teredo navalis.* Adults were not affected by exposures to cultured bacteria. The course of the disease in cultured larval populations was dramatic. Larval activity was reduced and bacteria "swarmed" within a few hours. Complete mortality occurred in as little as 18 hours.

Hatchery-produced oyster and clam larvae can be killed by fungi. Davis *et al.* (1954) isolated a fungus, later described as *Sirolpidium zoophthorum* by Vishniac (1955), which produced occasional epizootics that killed most of the cultured larval population within 4 days. Larval and juvenile bivalves were infected; growth ceased, and death followed soon after infection. Infected larval cultures contain large numbers of motile, biflagellate zoospores of the pathogen, and the authors suggested that similar epizootics could occur among bivalve larvae in natural waters.

A number of diseases and parasites of the eggs of marine invertebrates are known, and many others undoubtedly exist. Eggs of sea mussels from the North American coast are occasionally infected with a haplosporidan, *Chytridiopsis mytilovum.* The parasite and several of its life history stages were first described by Field (1923), and additional information was provided by Sprague (1965b).

The parasite had a high prevalence in some samples, although the proportion of infected eggs to normal eggs in any individual was low. The same or a closely related haplosporidan was seen by De Vincentiis and Renzoni (1963) in eggs of the Mediterranean edible mussel, *Mytilus galloprovincialis* L., from the Gulf of Naples, and another haplosporidan, *Chytridiopsis ovicola,* has been reported from eggs of the European oyster (Léger and Hollande, 1917).

A fungus, *Lagenidium callinectes* Couch, parasitizes eggs of blue crabs, *Callinectes sapidus,* from lower Chesapeake Bay (Couch, 1942;

Sandoz *et al.*, 1944; Sandoz and Rogers, 1944; Newcombe and Rogers, 1947; Rogers-Talbert, 1948). Infected eggs either failed to hatch, or gave rise to abnormal zoea larvae. Infection levels were as high as 90% of a sample of ovigerous female crabs, and up to 25% of the eggs in a sponge (egg mass) were parasitized. Penetration of the egg mass was slow and did not exceed 3 mm. This, combined with the short (2-week) incubation time, permitted normal development of much of the egg mass internal to the infection. Experimentally, the fungus developed normally in salinities from 5 to 30%. It was transmitted experimentally to the eggs of two other species of crabs (the oyster crab and the mud crab, *Neopanope texiana* Rathbun) inhabiting the same area in Chesapeake Bay. Atkins (1954, 1955) described two other fungi, *Plectospira dubia* and *Pythium thalassium,* which infect eggs of pea crabs and other Crustacea.

Crab eggs are sometimes parasitized by copepods. As examples, *Choniosphaera cancrorum* occurs on the egg masses of American rock crabs, *Cancer borealis* and *C. irroratus* (Connolly, 1929), and *Choniosphaera indica* occurs on the gills and egg masses of the Indian edible crab, *Neptunus sanguinolentus* (Gnanamuthu, 1954). Larvae of *C. indica* were found between the crab's gill lamellae; they probably feed on tissue fluids, whereas adults apparently sucked out the fluids of the crab eggs.

The suctorian, *Ephelota gemmipara* Hertwig, was reported to infect and destroy lobster eggs in Norwegian hatcheries (Dannevig, 1928, 1939). The protozoan was found on newly caught females, and increased tremendously in hatching boxes. Dannevig attributed substantial decreases (up to 90%) in production of larvae to the effects of the parasite, but found it abundant only in certain years.

Survival of lobster eggs and larvae hatched under artificial conditions can be affected by other organisms. Havinga (1921) described the attachment of a small green annelid worm, *Histriobdella homari* Van Beneden, to the eggs and to all parts of the bodies of larval and adult lobsters in Norway. He attributed poor success in production of larvae to effects of the worm. Massive numbers of the same parasite had been observed earlier on eggs of lobsters held in floating boxes at Korshavn, Norway, where it was held responsible for destruction of the brood (Sund, 1914, 1915). Every female lobster was infested with thousands of worms, which also occurred on larvae. Although *H. homari* had not been reported previously from American lobsters, Uzmann (1967) recently found it to be widely distributed on the gills of lobsters in New England coastal waters from Maine to Connecticut, and on samples from Georges Bank as well.

Evidence of disease and mortality in eggs or larvae is difficult to acquire from the natural environment. Eggs are normally coated with microorganisms of many kinds, and it is difficult to determine if a larva was alive or dead when taken in a plankton net, unless decomposition is advanced. Microbial pathogens may be masked by saprophytic and other organisms that quickly invade dead eggs and larvae. As mentioned by Oppenheimer (1962), it is possible that young forms are more susceptible to microbial attack than adults, and that fluctuations in year class strength may be shaped in part by variations in disease-caused mortality.

F. CONTROL OF DISEASES OF MARINE ANIMALS

The original, persistent, and largely erroneous feeling about disease in marine populations is that little can be done about it. This pessimistic attitude is definitely unwarranted for species that live inshore, particularly the sedentary invertebrates, for whom practical measures of disease control are possible and have already been applied in some situations. Possible methods for disease control in invertebrates include the following:

(1) The transfer of susceptible animals into epizootic areas, or of individuals from such areas, should be prevented. Because each disease is discrete in terms of transmission and infectivity, risks of transfer will vary as well. When intermediate or alternate hosts play a significant role in maintaining the disease in a given geographical area, transfer of infected individuals to other areas where these hosts are absent may be a reasonable management procedure. Diseases that have been demonstrated experimentally to be transmitted directly, however, such as *Dermocystidium* infections of oysters, may be maintained at epizootic levels by repeated introduction of susceptible animals.

(2) Disease-resistant stocks should be developed by selective breeding of survivors. Epizootics of several oyster diseases have apparently produced increased resistance among survivors. During the outbreak of Malpeque disease in oysters of Prince Edward Island (Canada), resistance developed to an unidentified pathogen, and stocks returned to previous levels of abundance after several decades. That the pathogen is still present, is indicated by deaths of susceptible oysters from other geographical areas introduced into Prince Edward Island waters. Resistant stocks were drawn upon to repopulate other oyster-growing areas of the Gulf of Saint Lawrence that had been subsequently decimated by the same disease.

Evidence is accumulating that increased resistance to the haplo-sporidan pathogen, *Minchinia nelsoni,* is developing among oysters that have survived the disease in the Middle Atlantic States. The disease has been at epizootic levels in some Chesapeake Bay populations for several years. Perhaps resistant strains can be developed with presently available hatchery techniques. Aggregation of survivors on natural beds to which adequate cultch has been added could also do much to improve re-production, spatfall, and return to full production.

(3) Basic information about the life history and ecology of the disease agent must be accumulated, to define vulnerable stages or restrictive environmental requirements. As an example, several oyster pathogens, such as *M. nelsoni,* are limited to salinities in excess of 15%$_{00}$. Plantings during epizootics can be restricted to low salinity areas, and temporary transfer of infected stocks to low salinities may retard or eliminate infections. Mechanical and chemical treatments can also reduce disease prevalence. Effects of gaffkaemia on impounded lobster popu-lations have been reduced by treating bottom muds of pounds with calcium hypochlorite. Damages of *Dermocystidium* disease to oysters have been lessened by planting oysters thinly on the beds, by harvesting within 2 years, and by planting and harvesting at prescribed seasons, to take advantage of the decrease in pathogen activity during the colder months.

Korringa (1959) outlined an extensive program to control the spread of the parasitic copepod *Mytilicola* in cultivated mussel stocks of The Netherlands. Included were extensive dredging of adjacent natural beds, transfer of lightly infected stocks, and destruction of heavily infested beds.

Korringa (1951a) found shell disease of oysters to be caused by a fungus that perforated the shell and that thrived on old shells. He at-tributed the outbreak of shell disease in 1930 in The Netherlands to the practice of spreading enormous quantities of cockle shells on the beds. The disease declined when the spat collectors were placed in areas free of the disease, when old shells were cleared from beds, and when infected young oysters were dipped in mercuric disinfectant (Korringa, 1948, 1949, 1951b).

Biological control of other hosts in the life cycle of parasites, or bio-logical control of the parasite itself, are also possible approaches.

(4) Production could be maintained in artificial environments where disease can be controlled. Some progress has been made in this direction with the development of hatchery methods of producing seed oysters and clams (Loosanoff and Davis, 1963). Bacterial and fungal epizootics in larval culture tanks can be prevented, or their effects reduced, by ultraviolet treatment of filtered seawater, antibiotic treatment of sea-

water in standing water or recirculated cultures, maintenance of general cleanliness of all utensils used in handling larvae, ultraviolet treatment of phytoplankton food derived from impure mass cultures, and use of bacteria-free phytoplankton cultures or sterilized artificial diets.

Shellfish production in artificial ponds (Shaw, 1965) offers distinct possibilities for disease and predator control, beginning with disease-free and disease-resistant brood stock and progressing to filtration and ultra-violet treatment of recirculated water; important also are careful control of contaminants in mass phytoplankton cultures, and elimination of shell-fish associates that act as alternate or intermediate hosts of disease agents.

Among the inshore fishes, partial disease control could be effected by the following:

1. A species could be deliberately overfished when evidence of an incipient epizootic is found, or when particular fishing areas are found to contain large proportions of diseased fish. Such mass removal could reduce the infection pressure and opportunity for contact of diseased and non-diseased individuals. It would also reduce economic losses by utilizing individuals who would otherwise die in the natural environment and be unavailable to man.

2. For particular microbial diseases, such as *Ichthyophonus* disease of sea herring, in which periodic epizootics occur, population resistance levels might be artificially maintained at a level high enough to prevent outbreaks, by deliberate seeding of inshore areas with cultured pathogens. The demonstration of specific immunological competence in fish indicates that controlling factors in epizootics are not fundamentally different from those for other vertebrate groups. Individual variability in susceptibility to pathogens has been demonstrated, and the course of certain fish diseases shown to be alterable by environmental factors such as temperature and diet.

3. Great care must be taken in introductions of marine or estuarine species from other areas, to ensure that disease organisms capable of producing epizootics in endemic species are not introduced simultaneously. Introductions of adult fish should be absolutely prohibited unless careful examination is made by fish pathologists of the species to be introduced.

4. Procedures which prevent return of viscera or entire diseased fish to the natural environment could prevent spread of infection, particularly of Myxosporida, Microsporida, larval nematodes, and larval cestodes. Polyanski (1955), discussing parasites of Barents Sea fishes, proposed an elementary method to control the increase of visceral nematodes, particularly *Contracoecum aduncum* and *Anisakis* sp. Cleaning trawled fish at sea or at coastal sites leads to discarding of encysted worms in the sea. Such worms can continue developing in juvenile cod and haddock

which gather to feed on fish offal. Expansion of the fishery should lead to increased infestation unless the simple measures are taken of scalding fish offal before it is dumped overboard from trawlers or shore facilities, or burying offal on land.

Little basis exists for pessimism as to the possibility of disease control in natural populations of marine animals, despite the seeming immensity of the problem. True, we now stand in marine disease studies almost where our ancestors of the Middle Ages did when confronted with the great pestilences of those days. Yet the advances made since then in the understanding and control of human diseases suggest that technology and techniques impossible to foresee now can lead to manipulation of the marine environment and the factors that influence population size of marine fish. Some approaches have already been suggested. These are, of course, based on present knowledge and do not constitute a legitimate portrayal of future control based on the acquisition of new information.

REFERENCES

Atkins, D. (1954). A marine fungus *Plectospira dubia* n. sp. (Saprolegniaceae), infecting crustacean eggs and small Crustacea. *J. Marine Biol. Assoc. U. K.* **33**, 721–732.

Atkins, D. (1955). *Pythium thalassium* n. sp. infecting the egg-mass of the pea-crab *Pinnotheres pisum*. *Brit. Mycol. Soc. Trans.* **38**, 31–46.

Bruun, A. F., and Heiberg, B. (1932). The "Red Disease" of the eel in Danish waters. *Medd. Komm. Havundersøg., Fiskeri* **9**, 1–17.

Bruun, A. F., and Heiberg, B. (1935). Weitere Untersuchungen über die Rotseuche des Aales in den dänischen Gewässern. *Z. Fischerei* **33**, 379–382.

Connolly, C. J. (1929). A new copepod parasite *Choniosphaera·cancrorum*, gen. et sp. n., representing a new genus, and its larval development. *Proc. Zool. Soc. London* pp. 415–427.

Couch, J. N. (1942). A new fungus on crab eggs. *J. Elisha Mitchell Sci. Soc.* **58**, 158–162.

Cox, P. (1916). Investigation of a disease of the herring (*Clupea harengus*) in the Gulf of St. Lawrence, 1914. *Contrib. Can. Biol. Fisheries 1914–1915* 81–85.

Dannevig, A. (1928). Beretning om Flødevigens utklekningsanstalt for 1926/1927. *Arsberet. Vedkom. Norg. Fiskerier* pp. 150–156.

Dannevig, A. (1939). Beretning for Flødevigens utklekningsanstalt 1936–37. *Arsberet. Vedkom. Norg. Fiskerier* pp. 70–75.

Dannevig, A., and Hansen, S. (1952). Faktorer av betydning for fiskeeggenes og fiskeyngelens oppvekst. *Fiskeridirektorat. Skrifter Havundersøk.* **10**, 5–36.

Davis, H. C., Loosanoff, V. L., Weston, W. H., and Martin, C. (1954). A fungus disease in clam and oyster larvae. *Science* **120**, 36–38.

De Vincentiis, and Renzoni, A. (1963). Sulla presenza di uno sporozoo in ovociti di *Mytilus galloprovincialis*. Lam. *Arch. Zool. Ital.* **47**, 21–26.

Dogiel, V. A., and Lutta, A. S. (1937). On the death of sturgeon in the Aral Sea in 1936. (In Russian.) *Ryb. Khoz.* **12**, 26–27.

Drew, H. (1909). Some notes on parasitic and other diseases of fish. A new species of *Plistophora* invading the muscles of a cod. *Parasitology* 2, 193–194.

Field, I. A. (1923). Biology and economic value of the sea mussel *Mytilus edulis*. *U. S. Bur. Fisheries, Bull.* 38, 127–259.

Fish, F. W. (1934). A fungus disease in fishes of the Gulf of Maine. *Parasitology* 26, 1–16.

Ghittino, P. (1963). Les maladies des poissons en Italie. *Bull. Office Intern. Epizooties* 59, 59–87.

Gnanamuthu, C. P. (1954). *Choniosphaera indica,* a copepod parasitic on the crab *Neptunus* sp. *Parasitology* 44, 371–378.

Guillard, R. R. L. (1959). Further evidence of the destruction of bivalve larvae by bacteria. *Biol. Bull.* 117, 258–266.

Hargis, W. J. (1958). Parasites and fishery problems. *Proc. Gulf Caribbean Fishery Inst.* pp. 70–75.

Havinga, B. (1921). Rapport over de kreeftenvisserij in Zeeland en de kunstmatige kreeftenteelt. *Meded. Visscherijinspect.* 30, 1–51.

Hofer, B. (1904). "Handbuch der Fischkrankheiten," 395 pp. Verlag Allgemeine Fisch.-Ztg., München.

Kabata, Z. (1958). *Lernaeocera obtusa* n. sp. Its biology and its effects on the haddock. *Marine Res.* No. 3, 26 pp.

Kohler, A. C. (1961). Variations in the growth of Atlantic cod (*Gadus morhua* L.). Ph.D. Thesis, McGill University, Montreal.

Korringa, P. (1948). Shell disease in *Ostrea edulis*—its dangers, its cause, its control. *Conv. Add. Natl. Shellfish. Assoc.* pp. 86–94.

Korringa, P. (1949). Nieuwe aanwijzingen voor de bestrijding van slipper en schelpziekte. *Visserijnieuws* 2, 90–94.

Korringa, P. (1951a). Investigations on shell-disease in the oyster, *Ostrea edulis* L. *Cons. Perm. Intern. Explor. Mer, Rappt. Proces-Verbaux Reun.* 128, No. 2, 50–54.

Korringa, P. (1951b). Voorzetting van de strijd tegen de schelpziekte in de oesters. *Visserijnieuws* 3, No. 12, Suppl., 1–8.

Korringa, P. (1959). Checking *Mytilicola's* advance in the Dutch Waddensea. *Cons. Perm. Intern. Explor. Mer, 47th Meeting 1959, Shellfish Comm. Rept. No.* 87, 3 pp. (mimeo.).

Legault, R. O., and Delisle, C. (1967). Acute infection by *Glugea hertwigi* Weissenberg in young-of-the-year rainbow smelt *Osmerus eperlanus mordax* (Mitchill). *Can. J. Zool.* 45, 1291–1292.

Léger, L., and Hollande, A. C. (1917). Sur un nouveau protiste a facies de *Chytridiopsis*, parasite des ovules de l'Huitre. *Compt. Rend. Soc. Biol.* (*Paris*) 80, 61–64.

Loosanoff, V. L., and Davis, H. C. (1963). Rearing of bivalve mollusks. *Advan. Marine Biol.* 1, 1–136.

Mann, H. (1954). Die wirtschaftliche Bedeutung von Krankheiten bei Seefischen. *Fischwirtschaft* (*Bremerhaven*) 6, 38–39.

Mattheis, T. (1960). Das Aalsterben an der Ostseeküste zwischen Usedom und Wismar im Sommer 1959. *Deut. Fischereiztg.* (*Radebeul*) 7, 23–25.

Newcombe, C. L., and Rogers, M. R. (1947). Studies of a fungus parasite that infects blue crab eggs. *Turtox News* 25, 1–7.

Oppenheimer, C. H. (1962). On marine fish diseases. *In* "Fish as Food" (G. Borgstrom, ed.), Vol. 2, p. 541. Academic Press, New York.

Pinto, J. S. (1956). Parasitic castration in males of *Sardina pilchardus* (Walb.) due to testicular infestation by the coccidia *Eimeria sardinae* (Thélohan). *Rev. Fac. Cien., Univ. Lisboa* **C5**, 209–224.

Plehn, M., and Mulsow, K. (1911). Erreger der "Taumelkrankheiten" der Salmoniden. *Zentr. Bakteriol., Parasitenk., Abt. I. Orig.* **59**, 63–68.

Polyanski, Y. I. (1955). Contributions to the parasitology of fishes of the northern seas of the USSR. (In Russian.) *Tr. Zool. Inst., Akad. Nauk SSSR* **19**, 5–170.

Priebe, K. (1963). Einige wenig bekannte parasitologische, lebensmittelhygienisch bedeutsame Befunde bei Meeresfischen. *Arch. Lebensmittelhyg.* **14**, 257–260.

Raney, E. C. (1952). The life history of the striped bass, *Roccus saxatilis* (Walbaum). *Bull. Bingham Oceanog. Collection* **14**, 5–97.

Rogers-Talbert, R. (1948). The fungus *Lagenidium callinectes* Couch (1942) on eggs of the blue crab in Chesapeake Bay. *Biol. Bull.* **95**, 214–228.

Rosenthal, H. (1967). Parasites in larvae of the herring (*Clupea harengus* L.) fed with wild plankton. *Marine Biol.* **1**, 10–15.

Roskam, R. T. (1967). *Anisakis* and *Contracaecum* larvae in North Sea herring. *Cons. Intern. Explor. Mer, C. M. Pelagic Fish (N) Comm., Paper* No. 19, 3 pp. (mimeo.).

Sandoz, M. D., and Rogers, M. R. (1944). The effect of environmental factors on hatching, moulting, and survival of zoea larvae of the blue crab, *Callinectes sapidus* Rathbun. *Ecology* **25**, 216–228.

Sandoz, M., Rogers, M. R., and Newcombe, C. L. (1944). Fungus infection of eggs of the blue crab *Callinectes sapidus* Rathbun. *Science* **99**, 124–125.

Scattergood, L. W. (1948). A report on the appearance of the fungus *Ichthyosporidium hoferi* in the herring of the Northwest Atlantic. *U. S. Fish Wildlife Serv., Spec. Sci. Rept., Fisheries* **58**, 1–33.

Shaw, W. N. (1965). Pond culture of oysters—past, present, and future. *Trans. North Am. Wildlife Conf.* **30**, 114–120.

Sindermann, C. J. (1956). Diseases of fishes of the western North Atlantic. IV. Fungus disease and resultant mortalities of herring in the Gulf of Saint Lawrence in 1955. *Maine Dept. Sea Shore Fish., Res. Bull.* 25, 1–23.

Sindermann, C. J. (1958). An epizootic in Gulf of Saint Lawrence fishes. *Trans. North Am. Wildlife Conf.* **23**, 349–360.

Sindermann, C. J. (1961). Sporozoan parasites of sea herring. *J. Parasitol.* **47**, Suppl., 34 (abstr.).

Sindermann, C. J. (1963). Disease in marine populations. *Trans. North Am. Wildlife Conf.* **28**, 336–356.

Sindermann, C. J., and Scattergood, L. W. (1954). Disease of fishes of the western North Atlantic. II. *Ichthyosporidium* disease of the sea herring (*Clupea harengus*). *Maine Dept. Sea Shore Fish., Res. Bull.* 19, 1–40.

Sprague, V. (1965a). *Ichthyosporidium* Caullery and Mesnil, 1905, the name of a genus of fungi or a genus of sporozoans. *Syst. Zool.* **14**, 110–114.

Sprague, V. (1965b). Observations on *Chytridiopsis mytilovum* (Field), formerly *Haplosporidium mytilovum* Field (Microsporida?). *J. Protozool.* **12**, 385–389.

Sund, O. (1914). Beretning om anlaeg av statens hummeravlsstation og driften i 1913. *Arsberet. Vedkom. Norg. Fiskerier* No. 4, 525–532.

Sund, O. (1915). Statens hummeravlsstation, Korshavn. *Arsberet. Vedkom. Norg. Fiskerier* No. 2, 176–181.

Tibbo, S. N., and Graham, T. R. (1963). Biological changes in herring stocks following an epizootic. *J. Fisheries Res. Board Can.* **20**, 435–449.

Tubiash, H. S., Chanley, P. E., and Leifson, E. (1965). Bacillary necrosis, a disease of larval and juvenile bivalve mollusks. I. Etiology and epizootiology. *J. Bacteriol.* **90,** 1036–1044.

Uzmann, J. R. (1967). *Histriobdella homari* (Annelida: Polychaeta) in the American lobster, *Homarus americanus. J. Parasitol.* **53,** 210–211.

Van Banning, P. (1967). Nematodes in plankton samples from the North Sea. *Cons. Intern. Explor. Mer, C. M. Pelagic Fish (N) Comm., Paper* No. 20, 5 pp. (mimeo.).

Vishniac, H. S. (1955). The morphology and nutrition of a new species of *Sirolpidium. Mycologia* **47,** 633–645.

Williams, H. H. (1963). Parasitic worms in marine fishes: A neglected study. *New Scientist* **12,** 156–159.

IX

Future Studies of Diseases in the Marine Environment

Because of the complexity and enormity of the ocean ecosystem, disease problems are difficult to approach. As with other marine problems, it is likely that greatest advances will be made when descriptive studies can be combined with experimentation in circumscribed bodies of water such as aquaria, saltwater ponds, and artificially restricted estuaries and other arms of the sea. Although it is difficult to predict the future course of research and the development of knowledge about marine fish diseases, it is comparatively easy to itemize areas that require exploration. Some suggestions are outlined below.

(1) Studies of diseases and parasites must be an essential part of our progress in marine aquaculture. A significant body of literature already exists about diseases in marine aquaria, and systems of control—many empirical, and most based on modifications of techniques developed for freshwater fishes—have been developed. It is becoming apparent from the work being done on diseases of cultured marine fish in Japan that many of the organisms already known as pathogens in marine aquaria will also be important in marine aquaculture.

Parasitology has proved of great importance to improvement of agricultural practices. As examples, control of parasitic worms and infectious diseases of domesticated plants and animals has resulted in great increases in yields. Increases result from reduction in mortalities and reduction in weight loss due to parasitization. Parasites of fish, particularly the larger helminths, consume a significant part of marine food production, as can be easily seen by comparing emaciated, parasitized fish, such as cod, haddock, or whiting, with normal fish of the same age. Consequently, one of the objectives of aquaculture research, as pointed out by Williams (1963), must be control of worm parasites of food fishes. Approaches might be elimination of intermediate hosts of parasites which mature in fish, or elimination of definitive hosts of parasites which occur as larvae in fish. Control of parasites and diseases in the open sea may be difficult, but control in coastal waters is a distinct possibility. Reduction in prevalences would probably be the initial goal in inshore natural waters, rather than eradication. Certain coastal areas have much higher than average prevalences of certain parasites, often because of the presence of infected intermediate or definitive hosts. Such areas could be deliberately and systematically overfished for species harboring parasites, whether the hosts are of economic significance or not. If overfishing is not feasible, such areas could be avoided when returning cultured juvenile fish to the sea.

Young animals—the ones that will be the principal concern of aquaculturists—are often particularly vulnerable to disease, especially when reared under crowded conditions. Attention must be paid to diseases and parasites of eggs, larvae, and juveniles of marine animals, since we already have excellent examples of deleterious effects of disease on early life-history stages in natural and captive populations. In addition to the examples cited in chapter VIII, there are numerous poorly documented indications of mass deaths of juvenile shellfish. Information from fishery sources indicates that recently set oyster spat have died in late autumn in Matsushima Bay, northern Japan, in recent years, and that newly set oyster spat died in late summer in Long Island Sound in the mid-1940's.

(2) The role of parasites and diseases in reducing abundance of noncommercial food chain organisms should be examined in great detail, with long-term, ecologically based research particularly oriented toward infectious diseases. The scattered information that now exists about a few epizootics in noncommercial species, and the existing data on parasites of such species should be compiled. Great epizootics could sweep through populations at various trophic levels in the sea, drastically reducing abundance, without coming to the attention of marine scientists. One hint of this possibility was called to my attention by Dr. Abraham Fleminger of the Scripps Institution of Oceanography (1964). He had found in plankton tows a significant prevalence of systematic fungus infections in calanoid copepods of the Pacific. The parasite was morphologically similar to *Ichthyophonus*, which had been described earlier (Jepps, 1937) from copepods in North European waters.

More definitive evidence of disease and associated mass mortalities of copepods was reported by Vallin (1951). An epizootic in populations of *Eurytemora hirundoides* (Nordquist) on the Swedish coast of the northern Baltic in 1950 was apparently caused by a fungus pathogen, tentatively identified as a new species of *Leptolegnia* (later described as *L. baltica* by Höhnk and Vallin, 1953). *Eurytemora hirundoides* is the inner Baltic's most common and abundant copepod during the warmer months of the year, constituting from 50 to 90% of all copepods in plankton tows. After the 1950 mortalities the species was much less abundant in samples. Vallin's description of the mortalities is dramatic:

At the beginning of August 1950 it was reported that herring fishermen in the Botten Sea, off Sundsvall, had found their nets to be clogged with a sticky substance. When the tackle was taken out of the water the substance soon began to rot and smell. It was suspected that its cause might be industrial pollution from cellulose plants. Samples of the material scraped off the nets, some treated with formalin, were however found to consist of dead plankton crustaceans. A single species of copepod—*Eurytemora hirundoides* (Nordquist)—formed almost 100% of the substance. . . . Death of the plankton . . . was first reported from fishing grounds east of the island of Alnö, off Sundsvall, at the beginning of August. Fishermen found such large quantities of dead *Eurytemora* on their nets that they could easily scrape it off by the quart. At the same time the local fishery assistant stated that the sea water in wide areas was made turbid by a lot of "small dead white eggs," what instead of that must have been the killed copepods. Within a few days the same phenomenon was reported from other fishing waters. . . . The area, then, stretched for some 70 km in the outer skerries off Sundsvall.

Reports were also received that the mortality was observed on the Finnish coast north of Åland.

Mortalities recurred in 1951, at a reduced level and a month later than in 1950. The severe effects of the disease on *Eurytemora* populations were indicated by reductions in percentages of the species in plankton tows at Sundsvall to only 13%, from an expected 80% characteristic of pre-epizootic years. High river discharges in the summer of 1950, combined with exceptionally high surface-water temperatures, were thought to favor the rapid growth of the pathogen. The fungus is a member of the Saprolegniaceae, which are normally parasitic on freshwater organisms. The surface salinities in the epizootic area ranged from 4 to 6%₀. Lack of infections in other copepods sampled and the very selective nature of mortalities strongly indicate an epizootic due to a pathogen specific for *Eurytemora hirundoides*.

Eurytemora is an important food for herring, *Clupea harengus*, and other pelagic species of the area. Widespread mortalities at the trophic level of copepods could materially reduce the food supply for these commercial fishes, in addition to clogging and fouling nets, or causing their rapid decay.

(3) The internal defense mechanisms of marine animals—fish and shellfish—should be examined more completely. Understanding of resistance of marine invertebrates to disease offers exciting avenues of research, since available evidence suggests existence of principles not yet elucidated. Survival in a microbe-rich environment, without the specific antibody responses of vertebrates, suggests existence in nonvertebrates of possibly varied but very effective internal defense mechanisms.

(4) One of the greatest needs in marine disease research is for continuity of observations, so that changes in prevalence of recognized diseases, particularly those known to occur in epizootic proportions, can be documented over extended periods. These observations should be accompanied by detailed studies of such factors as food and temperature in the environment of host populations and of mechanisms of resistance to known pathogens. Acquisition of continuous information about the size of the host populations would also be an important facet of the studies.

(5) Another critical question concerns the effects of disease on the very early life-history stages of marine animals in natural waters. It is generally accepted that much of the mortality of a given year class occurs in the embryonic and larval stages. Variables such as oxygen, temperature, salinity, and food supply are undoubtedly important, as is the very obvious and extensive predation on eggs and larvae. Effects of disease on early life-history stages in natural waters, which may also be significant, are less clearly understood, but are amenable to descriptive and experimental studies.

(6) Another research area deserving greater attention concerns the role of viruses and bacteria in marine populations. Enough evidence is already available to prove that bacteria can be significant primary or secondary invaders, and causes of mortality in natural as well as captive populations. Identification of bacterial pathogens is not simple; the classification is a present confused; reinfection from cultured organisms is often unsuccessful; and disease-free experimental animals that have not been exposed in the past to the same or related organisms may be very difficult to obtain. Other basic and related problems immediately present themselves—such as the role of marine bacteriophages in populations of bacteria potentially pathogenic to marine animals (Spencer, 1963), and the role of antibiotics elaborated by many marine organisms in suppressing bacterial populations (Lucas, 1955; Nielsen, 1955). Knowledge of viruses as pathogens of marine fish and shellfish is even more rudimentary than is that for bacteria, except for tumor-inducing agents in fish. Currently available established cell cultures of marine fish origin should do much to improve our understanding of viruses in the oceans. We need

comparable established cell lines of invertebrate origin. At present there is no generally available cell line from any marine invertebrate, although several recent papers have reported successful long-term maintenance of certain invertebrate tissues. Viruses in marine invertebrates, with but a single exception, are unknown. It would be very surprising if virus diseases do not exist in populations of many invertebrates.

In conclusion, it can be seen that, despite the rapidly expanding body of literature on parasites and diseases of marine animals, the unknown still by far transcends the known. With the impetus provided by increasing need for protein from the sea and by the development of marine aquaculture, we can except significant increases in global commitment to research on factors such as disease, which act to thwart human exploitation of the marine environment.

REFERENCES

Fleminger, A. (1964). Personal communication.

Höhnk, V. W., and Vallin, S. (1953). Epidemisches Absterben von *Eurytemora* im Bottnischen Meerbusen, ver ursacht durch *Leptolegnia baltica* nov. spec. *Veroeffentl. Inst. Meeresforsch. Bremerhaven* 2, 215–223.

Jepps, M. W. (1937). On the protozoan parasites of *Calanus finmarchicus* in the Clyde Sea area. *Quart. J. Microscop. Sci.* 79, 589–658.

Lucas, C. E. (1955). External metabolites in the sea. *Deep-Sea Res.* 3, Suppl., 139–148.

Nielsen, E. S. (1955). The production of antibiotics by plankton algae and its effect upon bacterial activities in the sea. *Deep-Sea Res.* 3, Suppl., 281–286.

Spencer, R. (1963). Bacterial viruses in the sea. *In* "Symposium on Marine Microbiology" (C. H. Oppenheimer ed.), pp. 321. Thomas, Springfield, Illinois.

Vallin, S. (1951). Plankton mortality in the northern Baltic caused by a parasitic water-mould. *Rept. Inst. Freshwater Res. Drottingholm* 32, 139–148.

Williams, H. H. (1963). Parasitic worms in marine fishes: A neglected study. *New Scientist* 12, 156–159.

AUTHOR INDEX

Numbers in italics refer to pages on which the references are listed.

SUBJECT INDEX

A

Abalone, as nematode host, 146

Abnormalities, genetic and environmental, 74–79

Abothrium, 60

Abramis ballerus, 77

Acanthocephalans, infestation by, 61–63, 164

Acanthocheilinae, 300

Acanthoclinus quadridactylus, 51

Acanthocybium solandri, 56

Acanthoparyphium spinulosum, 127

Achatina fulica, 297

Achromobacter, 109, 158

Achromobacter punctatum, 280

Acipenser nudiventris, 57, 312

Acipenser stellatus, 57

Acquired immunity, defined, 280

Aequipecten irradians, 141, 272, 318

Aequipecten maximus, 141

Aeromonas, 109, 245, 318

Aeromonas hydrophila, 277

Aeromonas liquefaciens, 211

Aeromonas salmonicida, 277

Alewives
fungus infection in, 27
mass mortalities of, 211–212, 313

Alosa nordmani, 74

Alosa pontica, 74

Alosa pseudoharengus, 27, 211

Alosa sapidissima, 211

Alutera schoepfii, 11

American Fisheries Society, 5 n

Amoebocytes, 261–264

Anabothrium, 139

Anadromous species, diseases of, 2

Anarhichas lupus, 36, 48, 315

Anchorella, 165

Ancistrocoma myae, 138

Ancistrocoma pelseneeri, 123, 133, 138

Ancistruma mytili, 133

Angiostrongylus, 301

Angiostrongylus cantonensis, 296–297

Anguilla anguilla, 15, 31, 35

Anguilla bengalensis, 32

Anguilla mauritanica, 32

Anguilla reinhardtii, 32

Anisakiasis
from herring, 298–300, 316
human, 298–300

Anisakinae, 63

Anisakis, 64–65, 298–300, 322

Anisakis-like larvae, 301

Anisakis marina, 300

Anisakis phiseteris, 301

Anisakis simplex, 301

Anisakids, in herring, 316

Anophrys sarcophaga, 152, 269

Anthopleura elegantissima, 270

Antibacterial fluids, 269

Antibiotics, in ulcer disease, 235

Antibody-like defense mechanisms, 267

Antibody production
in fishes, 276–277, 291
immunization and, 280
in invertebrates, 273–274
in oysters, 269
in sharks, 270
in vertebrates, 270, 274–275

Antimicrobial substances, 270–271

Antitumor substances, 270

Aphanomyces, 246

Aphanomyces astaci, 148

Aquariology, first international congress of, 228
see also Marine aquaculture; Marine aquaria

Aral Sea sturgeon, nematodes in, 312

Argeia pugettensis, 171

crowding and, 4–5
defined, 2, 8–9, 106
in early life histories, 316–320
economic effects of, 315–316
environmental and physiological factors in, 6
epizootic, 4–6, 310–314, 328–329
erratic swimming as sign of, 314
factors in, 4
future studies of, 327–331
in hatcheries, 227–234
hyperplastic, 13
in humans and marine animals, 290–302
infectious, 2, 258
internal defense mechanisms and, 258–281
invasive, 5
of marine vs. freshwater species, 4
in marine aquaria, 3
mass mortalities and, 5, 204–221, 310–313
microbial, *see* Microbial diseases
neoplastic, 13
reproductive capacity and, 314
resistance to, 258–281, 320
role of in marine populations, 4, 309–323
signs of, 314
spawning and, 314
susceptibility to, 258–259
world literature on, 2–5, 9
Diseased fish
disposal of, 322
rejection of by dealers, 315
Disease-resistant stocks, 3, 320
Distomum (Gymnophallus) somateriae, 133
Distomum margaritarum (= Gymnophallus margaritarum), 133
Dock shrimp, parasites of, 171
Dogs, salmon poisoning in, 16, 293
Dolphin
nematodes in, 301
trematodes in, 56
Donax, 126, 138–139
Donax gouldi, 139
Donax trunculus, 139
Donax variabilis, 139
Donax vittatus, 138–139
Dorosoma cepedianum, 212

Dorosoma petenense, 211–212
Dover sole, lymphocytes in, 238
Drepanopsetta hippoglossoides, 48
Drills, effects of, 144, 248
Drum fish
epidermoid carcinomas in, 75
tapeworms in, 58
Dussumeriidae, 205

E

Earthquakes, 204
Eccrinides, 151
Echeneibothrium, 139–140
Echinobothrium affine, 154
Echinocephalus pseudouncinatus, 146
Echinorhynchus gadi, 61
Echinorhynchus lageniformis, 61
Echinostephanus hispidus, 237
Echinostome trematode, 295
Economic effects, of fish diseases, 315–316
Eels
acanthocephalan infections of, 62
Blumenkohlkrankheit in, 14–15
coccidian infection of, 35
epizootic red disease in, 312
haemogregarine infections in, 35
hemoflagellates in, 31
human serum injection in, 280
"red" disease of, 5, 17, 236, 312
sarcomas in, 14–15
Eggs
destruction of by storms, 205–206, 209
diseases and parasites of, 318–320
Eimeria, 34
Eimeria anguillae, 35
Eimeria auxilis, 35
Eimeria brevoortiana, 34
Eimeria clupearum, 34
Eimeria cruciata, 34
Eimeria cristalloides, 35
Eimeria etrumei, 34
Eimeria gadi, 35
Eimeria gasterostei, 34
Eimeria motellae, 35
Eimeria nishin, 34
Eimeria sardinae, 33–34
Elasmobranchs, Myxosporida infections of, 41
Elytrophora brachyptera, 73
Endotoxin, 264

K

Kamchatkan salmon, Myxosporida infection of, 40
Kathetostoma giganteum, 126
Katsuwonus pelamis, 62
Kelp crab, parasites of, 155–156
Kelpfish, parasite of, 51
Kennebec River, alewife mortalities in, 212
Kidderia mytili, 133
Killifish
  lymphocystis in, 11
  Microsporida infections in, 49
  Pseudomonas infections of, 20
  sewer effluent and, 76
King crab
  bacterial disease of, 149
  parasites of, 156
Kingfish
  coccidian infections of, 34
  isopod parasitization of, 74
Kowari enclosures, Japan, 235, 237
"Krebspest" disease, 148
Kronborgia caridicola, 169
Kudoa, 36–37
Kudoa (=*Chloromyxum*) *clupeidae,* 37–39
Kudoa clupeidae, 37, 39, 43
Kudoa thyrsites, 40
Kurita Bay, Japan, vibrio disease in, 235–236

L

Labyrinthomyxa, 113
Labyrinthulales, 113
Lagenidium callinectes, 318
Lagenophrys, 152–153
Lagenophrys lunatus, 168
Lagodon rhomboides, 41
Larus argentatus, 52, 154
Larval cestodes, 5
Larval fishes, abnormal conditions in, 77–78
Larval flukes, 52–53
Larval worms, in marine fish, 56–60, 65
Leander serrifer, 171
Leander squilla, 168
Lebbeus polaris, 169
Lecithodendrium, 134

Leeches
  on Dover sole, 238
  hemoflagellates and, 31
Leiognathus fasciatus, 41
Leiostomus xanthurus, 48, 62
Leopard lobsters, 162
Lepeophtheirus nordmanni, 238
Lepeophtheirus pectoralis, 73
Lepeophtheirus salmonis, 72
Lepidopsetta bilineata, 61, 67
Lepidoteuthis grimaldii, 147
Lepisosteus spatula, 123
Leptolegnia, 329
Leptotheca, 41
Lernaeenicus sprattae, 69, 71
Lernaeocera branchialis, 68–70, 315, 317
Lernaeocera obtusata, 70
Lernaeoceridae, 68
Lernaeopoda, 237
Lethal genes, 204
Leuciscus waleckii, 74
Leucosphaera oxneri, 233
Leukocytes, in oysters, 110, 261
Leukocytosis, in oysters, 261
Limanda ferruginea, 47
Limanda herzensteini, 13
Limulus, 263–264
Liriopsis pygmaea, 156
Littleneck clams, parasitization in, 139–140
Littorina littorea, 52, 145, 220
Littorina pintado, 146
Littorina planaxis, 146
Livoneca (*Ichthyoxenos*) *amurensis,* 74
Livoneca ovalis, 73–74
Livoneca pontica, 74
Livoneca puhi, 74
Lobster eggs, infestations of, 319
Lobsters
  albinism in, 165–166
  color variation in, 166
  diseases of, 157–166
  gaffkaemia in, 239
  gill maggot in, 165
  hatchery diseases in, 246
  helminth diseases in, 164–165
  mass mortalities of, 313
  microbial diseases of, 158–164
  mortality of in culture, 239
  mottling disease in, 162
  phagocytosis in, 266